ROYAL HISTORICAL SOCIETY
STUDIES IN HISTORY
SERIES
No. 25

THE HOUSE OF GIBBS AND THE PERUVIAN GUANO MONOPOLY

Recent volumes published in this series include

For a complete list of the Series please see pp. 282-3.

THE HOUSE OF GIBBS
AND THE PERUVIAN
GUANO MONOPOLY

W. M. Mathew

LONDON
ROYAL HISTORICAL SOCIETY
1981

The Society records its gratitude to the following whose generosity made possible the initiation of this series: The British Academy; The Pilgrim Trust; The Twenty-Seven Foundation; The United States Embassy bicentennial funds; The Wolfson Trust; several private donors.

This volume is published with the help of a grant from the late Miss Isobel Thornley's Bequest to the University of London.

Printed in England
by Swift Printers (Sales) Ltd
London, E.C.1.

In memory of my
father, John Blane Mathew

CONTENTS

PREFACE

This book is about the fortunes of the guano trade over the two decades when it was largely in the hands of the London merchant house of Antony Gibbs & Sons: a trade that dominated the commercial and financial life of Peru for close on forty years, that provided advanced economies, particularly Britain, with a commodity of great consequence for agricultural improvement, and that, in crude volume and value terms, ranked as one of the most important Latin American export businesses.

The literature on the subject is not very substantial. Peruvian historians have treated it in a rather sketchy and over-generalized fashion, and have drawn on only a narrow range of sources. Their work, moreover, is only available in Spanish. In English, the most useful and widely-quoted account is the long second chapter of Jonathan Levin's *The Export Economies* (Cambridge, Mass., 1960): again, however, using only a limited body of primary materials, and offering a number of questionable conclusions which will be explicitly challenged in the pages that follow. Guano features hardly at all in studies of international trade or, more surprisingly, of agricultural improvement. Fertilizers generally have received only scant attention from agricultural historians, perhaps through some lofty disdain for such lowly commodities. Our knowledge of their role in British farming has advanced very little since Lord Ernle devoted a page or two to the subject in 1912 in his *English Farming Past and Present* and suggested, in a way that ought to have stimulated further enquiry, that the 'supply of concentrated portable manures. . .is the greatest achievement of modern agricultural science'. As for literature on the house of Gibbs, this is confined to a handful of volumes produced either by members of the Gibbs family or by authors commissioned to write short anniversary histories. Not much useful comment is provided on the guano trade or on its role in the growth of the firm.

No attempt, it should be stressed at the outset, has ben made to present here a systematic business history of Gibbs during their guano period, nor is any comprehensive analysis offered of the effects of the trade on the Peruvian economy or on the agriculture of consuming countries. There is, inevitably, a great deal of material in this book that relates to these questions, but the principal concern has been to offer rigorous analysis of the way in which Gibbs handled the trade and of the nature and implications of their relationship with the Peruvian government, the owner of the guano. It was a fascinating and unique association, of the greatest consequence for both parties, and one that can be examined in detail since we have access both to the Gibbs archive in London and official Peruvian papers in Lima.

The origins of the book lie in the middle chapters of a thesis accepted by the University of London in 1964. I owe thanks to the late Professor Arthur John of the London School of Economics who supervised my preliminary enquiries in the early 1960's and to the present Lord Aldenham of the house of Gibbs for allowing me to examine the firm's records while still in their possession. These, plus Foreign Office documents relating to Peru, comprised the principal primary sources for my thesis. A good deal of additional research has been undertaken over the intervening years. The transfer of the Gibbs archive to the Guildhall Library meant that I could, with the assistance of catalogues, study items of whose existence I had hitherto been unaware. I sought out more information on shipping and the agricultural market: the first in the Customs House Library in London and in the Liverpool Record Office, the second among the great mass of contemporary farming literature available in the British Library. I also undertook a more exhaustive scrutiny of Foreign Office material. Most important of all, I visited Lima in 1973 and was able to work on a wide range of primary and secondary sources in the Biblioteca Nacional, the Instituto Riva Aguero and the Archivo Nacional. I also had the opportunity to consult valuable items in the possession of Sra. Eloyda Garland Melián de Montero, Sr. Félix Denegri Luna, and Sr. Carlos Palacio Moreyra. In 1973 and 1974, additional sources were examined in the Baker and Widener Libraries of Harvard University and in the Bibliotheque Nationale, the Archives Nationales, and the Archivès du Ministère des Affaires Etrangères in Paris.

It would be impossible to thank all the people whose kindness and cooperation have enabled me to complete this study. My debts to the late Professor John and Lord Aldenham I have already acknowledged. In all the institutions where I have worked I have heavily taxed the patience of countless archivists, librarians and assistants. In particular I should like to express gratitude to Dr. A.E.J. Hollaender, former Archivist of the Guildhall Library in London. I must also acknowledge the assistance, hospitality and advice that I received from Bill Albert and Heraclio Bonilla while I was in Peru. Valued suggestions and encouragement, moreover, were offered me by the most eminent and sympathetic of Peruvian historians, Jorge Basadre. Bill Albert, Gerald Crompton and Richard Wilson took the time and trouble to read my manuscript and offer perceptive and useful advice. In Leicester, Norwich and St. Louis, Judith Watts, Patricia Charman, Judith Sparks, Valerie Striker and Patricia Minute undertook the labours of typing and retyping.

I have received much financial assistance from a number of institutions. My original postgraduate research was undertaken with the support of the Carnegie Trust for the Universities of Scotland. The cost of countless visits to London since the mid-1960s was borne by the Research Board of the University of Leicester and the School of Economic and Social Studies of the University of East Anglia. The very considerable expenses connected with my work in Lima, Paris and Boston were generously met by the Nuffield Foundation.

Finally, I must thank my wife and children for tolerating the diversion from life which the unnatural exercise of book-writing has entailed.

St. Louis, March 1980

ABBREVIATIONS

AgHR	*Agricultural History Review*
ANF	Archives Nationales de France (Paris)
AP	*L'Agriculteur Practicien*
DBCR	*De Bow's Commercial Review*
EHR	*Economic History Review*
ER	*Edinburgh Review*
FM	*Farmer's Magazine*
FO	British Foreign Office, General Correspondence and Embassy and Consular Archives (London).
GGC	Antony Gibbs & Sons, Ltd. Extracts of Correspondence between the London head office and others concerning the firm's Guano business (London).
GH	*Glasgow Herald*
Hac Arch	Ministerio de Hacienda, Archivo Histórico (Lima).
HAHR	*Hispanic American Historical Review*
HHGC	Antony Gibbs & Sons, Ltd. Out-letter books (private) of Henry Hucks Gibbs, 1845-1882 (London).
HMM	*Hunt's Merchant's Magazine*
HW	*Household Words*
JA	*Journal of Agriculture*
JE	*Journal des Economistes*
JLAS	*Journal of Latin American Studies*
JRAS	*Journal of the Royal Agricultural Society of England*
LAP	*Latin American Perspectives*
Lob Corr	*Correspondence Respecting the Guano Islands of Lobos De Tierra and Lobos de Afuera, 1833-1852*
LGL	Antony Gibbs & Sons, Ltd., London head office general ledgers (London).
LRS	*Lloyd's Register of Shipping*
MAE	Archives du Ministère des Affaires Etrangères, Correspondance Consulaire et Commerciale (Paris)
MLE	*Mark Lane Express*
MM	*Mariner's Mirror*
NM	*Nautical Magazine and Naval Chronicle*
NQ	*Notes and Queries*
Parl Debs	*Hansard, Parliamentary Debates*

PP	*Parliamentary Accounts and Papers*
PP *(British Loans)*	*Correspondence between Great Britain and Foreign Powers, and Communications from the British Government to Claimants, relative to Loans made by British Subjects, 1847-1853.*
RCUS	*Minutes of Evidence Taken Before the Royal Commission on Unseaworthy Ships, 1873.*
RHES	*Revue d'Histoire Economique et Sociale*
THAS	*Transactions of the Highland and Agricultural Society of Scotland.*
WGC	Antony Gibbs & Sons, Ltd. Copybook of *in*-letters addressed to William Gibbs, 1854-1855 (London).

INTRODUCTION

'So great is the value of this branch of the national riches, that without exaggeration it may be asserted that on its estimation and good handling depend the subsistence of the State, the maintenance of its credit, the future of its increase, and the preservation of public order'.

Manuel Ortiz de Zevallos,
Peruvian finance minister, 1858

ISSUES

The expansion of the Peruvian guano trade in the middle of the nineteenth century was accomplished with relatively little effort. Guano was not a commodity that had to be produced in the normal sense of the term. Birds deposited it and a few hundred labourers dug it. No processing was required and its location on small islands[1] meant that there were no significant costs in transporting it to ocean-going ships. It was, moreover, a very superior guano, the lack of rainfall on the coast preventing the removal of its nitrogenous component. Nitrogen is the most important of all plant foods and guanos from other, damper parts of the world contained much less of it. Peru, in fact, had a virtual world monopoly in nitrogenous guano — and with trades like nitrate of soda (also Peruvian) still relatively undeveloped and very little ammoniacal material coming out of European and American factories, that meant a monopoly in nitrogenous fertilizer generally.

The trade had two other monopolistic features. Guano had a single owner after 1842: the Peruvian government; and exporting was placed in the hands of contractors who were awarded exclusive selling rights in specified markets. Such a very tight form of organisation meant that the trade could, if so wished, be rigorously controlled from the centre and the natural commodity monopoly exploited to the full. Government ownership, moreover, meant that the rewards could be claimed by the Peruvian nation rather than dissipated among a host of foreign commercial adventurers. With so many advantages, Peru, according to one excited observer in 1857, was destined to become 'at once the richest and happiest nation on earth'.[2]

The trade, moreover, gave Peru for a time a position of consider-able prominence in international commodity and capital exchanges.

---

[1] See, *inter alia*, Robert Cushman Murphy, *Bird Islands of Peru* (New York and London, 1925), *passim*.

[2] Carlos Barroilhet, *Contestación al Señnor Ministro de Hacienda del Perú* (Paris, 1857), p. 38.

Over the decade 1855 to 1864 Britain received cargoes of Peruvian
guano to the value of over £20,000,000: a figure greater than that
recorded for any other commodity imported from a South American
country.[3] Between 1861 and 1875 the Peruvian government, its
credit enormously strengthened by guano earnings, floated more
paper on the London money market than any other Latin American
state: £41.7 million, compared with the £14.4 million of its closest
rival, Brazil.[4] And guano quickly came to dominate the Peruvian
export structure and to provide the state with the great bulk of its
revenues.

Despite the favourable circumstances and the rapid growth,
however, much of the interest of the guano trade lies in miscalculation,
failure and wasted opportunity. In the first place, the period of
expansion in the principal overseas market, Britain, lasted for less
than two decades. The trade began in 1840: the British sales peak
came as early as 1856. Thereafter the sequence was contraction,
partial recovery, then rapid decline. 'The real heyday of the guano
period had been passed', writes C. A. MacQueen of the mid-1860s,
'although the ultimate collapse did not take place until 15 years
later'.[5] Secondly, guano produced no breakthrough in Peruvian
economic growth. The treasury remained hard up, agriculture and
industry enjoyed no general and sustained prosperity, and in 1876 the
government was forced to default on its bonded debt. After the losses
and expenses of the War of the Pacific in 1879-83 and the petering out
of the trade around the same time, Peru lapsed into a condition of
inconsequence within the world economy. Guano had come and gone,
and to many it seemed that its principal legacy had been one of
debilitation. It was, commented an English observer in 1881, 'a good
thing for Peru that the accursed Age of Guano has been brought to a
close. . .'.[6]

To what extent, one wonders, can the blame be laid on foreigners?
There are two questions here, to some degree separate. One concerns
the possibly harmful activities of powerful individual foreigners such
as the house of Gibbs, which dominated the trade for two decades
after its inception. Secondly, there is the much more general question
of the possible damage done to an underdeveloped economy when it
forms close ties with the more powerful metropolitan economies.

[3]*Parliamentary Papers* (hereinafter *PP*), 1860, LXIV, pp. 326-8; 1861, LX, pp.
326-38; 1866, LXVII, pp. 296-312.

[4]L. H. Jenks, *The Migration of British Capital to 1875* (London, 1938), pp. 421-3.

[5]C. A. MacQueen, *Peruvian Public Finance* (Washington, 1926), p. 38.

[6]A. J. Duffield, *The Prospects of Peru* (London, 1881), p. 91.

Comprehensive treatment of the latter issue is well beyond the scope of this book, although the documentation that will be presented on the independently-conceived follies of the Peruvian government will, hopefully, serve as a corrective to any interpretation that presents Peru as exclusively the passive, innocent victim of economic imperialism. The historical experience of relatively backward economies over the last century or two[7] and the interpretative work of Myrdal, Baran, Emmanuel, dependency theorists and many others[8] certainly forces the most radical questioning of the old optimistic assumptions of liberal economics concerning the vitalising influences of foreign trade and investment. Peru did get drawn, through guano, into a world economy shaped and dominated by advanced capitalism, and the opportunities in particular for borrowing which London and other money markets held out to her proved highly destructive in the long run and were the cause of much of the trouble that befell the country in the guano period. 'The Government's treasury was always without a dollar', observed a guano merchant of the 1860s, Henry Witt; 'they owed much and every sum which entered vanished like smoke, to satisfy the urgent claims of hundreds of creditors'.[9] Governments, however, are not normally compelled to borrow against their will. The reason why they do so may lie principally with an imbalance between the need or wish to spend and the capacity to tax, and this in turn may be essentially the product of local economic, social and political circumstances. The weak, of course, will be taken advantage of when they form an association with the strong, but the association is not necessarily forced upon them.

The focus of the chapters that follow is on matters relating to these broad questions, but is specifically placed on the narrower issue of foreign mercantile activity in Peru. I shall examine the relationship between the principal guano contractors in the trade's earliest and most buoyant phase, the English firm of Gibbs, and the successive

[7] This has hardly been analysed in *general* fashion by economic historians. The most interesting of the recent brief accounts relevant to our period is E. J. Hobsbawm, *The Age of Capital, 1848-1875* (London, 1977 edn.), ch. 5. Hobsbawm places Peru and other relatively backward economies in the 'world of victims' and 'losers', societies 'at the mercy of the west' (pp. 143-4, 161).

[8] Gunnar Myrdal, *Economic Theory and Underdeveloped Regions* (London, 1957); Paul A. Baran, *The Political Economy of Growth* (London and New York, 1968); Arghiri Emmanuel, *Unequal Exchange: A Study of the Imperialism of Trade* (London and New York, 1972); Andre Gunder Frank, *Capitalism and Under-development in Latin America* (London and New York, 1967); R. H. Chilcote, 'A Critical Synthesis of Dependency Literature', *LAP*, I, no. 1 (1974), with extensive bibliography on pp. 21-9.

[9] Diaries of Henry Witt, VI, 1 January 1862. (I am grateful to Sra. Eloyda Garland Melián de Montero for making this very valuable and hitherto largely unseen manuscript available for my inspection).

governments which held power in Lima between 1840 and the early 1860s. By the late 1850s Gibbs controlled almost the entire European market and held monopoly rights for Africa, Australia and the West Indies as well. Hobsbawm, describing mid-nineteenth century Latin American economies, writes of 'the foreigners who dominated the import and export of their staples . . .'.[10] Fieldhouse observes how European traders and financiers at the time were able to obtain a 'stranglehold' on the 'defenceless, though politically independent, states of South America . . .'.[11] Here, it seems, we have the quite dramatic instance of a single foreigner running a very large export trade. But what, exactly, was the nature and degree of the dominance, and did strangulation in fact occur? A number of very precise questions must be posed. Who was really in charge of the trade: government or merchant? Who made the crucial decisions on marketing policy? How were the proceeds shared out? How much power and income accrued to the Peruvian government through its ownership of the guano? To what degree and in what ways did Gibbs help intensify the problematic indebtedness of the government? Did the interests of the English merchants, vigorously pursued, stand in the way of Peru's full exploitation of her natural monopoly in nitrogenous fertilizer? Did Gibbs act in bad faith, twisting their contracts, securing illegitimate returns, and eroding the income due to the government? To what extent were government and merchant villains together, striking collaborationist bargains of mutual convenience at the expense of the nation at large? Did Gibbs's presence in the trade complicate and delay the involvement of indigenous merchants who, if given rights to sell guano, could have expanded the funds of liquid capital circulating within the Peruvian economy? Why and how did Peru dislodge Gibbs from the business in 1861?

To date, historians have seen Gibbs as a firm of great power, guilty of a variety of misdemeanours, and partly responsible for the trade's failure to yield notable benefit to Peru. By the late 1840s, according to Fredrick Pike, 'Peru's economy was largely at the mercy of Antony Gibbs & Sons of London'.[12] In Heraclio Bonilla's view, the house of Gibbs, enjoying 'absolute control . . . over the sale of guano in Europe', came to hold in their hands 'the vital mainsprings of the Peruvian economy'.[13] Jonathan Levin argues that in two important

[10] Hobsbawm, p. 146; also p. 148.

[11] D. K. Fieldhouse, 'Imperialism: An Historiographical Revision', *EHR,* 2nd ser., 14, no. 2 (1961), p. 202.

[12] Fredrick B. Pike, *The Modern History of Peru* (London, 1967), p. 98.

[13] Heraclio Bonilla, 'Aspects de l'histoire économique et sociale du Pérou au XIXe siècle' (unpublished doctoral thesis, Paris, 1970), p. 216.

respects there was a major conflict of interest between government and contractors, and that in both the latter emerged victorious. These concerned intermediate costs and market prices. 'Every consignment contractor', he writes, 'organized for the government the operations of loading, charter, storage, and final sale, and was rewarded with a 2 or 3 per cent commission on the cost of these operations ... While the interest of the government lay in keeping costs down, the contractor's profit lay in raising the costs and thereby increasing his commission on them. As the guano trade continued under consignment, therefore, intermediate costs increased steadily'.[14] As for price policy, the government as 'owner of a wasting resource ... wanted the highest possible price per ton, consistent with large sales.... The contractors, however, received a commission on gross sales proceeds, and if gross sales proceeds could be increased by lowering the price per ton ... their interest lay in selling at a low price'.[15] Levin concludes that on both counts — 'the holding down of intermediate costs and the maintenance of high monopoly prices — the government suffered losses. Because the contractors' interests were allowed to diverge from the government's while the government lacked any effective means of enforcement, the government's interests suffered'.[16] These important and highly specific issues — pricing policy in particular — must be analysed at some length in the discussion that follows.

Unfavourable assessment of consignee power and behaviour did not have to await the historian. In 1849 Sir Robert Peel wrote to Lord Palmerston, then foreign secretary, that the monopoly-consignment system of exporting served only the interests of the merchants; its abandonment would be 'to the advantage of every party excepting the two Houses who have the monopoly'.[17] It was described as 'vicious' in 1859 by Luis Mesones, a Peruvian diplomat, involving extravagant charges and grave damage to the national treasury.[18] In the view of

[14] J. V. Levin, *The Export Economies* (Cambridge, Massachusetts, 1960), p. 68.
[15] *Ibid.,* p. 69.

[16] *Ibid.,* pp. 70-1. These arguments have been restated in recent accounts of the trade by Peruvian scholars: Jorge Basadre, *Historia de la República del Perú 1822-1933* (Lima, 6th edn., 1969), III, p. 162; Bonilla, pp. 226-7; Luis Pásara, *El Rol del Derecho en la época del guano* (Lima, 1970), p. 15; Ernesto Yepes del Castillo, *Perú 1820-1920; un siglo de desarrollo capitalista* (Lima, 1972), pp. 62-3. See also Roberto Cortés Conde, *The First Stages of Modernization in Spanish America* (New York, 1974), p. 20.

[17] British Foreign Office, General Correspondence and Embassy and Consular Archives relating to Peru (PRO FO61 and FO 177 respectively), FO 61/124, Peel to Palmerston, 12 July 1849.

[18] Luis Mesones, *El Ministerio de Hacienda del Perú en sus relaciones con los administradores del huano en Europa* (Besançon, 1859), p. 20.)

6

José Casimiro Ulloa, writing in the same year, the English house wielded 'the greatest despotism that a person or family could exercise over a nation'.[19] Gibbs's participation in guano exporting, in the words of one of the first merchants in the trade, Carlos Barroilhet, had been 'a complete disaster for Peru, a public calamity'.[20]

THE GIBBS HOUSES BEFORE 1840

In 1840, at the start of the guano trade, the Lima branch of Antony Gibbs & Sons, known as Gibbs Crawley & Company, was one of the most important European merchant houses in Peru, and the parent concern in London was, by English standards, a mercantile establishment of moderate size and considerable respectability. The latter firm had been founded in 1808, quite a time that is before the complete liberation of the Spanish empire in America. This fact of chronology meant that Gibbs's earliest contacts with South America were secured through their trade with Spain. The Lima branch was not set up until 1822.

The very first Gibbs firm was established in Exeter in 1778.[21] In and around that port the Gibbs family had been active for more than two centuries. Antony Gibbs, the founder of the Exeter firm, and of the London house thirty years later, was born there in 1756, the son of a landowner and surgeon. In 1774 he was apprenticed to a Mr. Brook who had a business in the city and conducted a considerable trade in woollen cloth with Spain. Four years later, with financial assistance from his father, Gibbs set up his own establishment, and like Brook concentrated his attention on the textile trade with Southern Europe. He also engaged in the manufacture of woollens. The late 1770s, however, proved a bad time for forming commercial links with Spain and Italy, Gibbs's two main markets. Exeter's serge trade with these countries, which had been growing rapidly in the 1760s and 1770s,

José Casimiro Ulloa, *Huano (Apuntes económicos y administrativos)* (Lima, 1859), p. 116.

[20]Carlos Barroilhet, *Opúsculo sobre el huano dedicado a la nación peruano* (Paris, 1857), p. 6.

[21]Where not otherwise indicated, the first part of this section is based on material supplied in five books dealing with the Gibbs family and firm: Henry H. Gibbs, *Pedigree of the Family of Gibbs* (London, 1890); John Arthur Gibbs, *Pedigree of the Family of Gibbs* (London, 1932)and *The History of Antony and Dorothea Gibbs and of their Contemporary Relatives, including the History of the Origin and Early Years of the House of Antony Gibbs & Sons* (London, 1922); Wilfred Maude, *Antony Gibbs & Sons Limited, Merchants and Bankers, 1808-1958* (London, 1958); Colin Jones, *Antony Gibbs & Sons Limited, A Record of 150 Years of Merchant Banking, 1808-1958* (London, 1958). Of these the most useful are the third and fourth named. The books are only specifically cited when directly quoted.

fell away dramatically in the 1780s.[22] By then, moreover, the city had lost its place as the main trading centre of the south-west: one of the biggest ports in England early in the century, it was 'now far down the list of ports of the kingdom, surpassed by places that had been unknown fishing villages in 1688'.[23] By 1789 Antony Gibbs was bankrupt, and in consequence decided to quit Devon and move to Spain. He lived in Madrid between 1789 and 1792, and from the latter year until 1807 journeyed back and forth between Spain, Portugal and England. His main business in these years was as a commercial agent in the Peninsula for British manufactures. In addition, he undertook some importing on his own account, and in 1793 entered into a partnership with Juan Pomar of Malaga, engaging with him in the export of local produce until 1803. As an agent, Gibbs's first headquarters were in the Spanish capital, but difficulties arising from the conflict with France forced him to move to Lisbon in 1797 and from there to Cadiz in 1802. With the outbreak of war between Britain and Spain in 1805, and the imposition of an embargo on all British property, he made his way back to Lisbon. Before he left he had arranged through his son Henry for a Spanish firm to hold his own and his principals' stocks in Cadiz, Seville and other Spanish ports, and some way of disposing of these had now to be found. The local markets were in a weak condition at the time and Gibbs's agents had little success in finding an adequate number of purchasers. As a result, his attention was drawn towards South America.

The goods were nominally in Spanish ownership and would have to be shipped in a Spanish vessel. With Britain operating a naval blockade of Cadiz, however, it was almost certain that any such ship would be seized as a prize of war. Gibbs, accordingly, travelled to London and with the assistance of his brother Sir Vicary Gibbs, then Solicitor-General, managed to secure a licence guaranteeing safe passage out of port and stipulating that the venture be a round trip from Spain to Lima and back to Britain. The choice of Peru as the American destination, for reasons that are not clear, was Antony's own. On 24 December 1806 the ship chartered for the voyage, *Hermosa Mexicana,* set sail on consignment to Antonio Baras of Lima. The enterprise proved a complex and trouble-afflicted affair, but it did mark the beginning of Gibbs's direct dealings with Peru. In July 1808 Antony instructed one of his sons, then in Spain, to take

---

[22] The operations of the French in the Mediterranean during the American war of independence have been suggested as one possible reason for this. W. G. Hoskins, *Industry, Trade and People in Exeter 1688-1800, with special reference to the Serge Industry* (Manchester, 1935), pp. 80-1 and Appendix B, Tables I, III(a) and III(b).

[23] *Ibid.,* pp. 109-10.

8

advantage of the contact with Baras in Lima and send him more consignments: 'that connection', he wrote, 'may eventually be of service'.[24]

Antony Gibbs had made his last trip to Spain in 1807, and in the following year was appointed as one of four commissioners to deal with Portuguese property sent to England during the war. The job obliged him to live in London and this, combined with the useful personal contacts with bodies in the City which it entailed, encouraged him to set up his own mercantile establishment in the capital, in partnership with his eldest son Henry. His second son William joined the business in 1813, the style of the house then becoming Antony Gibbs & Sons — as it was to remain for the next 135 years.[25] At about the same time, following the restoration of peace between Spain and Britain, the house of Antony Gibbs, Son & Branscombe[26] was opened in Cadiz. This new establishment enabled Antony to preserve and build on the connections formed in the Peninsula during the previous thirty years. Most of the business was with the Spanish market, but opportunities were also enlarged for trading with America. The house was well placed for securing South American produce for consignment to Gibbs in London, and for receiving British goods which could be re-exported to the trans-Atlantic colonies. In 1811 and 1812 substantial consignments were despatched on joint account with other houses to Buenos Aires and Rio de Janeiro. Correspondence was opened with agents in Vera Cruz in Mexico, and in 1811 Antonio Baras began sending them goods from Peru and placing orders for shipments back out to the Pacific. Own-account, joint-account and commission trading as a whole grew over the years that

[24] Quoted in J. A. Gibbs, *History*, p. 197.

[25] Both sons had already been working with their father for some time — a sign, no doubt, of the generally awkward state of the family's finances. Henry joined the business around 1800 when he was 15, and William two years later when he was only 12. William, who was to become head of the house during the guano period, resented the fact that his formal education had been cut short, but Henry pointed out that his father simply had not the money to send him to university and that in any case he might have become 'profligate and dissipated' in such an environment. (Antony Gibbs & Sons Ltd. Family archives and mss.:- Letters and miscellaneous papers. 1787-1907. Henry Gibbs to William Gibbs 10 February 1808). Antony Gibbs instructed his young sons to apply themselves seriously to their commercial tasks. They ought, he suggested, to use their spare time studying 'accompts, French, Spanish, and History' and not to waste it on frivolities like music and drawing — unnecessary 'for young men who have their bread to get by their attention and cleverness in business . . .'. (*Ibid.,* Antony Gibbs to Henry and William Gibbs, 24 January 1805).

[26] William Branscombe, a partner in Cadiz from 1808 until 1813, was an associate of some years' standing. He was well acquainted with the ways of business in Cadiz and had many useful connections there. See *ibid,* letter (author unknown) to Henry Gibbs, 13 September 1808.

followed and was boosted by the establishment of a third firm in 1818, Gibbs, Casson & Company of Gibralter.

With these overseas contacts and the progressive disintegration of the Spanish empire in America, it was perhaps inevitable that Gibbs should attempt to set themselves up in business on the other side of the ocean. Building on the foundations laid in 1806, the firms had established the most important of their American connections with Peru. By 1818-20 the London house had 14 clients outside Europe, of whom as many as 11 were resident in Lima. The Peruvian capital, therefore, was the most likely location for a branch in South America and in 1820 John Moens, son of the Dutch consul in Bristol, was sent out to test the lie of the land. The London house was then under the direction of Henry Gibbs, as it had been since Antony's death in 1815. It was still a very small establishment, employing only about half a dozen people, and it was felt that no-one from the Gibbs family could be spared for the trip. Moens's arrival in Lima in January 1821 pre-dated the achievement of complete Peruvian independence by almost four years. It appears that his mission was not simply to await Peruvian liberation and seize any trading opportunities arising from this, but also to take immediate advantage of certain favourable changes in colonial commercial policy. Spain's involvement in the war in Europe had seriously impaired her capacity to satisfy the commodity needs of her colonies, and with legitimate trading drastically reduced the colonial customs houses had suffered great reductions in revenue. The requirements of both market and treasury combined to force on the viceroy in Lima a toleration of direct commerce with Britain. By 1818 British vessels were entering Callao and disposing of their cargoes without notable effort being made to expel them. In 1819 Callao was officially opened to British trade for a period of two years and British merchants permitted to settle there.[27] Gibbs's representative hoped to exploit these new opportunities. He was instructed, among other things, to arrange for cargoes of precious metals and other Peruvian produce to be consigned to Gibbs's houses in Spain and London.

On 21 January 1822 the house of Gibbs, Crawley,[28] Moens and Company was set up in Lima, the event being publicised in advance by the parent concern in London. By mid-December Gibbs had distributed about 1,000 circulars. Members of the firm were sent to

[27]Dorothy Burne Goebel, 'British Trade to the Spanish Colonies, 1796-1823', *AHR*, 43, no. 2 (1938), pp. 318-9.

[28]One of the partners was to be Charles Crawley. He was a nephew of Antony Gibbs and had held a partnership in the London firm for some years. He only spent four years on the West Coast, however, in 1829-33.

the North of England, Scotland and the Continent to supply further information and appoint agents for securing consignments. In 1823 branches of the new house were set up in Guayaquil, the main port of Ecuador, and in Arequipa, the principal trading centre of southern Peru.[29] The principal functions of the Lima house, according to instructions from London, were the receipt of cargoes from Europe and the arrangement of return consignments on a commission basis. Speculative, own-account ventures were limited to $10,000[30] in outlay, unless special permission for something larger was forthcoming from London. The first Lima profit and loss account, dated 30 June 1824 and covering a period of just over two years, showed a positive balance of $83,416. The credit total amounted to $122,621 and of this $82,559 represented commission earnings from business done for just over 50 clients, the great majority of whom were British.[31]

Moens managed the Gibbs house in its earliest days, and was one of only a handful of foreign traders in Lima.[32] As it turned out, however, he was not particularly attentive to the fine details of enterprise or very good at recruiting reliable employees. Important correspondence and accounting work were neglected. In July 1824 the Gibbs brothers reduced his partnership interest from 25 per cent to 10 per cent, and from then on the Lima establishment was styled as Gibbs Crawley & Company. In the following year Gibbs decided to make John Hayne, who had been book-keeping for the London house, a partner in the South American firm and send him out to the West Coast to attend to the accounts there. Like Moens he was not related to the Gibbs family, although he did have tenuous personal associations, one of his aunts having been a maid to Antony Gibbs's mother-in-law. He reached Lima in October 1826. Moens finally departed in May 1829, leaving Hayne as head of the firm, a position he retained until 1847. In the last full accounting year of the pre-1840 period (1st November 1838 to 31st October 1839)[33] the Lima concern registered

[29] Two branches were also opened in Chile in 1825 and 1826: one in Valparaiso, the other in Santiago.

[30] In conformity with contemporary usage, I have used dollars and pesos synonymously throughout the book. Conversion to sterling was usually made at the rate of $5 to £1.

[31] Antony Gibbs & Sons, Ltd. Business archives:- South American branches. Lima, Peru. Accounts, 1819-1883 (hereinafter referred to as Lima Branch Accounts), File 1, 1819-1837.

[32] FO 61/3, Rowcroft to Canning, 23 September 1824; FO 61/26, Wilson to Palmerston, 15 January 1834; Also R. A. Humphreys, *British Consular Reports on the Trade and Politics of Latin America, 1824-26* (London, 1940), p. 108, n.1.

[33] There were two profit and loss accounts for the year, relating to successive periods of six months.

a profit of $80,462, or roughly £16,000. Credit items came to $134,313, with income from commission business yielding $80,404 or 60 per cent of the total. Profitable own-account ventures—in bullion, silver ore, wool, skins, bark, barilla, flour, and straw hats—brought in $14,440 (11 per cent). Other prominent credit items included bond speculation, interest and delcredere. At the end of the period, as at the beginning, Gibbs Crawley & Company were essentially commission merchants, with about four-fifths of their commission earnings deriving from sales of foreign produce in Lima.[34]

As for the parent house in London, profit and loss accounts (from which the year-by-year figures for 1820 to 1879 in Appendix III have been derived) reveal an income of only modest proportions in the period 1820-39,[35] with a marked downward trend over the first 15 years. The annual average net returns in 1820-4 stood at £5,617; in 1825-9 at £4,053; in 1830-4 at £1,778; and in 1835-9 at £21,183. Again we find a heavy emphasis on commission work. Annual average net earnings from commissions and brokerage in the four five-year periods between 1820 and 1839 were, in sequence, £4,441, £4,009, £3,736 and £8,856. Expressed as a percentage of total earnings (as distinct from profits) the figures were 41, 48, 61, and 30. The reversal of the upward trend apparent in the last figure was principally due to the appearance in Gibbs's accounts of profits from the South American firms following 1834 (annual average receipts in London for the five-year period being £12,999). By the 1820s and 1830s trading on own and joint account (in commodities like bark, bullion, copper, nitrate of soda, wool, textiles, coal and bar-iron) had been reduced to a position of relative inconsequence. It was, on balance, unprofitable in the 1820s, giving an average annual net loss of £418. In the 1830s it was remunerative, but only just, the annual average net gain being as little as £57. Earnings of a financial nature, on the other hand, were of increasing importance throughout the period and beyond. The annual average net figure for interest and discount receipts amounted to £1,033 in the 1820s and £1,537 in the 1830s,[36] the bulk of these coming from covered credits granted by Gibbs to the overseas clients with whom they traded. Delcredere income, likewise stemming from commodity transactions, was of little significance in the 1820s, but in the 1830s brought in on average just

[34]All figures in paragraph based on Lima Branch Accounts, File 2, 1837-47.

[35]No commercial correspondence has been found for these years. This part of the chapter is based almost entirely on accounts in Gibbs's ledgers. Antony Gibbs & Sons, Ltd. Business archives:- London head office general ledgers (hereinafter referred to as LGL), first ser. 3, 3a, 4, 5, 6, 7, 8.

[36]Gross figures were very much larger.

under £800 a year. Returns from investments were of very little account before 1840, for the simple reason that Gibbs had not yet begun to place large portions of their wealth in stocks and shares. They did, however, take some Great Western Railway shares in the mid-1830s, and these had quite a major impact on profit levels in the last year of the period, 1839, in consequence of a sharp fall in the value of the paper.[37]

In 1820 Gibbs registered a profit of £5,882. In 1839 the figure was £27,350. Gross earnings, as indicated in the general profit and loss accounts, amounted to £8,766 in the first year and £35,488 in the second. Over the same period net commission and brokerage earnings had grown from £4,180 to £13,055. Apart from this expansion, the principal change occurring over the two decades (as revealed by clients' accounts) was a marked shift of emphasis away from Europe towards America. By 1839 Gibbs had sizable dealings with about a couple of dozen correspondents in Spain, compared with about half as many again in Latin America. On the eve of the guano trade the firm's existence as a commercial concern revolved to a very marked degree around the commission trade with the West Coast. Its connections with European countries other than Spain were in essence an extension of that trade, in particular through re-exports of Peruvian bark. Its connections with Spain, though still substantial, were mainly a survival from the past.

What we find by the end of the 1830s is a successful trading house of modest size, confining itself to the safer lines of business. In the twenty years or so following 1820 there were three partners in the London firm: two of Antony Gibbs's three sons, Henry and William, and their cousin Charles Crawley. The number of people working in the London office had grown from about half a dozen in 1820 to 16 in 1840. They operated, it may be assumed, in accordance with what William Gibbs in 1842 termed 'sound, prudent and cautious maxims'.[38] It is probable, however, that a detached observer in these years would have counted it a firm of only very limited prospects. It had not emerged, and was showing no signs of emerging, as a merchant bank of any significance. Commission trading was not likely to yield any grand returns until the volumes of commodities handled assumed very

[37] See Jack Simmons (ed.), *The Birth of the Great Western Railway, Extracts from the Diary and Correspondence of George Henry Gibbs* (Bath, 1971), pp. 68-9, 71. The reason for this one excursion into the field of stock exchange investment probably lay in the fact that George Henry Gibbs, Antony's son and the head of the firm from 1815 until his death in 1842, was one of the promoters of the Great Western and a director of the company between 1835 and 1842. *Ibid., passim.*

[38] Antony Gibbs & Sons, Ltd. Extracts of correspondence between the London head office and others concerning the firm's Guano business. Letter of 1 December 1842.

substantial proportions. It might well have seemed that these volumes would never be large as long as the firm was importing mainly from the West Coast and exporting mainly to Spain. Spanish foreign trade in the first half of the nineteenth century was, according to one historian, in 'a stage of contraction', and a lot of foreign exchange was spent on commodities which Britain could not easily supply. In 1829 textiles accounted for under a quarter of total imports, and iron and steel products for only a fraction of one per cent.[39] Further difficulties arose in relation to invasion in the 1820s, civil war in the 1830s,[40] sluggish population growth,[41] and the maintenance throughout the 1820s and 30s of strongly protectionist commercial policies, especially harsh in the relation to goods carried in foreign vessels. In 1825 some 657 articles were placed on a prohibited list.[42]

PERUVIAN PROSPECTS

Unhappily for Gibbs, Peru also posed very major problems. There was, in the first place, the simple matter of distance. It took about three and a half months to sail from Falmouth to Callao in 1826, and even longer on the homeward journey because of the prevailing southerly winds in the Pacific.[43] The route, by Cape Horn, was about the same length as that to Calcutta or Singapore. This meant that freight and insurance rates were relatively high and that eight months at least elapsed between the despatch of market reports and the arrival of goods on the Peruvian coast.[44]

Difficulties also arose from acute political instability. According to the Peruvian foreign minister in 1834, his country had 'not enjoyed a tranquil moment' since independence.[45] 'The years between 1826 and

[39] Jaime Vicens Vives, *An Economic History of Spain* (Translated Frances M. López-Morillas, Princeton, 1969), pp. 693-8.

[40] *Ibid.*, pp. 705-6; Louis Bertrand and Sir Charles Petrie, *The History of Spain* (London, 2nd edn., 1952), pp. 313-4, 323-5.

[41] Vicens, pp. 617-8.

[42] *Ibid.*, pp. 705-6.

[43] Humphreys, pp. 161-2. (All references to Humphreys's book in this chapter relate to the reproduction therein of Charles Milner Ricketts's Consular Report from Peru, FO 61/8, 27 December 1826).

[44] The Panama route, although much shorter, was neither quicker, cheaper, nor safer. Land transportation across the isthmus meant considerable delays in both trans-shipment and movement, expensive freights since the journey was in three parts, and risk of damage to goods because of so much loading and unloading. FO 18/37, Wood to Canning, 28 February 1826.

[45] *Correspondence Between Great Britain and Foreign Powers, and Communications from the British Government to Claimants, Relative to Loans Made by British Subjects, 1823-1847. PP,* 1847, LXIX, p. 665. Matias León to Wilson, 15 July 1834.

1845', writes MacQueen, 'may be described as a time when political and military questions completely absorbed the attention of the people'.[46] Peru's was a government of soldiers. The post-imperial state had not developed organically and representatively out of the country's heterogeneous social structure. It was, rather, a military accretion, growing within what Yepes has termed *'el vacio administrativo-politico':*[47] an unstable and insubstantial[48] institution, dominated by a succession of army commanders, most of whom had acquired fame and pretension during the war of independence. It certainly was not shaped to any signifiant degree by the Peruvian bourgeoisie, for that had always been a very small class, and with the departure of Spanish merchants, mineowners and others after independence, its relative weakness and insignificance had become accentuated.[49] Bourgeois liberalism was not without its voices in early nineteenth century Peru, and it helped shape one or two constitutions, but its successes were not guaranteed durability and its focus was on issues such as the social and political rights of the Church and the relative powers of Congress and Executive[50] rather than on the proper forms of economic organisation and external economic relations. Its manner and ideology, moreover, appeared out of place in a turbulent military state. Belford Wilson, the British chargé d'affaires, contrasted the unending 'struggle between Military depotism' with 'the frenetic attempt to enthrone theoretical excellencies in a Country one degree removed in Civilisation from the Natives of the Coast of Guinea'.[51]

Had there been a substantial economic liberalism, this might have been reflected in the field of tariff policy. Fredrick Pike notes that 'since economic liberalism was unchallenged at the time by Peruvian statesmen, no thought was entertained of affording tariff protection to native industries'.[52] This is a questionable observation. Lack of

[46]MacQueen, p. 3.

[47]Yepes, p. 33.

[48]Between the mid-1820s and mid-1840s, according to Fredrick Pike, 'Centralized power virtually disappeared...' in Peru. *The United States and the Andean Republics: Peru, Bolivia, and Ecuador* (Cambridge, Mass. and London, 1977), p. 83.

[49]FO 61/8, Ricketts to Canning, 16 September 1826; Basil Hall, *Extracts from a Journal written on the Coasts of Chili, Peru, and Mexico, in the years 1820, 1821, 1822* (Edinburgh, 1824), II, pp. 87, 96; C. R. Markham, *A History of Peru* (London, 1892), p. 290. Yepes writes of *'la ausencia de una burguesia con pretensiones de poder nacionales'.* P. 33.

[50]Pike, *Peru*, ch. 3, *passim.*

[51]FO 61/26, Wilson to Palmerston, 15 January 1834; also Yepes, pp. 38-9. For continental perspective, see Hobsbawm, pp. 145-9.

[52]Pike, *Peru*, p. 65. (Pike, however, does acknowledge the existence of protective policies in his most recent book, *Andean Republics,* p. 82).

a challenge to a principle does not prove active commitment to it and even a liberal caudillo could be forced, by revenue considerations alone, to eschew free-trade policies. The Peruvian tariff was not at all generous to the merchant, and indeed provided the main source of government income into the 1850s, when guano gained the ascendancy.[53] Import duties, of course, posed further problems for foreign traders such as Gibbs. In 1825 the tax on textiles and hardware goods, embracing most British imports, stood at 35%.[54] In 1826 a new commercial code set a duty of 30% on most items. Baizes and other coarse woollens, rough cotton cloths, hats, boots, shoes, saddlery, soap, candles, hogslard and furniture, however, had to pay as much as 90%, spirits were taxed at 100% and wheat at 114%.[55] Protectionist sentiment, without question, underlay many of these duties, for Peru herself was producing most of the more heavily-taxed items.[56] Levels fell somewhat between 1833 and 1836,[57] but were pushed up again in 1839 (to a 25-40% range in the main). Export duties were also placed on bark.[58]

There was little that could be termed 'collaborationist' about the regimes in Lima. Belford Wilson wrote in 1834 about the 'inveterately rooted Colonial Prejudice against a liberal Commercial Policy and Foreigners in general'. He considered that 'at least one half of the Deputies of Congress, and Members of Government, consider them in the light of Public Robbers, as Enemies to the Community, and whose property is therefore lawful plunder'.[59] For a short time in the late 1830s foreigners were prohibited from engaging in retail trade and, by a local decree, ordered to shut down all their commercial

[53]MacQueen, p. 37; Shane J. Hunt, 'Growth and Guano in Nineteenth Century Peru' (unpublished discussion paper, Princeton University, February 1973), p. 70. I am grateful to Hunt for sending me a copy of this paper, and another one entitled 'Price and Quantum Estimates of Peruvian Exports, 1830-1962', dated January 1973, and for giving me permission to cite his findings.

[54]Humphreys, p. 144.

[55]Ibid., pp. 144, 147-8, 198-206. 'In all new governments', wrote Consul-General Ricketts, 'the means of raising a revenue by levying high duties is generally recurred to; but in no country perhaps have the effects of the imposition of them been more distinctly marked than in this'. Ibid., pp. 144-5.

[56]Many of the taxed imports were regarded, in the government's words, as 'prejudicial to the agriculture and industry of the State'. Ibid., p. 201. A number of outright prohibitions were introduced in 1828. Hunt, 'Guano', pp. 102-3.

[57]FO 61/26, Wilson to Palmerston, 15 January 1834; FO 61/53, Wilson to Palmerston, 29 September 1838.

[58]FO 61/71, Wilson to Palmerston 30 April 1840; FO 61/82, Wilson to Palmerston, 15 April 1841. For a tabulated summary of tariffs between 1826 and 1872, see Hunt, 'Guano', p. 102.

[59]FO 61/26, Wilson to Palmerston, 15 January 1834.

houses in the Department of Piura.[60] One deputy at a Congress held in Huancayo in 1839 asked that every foreign establishment in Peru be closed, merchants confined to within one mile of the ports, and consuls and agents from abroad forced to leave the country.[61] The only president who gained official approval from the British because of his attachment to some of the principles of economic liberalism was Andrés de Santa Cruz, head of the short-lived Peru-Bolivia Confederation, 1836-9.[62] He was, in Palmerston's words, a man of 'enlightened mind' and an admirable believer in 'a liberal system of Commercial Policy'.[63] But he was clearly identified as exceptional[64], and the Treaty of Amity, Commerce and Navigation which he signed with the British in 1837[65] was rejected by President Augustín Gamarra less than two years later.[66] Traders like Gibbs, in short, usually operated within a political environment that was variously hostile, illiberal, unstable and violent.

Peruvian governments, moreover, were almost always short of money: to such a degree, in MacQueen's opinion, that they were scarcely able to perform the simplest administrative functions.[67] As late as 1840 revenues totalled only 3,000,000 pesos (£600,000), of which 1,600,000 came from customs duties and the rest from the poll tax (mainly from Indians) and an assortment of small imposts on commerce and property.[68] This weakness must be stressed. Governments on the eve of the guano period were impoverished as well as illiberal. Having neither the funds nor the inclination, they had no developmental plans for their economy. The financial problem was greatly aggravated by the costly warfare which the various military regimes so frequently engaged in. In so far as the ruling soldiers

[60]FO 61/58, Wilson to Palmerston, 14 January 1839; Peruvian government to Wilson, 27 January 1839.

[61]FO 61/61, Wilson to Palmerston, 31 December 1839. For other comments on anti-foreign sentiment, see FO 61/53, Wilson to Palmerston, 29 September 1838 and FO 61/82, Wilson to Palmerston, 15 April 1841.

[62]See L.C. Kendall, 'Andrés de Santa Cruz and the Peru-Bolivian Confederation', *HAHR*, 16, no. 1 (1936).

[63]FO 61/43, Palmerston to Wilson, 30 October 1837.

[64]See, for example, FO 61/93, Cope to Wilson, 12 October 1842.

[65]The first between the two countries. L. Hertslet, *Treaties and Conventions* (London, 1840 edn.), V, pp. 383-92; also FO 61/44, Wilson to Palmerston, 17 January 1837; FO 61/43, Memorandum of 11 October 1837 and Palmerston to Wilson, 30 October 1837.

[66]FO 61/71, Wilson to Palmerston, 30 April 1840; also FO 61/58, Wilson to Palmerston, 14 February 1839.

[67]MacQueen, p. 37.

[68]*Ibid.*

operated according to some economic rationale, it was one, not of liberalism or *étatisme,* but of short-term financial expediency, with the funding of the army and the navy as the principal preoccupation of treasury ministers. Internal turmoil was incessant and intense, as one army officer after another tried to seize power. This was compounded by the wars that Peru fought with her neighbours: Colombia in 1828-9. Bolivia in 1828, 1835 and 1841, and Chile and Argentina in 1836-9. Political instability, according to MacQueen, caused a great deal of confusion in budgetary affairs: 'the fiscal history of those times, even if it had been recorded, could not be counted of importance.'[69] Large and irregular expenditures, combined with slender revenues, inevitably led to borrowing. As the internal and external debts had been in default since just after independence,[70] the only way to raise money in an emergency, real or contrived, was by forced loan or by coming to mutually convenient arrangements with individuals. The people with the largest amounts of cash were usually merchants, and the most attractive of these were the European traders with their relatively easy access to metropolitan credit.[71] Instead of such dependence being reduced after 1840, as the government received larger and larger sums of money from the sale of its guano overseas, it came to acquire, as we shall see, quite gigantic dimensions.

The condition of the political environment was a matter of great significance for the trader. So too, of course, was the strictly economic environment. 'The scene is dismal', wrote Consul-General Charles Milner Ricketts in 1826. 'The lands are waste . . . the population diminished . . . and tranquillity to be secured. The ground plan of improvement is not yet traced'. The market, in fact, was an extremely small and difficult one to sell in. Merchants could, individually, misjudge it and, collectively, oversupply it. Peru's population was estimated at one million in the mid 1820s[72] and at one-and-a-half million in the early 1840s.[73] The great majority of the people were sunk in the deepest poverty. They were, moreover, largely concentrated in the valleys and plateaux of the Peruvian interior and the difficulties and expense of transport to these regions were enormous. Large masses of the population beyond the Andean watershed lay right outside the market economy. Goods were carried by mule-train, and freight costs from Quilca on the coast to Arequipa, less than 100

[69]MacQueen, p. 4.

[70]W. M. Mathew, 'The First Anglo-Peruvian Debt and its Settlement', *JLAS,* 2, 1 (1970), *passim.*

[71]Yepes, pp. 45-6.

[72]Humphreys, p. 109.

[73]John MacGregor, *Commercial Statistics* (London, 1843-50), 111, p. 1253.

miles inland, were estimated around 1830 to stand at roughly three times those of the ocean voyage from England.[74] In addition, from what we know of the conditions of the Peruvian mercantile classes in the 1820s and 1830s, firms like Gibbs Crawley must have had to act fairly liberally in the granting of credit before they could dispose of their commodities. With the exit of so many of the old Spaniards after independence, the main people left to buy European goods tended to be individuals of very limited means. In the mid-1820s, the principal purchasers in Arequipa were four dozen impoverished shopkeepers.[75] Debts owing to British merchants in Peru amounted to around $2,000,000 in 1826.[76] 'The petty dealer', observed Ricketts, 'receives an advance of goods, the price charged to him is proportioned to the risk, he pays a little and receives more goods, and a constant running account with him is kept open'. No law existed to 'compel the debtor to pay his debts, or to give security for their liquidation'.[77] If matters did reach the courts, there was no guarantee of an impartial judgement. 'The Juez de Comercio, or judge of commerce', observed Haigh, 'almost always leans to the side of the shopkeeper, which is to his own interest'.[78] In their list of outstanding debts on 31 October 1829, Gibbs's Arequipa house had as many as 143 entries, representing a total sum of just under $170,000.[79] Between 1 January 1835 and 31 May 1837 bankruptcies among Peruvian merchants and shopkeepers in Lima were estimated at a value of $1,120,000, of which just under $1,000,000 represented money owing to British subjects.[80] Moreover, during the military conflicts of these years, attacks were made on the Customs House stores in Callao. Claims for damages registered with the Peruvian government for the period 1 January 1835 to 31 December 1839 amounted to $79,000. Of this total, $44,439 was accounted for by claims from Gibbs Crawley & Co. — $23,376 of which was acknowledged.[81] The firm was certainly able to remit profits to the parent concern in the late 1830s, as already indicated, but the London ledgers for the 1830s clearly show a growing number of bad debts. Debit entries of this sort for

---

[74] Samuel Haigh, *Sketches of Buenos Ayres, Chile and Peru* (London, 1831 edn.), p. 382.

[75] *Ibid.*, p. 379.

[76] Humphreys, p. 130.

[77] *Ibid.*

[78] Haigh, p. 380.

[79] Antony Gibbs & Sons, Ltd. Business archives:- South American branches. Arequipa, Peru. Accounts 1819-1877, File 1, 1819-1837.

[80] FO 61/53, Wilson to Palmerston, 29 September 1839.

[81] FO 61/61, Wilson to Palmerston, 31 December 1839.

1834-7 totalled £25,245, and Peruvian debtors were the main offenders.[82]

A further problem was the generally low exporting, and therefore importing, capacity of the Peruvian economy. Post-colonial dislocations, in internal production and in external relations, brought about what Pablo Macera has termed *una crisis de adaptación,* lasting into the middle of the century.[83] Exports at the end of the period under consideration here were, by the estimates of the British chargé d'affaires, less than £2 million in value: £1,632,870 in 1839[84] and £1,948,347 in 1840.[85] The commodity structure was dominated, as it had been since independence and during the colonial period as well, by bullion and specie. In 1840 these accounted for 71.2 per cent of the exports to Britain; of the remainder, wool made up 12.8 per cent, nitrate of soda 6.5, cotton 5.9, copper 1.8, and bark 1.6.[86] One of the principal features of the post-independence Peruvian economy was the failure of the mining industry to effect any radical increase of productive capacity from the low levels reached in the years immediately preceding independence. The establishment of the Republic was accompanied, in Basil Hall's words, by 'the ruin of the old Spaniards',[87] the people who had at least a portion of the capital necessary for investment to control flooding at the mines and extend the range of extractive enterprise. 'Nowhere', wrote Edmond Temple in 1830, 'has destruction been more mischievously active, more complete, and more manifest, than in the property of the *azoguéros* of Peru'.[88] In the view of the British consul-general in the mid 1820s, 'without the aid of British capital' there was little chance 'of effecting an extension of the produce of the mines'.[89] This foreign capital did in fact move in, in small quantities,[90] but, failing to produce immediate

[82]LGL, first ser., 6 and 7. The Lima and Arequipa houses, it seems, advanced credits (of an unspecified nature) to a variety of clients, and when full repayment was not forthcoming Gibbs in London carried 75 per cent of the loss.

[83]Pablo Macera, *Las Plantaciones Azucareras en el Perú, 1821-1875* (Lima, 1974), pp. xviii-xx.

[84]FO 61/71, Wilson to Palmerston, 30 April 1840.

[85]FO 61/82, Wilson to Palmerston, 15 April 1841.

[86]Calculated from figures in *ibid.*

[87]Hall, 11, p. 87; also Humphreys, p. 115.

[88]Edmond Temple, *Travels in Various Parts of Peru, Including a Year's Residence in Potosi* (London, 1830), I, p. 309; also John Fisher, *Silver Mines and Silver Miners in Colonial Peru, 1776-1824* (Liverpool, 1977), p. 120.

[89]Humphreys, p. 158.

[90]Henry English, *A General Guide to the Companies formed for Working Foreign Mines* (London, 1825), pp. 8-9, 20-3, 46-52, 76, 79, 90-5; *ibid., A Complete View of the Joint Stock Companies formed during the Years 1824 and 1825* (London, 1827).

dividends, it quickly retreated,[91] thus confirming John Miers's forecast in 1826 that most of the money placed in the confident new mining companies would 'be wasted in merely learning how they should conduct their operations to advantage and in acquiring the necessary experience of the country'.[92] As late as 1834 the amount of silver produced in Peru was only 79 per cent of the 1820 total.[93] Bonilla gives annual production figures for 1790-1834[94] which, converted into five-year averages, show a strong downward trend in the late colonial period and a weaker upward trend in the early republican period.[95]

The mining industry was beset by a damagingly wide range of difficulties: physical destruction in periods of military conflict, political uncertainty, shortage of fuel, expensive quicksilver (for amalgamation), lack of capital, crippling interest rates on the money that could be borrowed, backward production techniques, and deficient entrepreneurship.[96] As long as the mining industry remained in a depressed state, Peruvian trade as a whole languished. Other commodities were relatively insignificant as exports and for none of them was there apparent any real prospect of dramatic increases in production. Plantation agriculture, confined to little pockets of land along the coast, was afflicted by many of the same problems that held

pp. 4-5; anon., *An Inquiry into the Plans, Progress and Policy of the American Mining Companies* (London, 3rd edn., 1825), pp. 65-7; Hansard, *Parliamentary Debates,* new ser. XII, cols. 1049-73, 16 March 1825.

[91]FO 61/8, Ricketts to Canning, 16 September 1826; FO 61/11, Ricketts to Canning, 14 May 1827; H. W. Dickinson and Arthur Titley, *Richard Trevithick* (Cambridge, 1934), p. 187.

[92]John Miers, *Travels in Chile and La Plata* (London, 1826), 11, p. 381.

[93]Bonilla, p. 25. 1820 was, admittedly, a good year, but no better than 1808, 1809 or 1811. See Fisher, p. 125.

[94]Bonilla, p. 25.

[95]The official figures, in *marcos de 8 onzas,* are 1790-4, 520, 498; 1795-9, 556, 751; 1800-4, 529, 014; 1805-9, 432, 924; 1810-4, 374,652; 1815-9, 368, 783; 1820-4, 151, 253; (1821-4, 81, 548); 1825-9, 207, 571; 1830-4, 300, 490. The post-independence upward trend appears to have continued up to the end of the 1830s and beyond. See Hunt, 'Exports', p. 64 and 'Guano', pp. 36-7. Fisher's figures for the years up to 1824 are roughly similar to Bonilla's, the only large differences coming in 1805-9 and 1815-9 with averages of 375, 769 and 270, 630 respectively. Fisher, pp. 124-5.

[96]FO 61/8, Ricketts to Canning, 16 September 1826; FO 61/12, Pentland to Ricketts, 2 December 1827; FO 61/39, Wilson to Palmerston, 20 July 1836; FO 61/52, Wilson to Palmerston, 29 March 1838; FO 61/71, Wilson to Palmerston, 30 April 1840; FO 97/284, Wilson to Canning, 27 August 1842; Temple, 1, pp. 357-60; Archibald Smith, *Peru as it is* (London 1839), II, pp. 3-24, 173; J. J. von Tschudi, *Travels in Peru During the Years 1838-1842* (London, 1847), pp. 283-4, 329-42; C. R. Markham, *Travels in Peru and India* (London, 1862), pp. 99-100; Levin, pp. 36-8; Hunt, 'Guano', pp. 43-51.

back progress at the mines.[97] Production of bark and wool was conducted according to primitive and exhaustive methods.[98] Nitrate of soda was still a very new article of commerce and was catering for only a small market, industrial rather than agricultural, in Europe.[99] Exports of these various commodities did, nonetheless, generally increase over the period, as they were almost bound to considering the extremely low levels prevailing immediately after independence.[100] The wool trade in particular entered a phase of some buoyancy in the late 1830s,[101] due mainly to the appearance of alpaca wool as an article of external commerce, directed principally to the Bradford area where Titus Salt was pioneering the manufacture of cloth with a cotton warp and an alpaca weft.[102] Generally speaking, however, Peruvian commerce in this period was in a very retarded and unpromising condition, and flowed from only a tiny portion of the country's total economic activity, the great bulk of this being either subsistence in nature or directed towards local markets. Gibbs's intention to make this unstable, impoverished and private corner of South America the main base of their mercantile operations must have been taken in London commercial circles as token of very limited ambition. What no-one knew, least of all Gibbs, was that they had placed themselves in a position, and acquired enough cash, contact and experience, to gain entry into one of the great trades of the nineteenth century — a trade organised in a way that presented unique opportunities to those few merchant houses granted rights of participation. It was perhaps the conclusive sign of the modesty of Antony Gibbs & Sons' objectives that they entered the guano business with the greatest reluctance and the most profound misgivings.

[97] Smith, II, pp. 172-3; Humphreys, p. 123; Jean Piel, 'The Place of the Peasantry in the National Life of Peru in the Nineteenth Century', *P & P*, 46 (1970), p. 122; Hunt, 'Guano', pp. 33, 36, 54; Macera, pp. xviii-xiv.

[98] FO 61/23, Wilson to Palmerston, 15 January 1834; FO 61/53, Wilson to Palmerston, 29 September 1838; Tschudi, pp. 307-15; Markham, *Travels*, pp. 10-1, 14-5, 33-6, 44-5; Gustave Planchon, *Des Quinquinas* (Paris and Montpellier, 1864), pp. 56-63.

[99] FO 61/23, Wilson to Palmerston, 10 March 1833; FO 61/53, Wilson to Palmerston, 29 September 1838; Board of Trade 2/5, Wilson to Palmerston, 13 August 1839; FO 61/71, Wilson to Palmerston, 24 March 1840; FO 61/71, Wilson to Palmerston, 30 April 1840; Charles Darwin, *Voyage of H.M.S. 'Beagle' Round the World* (London, 7th edn., 1890), pp. 263-5.

[101] For figures, see Humphreys, table facing p. 206; Hunt, 'Exports', pp. 57, 64.

[101] Bonilla, pp. 26, 33.

[102] Board of Trade 2/5, Wilson to Palmerston, 14 August 1839; FO 61/71, Wilson to Palmerston, 25 March 1840; FO 61/71, Wilson to Palmerston, 30 April 1840; FO 61/82, Wilson to Palmerston, 15 April 1841; FO 61/110, Crompton to Aberdeen, 20 March 1845; R. Balgarnie, *Sir Titus Salt* (London, 1877), pp. 64-72.

1

THE START OF THE GUANO TRADE, 1840-2

'The Government took advantage of the avidity of the Monopolists and Speculators'.

Thomas Crompton, British vice-consul in Islay, 1842

THE FIRST GUANO CONTRACT, 1840: QUIROS & CO

'In consideration of the payment by Instalments during 6 years, of the sum of $60,000 = £12,000', wrote the British chargé d'affaires, Belford Wilson, in his report on Peruvian trade in 1840, 'a Supreme Resolution was issued on the 10th of November, granting to Don Francisco Quiros an exclusive Privilege for Six Years to export to Foreign Countries "Huano" (excrement of Birds) from the Islands situated along the Peruvian Coast'.[1] This marked the official beginning of the guano trade. Quiros was a prominent Peruvian entrepreneur and the president of the Lima Chamber of Commerce.[2] With him in the venture were Carlos Barroilhet, a man of obscure origin, Aquiles Allier, described by Wilson as 'a French-Peruvian Stock Jobber', the French firm of Dutez & Co., and the Liverpool house of William Myers & Co.[3]

It seems curious, in the light of Peru's economic problems, that the start of the guano trade was delayed this long. The bird manure had been known and used in Peru for centuries.[4] It was, as noted earlier, located on coastal promontories and small off-shore islands, meaning that internal transport costs, enormously high in Peru, could hardly deter its exploitation and that it lay well away from the main areas of military conflict. Production costs were minimal. Guano was a natural product; it was dug rather than mined; and it required no processing. It was, moreover, an extremely effective fertilizer. This had already been proved, not only by application in Peru but by analysis in Europe. Samples removed by Humboldt were examined in

---

[1]FO 61/82, Wilson to Palmerston, 15 April 1841.

[2]Levin, p. 49.

[3]FO 61/82, Wilson to Palmerston, 15 April 1841; Barroilhet, *Opúsculo*, p. 11.

[4]See, for instance, William Walton, 'Guano, Its History and Uses Among the Peruvians', *JA* (October 1844), pp. 592-637.

France as early as 1806: 'from its composition', wrote Sir Humphrey Davy in 1813, 'it might be supposed to be a very powerful manure,'[5] The fertilizer, it was noted by the chemists, was particularly rich in nitrogen and phosphorous, two of the three essential plant foods. Its relatively high nitrogen content was its most distinctive virtue: the result of aridity along the Peruvian coast. In damper conditions much of the organic matter would have been lost through fermentation and removal in solution by rain water.

Three factors in particular account for the delay: the restricted character of the British fertilizer market, high ocean transport costs, and a degree of timidity among merchants in Peru. It certainly can no longer be argued that British farming was in a universally depressed and unprogressive condition in the two decades following the end of the Napoleonic Wars.[6] A great variety of articles had been bought and sold as manures for centuries,[7] and in the 1820s and 1830s bones especially were growing rapidly in popularity as an application in the mixed-farming systems of north-eastern Britain and in Cheshire dairy farming, a sizable portion of them being imported from the Continent.[8] Nevertheless, the British farming community at large still depended very heavily on its own internally-produced animal manure for the replenishment of the land, and there existed a traditional, and to some extent healthy, preference for this well-tried and bulky application which improved the structure as well as the fertility of the soil. As late as 1860 it was calculated that around 60 million tons of farmyard manure were applied to British crops each year, a figure enormously in excess of that for all purchased fertilizers taken together.[9] As for freight costs, it was considered by most merchants in the 1830s,

[5] Sir Humphrey Davey, *Elements of Agricultural Chemistry* (London, 1813), pp. 258-9. See also W. A. Smeaton, *Fourcroy, Chemist and Revolutionary, 1755-1809* (Cambridge, 1962), p. 158.

[6] See, for example, E. L. Jones, *The Development of English Agriculture, 1815-1873* (London, 1968), pp. 13-7; D. C. Moore, 'The Corn Laws and High Farming', *EHR*, 2nd ser., 18, no. 3 (1965), pp. 545-8.

[7] See, *inter alia*, J. C. Loudon, *An Encyclopaedia of Agriculture* (London, 1825), pp. 328-42; Joan Thirsk (ed.), *The Agrarian History of England and Wales, IV, 1500-1640* (Cambridge, 1967), pp. 167-8; Eric Kerridge, *The Agricultural Revolution* (London, 1967), pp. 240-8.

[8] For general accounts, see C. W. Johnson, *The Use of Crushed Bones as Manure* (London 3rd edn., 1836); John M. Wilson (ed.), *The Rural Cyclopedia* (Edinburgh, 1847), I, pp. 473-85; John C. Morton (ed.), *A Cyclopedia of Agriculture* (Glasgow, Edinburgh & London, 1855), II, pp. 257-304. Also F. M. L. Thompson, 'The Second Agricultural Revolution, 1815-1880', *EHR*, 2nd ser., 21, no. 1 (1968), pp. 66, 68-70, 75.

[9] T. Anderson, 'Instructions to Farmers on the Reading of Analyses and the Valuation of Manures', *THAS*, new ser., 18 (1859-61), p. 433.

according to Carlos Barroilhet, that 'the extreme cheapness of fertilizers in Europe, and the inevitable costliness of transporting the guano' ruled out any possibility of a viable export trade.[10] Guano belonged to the category of bulky, relatively low-value articles which featured hardly at all in long-distance commerce in the early nineteenth century. Bones could be carried economically to Britain over the short North Sea routes, but the most serious doubts must have been entertained about the profitability of transporting (and insuring) guano on the three to four month journey down the Pacific coast, round Cape Horn, and north-east across virtually the entire latitudinal stretch of the Atlantic. Even after the trade began, freight rates on each ton could on occasions amount to more than half the market price. As for lack of enterprise among merchants in Peru, this perhaps ought to be seen largely as a function of the first two factors. It might, however, be viewed as to some extent independent,[11] for it should not have been beyond the capacity of merchant houses, witnessing the half-empty holds of vessels leaving Peru for Europe,[12] to have despatched more than the occasional sample of fertilizer of established merit. Such samples were sent off by Barroilhet, Allier, Gibbs Crawley and a merchant by the name of Sarratea in the 1830s,[13] and possibly by others as well, but this sort of market probing was far too tentative and small-scale to have any significant commercial consequences. The odd package could prove virtually nothing about the commodity's general marketability. Someone had to take the risk of sending a cargo or more, so that a large number of practical and well-publicized experiments could take place in the intended markets.

By his own account, the one man who had the necessary faith and vision was Carlos Barroilhet. He had witnessed guano's effects in Peru and believed that 'the base manure could well be transformed into the purest gold'. The problem of freight costs had been exaggerated. Guano could be carried more cheaply to Europe than to the

---

[10]Barroilhet, *Opúsculo*, p. 10; also pp. 17-8.

[11]See, for example, *ibid.*, p. 10 and Aquiles Allier, *Alcance al Comercio Numero 742 Sobre la Cuestion del Huano* (Lima, 1841), p. 15.

[12]'Les navires qui reviennent du Pérou', observed a French journal in 1842, 'manquent généralement de chargements pour leur retour; les métaux précieux peuvent bien servir de contre-valeur aux envois qui ont été faits, mais ils ne remplissent point un navire; le cotton, qui est un produit nouveau pour ce pays, la laine, le quinquina, sont eux-mêmes des articles insuffisants pour alimenter un tonnage important'. 'Huano, Nouvel Engrais Venant du Pérou', *JÉ*, 1st ser., 2 (1842), p. 93. See also J. P. Faivre, *L'Expansion Française dans le Pacifique de 1800 à 1842* (Paris, 1953), p. 365.

[13]Antony Gibbs & Sons, Ltd. Extracts of correspondence between the London head office and others concerning the firm's Guano business. Letter of 6 February 1841; Alejandro Cochet, *Al Soberano Congreso* (Lima, 1849), p. 13; Barroilhet, *Opúsculo*, p. 11; Allier, p. 8; Maude, p. 27.

Arequipa region,[14] where it was already in use as a manure. British farmers were buying some Peruvian nitrate at considerable expense, so why not guano as well?[15] The crucial step, linking this sort of conviction in Peru with real effort at the European end to give guano a fair trial, was the decision by Barroilhet and Aquiles Allier to ask Horace Bland, an English merchant resident in Valparaiso, to pass on some samples to his associate in Liverpool, William Myers.[16] This happened around 1837-8. Myers turned out to be just the man to gauge the market. He had farming interests himself and took up the examination of guano's potential with considerable enthusiasm. The fertilizer was shared out among a number of farmers in the vicinity of Liverpool and the results proved most encouraging. Myers asked for further supplies and arranged for more sophisticated trials in which guano's effects could be measured on particular crops and soils. The outcome of these experiments added strength to his conviction that there might well be money in the new fertilizer. He told the enthusiasts back in Lima that guano would probably sell for £24 or more a ton and offered them his financial backing in starting the trade.[17]

Myers's authorization for an approach to the government to secure exclusive trading rights arrived in Lima in the autumn of 1840. The prospects for success were in one sense quite good. The granting of monopolies was consistent with Peruvian tradition, being an important source of revenue for the state,[18] and the habit had, as it happened, become quite pronounced under the incumbent Gamarra regime.[19] On the other hand, there was an apparent reluctance to grant privileges of this sort to foreigners.[20] The prevailing climate of opinion in Peru, Bonilla writes, 'was not propitious for direct dealings between the Peruvian government and foreign merchants . . . . A direct concession for the working of the guano deposits would have aroused public hostility'.[21] In such circumstances a respectable Peruvian front

---

[14]This was almost certainly correct. See observations on relative costs of ocean and overland transport above, pp. 17-8.

[15]Barroilhet, *Opúsculo*, p. 18.

[16]*Ibid.*, pp. 12, 18; Allier, p. 8.

[17]Barroilhet, *Opúsculo*, p. 18; also Allier, p. 8.

[18]Levin, pp. 50-1.

[19]FO 61/82, Wilson to Palmerston, 15 April 1841.

[20]The British chargé d'affaires indeed viewed the very practice of handing out monopoly rights as 'part of a series of ridiculous attempts making [sic] by the Government of General Gamarra to exclude Foreigners from any participation in the benefits that may be deserved from the Speculations in the Peruvian Native Productions'. *Ibid.* See also FO 61/71, Wilson to Palmerston, 30 April 1840.

[21]Bonilla, pp. 204-5. See also J. P. Faivre, 'Le Début des Exportations du Guano Péruvien', *RHES*, 37 (1959), p. 118.

man was required. Francisco de Quiros, a man of local prominence who also had some useful money to hand, was selected. His name does not appear in accounts of the earlier market probes, so one can assume that he came into the guano business on invitation rather than on personal initiative.[22] The details were worked out with the finance minister, Ramón Castilla.[23] The merchants were given exclusive rights to sell guano from the Peruvian islands in any market they chose for a period of six years, and no limits whatever were set upon the amount to be exported. The sum of 40,000 pesos was to be paid at once to the government, 10,000 more at the end of the first year, and a further 10,000 at the end of the second.[24] Less than a month later, on 4 December 1840, the duration of the monopoly was extended by an extra three years, on the understanding that at the start of this period a further 15,000 pesos would be given to the government, with another 15,000 coming 18 months later.[25] On 17 December it was decreed that the trading rights applied to all the deposits in existence along the coast of Peru, whether they be on islands or not.[26] All these arrangements were made in Quiros's name and his alone.

The Gamarra regime was charging 90,000 pesos, or £18,000, for trading rights extending over almost a decade. Of the 40,000 pesos that were required immediately, 38,500 were taken in the form of depreciated debt certificates which Allier had been holding and which were accepted at face value.[27] The initial cash payment received by the government, therefore, amounted to no more than 1,500 pesos or about £300. Figures such as these suggest that the government was in a state of almost total ignorance as to guano's potential profitability as an export commodity. Allier relates how two of the government men who took part in the contract negotiations, Dr. Charún and Col. Iguaín, 'were astounded that D. Francisco Quiros should offer so much money for something so valueless . . .'.[28] No effort was made to

---

[22] According to Barroilhet, Quiros made his approaches to the government 'on behalf of Allier'. The contract that followed, Cochet wrote, was essentially Allier's, but was made 'under the pseudonym of Quiros . . .'. Barroilhet, *Opúsculo*, p. 18; Cochet, p. 14.

[23] Allier, p. 8.

[24] P. E. Dancuart and J. M. Rodríguez (eds.), *Anales de la Hacienda Pública del Perú. Leyes, Decretos, Reglamentos y Resoluciones; Aranceles, Presupuestos, Asientos y Contratos que constituyen la Legislación y la Historia Fiscal de la República* (Lima 1902-1920) [hereinafter *Anales*], III, pp. 103-5.

[25] *Ibid.*, p. 126.

[26] *Ibid.*, p. 127.

[27] FO 61/81, Wilson to Palmerston, 22 December 1841; Bonilla, p. 205; Levin, pp. 51-2.

[28] Allier, p. 15.

enlighten them as to the success of Myers's experiments.[29] There was, however, a major weakness in the merchants' position. A government had the crude power to tear up a contract, and as Peruvian administrations were chronically short of funds they could be expected to seek much larger returns from guano if the commodity proved marketable on a large and profitable scale. Already the deposits were being viewed as State property.[30] The merchants apparently were fully aware of the dangers, being, in Barroilhet's words, 'in no doubt that, when the Government learned of the high price at which guano sold in England and applied the principle of *lesión enorme* provided for in law, the contract would be annulled without compensation'.[31]

During this first year of the trade the contractors despatched 22 vessels (19 of them to Britain) carrying a total of 7,723 tons of guano.[32] The first to leave was the *Bonanza*, a 176-ton British ship which cleared from Callao on 3 March 1841.[33] Two more were sent off in April, one in May, two in June, one in July, and four in August. The pace speeded up towards the end of the year, no doubt partly in anticipation of the scrapping of the contract, 11 vessels being sent off in October and November.[34] The response in Britain was immediately favourable. In July guano was referred to in *The Liverpool Times* as 'the most powerful and concentrated of all manures'.[35] In October James Johnston, professor of chemistry at Durham University, pronounced that it contained 'the greater part of the ingredients which are necessary to the growth of almost every variety of crop'.[36] For

[29] See Cochet, p. 5; *Exposición que Don Francisco Quiros y Don Aquiles Allier Elevan al Soberano Congreso* (Lima, 1845) (hereinafter Quiros y Allier), p. 5 (I am grateful to Sr. Carlos Palacios Moreyra for providing me with a copy of this informative pamphlet).

[30] See, for example, article I of the contract, *Anales*, III, p. 104; also *ibid.*, p. 127. For further remarks on the subject, see Levin, p. 52.

[31] Barroilhet, *Opúsculo*, p. 19.

[32] Ministerio de Hacienda. Archivo Histórico (hereinafter Hac Arch), Año 1842, Razón General de los cargamentos de huano Remitidos á Europa por Quiros y Ca. Belford Wilson gives the higher figures of 8,602 tons but includes at least one vessel sailing from a Peruvian port with Bolivian guano. FO 61/81, Wilson to Palmerston, 22 December 1841.

[33] FO 61/87, Sealey to Palmerston, 1 January 1842.

[34] Razón General, *loc. cit.* Somewhat different dating appears in FO 61/87, Sealey to Palmerston, 1 January 1842, but the same clustering in the late months of 1841 is clearly shown.

[35] Quoted in *The Times*, 30 July 1841, p. 4.

[36] James Johnston, 'On Guano', *JRAS*, 2 (1841), p. 319. Thomas Way, when he was consulting chemist to the Royal Agricultural Society, calculated that an average specimen of Peruvian guano contained 17.41 per cent ammonia, 24.12 per cent phosphate of lime, and 3.5 per cent potash. See his 'On the Composition and Money Value of the Different Varieties of Guano', *JRAS*, 10 (1859), pp. 196-230.

Cuthbert Johnson, in the same month, there was 'no doubt but that this is a very powerful manure; the very composition of its salts would indicate that fact'.[37] Impressive testimonials were matched by the prices which the new fertilizer fetched. One cannot talk of any single price, for the market was as yet very small and fragmentary, but returns generally were encouragingly high. Gibbs in London noted in July 1841 that *Bonanza* guano had been selling at between 14s. and 16s. per cwt., i.e. up to £16 per ton.[38] James Johnston, a month or two later, wrote of a market value (retail) of £25.[39] Two October letters in the Gibbs correspondence referred to retail levels equivalent to between £24 and £26 a ton.[40] In November Gibbs Crawley wrote of reports from England indicating prices of between £18 and £28[41] and in December, of news from Myers concerning sales at £18 'and 7,000 to arrive at same'.[42] This latter transaction had been made with the London firm of MacDonald & Co., which had been one of the earliest importers of Peruvian nitrate.[43] They also acquired the right to buy additional guano under the same terms if they so chose.[44] Despite the fact that the arrangement was highly conditional, depending on MacDonald's ability to resell at a profit,[45] it did seem to confirm that there existed a sizable and willing market in Britain.

[37] Cuthbert Johnson, 'On the Guano', *FM,* 2nd ser., 4 (October 1841), p. 266; also *ibid., Modern Agricultural Improvements* (London, 1847), pp. 135-6 (for details of experiments in 1841); Joshua Trimmer, *Practical Chemistry for Farmers and Landowners* (London, 1842), p. 178.

[38] Antony Gibbs & Sons, Ltd. Extracts of correspondence between the London head office and others concerning the firm's Guano business. Folder 2, letter of 1 July 1841. Hereinafter references to these extracts will take the following form (using the letter cited here as an example): GGC (i.e. Gibbs's Guano Correspondence), 1 July 1841. There are, in all, three folders. 1: Extracts from the Private Correspondence of Antony Gibbs & Sons with Gibbs Crawley & Co. and William Gibbs & Co. (style of South American branches after 1 May 1847) on the subject of Huano Especially with reference to the Price from 1841 to 1856. 2: Extracts of Correspondence between ourselves and Our Lima House and others, on the subject of the Guano Business, and chiefly with reference to the Price — ranging from Novr 25 1840 to June 30 1856. 3: Extracts from the Correspondence of William Joseph Myers and others and William Gibbs on the subject of the Guano Business between the years 1842 and 1849. (It will be noted that this important source comprises extracts. One cannot, therefore, be absolutely certain that all the quotations used in the text are exact representations of the original comments).

[39] Johnston, p. 319.

[40] GGC, 1 and 15 October 1841.

[41] *Ibid.,* 23 November 1841.

[42] *Ibid.,* 17 December 1841; also 4 February 1842.

[43] Quiros y Allier, pp. 6, 10.

[44] *Ibid.,* p. 6; Barroilhet, *Opúsculo,* p. 19.

[45] Witt Diaries, 1, 19 July to 17 November 1842.

A very rough guess might place the average wholesale price at around £18 per ton. Setting this against the cost of getting guano onto the British market, one can get some idea of the profitability of the trade in its first year. According to Belford Wilson, digging and loading expenses came to about 11s. 6d. per ton. Freights cost £4 17s. on average, and another 11s. 6d. was required for warehousing, insurance, sales commissions etc. in Britain.[46] Expenses, therefore, totalled £6, leaving a profit (excluding deductions for small fixed capital costs and a variety of incidental expenditures in Lima, which Wilson did not estimate) of around £12 per ton. Not much more than a couple of dozen tons, therefore, would reimburse the contractors for the initial cash payment they had made to the government. Figures of this sort explain why people in Peru came to feel that guano 'would prove a second Potosí'[47] and that Quiros and his friends had acquired control of the trade for an absurdly low rental.

The slender defences around the 1840 contract were quite overwhelmed in November 1841. Towards the end of that month the *Dyson* sailed into Callao carrying a cargo of coal and news that guano had been selling at prices as high as £28 per ton.[48] It docked on 26 November. So too did the *Minstrel Boy* and the *Enchantress*. All three had come from Liverpool, and seem to have been the first vessels to leave Britain for Callao after Peruvian manure had been unloaded and sold.[49] Information that the contractors had thus far been able to keep to themselves was now available to the public. Accusations of trickery and deceit were widely levelled against Quiros and Allier and clamorous demands made, inside as well as outside official circles, for the termination of their contract.[50] Some moves, however, had been made by the government even before the *Dyson* arrived. This alertness probably resulted from a number of factors — the sight of so many ships leaving Callao laden with fertilizer (as many as seven in October),[51] the efforts of one Alejandro Cochet to advance his own claims over guano and, in the process, to cast dark aspersions on the conduct of the present

[46] FO 61/83, Wilson to Palmerston, 22 December 1841.

[47] FO 61/94, Crompton to Aberdeen, 14 December 1842.

[48] Levin, p. 52: *Anales,* III, p. 24; Allier, p. 16; Quiros y Allier, p. 45; Hac Arch, Año 1845, Memoria Sobre La Negociación Del Guano (Por El Encargado De La Cuenta De Ella, Contador Dn. Pedro José Carillo).

[49] Data supplied in FO 61/87, Sealey to Palmerston, 1 January 1842 ('Return of the British Trade at the Principal Ports within the Consulate General of Peru, during the Year ending the 31st December 1841').

[50] Allier, p. 16; Quiros y Allier, p. 6.

[51] Razón General, *loc. cit.*

traders,[52] and the arrival of vessels from Britain and of fast steamships from Valparaiso in October and early November which might well have brought word of the disposal of a cargo of Bolivian guano from the *Charles Eyes* which had docked in Liverpool two months ahead of the *Bonanza*.[53] As far back as 1 September (and perhaps earlier)[54] the *Consejo de Estado* had advised the Executive to scrap the original Quiros contract.[55] This pressure continued over the weeks that followed, and in mid-November Gibbs Crawley reported that guano was 'becoming very important' and that annulment was being seriously discussed.[56] On 23 November they wrote that some radical change was imminent, the *Consejo* having again strongly advised cancellation[57] and the new president, Manuel Menéndez, favouring at least some major modifications of the existing arrangements.[58] The information brought in by the *Dyson* was probably the last straw, creating the *explosión furiosa*,[59] the *commoción electrica*[60] which the government had to quell as quickly as it could. The first guano contract was annulled on 27 November.

[52] Cochet, *passim*. For further comment on Cochet and his impact, see Levin, p. 48, no. 67; Pierre Larousse, *Dictionnaire Universel du XIXe Siècle* (Paris, 1866), p. 1573.

[53] Data on Callao arrivals from FO 61/87, Sealey to Palmerston, 1 January 1842. For pre-*Dyson* references to British sales, see GGC, 13 and 23 November 1841. Information on *Charles Eyes* from FO 61/81, Wilson to Palmerston, 22 December 1841; also FO 61/82, Wilson to Palmerston, 15 April 1841 and FO 61/94, Crompton to Aberdeen, 14 December 1842. This indeed was the cargo that launched the international guano trade. It is not at all clear who arranged for its despatch, but Quiros or Barroilhet, or both, may have had a hand in it. Contracts were later arranged with some of the merchants in the Peruvian trade (Quiros Allier & Co. in particular) and the Gibbs Crawley establishment in Valparaiso, and Antony Gibbs and W. J. Myers attended to sales in Britain. References to Bolivian guano in the Gibbs archive, however, are infrequent, fragmentary, and not at all informative. The trade never assumed important dimensions. In 1846-50, for example, British guano imports from Bolivia were, in volume, only one-thirtieth of those from Peru, and were generally of inferior quality. For early developments, see FO 16/46, Walpole to Aberdeen, 12 April 1842; FO 61/82, Wilson to Palmerston, 15 April 1841; FO 61/81, Wilson to Palmerston, 22 December 1841; FO 61/101, Gibbs and Myers to Sandon, 24 March 1843; FO 61/126, Billinghurst to Adams, 2 December 1844; FO 126/11, Masterton to Bidwell, 15 March and 25 November 1842; 27 April and 10 August 1843; FO 126/13, Masterton to Aberdeen, 21 February 1845; Archives du Ministère des Affaires Etrangères, Correspondance Consulaire et Commerciale (hereinafter MAE), Chuquisaca 3, Villamus to Guizot, 24 February 1842; Witt Diaries, 1, 19 July to 17 November 1842.

[54] See Cochet, pp. 7-8.

[55] Memoria Sobre La Negociación Del Guano, *loc. cit.*

[56] GGC, 16 November 1841; also Cochet, pp. 8-9.

[57] The *Consejo* had also been suggesting that the only legal way to dispose of 'natural assets' was through public sales and not through loan contracts. See GGC, 23 November and 17 December 1841.

[58] *Ibid.*, 23 November 1841.

[59] Allier, p. 16.

[60] Barroilhet, *Opúsculo*, p. 19.

THE SECOND CONTRACT, 1841: QUIROS ALLIER & CO

The annulment was made, in Belford Wilson's words, 'on the plea, warranted by Spanish Law, of enormous Lesion to the State; the Government at the time of granting the Monopoly not having been aware of the Value of "Huano" as a Return'.[61] The government, in short, wanted to gain an income from the trade more commensurate with its current profitability. This was important towards the end of 1841 because of the increased expenditures likely to ensue from the conflict that had begun with Bolivia. The factors underlying this struggle are of little relevance here.[62] Suffice to note a significant point of chronology: that Peru officially declared war on Bolivia on the very same day that the guano contract was cancelled.[63] A request was immediately made for fresh proposals 'on the condition that, within Eight days after the celebration of the Contract, a Sum of Money shall be paid in to the Treasury sufficient to defray the urgent Expenses of the State'.[64] As Wilson saw it, guano was 'about to be made use of for waging a War against a neighbouring Republic'.[65]

The immediate response to the government's request for fresh offers was not, as it happened, particularly encouraging. The British firm of Maclean Rowe & Co. asked to take the business on consignment at a commission of 2½% and to advance 20 pesos per ton to the government before shipment. This proposal was turned down,[66] and the government itself began to make suggestions. It 'wished us to take it', wrote John Hayne, the head of Gibbs Crawley, in December 1841, 'and I was desirous of it; but Government wanted an advance of $125,000 down and $50,000 a month for a certain time' — terms which Hayne rejected.[67] Quiros Allier & Co. (as

[61] FO 61/81, Wilson to Palmerston, 22 December 1841.

[62] 'Crisis was the normal state of affairs in Peru and Bolivia after the collapse of the confederation', writes R. N. Burr. 'General Agustin Gamarra, president of Peru, remained as dedicated as ever to confederation, notwithstanding his personal participation in the Expedition of Restoration. From 1839 to mid-1841 Gamarra worked unceasingly for that objective. Tragic Bolivia, torn by internal disorder after the downfall of Santa Cruz, was ripe for Peruvian intervention'. *By Reason or Force. Chile and the Balancing of Power in South America, 1830-1905* (Berkeley and Los Angeles, 1965), p. 64.

[63] FO 177/16, Wilson to Peruvian foreign minister, 1 December 1841. Peru, however, had invaded Bolivia some weeks earlier, and President Gamarra had already been killed at the battle of Ingavi. See Burr, p. 67; Pike, *Peru*, p. 85.

[64] Quoted in FO 177/16, Wilson to Peruvian foreign minister, 1 December 1841.

[65] *Ibid.*, also GGC, 18 December 1841, in which Gibbs Crawley & Co. reported, 'Government want all their revenues for military purposes'.

[66] GGC, 17 December 1841.

[67] *Ibid.*

they were now known) — comprising Quiros, Allier, Dutez, Barroilhet and Horace Bland,[68] Myers's West Coast associate — then made their move, offering to advance 87,000 pesos at once and 50,000 pesos for each of the following four months, all of it in cash.[69] Despite the attractions of this offer, the government accorded it only a conditional acceptance, reserving the right to consult Pedro de Candamo,[70] a Chilean merchant in Lima, before coming to any final decision. Candamo was duly contacted and he in turn, possibly at the government's suggestion, got in touch with Gibbs Crawley, proposing that the latter take a one-third share in a bid for guano, with the remaining third being carried by the French house of Puymerol Poumarroux & Co.[71] For the second time in a matter of days Gibbs resisted temptation. Initially their inclination was to join Candamo, but on reflection they considered it would be prudent to find out first from President Menéndez precisely what the terms of the Quiros offer were. When they were told that the proposed advances were interest free, that the amount to be exported was limited to 20,000 tons, that Quiros had agreed 'to place two steamers in Callao of 400 tons each in 12 months', they decided once again to remain aloof. 'I determined,' wrote Hayne, 'that we could not better such a proposal'.[72] On the following morning, of 8 December, the government published its contract with Quiros Allier & Co. To Hayne's surprise, the terms were not those indicated to him by the Peruvian president.[73] They were in certain important respects considerably better from the contractors' point of view. The arrangement placed virtually no limit[74] on the amount of guano to be exported; it was the period rather than the quantity that was stipulated, and this was set at one year with the option to continue for a further four if both government and merchants so desired. As for the steamers that Quiros Allier had to hand over to the government, these were to be paid for out of the proceeds of guano sales, and were to be used to protect the Chincha deposits. And although no interest was to be paid on their advances, amounting to 287,000 pesos, Quiros & Co. were to be given a cargo

[68]GGC, 21 August 1842.

[69]Ibid., 17 December 1841.

[70]Candamo was a merchant with whom the Gibbs firm had already engaged in joint-account ventures.

[71]GGC, 17 December 1841.

[72]Ibid.

[73]See ibid. The contract is reproduced in full in Anales, III, pp. 153-5.

[74]The 20,000 ton ceiling would only apply in the unlikely circumstance of a government survey of the deposits revealing that supplies of guano were deficient and likely to be exhausted within a short space of time.

of guano by way of compensation. The terms of the contract also surprised Quiros Allier & Co., being in fact *less* favourable than they had been led to expect. When they had had their discussions with the government — Quiros with President Menéndez, Allier with General Lafuente, and both with Dr. Cano the finance minister — they had agreed to make a large loan and hand over a share of the profits on the assumption that their contract would be for five years and for all foreign markets. But the contract, as published, only guaranteed one year and limited the selling area to Europe. Quiros and Allier immediately called on Menéndez to complain about this apparent trickery, and were told (so they relate) not to worry about the period: the monopoly, they could rest assured, would be theirs for the full five years.[75]

The government, eager to obtain good terms, seems to have been trying to play one group off against the other. When Menéndez exaggerated the generosity of the Quiros Allier offer in his conversation with John Hayne he was perhaps hoping that the latter would be tempted to make proposals much more advantageous to the government than any that had come from the other merchants. And the very fact that he was talking to Gibbs Crawley and to Candamo after Quiros Allier & Co. had placed their offer on the table undoubtedly served to draw the latter's attention to the insecurity of their position and made them more likely to accept harsher contract terms. It is also entirely possible that the final revisions to the Quiros Allier contract were undertaken in direct consequence of the conversation between Menéndez and Hayne. The president had no doubt been aware that this relatively wealthy foreign house, with good connections in the London money market, was interested in joining the business, and accordingly went out of his way to make chinks in the Quiros Allier monopoly so that Gibbs money might be tapped in the future.[76] 'The Government', wrote an official a few years later, 'substituted *Europe* for the word *foreign* that Quiros and Allier had used in their contract, regarding such an alteration as expedient. . .'.[77] Quiros Allier & Co. received their new, if somewhat blemished, contract, having already commenced payment on the 287,000 peso loan with funds from the sale of bills drawn against Myers's present and

[75]Quiros y Allier, pp. 6-8.

[76]It may even be that Hayne himself suggested the revisions, indicating how these might facilitate some early contribution from his own firm. The insertion of the words 'to Europe', Barroilhet later contended, was the work of 'a hidden hand', by which he clearly meant one or more of Quiros Allier's mercantile opponents. *Opúsculo*, p. 20.

[77]Memoria Sobre La Negociación Del Guano, *loc. cit.*

anticipated guano proceeds.[78] One of the principal purchasers of these drafts, somewhat ironically, was Gibbs Crawley & Co.[79] The matter was still not finally settled, however, for the law allowed other merchants nine days to come forward with better contract proposals if they so chose.[80] And indeed on the day following the publication of the Quiros Allier terms, Gibbs Crawley & Co., Pedro de Candamo, and Puymerol Poumarroux & Co., acting together, did submit their own clear terms: an immediate advance of 100,000 pesos (compared with Quiros's initial 87,000), 68 per cent of the profits to the government in the first year and 70 per cent in the remaining four (compared with Quiros's 64 per cent and 66 per cent).[81] A week later the government declared its rejection of this offer.[82] It would seem likely that it did not so much want the Quiros group replaced by another set of merchants as a fusion, so that the loan money available could be maximized. The task was to keep Quiros Allier in the business and to graft the other merchants on to their enterprise.

Back in England Antony Gibbs & Sons had no regrets whatever about their branch's exclusion. In mid-March 1842, by which time they had heard of the November annulment and Gibbs Crawley's desire to get into the trade, they wrote of guano: 'we have so little confidence in it that we would not risk 10 farthings a ton, on consignment, and if it were consigned to us we should always wish to have the power to abandon for freight'.[83] Two weeks later, on 1 April, fully informed now on the arrangement of the second contract, William Gibbs wrote: '*Congratulate* you sincerely on your *failure*. . . your non success a great relief to us'.[84] In another letter, also dated 1 April, he remarked: 'The *Result* may be ultimately as brilliant as the Limeños expect, but that no more justifies a speculation in it *now,* than *success* does *gambling*. You have been misled by others' reports. Look to *us* for the future.'[85] The London house appears to have assumed that the question of guano contracts was closed for the time being. What they did not fully appreciate was that guano's initial

[78]Witt Diaries, I, 19 July to 17 November 1842; GGC, 21 August 1842. Quiros, incidentally, renounced all claims to the 40,000 pesos paid under the earlier contract. *Anales*, III, p. 24.

[79]See table in Quiros y Allier, p. 23.

[80] *Ibid.*, p. 8.

[81]GGC, 17 December 1841.

[82]*Anales*, III, p. 25; also GGC, 17 and 18 December 1841.

[83]GGC, 15 March 1842.

[84]*Ibid.*, 1 April 1842; also 7 April 1842.

[85]*Ibid.*, 1 April 1842.

success in the British market had acted dramatically on the minds of both government and merchants in Peru. Government in the past had been crippled by war and inadequate revenue, and the mercantile community had been labouring away for years within the circumscriptions of a small, sluggish, and very backward economy. For both, guano seemed to offer new hope for the future. Excitement and anticipation, combined with a degree of uncertainty as to guano's true worth in distant markets, had produced a very fluid situation in Peru.

The proposals made by Gibbs Crawley and their associates gave the government a further opportunity to extract additional favours from the old contractors. Menéndez now told them that he would keep them in the trade on the condition that they provided a complete set of uniforms for a cavalry regiment. The helmets, dress coats, pants and epaulets cost them — so they claimed — 8,000 pesos.[86] The Quiros group knew full well that their position was extremely precarious, and that the government's behaviour was thoroughly opportunistic. Towards the end of 1841 Aquiles Allier produced a pamphlet complaining of the continuing uncertainty and warning that if the government scrapped this new contract, not only would it bring discredit on its name but it would expose Peruvian guano to competition from Bolivia. Allier and his associates now held a Bolivian as well as a Peruvian contract;[87] if they lost the latter, then their successors would have to face challenges from Bolivian guano in foreign markets, which could only drive down the price of Peruvian.[88] It was a fair argument and it further strengthened the case, as the government saw it, for a union of the two factions. The Bolivian flank had to be protected, so Quiros Allier had to be retained. Extra funds, however, were wanted, so the Gibbs group had also to be kept in the game.

A fresh turn of the screw on the contractors, further accelerating the movement towards amalgamation, was applied a few days later. On 23 December Gibbs Crawley reported that the French house with whom they had been associated in their bid for the second contract, Puymerol Poumarroux & Co., had just been given exclusive rights to export guano to the United States.[89] Other sources indicate that Gibbs themselves were also party to this arrangement.[90] Quiros and

[86] Quiros y Allier, pp. 8-9, 22.

[87] See p. 30, n. 53.

[88] Allier, pp. 19-21.

[89] GGC, 23 December 1841.

[90] See for example, Barroilhet, *Opúsculo*, p. 20.

Allier were opposed to the acceptance of these proposals',[91] one of their fears apparently being that the guano would be re-exported from North America to Europe, thus damaging their own trade.[92] The pressure on them intensified on 29 December when the government published proposals it had just received for a loan of 150,000 pesos in return for exporting rights after the single guaranteed year of the Quiros Allier contract had come to an end — this despite Menéndez's assurances that the contract would in fact last for five years. Some days later, Quiros and Allier recounted, 'meeting a request to be present at seven in the evening at the house of the President... we were informed by His Excellency, in the company of his Ministers, of the Government's decision to make use of the four voluntary years of our contract, and that we and the other houses with whom it wished to do business were to come together and work out the terms of an agreement'.[93]

Quiros and Allier now realised for certain that their monopoly would have to be shared: 'we knew that there remained to us now no way of holding our position, save through union with our opponents'. The other merchants had offered a loan of 200,000 pesos and this had been sufficient 'to overcome the scruples of Señor Menéndez and his Ministers'. If their contract was to be ended after just one year, they might be unable to ship and sell enough guano to cover their advances to the government.[94] Gibbs Crawley reported to London that Quiros Allier had finally crumbled 'because Puymerol Poumarroux & Co. opposed them so vehemently and because they felt that their own contract being only binding for one year... might be upset if Puymerol Poumarroux & Co. chose, and moreover it was *only for Europe*. In the end an agreement was formally signed between them and the others'.[95] 'The others' included Gibbs Crawley themselves.

THE THIRD GUANO CONTRACT, 1842: ENTRY OF GIBBS

Details of the new joint proposals made by Quiros Allier & Co., Gibbs Crawley & Co., and their respective associates were made public on January 29th 1842 and some time was allowed, as the law

[91] Memoria Sobre La Negociación Del Guano, *loc. cit.*

[92] Barroilhet, *Opúsculo,* p. 20.

[93] Quiros y Allier, p. 9; also Memoria Sobre La Negociación Dél Guano, *loc. cit.*

[94] Quiros y Allier, p. 10.

[95] These are Henry Gibbs's words. He apparently took a number of the letters of January and February 1842 dealing with the events immediately preceding Gibbs Crawley's entry into the trade and made a short précis of them. Dates for the individual letters are not given. Reference hereinafter: GGC, H. H. Gibbs's abstract.

stipulated, for others to come forward with better offers. No party, however, was able to improve on the loan which the Quiros-Gibbs group had agreed to make.[96] With the war against Bolivia still in operation, and Peru faring badly, such loans were, in the government's words, 'of Vital Interest to maintain the Army'.[97]

Article I of the contract, dated 19 February 1842, referred to the establishment of a corporation comprising the Peruvian government, Quiros Allier & Co., Puymerol Poumarroux & Co., and Gibbs Crawley & Co.[98] The corporation was to hold the monopoly of guano exports to all foreign countries for an obligatory period of five years from 27 December 1841. Quiros Allier & Co.'s undertaking of 8 December to advance 287,000 pesos was reincorporated in the fresh contract; in addition, the new parties were to advance 200,000 pesos within three months, giving the government a total loan of 487,000 pesos, or roughly £97,000. It was stipulated, moreover, that 40,000 tons of guano should be exported in 1842 and 20,000 tons in each of the four succeeding years. These figures could be adjusted for individual years, but a minimum of 120,000 tons had to be disposed of by the end of the five-year period. If it was not, then the contractors had no claims on whatever quantity remained unexported. An extra 1,300 tons (register) could be shipped by the contractors on their own account, representing interest on the loans advanced to the government.

The contractors had also to make the various payments necessary to remove and carry guano to markets overseas, reimbursing themselves after sales. From the proceeds the government was to get the first £6 per register ton (receiving this in fact the moment guano was embarked) and three-quarters of any profits in excess of that figure. The initial £6 — equivalent to £4 10s. per effective (actual) ton — was paid half in cash, a quarter in internal debt paper and a quarter in external debt paper. If net proceeds were £4 10s. or less per effective ton the government would take the entire amount. If they were £5, the contractors could expect 2s. 6d.; if £6, 7s. 6d.; if £7, 12s. 6d — and so on. Losses were to be divided in the same proportions as profits. If profits did accrue to the contractors, two-thirds of the total was to go

[96] Offers came in from Malcolm Rowe and from Hegan Hall & Co. *Ibid.*

[97] Quoted in FO 61/88, Sealey to Aberdeen, 9 March 1842.

[98] The contract is reproduced in *Anales*, III, pp. 155-9. See also FO 61/88, Sealey to Aberdeen, 9 March 1842. According to Gibbs the merchant houses of Candamo and Tabara, both of which had been on their side in the past weeks, were also involved, although their names do not appear in the public document. GGC, H. H. Gibbs's abstract.

to Quiros Allier & Co., and one-third to the others.[99] As for the consignments to Europe, two-thirds of the guano was to be handled by Myers in Liverpool and one-third by Gibbs in London: shortly after this (and the merchant profit sharing) was altered to half each.[100]

From the point of view of the contractors, these really were quite harsh terms. They indicate great optimism on the part of the merchants concerning guano's selling power:[101] sustained and intensified, no doubt, by the hot-house atmosphere surrounding the contract issue in Lima. They also demonstrate the government's ability to take full advantage of the guano fever afflicting the merchants. The latter took on all the entrepreneurial functions in the trade, they were committing themselves heavily over a number of years to a commodity as yet virtually untested in Europe and North America, and they had agreed to lend large sums of money to the government in advance of sales.[102] The latter promised to repay these loans out of Mint and Customs House funds if the venture proved unprofitable, but this could hardly be taken all that seriously in the light of its bad record with both its internal and external debts.[103] Internal debt paper, symptomatically, was fetching only 10-12 per cent of its face value on the market,[104] and bonds of the foreign debt were selling in London in March 1842 at 16½ per cent.[105] If the enterprise was profitable, they could only claim a return for their efforts when net proceeds exceeded £4 10s. per ton. There were,

[99]GGC, H.H. Gibbs's abstract, and 13 May 1842.

[100]*Ibid.,* H. H. Gibbs's abstract.

[101]See contractors' own retrospective comments in Hac Arch, Año 1841, Memorandum Para El Ministro De Hacienda Sobre El Negocio De Huano, 12 December 1842.

[102]It is not clear precisely how Gibbs Crawley raised the money for their loan to the government. In their first guano account, dated 30 April 1845, it is indicated that their share was 28 per cent. Since the loan under the 1842 contract amounted to 487,000 pesos, this would mean that they had to find 136,360 pesos or about £27,000. An examination of Antony Gibbs & Sons' accounts with their Lima branch for 1841 and 1842 reveals that sterling bills drawn under the 1842 account amounted to £48,210 in all, compared with only £24,670 in 1841. The timing of bill-drawing in 1842 does not indicate any very direct connection between lending to the government and borrowing from London (no more than 38 per cent of the bills by value being drawn in the first third of the year), but the fact that the 1842 total was almost double that for 1841 does at least suggest that Gibbs Crawley's entry into the guano trade led to a considerable depletion of their liquid assets, necessitating greater financial dependence on the parent house. Lima Branch Accounts, File 2, 1837-1847; LGL, first ser. 9.

[103]See, for instance, Mathew, pp. 81-98. Mint and Customs House revenues had been pledged as security for the government loans in Britain which had been in default since 1825. FO 61/118, Adams to Palmerston, 10 October 1848.

[104]See retrospective remarks in FO 177/68, Sulivan to Clarendon, 12 May 1857.

[105]Mathew, p. 86.

however, features of the contract which, in the immediate future at least, more or less guaranteed some income for the contractors. First, there was the substantial quantity of guano which they were permitted to ship exclusively on their own account in return for the loans. Second, there was the clause in the contract, deriving from the government's wish to begin retiring the national debt, which allowed the merchants to remit up to £3 of the funds due on each register ton in state bonds, accepted at par value. These, as just noted, could be picked up at very low prices. Even if net proceeds per register ton amounted to only £4 (in which case the government took all), the fact that half of this could be handed over in paper costing the contractors 7s. or less, meant that quite a sizable amount of money could be earned on, from the contractors' point of view, officially unprofitable sales.

ALARM IN ENGLAND AND PERU

Considering the London Gibbs's earlier expressions of doubt concerning the potential profitability of any trade in guano, it is not surprising to discover that they reacted with great dismay to the latest news of their branch house's activities in Lima. 'I had hoped', wrote William Gibbs in mid-May 1842, 'the maximum of madness had been reached! Nothing but mental delusion produced by Myers & Co.'s sanguine and exaggerated statements could have induced you to forsake the sound mercantile principles we have ever inculcated! Impossible to say *what* the loss will be....'.[106] The entry into the trade he later described as an 'act of insanity'.[107] It became clear in the spring that the general level of prices would settle at a level quite a bit lower than the old average of £18 or so.[108] In April Antony Gibbs & Sons informed Lima: 'Large holders have reduced to £15. Nothing doing. Not likely to answer in France'.[109] The retail price, they reported in May, was 'falling to £16 and £15 ... Price considered high by farmers, who therefore buy little. The season is passing'.[110] Guano, as a Peruvian official, Pedro Carillo, later recorded, failed 'to maintain its initial price . . . Sales proceeded slowly and farmers bought for experimental purposes only. . . .'.[111]

[106] GGC, 16 May 1842.

[107] *Ibid.*, 1 August 1842.

[108] *Ibid.*, 1 March and 1 April 1842.

[109] *Ibid.*, 15 April 1842.

[110] *Ibid.*, 13 May 1842.

[111] Memoria Sobre La Negociación Del Guano, *loc. cit.* For further comment on the alarming market situation, see Quiros y Allier, p. 10; Barroilhet, *Opúsculo*, pp. 20-2; *Memorandum Para El Ministro De Hacienda, loc. cit.*

One of the first to suffer inconvenience was MacDonald, the man who had agreed to buy 7,000 tons from Myers, as and when it was imported in 1841 and 1842. The terms of the arrangement, however, were such that MacDonald, faced with a deteriorating market, was able to dilute his obligations and cause the gravest embarrassment to Myers, and in turn to Quiros Allier & Co., who had drawn bills against the anticipated sales proceeds in order to pay their loan to the government under the second (and third) contract.[112] The original agreement with MacDonald was made in July 1841, just after the arrival of the *Bonanza.*[113] He appears to have purchased the guano from that vessel, and from the *Charles Eyes* as well,[114] and to have promised to take all the rest that came in at £18 per ton.[115] But this deal, which gave so much heart to the merchants in Lima, was not quite what it seemed at that far distance: 'the sale . . . had been under the condition', recorded Henry Witt, 'that it would only stand good, if MacDonald could resell. If not, he was not obliged to receive the huano. The latter turned out to be the case . . .'. It was, Witt contended, highly reprehensible of Myers not to give exact details of this curiously weak arrangement to Quiros in the first place.[116] According to Quiros and Allier, an additional factor causing Mac-Donald to reneaugue was the news that the original contract of 1840 had been scrapped, thereby appearing to erode his position as virtually the sole purchaser in the British market.[117] The arrangement collapsed round about March/April 1842,[118] and was replaced by one in which the quantity to be taken was reduced to 3,500 tons and the price to £14.[119] 7,000 at £18 would have grossed Myers £126,000. Half that amount at £14 would bring in only £49,000.

The result was that Myers, already over-extended on freight payments, was forced to protest bills drawn against him by Quiros Allier & Co.[120] The guano enterprise, launched with so much hope and further energized by Myers' own optimistic reports in 1841, had turned sour with alarming rapidity. News of Myers's refusal to pay the

[112]GGC, 21 August 1842.

[113]*Ibid.,* introductory synopsis to GGC, folder 2.

[114]*Ibid.,* 13 October 1841. See also above, p. 30.

[115]*Ibid.,* 13 May 1842.

[116]Witt Diaries, 1, 19 July to 17 November 1842.

[117]Quiros y Allier, pp. 10-1.

[118]See Barroilhet, *Opúsculo,* p. 20.

[119]GGC, 21 August 1842; introductory synopsis to folder 2.

[120]*Ibid.,* 21 August 1842.

bills reached Lima in August,[121] and landed Quiros and Allier in a most difficult predicament. 'The holders of these presented themselves before the *Tribunal de Consulado,* which carried rigour to extremes by ordering seals to be placed on the doors of our warehouses and offices, disgracing us in quite unmerited fashion...'.[122] The protested bills amounted to £34,457 in value, and in the disputes and claims that followed Quiros Allier & Co., so they relate, incurred expenses in excess of £8,000.[123] They made great play of the embarrassments in later years, blaming their predicament on the government's cancellation of their contract in November 1841 (thereby unsettling MacDonald), but according to Henry Witt the affair was soon sorted out. Guano sales in Britain picked up in the middle of 1842, Myers duly paid the bills, 'and as the Lima house had been treated with great indulgence by the holders of their paper, their credit did not suffer'.[124]

The MacDonald episode, however, had been a shock for Myers, as indeed had been the events in Lima which had forced him to share his selling monopoly with Antony Gibbs & Sons. His immediate reaction was to attempt an escape from a trade whose prospects were visibly darkening. Payments in connection with loans and freights now seemed excessive both in relation to market capacity and to the meagre profit opportunities offered by the 1842 contract. In May he made a vain effort to get Gibbs to take the entire business at the British end.[125] In June Gibbs reported, 'Myers writes to the Peruvian Consul that he won't take charge of his 2/3 and requests *him* to do so for the Government'. This appeal was also turned down.[126] Consular assistance, however, was provided in an attempt to pass the business on to a number of other firms — again without success: 'the Peruvian Consul in London', wrote Pedro Carillo, 'could not find a single house prepared to accept the consignment or lend a single peso against its value'.[127] Among the houses consulted were Baring, Cotesworth, Huth and Gower.[128] Such responses showed the degree of scepticism that detached merchants in Britain felt as to the prospects for a profitable trade in guano under the terms of the 1842 contract.

[121]*Ibid.*

[122]Quiros y Allier, p. 11; also Barroilhet, *Opúsculo,* p. 2.

[123]Quiros y Allier, p. 23.

[124]Witt Diaries, 1, 19 July to 17 November 1842.

[125]GGC, 16 May 1842.

[126]*Ibid.,* 2 June 1842; also 29 June 1844.

[127]Memoria Sobre La Negociación Del Guano, *loc. cit.*

[128]Witt Diaries, 1, 19 July to 17 November 1842; GGC, 29 June 1844.

Myers's conduct was severely frowned upon in Lima; it was, in Gibbs Crawley's view, 'unmercantile. He has led on his firm and is now trying to shift for himself. He must be a strange man!'[129] In the end, however, his problems were sorted out. Assisted by a mild recovery of sales towards the end of the season, he succeeded in winning some financial support from associates in London and Liverpool[130] and decided to stick with the trade.

John Hayne, however, was having regrets about his own behaviour and to some extent was trying to lay the blame at Myers's door. He and his colleagues in Lima were profoundly embarrassed by the letters of accusation arriving from London, and clearly felt, with some justification, that they had placed the standing of the whole Gibbs firm at considerable risk. 'Your early letters', Hayne wrote to London in August 1842, 'have shown me how much you will have disapproved of our conduct. I fear we have gotten into a serious scrape and should your opinion have remained unchanged by the time you had got fairly into the management, we must turn all our energies towards extricating ourselves — with your help'.[131] 'We have no excuse, but our being misled by Myers's advices and by our knowledge of its value here. Our delusion too was shared by every one in Lima . . .'.[132] Eight months later he was still apologising: 'we will never get into such a scrape again. It is our first error of consequence'.[133]

How justified was this gloom? Any answer, of course, must take account of Gibbs's own views as to how their firm ought to be developing and what the most promising fields of business activity were. It is fairly evident from the findings set out in the Introduction that Gibbs were a cautious and conservative house, concentrating their attention on the safer forms of mercantile enterprise. The only contradiction to this was their marked and increasing orientation towards dealings with South America. The trend, however, was the result of the fading commercial attractions of Spain and the almost inevitable trans-Atlantic extension of the old links with the metropolitan country. Therein lay the central dilemma of Antony Gibbs & Sons: could they reconcile their own conservative tendencies with the

[129]GGC, 8 August 1842.

[130]*Ibid.,* 12 July and 14 December 1842, 29 June 1844.

[131]*Ibid.,* 8 August 1842.

[132]*Ibid.,* 21 August 1842. When the contract was drawn up, the merchants recalled later in the year, they believed that 'the fertilizer had already entered into general consumption'. Memorandum Para El Ministro De Hacienda, *loc. cit.*

[133]GGC, 8 April 1843.

sort of imaginative, risk-taking activities that were necessary if the problematical South American connection were to become a source of major profit? It would seem that as late as the 1840s the parent house set a high premium on discretion. They appear to have been willing to settle for modest profit objectives and slow expansion. Gibbs Crawley's decision to move into the guano trade, in such a risky and potentially unrewarding fashion, was described, therefore, in a letter to Hayne, as 'your departure from those sound, prudent and cautious maxims which we have ever inculcated in you',[134] and Hayne was quick to assume the appropriate postures of remorse and contrition.

Nevertheless, even a house eager to take major risks in South American trade might have been somewhat alarmed by the commitments of the 1842 guano contract, as Myers's activities in the spring and summer of 1842 clearly show. The prospects regarding long-term price levels, as already noted, were not as bright as they had been the year before. This was not only because of the difference, to use Gibbs's words, between selling 'by way of sample' and selling 'for real consumption'[135] but because of the markedly downward trend of wheat prices in the early 1840s.[136] Wheat was not the only important recipient of bought fertilizers, but if they were used on a farm that had a wheat break and relied on grain for a major part of its income, then a fall in wheat prices could obviously have a dampening effect on fertilizer sales. Some farmers, of course, could cut through the problem of falling prices by increasing their efficiency and lowering their costs per unit of agricultural product, and fertilizers might assist here, as they certainly had done in the past,[137] but the appeal of expensive manures in such circumstances must have been very slight for all but the wealthiest and most experimentally-minded farmers. Guano, moreover, was a new and relatively untested manure. Praise from a few agriculturalists and chemists in 1841 did not provide a really adequate guarantee for future success. Farmers as yet knew little about how best to apply it, and whatever virtues it possessed could be obscured, initially at least, by misuse.[138] There was also legitimate uncertainty as to the degree of fresh competition which guano in Britain might have to face over the five-year contract period.

---

[134] *Ibid.,* 1 December 1842.

[135] *Ibid.,* 1 January 1842.

[136] Susan Fairlie, 'The Corn Laws and British Wheat Production, 1826-76', *EHR*, 2nd ser., 22, no. 1 (1969), p. 97, fig. 1.

[137] Jones, pp. 15-6.

[138] See, for example, *DBCR*, 33 (1855), p. 762.

The conditions required for the accumulation of guano were not necessarily confined to Peru and Bolivia, nitrate of soda was already in the market, and in the field of artificials the foundations had already been laid for the manufacture of superphosphate and other special manures.[139] Competition, wrote Gibbs in 1842, 'is our chief danger for it is plain agricultural Chemistry is in its infancy, and it is impossible to say what discoveries in it may be made'.[140]

Doubts, too, were entertained regarding the trustworthiness of the Peruvian government. 'The whole business', wrote Gibbs's London house before hearing of their branch's commitment to the trade, 'shews the gravest want of good faith on the part of the Government! Twice upsetting Q. & Co., and endeavouring to do so a 3rd time, to screw more money out of G.C. & Co. and their friends!'[141] A year or so later, concerned that the money Gibbs Crawley had advanced might not be recovered in full, they and Myers solicited the assistance of the British government, citing 'the fluctuating character of the Governments of the young South American states',[142] and requesting protection 'as circumstances hereafter may seem to demand or authorise'.[143] The foreign secretary, Lord Aberdeen, could not, however, 'see any reason for instructing Mr. Adams (the chargé in Lima)[144] specially to protect the monopoly which Messrs. Gibbs and

---

[139]Among the manures sold by one dealer early in 1844 were Potter's Guano ('a chemical composition founded on the analysis of the purest guano'), Petre Salt ('the residuum of a manufacture'), Urate of the London Manure Company ('earthy salts of bone combined with ammonia'), Sulphate of Ammonia, Phosphate of Lime, Phosphate of Ammonia, Muriate of Lime, Sulphate of Magnesia, Daniell's Bristol Manure ('vegetable matter, nitrate of soda, lime, ammonia, gas tar, and sulphur'), Clarke's Dessicated Compost, Watson's Compost, and Alexander's Compost ('contains, in a concentrated form, all the ingredients essential to the growth of plants'). 'Synopsis of Manures', *FM*, 2nd ser., 9 (March 1844), pp. 266-7.

[140]GGC, 2 May 1843.

[141]*Ibid.*, 9 April 1842. A contract with a government, they wrote in December, was by its very nature 'deficient in those characteristics we have always laid down for your speculations — Caution, prudence, circumspection etc'. *Ibid.*, 6 December 1842.

[142]Between Gamarra's death in 1841 and the seizure of power by Manuel Ignacio de Vivanco in 1843 there occurred, in Pike's words, 'a series of incredibly complex insurrections and insurrections within insurrections', in the course of which several men held the presidency for short periods. Vivanco himself fell to a revolt in 1844. Pike, *Peru*, pp. 87-8. See also Sir Robert Marett, *Peru* (London, 1969), p. 90; José Rufino Echenique, *Memorias Para La Historia Del Perú, 1808-1878* (Lima, 1952), 1, pp. 119-40; FO 61/108, Adams to Aberdeen, 8 February and 18 May 1845.

[143]FO 61/101, Gibbs and Myers to Sandon, 24 March 1843.

[144]William Pitt Adams arrived in Peru in January 1844 (more than two years after Belford Wilson had left) and held the post until his death in September 1852. See S. T. Bindoff, E. F. Malcolm Smith and C. K. Webster, *British Diplomatic Representatives 1789-1852* (London, 1934), p. 88.

Messrs. Myers have secured to themselves'.[145] Finally, Gibbs probably also wondered what sort of future lay ahead of them working as joint consignees with Myers. They must have anticipated, with some concern, the possibility of dispute and friction arising over the handling of the trade, especially since Myers would be regarding them as intruders in what had once been his own seemingly splendid private preserve. 'I wish we were independent', wrote William Gibbs in December 1842.[146]

Given this range of well-founded anxieties, it does seem a little strange that Gibbs in London failed to take effective action to prevent Gibbs Crawley & Co. becoming involved in the guano trade. One factor, of course, was the inevitably large degree of independence enjoyed by a branch house operating at such a great distance from London. Also of importance, it would seem, was the parent concern's failure to see just how eager their branch was to get into the trade, and make their objections to such possible participation really explicit. On the question of distance, it was unfortunate for Gibbs (at least in relation to short-term perspectives) that the start of the guano trade predated by a few years the speeding up of mail services effected by the Pacific Steam Navigation Company.[147] As it was, by the time that Gibbs in London had written their reply to a letter from Lima dated 30 September 1841 Gibbs Crawley were already making arrangements for their entry into the guano trade in mid-February 1842. It was 16 May 1842 before London could spell out its reaction to the February contract, and mid-August before Lima knew of the parent concern's distress. The two houses could keep up satisfactory communications on matters of long-term policy, but on an issue like the guano contract, unanticipated in anyone's plans, and demanding quick decisions in a rapid series of offers and negotiations among the interested parties, there was no time for consultation with London. By the same token, market reports from Britain were many months out of date by the time they arrived in Peru.

It does seem, however, that Antony Gibbs & Sons, presumably aware of the risks inherent in the communication problem, did not take the trouble to find out precisely what was going on in Lima and what their branch house's objectives were concerning guano, and to state quite categorically their opposition to involvement in the trade

[145]FO 61/101, Canning to Sandon, 20 May 1843.

[146]GGC, 14 December 1842.

[147]Arthur C. Wardle, *Steam Conquers the Pacific* (London, 1940), *passim.* See also *Documents Relating to Steam Navigation in the Pacific* (presented as bound volume, Lima, 1836); T. A. Bushell, *Royal Mail. A Centenary History of the Royal Mail Line 1839-1939* (London, 1939), pp. 6-53.

on the sorts of terms being mooted. At the start, they almost seemed to be giving tacit encouragement. 'Let us know all you can about the Article', wrote Hayne in February 1841, revealing an interest in the trade a full year before his house contracted to handle the fertilizer.[148] Replying in July 1841 William Gibbs observed, 'Huano seems likely to become a valuable manure'.[149] But in four later letters, one in mid-October 1841 and three in January and February 1842, each one in reply to notes from Lima speaking of guano and its attractions, they made no reference whatever to the manure.[150] 'Wonder you don't report on Guano', Gibbs Crawley wrote in January 1842, 'which besides being of immense importance, seems, by the papers, to have awakened great interest in London as well as Lima'.[151] Gibbs in London, could see no point in such criticism: 'No fault of ours that we gave no details. There were none to give — and even now *results* are in the dark. Could not dream that Q.A. being in quiet possession you would participate. Henceforward Silence is Dissent!'[152] Silence, however, being ambiguous, had been a pretty useless guide to Hayne and his colleagues in Lima. Perhaps feeling a little guilty at their failure to provide adequate advice in time, Gibbs in London quite quickly regained their composure. 'No exertions shall be wanting on my part', wrote William Gibbs on December 2nd 1842, 'to get you out with as little loss as may be;'[153] and, on December 6th: 'I assure you I have *no* bad feeling, and I will leave no stone unturned to extend consumption and bring the affair successfully through. Have advertised in 40 papers.'[154] This was a source of some comfort to Gibbs Crawley in Lima. 'Our minds are quite set at rest', they wrote a few months later, 'by seeing the energetic way in which both you and Myers are working at the business'.[155]

Gibbs's remarks in May 1842 about there being no details to supply on guano indicate that they had simply not taken the trouble to seek out any information, for there was plenty to be found in the newspapers and farming journals of the day. Despite the numerous and serious uncertainties surrounding the trade, there were in fact

[148]GGC, 6 February 1841.

[149]*Ibid.*, 30 July 1841.

[150]*Ibid.*, 14 October 1841, 1 January, 15 and 24 February 1842.

[151]*Ibid.*, 13 January 1842; also 8 December 1841.

[152]*Ibid.*, 13 May 1842. See also 15 March and 1 December 1842.

[153]*Ibid.*, 2 December 1842.

[154]*Ibid.*, 6 December 1842.

[155]*Ibid.*, 18 May 1843.

some grounds for cautious optimism: little prospect of large profits, but at least some indications that serious losses could be avoided and that modest commissions could be earned on the various services required of them in the market. The interest in agricultural chemistry in the early 1840s was widening steadily under the influence of the growing body of literature available to farmers, and, indeed, of the very appearance of new fertilizers like guano. The habit of purchasing light, concentrated applications had already caught on in some areas, thanks largely to the success of bone manuring. And there was no farmer or agricultural chemist who argued systematically against the use of guano, or produced a list of damning experiments. No-one could predict to what levels prices would have to fall before a decent-sized market would appear. In this, as in so many other respects, the future was very uncertain, but almost everyone accepted that guano was a good manure. 'That it may succeed in adding fertility to the soils of our country', wrote a distinguished chemist of the time, 'will be the ardent wish of every true Englishman; that it promises well, no one will doubt who attends carefully to its chemical composition; and it is more than probable that . . . a valuable fertilizer will be added to the manures already in the English farmer's possession'.[156]

The pendulum of expectation must have swung quite widely in the minds of the consignees when they assessed their predicament coolly and objectively. It was one thing to read flattering remarks about guano in books and farming journals; it was quite another to dispose of 120,000 tons in five years at prices that would guarantee profitable returns. Gibbs and Myers still had a very long way to go, and any success in Britain had to be backed up by fair treatment from the Peruvian government.

GOVERNMENT AND CONTRACTORS

The future was very unpredictable, and the contractors, having signed the agreement of February 1842, stood to lose heavily if the trade proved a failure. In the bipartite relationship the government was, without question, the stronger party. It was the undisputed owner of the guano, it was required to perform no entrepreneurial functions, it had secured for itself the lion's share of any ensuing profits, and it had acquired loans amounting to hundreds of thousands of pesos in advance of sales. The monopoly-contract system of export had been devised on the initiative of the merchants but the government had succeeded in quickly reshaping it to ensure that its own interests were

[156]C. W. Johnson, *The Farmer's Encyclopaedia* (London, 1842), pp. 595-6.

guarded and advanced above all others. It had, in short, managed to get the better of the contractors and had done so largely by stimulating competition among groups of merchants eager to participate in the trade and making full use of its position as owner of the commodity. Thomas Crompton, the British vice-consul in Islay, was probably correct when he wrote that the government simply 'took advantage of the avidity of the Monopolists and Speculators'.[157]

Most of these 'speculators' were, of course, foreign merchant houses, and the reasons for their prominence require consideration. One cannot cite production costs as a factor of very great significance. European merchants in Lima were certainly larger and wealthier on the whole than their Peruvian counterparts, and could more easily tap funds of capital in the main financial centres overseas. With the assistance of their parent concerns they were also better able to secure the necessary shipping capacity. But such advantages counted for little in the digging and loading of guano. Compared with the mining industry, still largely in Peruvian hands, extraction and transport costs in guano were trifling. Equipment and housing on the guano islands was primitive and inexpensive, and the costs of digging and loading, according to the 1841 estimate already cited, came to only 11s. 6d. per ton, of which by far the largest component was expenditure on bags.[158] Another factor that can be dismissed is British diplomatic intervention. Leland Jenks raises the point with reference to the 1842 contract. 'What assistance', he writes, 'British diplomacy rendered in arranging this matter, if any, is not known.'[159] Belford Wilson, the chargé d'affaires, was certainly eager to get the Peruvian government to settle things in such a way that money could be made available for the repayment of British bondholders,[160] but he was hardly a supporter of monopoly arrangements as such. He had, he remarked in 1841, 'been instructed that, whatever may be the pretence under which the Government near which he is accredited may propose to establish a Monopoly, that it will be his duty, at all times, to use his best endeavours to dissuade that Government from entertaining or encouraging any such Project'.[161] Some years later, writing of his attempts to get the trade thrown open, he recalled that these had been foiled by the government's desire to arrange contracts

[157]FO 61/94, Crompton to Aberdeen, 14 December 1842.

[158]FO 61/183, Wilson to Palmerston, 22 December 1841.

[159]Jenks, p. 120.

[160]Mathew, pp. 84-6.

[161] FO 177/16, Wilson to Peruvian foreign minister, 1 December 1841.

whereby they could come by the large loans required for the prosecution of the war against Bolivia.[162] He might also have added that since he left Peru in December 1841 he simply was not around to publicize his views when the main (February 1842) contract was being drawn up.[163]

Exploitation costs and diplomatic pressure, therefore, can both be discounted as factors explaining why foreigners were so conspicuous in the trade. The principal reason, apart from the fact that it was largely they who had taken the first crucial initiatives to set the trade in motion, was that, as Wilson pointed out, they were able to supply the government with large and immediate cash advances. In this respect, given the size of the loans required and the relative ease with which they could draw bills on their associates and parent concerns in Europe,[164] they had a clear advantage over any possible Peruvian rivals. As the preceding discussion has made clear, the question of loans was a fundamental determinant of contract allocation. This was so, in the most general terms, because of the government's eagerness to cash in at once on guano after long years of indigence and financial uncertainty. By being prepared to place fresh resources at the government's disposal, foreign merchants were, in the physical sense at least, able to take over the running of the trade. More specifically, there were the funds required to prosecute the war against Bolivia. It was this particular circumstance of conflict with a neighbouring state that made it urgently necessary for the government to find some quick and effective method of raising large quantities of cash. The most timely opportunities presented themselves in the manipulation of guano contracts. A document in the *Ministerio de Hacienda* archive itemizes the ways in which the 487,000 pesos loan from the third contract was disbursed. There are 44 entries in the account; 34 of these, representing 410, 877 pesos (84 per cent), relate to expenditures

---

[162]FO 16/137, Wilson to Stanley, 9 June 1852. Also cited were 'the personal and pecuniary Interests of the then corrupt Administration of Peru and of the wealthy Foreigners who desired to obtain the Monopoly'.

[163]This is clear from the correspondence in FO 177/126. See too Bindoff, Smith and Webster, p. 88. These authors point out that Wilson was also absent from Peru between September 1840 and January 1841, during which period, of course, the very first guano contract was arranged.

[164]And find funds of their own in Peru. Gibbs Crawley & Co.'s Lima house, as noted in the Introduction, recorded a profit of over 80,000 pesos for their last financial year of the 1830s.

[165]Hac Arch Año 1842, Razón que manifiesta las cantidades que han ingresado en laTesorería grãl. por adelantos sobre la extracción del Huano, y su inversion desde diciembre de 1841 hasta junio de 1842.

unambiguously connected with military activity — army salaries and wages, provisions, rifles, sabres, cannons, shrapnel, saddlery, horse-shoes, uniforms, ponchos, straw mattresses, water bottles, and various other 'articles for the Army'.[165]

It would, however, be foolish to ignore the fact that the government's position, in particular with respect to advances, was problematical. The question of interest burdens is not all that consequential, for the government did not have to find hard cash for interest payments; it simply awarded the contractors some free guano. More important was the danger that such advances would help create a form of organization and a set of dependent relationships that would become self-perpetuating and, therefore, a possible source of embarrassment in the future.[166] In addition, Peruvian governments, by being able to raise such large sums of money in a period when their grasp of the levers of power was uncertain, when they were obliged through considerations of expediency to give financial and other rewards to their supporters, and when they were liable either by design or misfortune to be frequently engaged in external and internal wars, were always faced with temptations to dissipate the funds they acquired in unproductive expenditures[167] and in the prosecution of schemes likely to enlarge rather than diminish their budgetary problems. As we have seen, the form and shape of the 1841 and 1842 contracts were to a very considerable degree the product of the war with Bolivia. It was this linking of the guano trade with the insecurities and assertive military dispositions of the Peruvian government that was the principal defect of the arrangements as concluded. It was a flaw that was to plague the trade in the future and seriously jeopardize its success.

[166]See retrospective observations in FO 61/144, Gómez Sánchez to Sulivan, 10 October 1854, cited in W. M. Mathew, 'Foreign Contractors and the Peruvian Government at the Outset of the Guano Trade', *HAHR,* 52, no. 4 (1972), pp. 619-20.

[167]In so far as enlarged military and administrative outlays helped on occasions to strengthen the hand, and therefore the staying power, of incumbent governments, they have also been seen as having the beneficial effect of promoting political stability. See Juan Maiguàshca, *A Reinterpretation of the Guano Age 1840-1880* (unpublished Oxford D.Phil. thesis, 1967), pp. 41-3; Pike, *Andean Republics,* pp. 83-6.

2

THE BRITISH TRADE, 1842-9:
CHALLENGES, CONFLICTS, AND
GROWTH

'The business is one of *price*, and price *only*'.

W.J. Myers, 23 September 1845

MAKING A MARKET, 1842-3

Gibbs's first eight years in the business were, on balance, successful. By the end of the 1840s guano had established itself as the British farmers' favourite light fertilizer, and the London house had managed to shed most of its earlier anxieties concerning its entanglement in the trade. These years did, nevertheless, comprise a generally troublesome and awkward period for Gibbs. Most of the difficulties that had been anticipated in 1842 were in fact realized. There were, among other things, the problems of selling guano in an initially unresponsive market, of making the trade remunerative for both government and contractors, of dealing with competition, of preserving contractual agreements, and of overcoming mutual tensions and suspicions amongst the various participating parties.

Initially, the main task was the establishment of an effective working relationship with Myers in Liverpool. Together they had to devise policies for dealing with the immediate problem of selling in a depressed market and the longer-term matter of disposing of 120,000 register tons of guano in Britain and Europe before the end of 1846. In 1842 the market was quite clearly overstocked. Official trade statistics show that British guano imports from Peru and Bolivia totalled 14,231 tons, compared with only 2,062 tons in 1841.[1] As early as May 1842 Gibbs wrote of their agreement with Myers that fresh shipments be stopped at once,[2] if only to save on warehousing costs. Myers, in fact, had issued instructions to curtail supplies as early as January.[3] Britain, moreover, was virtually the only market in which guano could be sold; in December Gibbs cited France,

---

[1]*PP*, 1851, LIII, p. 309. The 1841 figure is very much lower than Belford Wilson's estimate of Peruvian guano exports in that year, cited in the previous chapter. This is probably due to the length of the journey between Peru and Britain. A large portion of the 1841 exports did not become British imports until 1842.

[2]GGC, 13 May 1842.

[3]*Ibid.*, 23 June and 12 July 1842.

Germany and Italy as three in which guano was 'unsaleable'.[4]
For Britain, Myers's estimate in June was that at the very most only
about 1,500 tons had gone into consumption.[5] 'We have plenty of
enquiries but no orders,' Gibbs wrote towards the end of November.[6]

The most crucial decisions the consignees had to take concerned
pricing (and given the Levin thesis cited earlier we shall have to look at
these closely for the decade as a whole). Gibbs's argument, which
they expounded with considerable frequency, was that prices had to
be relatively low in order to promote the growth of a market big
enough to absorb the quantity of guano contracted: 'better to sell much
with a small profit', they suggested, 'than for the Huano to be eaten up
with rent and charges'.[7]   In August 1842 they agreed with Myers on a
fixed scale based on current market returns. For lots of 5 tons and
under the price was to be £15; for amounts between 5 and 24 tons,
£14; for quantities in excess of 24 tons, £13; and for whole cargoes,
£12.[8] This, however, proved to be too ambitious and a further
downward drift[9] was formalised in a new scale in January 1843: £12
for 1 to 15 tons; £11 for 16 to 29 tons; and £10 for 30 tons and over.[10]
Gibbs's view was that they should go lower still.[11] The Lima house,
expressing disappointment over the changes, observed in a letter of
May 1843 that Myers 'always writes as if these reductions were
forced upon him against his will: and true or imaginary this begins to
leave a bad impression on Quiros Allier & Co'.[12]

Exchanges on price policy between Myers and Gibbs continued in
the early months of 1843. The January scale, Gibbs observed in the
last week of February, 'has expired by lapse of time'.[13] They also felt
that there should be uniformity in prices between London and
Liverpool and what they termed the 'outports' such as Bristol and
Glasgow where a higher price scale was in operation.[14]   This did not

[4]*Ibid.*, 2 December 1842; also 13 May and 1 June 1842.

[5]*Ibid.*, 27 June 1842.

[6]*Ibid.*, 25 November 1842; also 6 December 1842 and 2 January 1843.

[7]*Ibid.*, 30 September 1842.

[8]See *ibid.*, 10 September 1842.

[9]*Ibid.*, 29 September, 2 November, 15 December 1842.

[10]*Ibid.*, 2 January 1843.

[11]*Ibid.*, 4 January 1843.

[12]*Ibid.*, 6 May 1843; also 18 May 1843.

[13]*Ibid.*, 22 February 1843.

[14]*Ibid.*, 5 January and 22 February 1843.

appeal to Myers; 'it would be virtually a further reduction and we consider that we are now too low'.[15] But 'in the nature of things', he acknowledged, 'if *you* reduce we *must* follow'.[16] The general objective of the consignees, Gibbs suggested at the end of February, ought to be the promotion of 'steady, large and increasing annual sales. To spread the want throughout the country, we must spread the manure even at a slight sacrifice; and to do this we must in a manner *force* dealers and consumers to buy.'[17] Myers, however, was determined not to go below the current £10 floor,[18] and this Gibbs came round to accepting, in part because they had to agree that major changes were not really advisable during the purchasing season.[19] Some small alterations, though, were brought into force in March: the minimum price of £10 was to apply to lots of 20 tons and over (instead of 30 and over); the £11 range was made to apply to lots of 5 to 20 tons (instead of 15 to 30); and the minimum price at the outports was to come down from £11 to £10 10s.[20] And there the matter appears to have rested for the remainder of the year.

Unlike 1842, therefore, 1843 was not a year of notable price changes. The downward trend had clearly been checked. This, without question, was the product of improving guano sales — which in turn might be connected with the original price reductions.[21] 'I think guano is the favourite manure', wrote William Gibbs in March.[22] In 1843 his house had been able to produce a sizable pamphlet giving details of guano's successful application to a wide range of crops, as documented in newspapers and farming journals.[23] Most of the experiments cited had been carried out in the Midland and Northern counties of England, and the crop most frequently referred to was the turnip, although information was also provided on yield improvements in wheat, oats, barley, potatoes, grass, clover, and hops. Guano was having some success in dislodging the old favourite, bones. According to one Hampshire farmer, it had 'quite given bone-

[15] *Ibid.*, 9 January 1843.

[16] *Ibid.*, 27 February 1843.

[17] *Ibid.*, 28 February 1843.

[18] *Ibid.*, 2 March 1843.

[19] *Ibid.*, 1 March 1843

[20] *Ibid.*, 8 and 11 March 1843.

[21] It would certainly be difficult to attribute the improvement to any significant upswing in agricultural prosperity. See Fairlie, p. 97; Arthur D. Gayer, W. W. Rostow, Anna Jacobsen Schwartz, *The Growth and Fluctuations of the British Economy 1790-1850* (Oxford, 1953), 1, p. 327, n. 3.

[22] GGC, 31 March 1843; also 2 May 1843.

[23] Antony Gibbs & Sons, *Guano: Its Analysis and Effects; Illustrated by the Latest Experiments* (London, 1843).

dust the go-by'.[24] The amount of guano required for any given area, observed John Dudgeon of Kelso, was, 'it may be safely said, as to bones, as one to four . . . The powerful effects of guano, as compared with its price, as well as the economy of time and labour in its application — from the small quantity necessary — promise, in the present depressed state of agricultural produce, to come in good stead to the farmer'.[25] Gibbs had also, though, to take note of the fact that there were quite a few reports of failure from different parts of the country. These they attempted to 'neutralise by discovering the cause'.[26] Britain, moreover, still provided the only effective market. The solitary reference to continental business in the 1843 correspondence spoke of 'low sale in Trieste'.[27]

The selling season, as before, ended with the completion of turnip sowing in June.[28] One feature of the business in 1843 was that the bulk of it appears to have been handled by Myers. The general situation for guano was encouraging, but Gibbs were finding it difficult to do much trade in the London area.[29] 'The cause of his [Myers] passing us', they informed Lima, 'is that he was first in the field, and is more easy in giving credit than we think it right to be'.[30]

[24]Quoted in William Horatio Potter, 'On the Use of Guano', *FM,* 2nd ser., 5 (June 1842), p. 435. See also Philip Pusey, 'On the Progress of Agricultural Knowledge during the last Four Years', *JRAS,* 3 (1842), P. 212.

[25]John Dudgeon, 'Report of Comparative Trials with Guano as a Manure for Turnips', *FM,* 2nd ser., 8 (November 1843), p. 374. See also James Napier, 'Guano', *FM,* 2nd ser., 7 (March 1843), p. 185. Cuthbert Johnson, remarking on guano's superiority to bones, observed that its introduction had brought the day closer 'when a person should carry in his pocket manure sufficient for an acre of land' (a frequently-mentioned fantasy among farmers and chemists of the day). *Agricultural Improvements,* p. 137. In 1844 A.J. Bernays warmly commended guano to the bone-using farmers of Cheshire. *Two Lectures on the Theory of Agriculture and on Farming as practised in Cheshire* (London, 1844), p. 15.

[26]GGC, 1 March 1843. Some of the failures may have been the product of unfamiliariy with the fertilizer, and consequent misuse — a point raised in the previous chapter. Writing of Irish experiments, Cuthbert Johnson noted in 1843 that they had been 'attended with all the disadvantages arising from a first attempt with a new manure'. 'On Guano', *FM,* 2nd ser., 7 (March 1843), p. 173. A great deal could be lost if it was applied on a windy day, or laid on excessively light, free-draining soils. If the growing season was dry, it could be ineffective in boosting yields, and could in fact damage the crop. And when applied to cereals, it could easily produce too much straw and place the crop in danger of lodging. See, *inter alia,* William Palin, 'The Farming of Cheshire', *JRAS,* 5 (1845), p. 91; G. H. Andrews, *Modern Husbandry: A Practical and Scientific Treatise on Agriculture* (London, 1853), p. 214; Charles A. Cameron, *Chemistry of Agriculture* (Dublin, 1857), p. 121; Thomas Anderson, *Elements of Agricultural Chemistry* (Edinburgh, 1860), pp. 215-6; Morton, 11, p. 1141.

[27]GGC, 31 August 1843.

[28]See, for example, *ibid,* 1 July 1843.

[29]*Ibid.,* 28 February and 3 April 1843.

[30]*Ibid.,* 4 December 1843.

The latter remark reflects again on the innate caution and conservatism of the London Gibbs, 'We consider *no* credit should be given', they told Myers in March.[31] Myers had no objections to such tightness in London, but refused to apply the same to his own territory in the north, commenting that he wanted to give encouragement to dealers.[32] The two houses, therefore, were adopting different approaches to the question of boosting sales. Gibbs, assuming the posture of sober theorists, argued a logical case for price reductions. Myers, more of a speculator by instinct, preferred to gamble for higher prices and higher returns, sweetening his pill with generous terms.

Overall, the situation had improved sufficiently for both houses to consider the feasibility of a resumption of shipments. Myers had been thinking along these lines as early as the spring of 1843,[33] and in June Gibbs suggested a 'moderate renewal of Shipments' to their house in Lima.[34] There was a risk, they wrote, that 'our hopes may be frustrated, yet if they should not and there should be no supplies, farmers would be driven to other manures'.[35] As usual, Gibbs expressed their optimism in very guarded terms, but the decision they and Myers took was a firm one, and was naturally welcomed in Lima.[36] By the early autumn Gibbs had chartered for 7,500 tons, and Myers for 2,597.[37] It seemed at last that the guano trade was about to enter a period of steady, if modest, expansion. Unfortunately, as 1842 had been largely a wasted year, witnessing little more than the emergence of realistic price policies, there remained a lot of catching up to be done. The guano contract, after all, was due to expire at the end of 1846; under it, only about 7,500 tons had been exported by September 1843,[38] leaving well over 100,000 tons to be disposed of in the remaining three years. The simple solution to this problem was to get the contract period extended, and in January 1843 Gibbs Crawley wrote that such a request had been placed before the Peruvian government.[39] This had taken the form of a memorandum from the merchants (dated 12 December 1842) drawing the finance minister's attention to the initially weak condition of the market and to

[31] *Ibid.*, 8 March 1843.

[32] *Ibid.*, 11 March 1843.

[33] See *ibid*, 27 June 1843.

[34] *Ibid.*, 3 June 1843.

[35] *Ibid.*

[36] *Ibid.*, 16 and 29 September 1843.

[37] *Ibid.*, 15 and 16 September 1843.

[38] *Ibid.*, 13 September 1843.

[39] *Ibid.*, 5 January 1843.

the excessive quantity of guano already lying there unsold. The condition of the business generally they described as 'hazardous'. Their argument was that an extension of the contract period would avoid the necessity of a drastic reduction in prices to find customers for the guano. Short of such a fall, there seemed no hope whatever of selling 120,000 tons within the stipulated period. The contractors also asked for a monetary interest payment on their advance to be substituted for the free guano which could only add to the excess-supply problem. With a monthly cash return on their loans they would not mind a slow sales tempo.[40] The contractors, of course, had an interest in keeping prices tolerably high and avoiding rushed sales at cheap rates so that there would be profit margins sufficient to permit full repayment of their loans.[41]

The proposals were rejected.[42] A further memorandum was submitted on March 7th 1843 and led to a series of conversations between merchants and ministers.[43] The latter, however, needed a good deal of persuading. 'I am straining every nerve', John Hayne wrote four months later, 'for an extension of our contract without which we could never get back our advances'.[44] Success came at last in September. The government still refused to give an interest payment on the loan,[45] but did yield on the contract period. 'We have had an extension of 3 years granted for our 120,000 Tons,' reported Hayne, 'making in all 8 years from December 17 1841. We have still then 6 years from 17 December next to ship the 112457 Tons remaining, or about 18500 Tons a year. I am very glad to hear from Bland (just arrived) that . . . . you have now no doubt that henceforward we shall be able to sell 20 or 30,000 Tons a year.'[46] Three days later he informed London that the decree for the extension had been officially signed.[47] The good news reached England just before the end of the year.[48]

[40] Memorandum Para El Ministro De Hacienda, *loc. cit.*

[41] Only half of the proceeds due to the government, i.e. the half in cash, was available for the repayment of contractor loans. The rest was designated for debt retirement. See *Anales,* III, p. 157.

[42] See Memoria Sobre La Negociación Del Guano, *loc. cit.*

[43] *Ibid.*

[44] *Ibid.,* 15 July; also 14 August 1843.

[45] Memoria Sobre La Negociación, *loc. cit.*

[46] GGC, 13 September 1843.

[47] *Ibid.,* 16 September 1843.

[48] See *ibid.,* 30 December 1843.

COMPETITION AND GLUT, 1843-7

The autumn of 1843 saw the end of one highly problematical period and the beginning of a new one. In mid-October Gibbs wrote to Lima of the 'alarming prospects of African competition'.[49] Competition had always been anticipated with some apprehension, but it was probably assumed that the threat would come largely from known enemies, or that any new foe would enter the field slowly and with fair warning. The worst possible eventuality, however, seemed to be materializing: the sudden appearance of another natural guano: of a relatively short-distance oceanic fertilizer trade in which the participating merchants had to bear none of the burdens of contractual obligations to a foreign government.

The new guano adventure was concentrated on the uninhabited and unclaimed island of Ichaboe, 'a barren rock, about a mile in circumference'[50] three miles off the coast of south west Africa. Although the manure, for climatic reasons, was inherently less valuable than Peruvian guano, bearing a much lower quantity of nitrogen,[51] it was, nevertheless, just lying there for the taking. The trade apparently began at the suggestion of Andrew Livingstone, a retired master-mariner of Liverpool, who had read about the deposits in a book by an American traveller, Benjamin Morrell.[52] Three vessels set sail for Ichaboe in 1842 and one succeeded in obtaining a small cargo of 175 tons which was successfully disposed of, partly in Dumfries and partly in Liverpool, in July 1843.[53] Interest spread rapidly among merchants and shipowners, the latter being eager to find employment for their vessels in a period of serious depression in the shipping industry.[54] By the end of September at least eight more ships had left British ports for Ichaboe.[55] Six months later 16 had returned with cargoes.[56] In March 1844 the master of one vessel estimated that there were probably 'about 200,000 tons of good guano on the island'.[57] 'So much guano is being discovered', Gibbs

[49] *Ibid.*, 14 October 1843; also 26 July, 11 and 26 August, 22 September 1843.

[50] *The Times,* 21 May 1844, p. 7.

[51] According to Ure and Tesche the average ammoniacal content of the 11 specimens they examined was 7.3 per cent, the range being 4.5 to 9.5 per cent. The equivalent range for Peruvian (14 samples), according to Way in 1849, was 16.82 to 18.94 per cent. See Morton, V, pp. 1012-3. The slightly less arid climate of the area was the main factor here.

[52] Benjamin Morrell, *A Narrative of Four Voyages* (London and Liverpool, 1832), cited in Robert Craig, 'The African Guano Trade', *MM,* 50 (1964).

[53] Craig, pp. 28-31.

[54] *Ibid.*, pp. 50-1; Gayer, Rostow, Schwartz, 1, p. 319.

[55] Craig, pp. 31-2.

[56] *Ibid.*

[57] *Ibid.*, p. 32.

observed, 'that we must give up all hopes of *Monopoly*'.[58] By the beginning of May 1844 more than a hundred ships had removed a total of 33,000 tons.[59] 'The African Mania is spreading', Gibbs informed Lima on May 13th, 'and we are threatened with an import of 120,000 Tons!'[60] The number of vessels either loading or lying off Ichaboe increased from 46 on 26 May to about 100 on 19 July, to 240 at the end of August, to around 300 on 28 September, and to a peak of 460 in early December.[61] At the end of January 1845 Gibbs gave a figure of 220,000 tons for 'present and expected stock of African'.[62]

For about a year-and-a-half after the first African arrivals, therefore, the new trade increased quite relentlessly to assume, by the standards of the times, quite massive proportions. It came as a powerful body blow to the Peruvian traders, just as they were beginning to overcome some of their initial troubles. They had succeeded in creating an embryonic guano market in Britain. Now others were moving in to exploit it. Fortunately, however, their presence was not to prove as durable as Gibbs had originally feared. Towards the end of 1844, when the congestion of shipping around Ichaboe was reaching its greatest intensity, the first reports of impending exhaustion began to circulate. 'I'd not by any means recommended chartering any more vessels for Ichaboe;' wrote one ship's captain from the African coast in September. '. . . from calculations there is only 112,000 tons of guano upon the island, and there is now in the roads 98,000 tons of shipping'.[63] In December the *Liverpool Albion* gave 'positive news of the beginning of the end of Ichaboe'.[64] What was left was quickly removed by those near the head of the great queue of ships, and by February 1845 the island was more or less cleared.[65]

There were plenty of other guano islands around the coast of Africa, but none provided a substitute for Ichaboe. The neighbouring islands of Possession, Angra Penqueña, Mercury, and Hollam's Bird held little appeal, much of the guano was of very poor quality,

[58]GGC, 17 February 1844.

[59]Craig, p. 33.

[60]GGC, 13 May 1844; also 5 July 1844.

[61]Craig, p. 35. See also *The Times*, 17 April 1851, pp. 6-7, where it is remarked in a letter that Ichaboe in 1844 provided more employment for British shipping than India and China together.

[62]GGC, 31 January 1845.

[63]Letter dated 11 September 1844 in *The Times*, 3 December 1844, p. 5.

[64]Quoted in *ibid.*, 31 December 1844, p. 7.

[65]Craig, p. 45; also *The Times*, 22 October 1845, p. 7.

some of it had already been removed, and heavy surf impeded access and loading.[66] The only one of any notable commercial importance was Malagas in Saldanha Bay, a few hundred miles to the south. One captain reported to the owner of his vessel in the spring of 1845 that there were about 85 ships at or in the vicinity of the island.[67] The trade, however, was very short-lived, more or less expiring by the end of the year. More fertilizer was found just round the corner from the Cape, in Algoa Bay, although again the deposits were insubstantial.[68] Some was also discovered along the Arabian coast,[69] Latham Island in particular being frequently cited as an important source in 1844 and 1845,[70] and although such discoveries were insignificant commercially they must have had an unsettling effect on the Peruvian consignees, as must the vigorous way in which new supplies were being sought. One vessel returning from Bombay had been ordered to scour the coast of east Africa from the Gulf of Aden to the Cape.[71] Another took the trouble to examine between two and three hundred islands in the Red sea.[72] In January 1845, William Walton observed as 'proof of the spirit with which this new trade is pursued in Liverpool' that a new chart of the world had just been published in the city 'exhibiting the certain and probably guano islands and coasts'.[73] Notes also appeared in the press on Labrador guano[74] and on

[66] *The Times,* 26 February 1844, p. 2; 3 December 1844, p. 5; 31 December 1844, p. 7. Craig, p. 45; T. E. Eden, *The Search for Nitre, and the True Nature of Guano, being an Account of a Voyage to the South-West Coast of Africa* (London, Liverpool and Glasgow, 1846), pp. 72-119.

[67] Quoted in *The Times,* 2 July 1845, p. 5; see also 30 May 1845, p. 8.

[68] 46,848 tons of guano were imported from 'British possessions in South Africa' in 1845, according to official figures. In 1846 this fell to 4,718 tons and in 1847 to 184 tons. *PP,* 1851, L111, p. 309.

[69] GGC, 24 October 1844.

[70] *The Times,* 30 October 1844, p. 6; 31 December 1844, p. 7; 2 April 1845, p. 7.

[71] *Ibid.,* 30 October 1844, p. 6. For a colourful account of events on the coast see 'The Perils of the Guano Trade' in *ibid.,* 26 September 1844, p. 8.

[72] *Ibid.,* 9 December 1845, p. 4. Only three, however, had any guano, and the quantities were so small and scattered that it did not seem worthwhile stopping to load. On St. Paul's rocks, in the middle of the Atlantic just north of the Equator, the captain of a British vessel homeward-bound from Buenos Aires found a letter in a bottle written by an agent for a Glasgow firm and dated April 17th 1845: 'I got here this day and there is no guano, so you must all proceed to where your latter instructions order you, as this was the last place to where I was to proceed for guano.... Wishing you all a prosperous voyage and good freights, I am yours in poor spirits, Oliver Campbell', *Ibid.,* 30 July 1845, p. 5. The mid-Atlantic, however, was not entirely barren of workable deposits. Small quantities were imported from St. Helena in 1844-7. *PP,* 1851, L111, p. 309.

[73] Walton, p. 629; also Eden, *passim.*

[74] *The Times,* 11 November 1844, p. 6.

Caithness guano,[75] and Myers wrote in February 1845 of the sizable deposits that were being worked in Chile.[76] References to importations from Patagonia began to appear in the Gibbs correspondence in the summer of 1846.[77] By that time, however, the Africa bubble had burst: 'no African is now coming', Gibbs observed in March.[78] Although they did not know it at the time, the experience of intense competition from other guanos would never be repeated. Despite its energetic pursuit by shippers eager for the further employment of their vessels, the other Ichaboe which 'would be worth half a million of sterling gold coin'[79] was never found.

While it lasted, however, the experience had been a nasty one, posing the most serious problems for the Peruvian consignees. Total imports from Africa had amounted to the enormous figure of 454,760 tons, Gibbs recorded in July 1846, Ichaboe by itself supplying about 350,000 tons.[80] In 1845 alone African imports came to 254,527 tons. In the same year 14,101 tons were brought in from Peru and Bolivia. With small amounts from other sources, also South American in the main, the sum came to 283,000 — coming on for three times the 1844 total of 104,251, which in turn had represented a massive increase on the small 1843 figure of 3,002.[81] At this early stage in the guano trade, could such quantities find a market? And, more specifically, could Gibbs and Myers hope to do any business at all without a drastic cut in prices?

In one sense the Peruvian consignees were in a fairly strong position for theirs was the more valuable manure, its relatively high nitrogen and phosphorous content enabling it to be applied effectively to a wide range of crops. On the other hand, African guano, relatively deficient in nitrogen and imported under highly competitive circumstances, was a cheaper manure. Although less versatile, it was quite suitable for the highly important turnip crop and its comparatively low price held considerable appeal for farmers in the mid-1840s. The year

[75] *Ibid.*, 28 December 1843, p. 7.

[76] GGC, 7 February 1845. Guano in fact came in from Chile more or less throughout the 1840s, the annual average figure for 1841-9 standing at 6,774 tons. The peak year was 1845 with an importation of 11,656 tons. *PP*, 1851, L111, p. 309.

[77] GGC, 16 June 1846. Imports began in 1846 and were really only of significance in that year and in 1847, the total figure for the two years being 48,404 tons. *PP*, 1851, L111, p. 309.

[78] GGC, 23 March 1846.

[79] Quoted in *The Times*, 30 October 1844, p. 6.

[80] GGC, 16 July 1846.

[81] *PP*, 1851, L111, p. 309.

1844, which saw a total African importation of 77,151 tons (compared with only 175 tons in 1843),[82] was not so difficult for the Peruvian consignees as might have been expected. This was because Ichaboe imports were not particularly heavy in the first six months when the market was most active. The price differential between African and Peruvian, for the moment at least, remained surprisingly slight.[83] Indeed, about the only serious source of vexation during the 1844 season was the *shortage* of Peruvian guano, and the inability of the consignees to meet the demand that had arisen. It was clear that the resumption of shipments in the autumn of 1843 had been undertaken on an insufficiently ambitious scale.[84] 'Very much pleased to hear it has been all cleared', wrote John Hayne from Lima in July, 'but I wish we had placed 15 or 20,000 Tons of ours in England to meet the brisk demand now beginning'.[85] Gibbs and Myers, not surprisingly, held easily to the £10 level and were even considering the possibility of a rise to make the price differential with African approximate more closely to the value differential. Gibbs's opinion in the spring was that as long as African sold at £7 or more, Peruvian would be competitive at £10.[86] For the moment, however, they had no guano to sell.[87]

Circumstances, however, were changing by the summer. The large numbers of vessels that had left British ports in the spring for south west Africa were arriving home and unloading their cargoes. In July Gibbs wrote despairingly of 'immense importations'.[88] The influx of African guano coincided, rather absurdly, with the seasonal contraction of the fertilizer market. The adventure had been no cool, soberly-judged affair: rather a wild, speculative rush. Inevitably prices started to wobble. In June African had stood at £10 and over.[89] By August it was selling at half that level.[90] Some recovery followed, but the maximum never seems to have got much above £6 10s. over

[82] *Ibid.*

[83] Craig, pp. 30 and 48; GGC, 22 February, 1 March, 18 and 20 April, 13 May and 3 June 1844.

[84] GGC, 16 and 29 January, 7 February, 3, 18, 19, 20 and 25 April 1844.

[85] *Ibid.*, 18 July 1844.

[86] *Ibid.*, 1 and 2 April 1844. This tallies with A. J. Bernays's judgement that 'when equal quantities of Peruvian and African Guano are applied to land, the former is preferable. But when African Guano is to be had at £7 per ton, and Peruvian at £10 10s., the former is more economical'. *A Lecture on the Application of Chemistry to the Details of Practical Farming* (London, 1845), p. 44.

[87] GGC, 22 April; also 1 May 1844.

[88] *Ibid.*, 5 July 1844.

[89] *Ibid.*, 3 June 1844.

[90] Craig, p. 49; also GGC, 22 July 1844 and *The Times*, 10 July 1844, p. 8.

the remainder of the year.[91] This was below the level which the Peruvian consignees thought necessary for the successful maintenance of their own £10. The crisis had materialized. 'We must endure it till the season', wrote Myers in July. 'If we can't sell then, it will be clear that we can't maintain £10. African must regulate price.'[92] Gibbs agreed,[93] but were by no means convinced that any alteration would be necessary or desirable. '*If* we were persuaded that the African is inexhaustible, we should have to lower our price so as to discourage importations; if we don't know this, our policy is to *maintain the price*. . . No compromise to continue Peruvian sale!'[94]

The course of events over the next two or three years was to show that this qualified optimism was quite misplaced. The principal difficulty that materialized for the Peruvian business in the mid-1840s was the clogging of the market by African guano and so-called 'second-hand' Peruvian stocks for a long time after the Ichaboe trade had petered out. African imports reached their peak in 1845 when 254,527 tons came into Britain.[95] The quantity, however, was vastly in excess of agricultural demand,[96] and in mid-October Gibbs estimated African stocks at around 140,000 tons.[97] By then, with the oceanic trade virtually at an end, there appears to have been much speculative retention of African guano in anticipation of scarcity and high prices in 1846.[98] The dearth, however, was slow to materialize. In March 1846 Gibbs complained of the still 'immense stock of African',[99] and although only 10,000 tons of fresh supplies came in during the year, these were accompanied by close on 40,000 tons from the newly-worked deposits in Patagonia.[100] 'Patagonian is poor stuff', commented William Gibbs in June 1846, 'but the cost of placing it here is little and *at a price* it must greatly interfere with us'.[101]

[91]GGC, 19 and 27 September, 16 and 17 October, 7 November, 16 and 24 December 1844; *The Times,* 15 October 1844, p. 7; 18 October 1844, p. 5; 30 October 1844, p. 7; 5 November 1844, p. 4; 6 November 1844, p. 4; 11 November 1844, p. 6; 18 November 1844, p. 3; 21 November 1844, p. 6; 26 November 1844, p. 6; 10 December 1844, p. 6; Walton, p. 635; Craig, p. 49.

[92]GGC, 27 July 1844.

[93]*Ibid.,* 29 July 1844; also 13 July and 1 August 1844.

[94]*Ibid.,* 20 December 1844.

[95]*PP,* 1851, LIII, p. 309.

[96]See, e.g., *The Times,* 1 May 1845, p. 8.

[97]GGC, 16 October 1845.

[98]See *ibid.,* 16 September 1845.

[99]*Ibid.,* 23 March 1846.

[100]*PP,* 1851, LIII, p. 309.

[101]GGC, 16 June 1846.

By the end of the year more than 30,000 tons of non-Peruvian guano lay in Liverpool alone,[102] and old Ichaboe stocks in Scottish ports were estimated at 41,178 tons.[103] In January 1847 Gibbs observed that so-called 'inferior' guanos made up the great bulk of the unsold stocks of 160,000 in the country as a whole.[104]

The African price fall in the summer of 1844 was an off-season affair and did not prove permanent. Prices jogged up and down a good deal, and the virtual ending of the trade in 1845, combined with the spreading out of sales over the years that followed, served to keep them at moderate levels: usually within the £6 10s. to £7 10s. range.[105] There was a brief collapse again following the heavy importations of the spring of 1845,[106] with Gibbs reporting 'panic' among the 'African Speculators' in May when prices in London were averaging £5 5s.,[107] but by September rates as high as £7 10s. were being quoted,[108] and there is no evidence of any significantly large price dips thereafter. The main direct source of concern for Gibbs and Myers was the problem of 'second-hand' Peruvian guano, which had been sold to middlemen at the standard wholesale price of £10, but then passed on to consumers in a glutted market at a cheaper rate. This, of course, meant losses for the intermediaries and a growing paralysis of the wholesale business. The problem first manifested itself during the acceleration of the African trade in the 1845 season. Some middlemen were unloading their Peruvian stocks at prices of between £7 2s. 6d. and £8 2s. 6d.[109] in May, and the second-hand price remained lower than the wholesale price for the rest of the year.[110] The business, commented Myers in March 1846, was being 'taken out of our hands'.[111] Second-hand prices were still depressed,[112] remaining so throughout 1846, and a lot of selling from what Gibbs described as 'bankrupt Stocks'[113] continued in 1847.[114] Much of the guano had

[102] *The Times*, 10 January 1848, p. 3.

[103] *JA* (January 1847), p. 578.

[104] GGC, 15 January 1847.

[105] *Ibid.*, 29 January, 10 and 27 February, 8 August, 16 September and 4 October 1845; 16 March and 11 May 1846; also Liverpool Commodity Market Report quoted in Craig, p. 49.

[106] Craig, p. 50; GGC, 3 May and 11 June 1845.

[107] GGC, 16 May 1845.

[108] *Ibid.*, 16 September 1845.

[109] *Ibid.*, 15, 16 and 21 May 1845.

[110] *Ibid.*, 11 and 16 June, 15 August, 16 October, 6 and 15 November 1845.

[111] *Ibid.*, 28 March 1846; also 19 March and 2 April 1846.

[112] *Ibid.*, 16 January, 12 February, 14, 18 and 26 March 1846.

[113] *Ibid.*, 30 September 1847.

[114] *Ibid.*, 13 March, 16 April, 15 June, 13 and 16 August 1847.

been taken in the first instance by speculators rather than regular guano dealers.[115] This appears odd, since the scale of importation from Africa might have seemed more likely to depress than to elevate prices, and make Peruvian guano in particular a bad buy for the speculator. There are a number of possible explanatory factors here. First, the African trade was just one, albeit the major, part of a guano rush in the early and mid-1840s. Obtaining manure, either from islands in Africa or from wholesalers in Britain, had become widespread practice among merchants and financiers seeking quick profit. Secondly, the rapid widening of the business almost certainly brought men on to the market who were ill-acquainted with the nature and limits of fertilizer consumption among farmers. Thirdly, it may have been rationally judged that the widespread use of cheap African guano would increase market receptivity to _all_ sorts of guano, including the more versatile, if more expensive, varieties such as Peruvian. Fourthly, it was generally anticipated that the African trade would not last more than a year or two: there was, accordingly, an expectation of shortage and substantial price increases. The main misjudgements were in relation to the size of the market and the timing of the guano dearth. Severe scarcity never really materialized. Stocks were run down only slowly; supplementary guano came in from Patagonia; the Peruvian trade expanded as the African trade faded (imports rising from 14,101 tons in 1845 to 22,410 in 1846 and 57,762 in 1847);[116] and purchasing power contracted in 1847 as a result of national economic circumstances. One might sum up the somewhat paradoxical predicament of the Peruvian consignees by saying that dealers clearly had confidence in their guano, but that the manifestation of that confidence, in the context of an extravagant trading boom, only served to delay the Peruvian recovery.

Both consignees, aware of the hopeful elements implicit in the crisis, were eager to stick with their £10 minimum wholesale price for as long as possible. Indeed, responding to temporarily good sales and low stocks in early 1845,[117] they pushed up to £10 10s. for a few weeks.[118] At £10, declared William Gibbs, they 'must be firm as a rock'.[119] If they lowered further, he wrote to Lima in June 1845, 'It is impossible to say where it might go. I still flatter myself we may get

[115]See _ibid.,_ 16 July 1847.

[116]_PP,_ 1851, LIII, p. 309.

[117]_The Times,_ 27 January 1845, p. 7; GGC, 29 January, 8, 10, 12 and 26 February, 15 March 1845.

[118]GGC, 3 6, 15 and 27 March, 3 May 1845.

[119]_Ibid.,_ 5 May 1845.

£10 when demand rises.'[120] These, of course, were the words of a man who was presently selling nothing. Why, Myers asked with rhetorical flourish, had they only sold 10,000 tons over the whole season? 'Because we didn't choose to sell it!. We asked a price higher than its market value in proportion to African, and of course farmers bought the latter. . . . The business is one of *price,* and price *only.*'[121] Trifling sales were effected in the off-season months of 1845,[122] and with second-hand Peruvian selling at such low prices, a pretty drastic cut would have been needed in the wholesale rate to retrieve any buoyancy for the business.

Sales remained inconsequential in the early months of 1846.[123] As stocks were now high,[124] a decision was taken around March to suspend further shipments.[125] This, of course, merely helped avoid further aggravation of the difficulty: the central problem was what to do with the stocks in hand. Considerations of appropriate policy at last focused on prices. Myers, as it turned out, was now the pessimist and Gibbs the optimist. Myers's view was that the situation had finally become intolerable and that as consignees he and Gibbs stood to gain absolutely nothing from a standstill in sales. He was, as Gibbs phrased it, 'most anxious to meet the market',[126] and on 24 April 1846 he announced his decision to act unilaterally and adopt a new price scale at the beginning of the following week: £9 for 30 tons and upwards, £9 10s. for 15 to 30 tons, and £10 for less than 15 tons.[127] Gibbs's view was that it was a bit late to consider reductions. At present, they argued, 'we could probably not sell at any price, hurt ourselves, and do no good. Our *steadiness* of price would be gone and we should make enemies of our buyers of this season at £10.'[128] They had to admit that it was extremely difficult to sell anything at £10 while old stocks sold at £9. 10s., but these latter, they felt, were 'fast disappearing, and as the remaining holders of them must make sales, if we offer at £8 they will assuredly come in at £7 10s'.[129] Once Myers

[120]*Ibid.,* 16 June 1845.

[121]*Ibid.,* 23 September 1845.

[122]*Ibid.,* 15 July and 16 October 1845.

[123]*Ibid.,* 28 March and 2 April 1846.

[124]*Ibid.,* 28 March 1846.

[125]*Ibid.,* 23 March, 11 June and 11 August 1846.

[126]*Ibid.,* 15 May 1846.

[127]*Ibid.,* 24 April 1846.

[128]*Ibid.,* 19 and 23 March 1846.

[129]*Ibid.,* 26 March 1846; also 1, 3 and 25 April 1846.

had lowered, however, they were forced to follow suit.[130] And further reductions were to come. Only five days after announcing the impending implementation of the £9 minimum, Myers wrote, 'We now fix £8 10s. for 30 Tons and £9 for smaller Lots'.[131] Gibbs suggested a minimum of £8 and a maximum of £10.[132] Myers replied that he would settle for a scale of £8 10s., £9, and £10[133] (the quantity categories presumably being the same as before).

The fall turned out to be only a qualified success,[134] but the consignees were not too worried.[135] Stocks of old African and second-hand Peruvian were running down sufficiently fast to leave room again for wholesale trading. Gibbs and Myers reported brisk business right from the beginning of the year,[136] and although they ran up against some frustrating market blockages in the spring and early summer,[137] they were able to view the season as a whole with some satisfaction. In September, Myers estimated that consumption of first and second-hand Peruvian and Bolivian guano in January-June 1847 had amounted to a very substantial 70,000 tons.[138] The pace of chartering was stepped up in the winter,[139] and only eight months after the much-delayed price reduction the level started to move up again,[140] culminating in a new scale at the end of January 1847: £10 for 30 tons and over and £11 10s. for smaller quantities.[141]

By the summer, however, the mood had lapsed back into gloom, this time for reasons that had little to do with competition. As early as May, Gibbs, explaining to Lima the fall in their monthly sales, had made reference to 'the scarceness of money'.[142] Gibbs Crawley replied that in their view 'the monetary crisis had *much* to do with the slackness of sales, but it could not have been the *only* cause. We fear guano itself is losing its hold on the farmers!'[143] The latter point was

[130] *Ibid,.* 27 April 1846.
[131] *Ibid.,* 29 April 1846.
[132] *Ibid.,* 30 April 1846.
[133] *Ibid.,* 1 May 1846.
[134] *Ibid.,* 15, 23 and 27 May, 16 June and 11 September 1846.
[135] *Ibid.,* 30 November and 16 December 1846.
[136] *Ibid.,* 6, 15 and 23 January, 16 February, 16 March 1847.
[137] *Ibid.,* 13 March, 10 April, 15 May, 15 and 16 June 1847.
[138] *Ibid.,* 22 September 1847.
[139] *Ibid.,* 10 February 1847.
[140] *Ibid.,* 30 December 1846, 2, 6, 7 and 15 January 1847.
[141] *Ibid.,* 29 January 1847; also 16 February 1847.
[142] *Ibid.,* 15 May 1847.
[143] *Ibid.,* 11 July 1847.

unduly pessimistic, but the references to tight money and relatively low agricultural purchasing power were based on fact and were the first of many such observations made during the rest of the year. In October, Horace Bland, Myers's associate, wrote that consumption of Peruvian guano depended on its price, competition from other manures, the means of farmers, and the 'state of Trade'. With reference to the latter, he observed, 'there is no confidence, credit, or speculation. Everybody expects a worse state of things, and nobody buys.'[144] Financial troubles obviously made it more difficult for dealers and farmers to secure the credit they may have required for purchasing guano, and cast uncertainties over agricultural commodity markets. And poor grain prices, the result of heavy wheat imports and a good harvest,[145] had an extra dampening effect on the market — just as high grain prices, conversely, had helped enliven the market in the early months of the year.

In such circumstances, sales of Peruvian guano slumped to levels lower than anticipated,[146] even allowing for the fact that these were off-season months. The minimum wholesale price of Peruvian guano (for private sales, which comprised the great bulk of all transactions) had been at £10 since late January, and in July the price had been raised to £10 5s. in the outports.[147] By September, however, Myers was urging a reduction. Stocks, he pointed out, were large; a great deal of fresh Peruvian was on its way; some second-hand guano was still selling at £9 10s. and £9 12s. 6d.; and the market situation was highly uncertain.[148] His reasons were sound enough, but perhaps the most important factor in his mind was his intention to quit the trade in the near future. The background to this decision we shall consider later. For the moment the point of relevance is that Myers was, by September, losing interest in the long-term prospects of the business and was eager to sell off his stocks as quickly as possible. William Gibbs, however, from his own quite different standpoint, found reasons for objecting to Myers's proposals. Any reduction, he wrote, would 'involve a loss to our friends in Lima', and would be a purely 'gratuitous sacrifice'.[149] In mid-October George Davy informed Hayne in Lima that Myers was 'determined not to hold over . . . None of Mr. Gibbs' arguments could move him . . . His determination looks

---

[144] *Ibid.,* 14 October 1847; see also 13 August 1847.

[145] See Thomas Tooke, *A History of Prices . . . from 1839 to 1847 inclusive* (London, 1848), pp. 32, 413.

[146] GGC, 14 and 16 October, 16 November 1847.

[147] *Ibid.,* 16 July 1847.

[148] *Ibid.,* 22 September 1847; also 14 October 1847.

[149] *Ibid.,* 30 September 1847.

very little like joint management I assure you.'[150] It was, however, gradually coming to be recognized that Myers had a case after all. 'As to price', wrote Davy, 'he (William Gibbs) is not perhaps so strong in his belief of the quantity that could be sold at £10'.[151] Such uncertainty made it easier for Gibbs to follow Myers, as he would have had to do anyhow. The reduction, which came into effect around the middle of October, was as Gibbs phrased it, 'Both sanctioned *and* forced on me'.[152] The new scale, not quite so generous as Myers had originally proposed, was £9 for 30 tons and over, and £10 10s. for amounts of under 30 tons. Prices at the outports were £9 5s. and £10 15s. respectively.[153] On 4 November Myers reported that he had sold four cargoes to arrive at £9 5s.,[154] and on 18 December pronounced: 'Our reduction of prices has answered admirably'.[155] Gibbs, however, were a little grieved by some of Myers's sales techniques. He was selling at the agreed prices 'subject to there being no fall at time of arrival — so that in case of a rise buyer has advantage of the fixed price, and in case of fall is spared the corresponding disadvantage. This is unfair to us, and unmercantile.'[156] But the problem of harmonizing policy with Myers was not going to last very much longer. 'I take my leave of guano', he wrote to Gibbs on 25 October 'for *I* will make no future contract; and if you like it all, I shall be very glad to see it in your hands'.[157]

And thus the period of the 1842 guano contract came to an end, although imports and sales were to continue for some considerable time after the terminal date. Prospects for the years ahead were, on the whole, fairly bright. Both Gibbs and Myers, as we shall see, had tried in 1847 — one successfully, the other unsuccessfully — to secure a fresh contract for themselves, suggesting clearly that neither of them had any very serious doubts about the long-term profitability of the trade. References to competition from other guanos and from manufactured fertilizers appear only occasionally in Gibbs's correspondence for 1847. It was obviously felt that for some considerable period in the future the fertilizer market would be dominated by Peruvian guano. There were still second-hand stocks around towards

---

[150]*Ibid.*, 15 October 1847.
[151]*Ibid.*, also 13 November 1847.
[152]*Ibid.*, 18 October 1847.
[153]*Ibid.*, 23 October and 16 November 1847.
[154]*Ibid.*, 4 November 1847.
[155]*Ibid.*, 18 December 1847.
[156]*Ibid.*, 15 December 1847.
[157]*Ibid.*, 25 October 1847.

the end of the year, and large amounts of 'inferiors' as well, but Gibbs at least did not regard any forthcoming difficulties as worthy of much discussion. The crisis of competition had, in their view, passed.[158] They considered, on balance, that there had been no need for the recent reduction in prices which Myers proposed and then carried into effect. They wrote of 'the progressive increase in Sales' which was likely to occur.[159] As to consumption in 1848, they considered '50,000 Tons a low and therefore prudent estimate'.[160]

DISPUTES: GOVERNMENT, CONTRACTORS AND CONSIGNEES

There was a good deal of friction in the 1840s among the various parties to the 1842 contract. The disagreement between Gibbs and Myers over prices has already been dealt with and can be viewed as largely inevitable, considering the problems of joint management in a difficult market. The greatest intensity of ill-feeling, in fact, arose not between London and Liverpool, but between England and Peru. Disputes centred on two of the important issues alluded to in the introductory chapter: prices and intermediate costs. To begin with, however, brief consideration can be given to a rather different matter, concerning the basic terms under which the trade was conducted. The original contract of February 1842 stipulated that 120,000 tons should be sold abroad by December 1846. In consequence of the trifling sales effected in the first year or two, the contractors, as we have seen, succeeded in securing a three-year extension in September 1843. Not very long after, however, the government decided to scrap the agreement: the sort of move that Gibbs and Myers had always thought possible (thus their appeal to Lord Aberdeen in 1843).[161] The original extension had been arranged during the presidency of Manuel Vivanco. Less than a year later Vivanco had been replaced by Menéndez and his various acts, the guano *prórroga* among them, declared null.[162] Pedro Carillo, commenting on the extension granted by 'the illegal Government' in his 1845 *Memoria* on the business, advised in his capacity as official guano accountant that the extension ought to be upheld since rushed sales at presently high freights and low prices would only serve to lower the unit returns to the government.[163]

[158]*Ibid.*, 30 September 1847.

[159]*Ibid.*

[160]GGC, 13 November 1847.

[161]See above, p.44.

[162]GGC, 16 October 1844.

[163]Memoria Sobre La Negociación Del Guano, *loc. cit.*

The government, however, now under Ramón Castilla,[164] thought differently and the contractors felt obliged to seek — apparently without effect[165] — the support of the British chargé d'affaires in Lima and the commander-in-chief of the British naval squadron in the Pacific.[166]

Towards the end of August 1845, if not before, the Castilla administration decided to turn the affair to its own advantage. 'The Government want a loan of $200,000', wrote Hayne on 3 September 'and hope to get it as a new advance on Huano — something we must give to ensure our proroga [sic]. I should not mind $50,000'.[167] In October the finance minister, Manuel del Rio, submitted a report to Congress in which he drew attention to the perilous state of the new government's finances[168] and to the consequent need for a further substantial loan from the contractors.[169] Hayne reported in December that an advance had indeed been authorized, but that the resolution passed on the subject 'does not confirm the proroga'.[170] At the end of January 1846 he explained how he had just offered the president '$100,000 down — and 100000 in a fortnight and 100000 more if you could sell in Spring at £10'.[171] The proposal was rejected. 'Castilla put himself in a great passion; broke with the Contractors entirely, and is to call a meeting of Natives tonight!.... No chance of getting our proroga now.'[172] Within a week of his outburst, however, Castilla, presumably unable to raise enough cash from Peruvian merchants, came back to the contractors and offered them an extension for one year (not three, as in the earlier arrangement), with the promise of extra time if required, in return for a loan of 300,000 pesos[173] at ½ per cent per month.[174] 'I think you will have to avail

---

[164]This had been a period of frequent changes of government, stablised only by Castilla's accession. See Andrés de Santa-Cruz Schuhkrafft, *Cuadros Sinópticos De Los Gobernantes De La República De Bolivia . . . Y De La Del Perú* (La Paz, 1956), pp. 92-5 and below, Appendix I.

[165]All the possibly relevant volumes of FO 61 and FO 177 have been consulted and no material whatever has been found relating to these approaches.

[166]GGC, 16 October 1845.

[167]*Ibid.,* 3 September 1845.

[168]With the aid of some very odd figures on guano returns.

[169]*Anales,* III, pp. 25-6; also FO 61/112, Barton to Aberdeen, 2 March 1846.

[170]GGC, 3 December 1845.

[171]*Ibid.,* 31 January 1846.

[172]*Ibid.*

[173]A third to be paid at once, another third after 15 days, and the remaining third after 45 days. *Anales,* IV, p. 22; FO 61/112, Barton to Aberdeen, 2 March 1846. Gibbs Crawley & Co. were responsible for finding 28 per cent of the sum: 84,000 pesos, or around £17,000. Lima Branch Accounts, File 2, 1837-1847.

[174]GGC, 7 February 1846.

yourselves of Castilla's promise', wrote William Gibbs when he heard of the proposals.[175] Hayne and the other parties had already done so[176] Myers, however, felt that the promise would be quickly forgotten if other parties offered a fresh loan in exchange for exporting rights after the end of the first extra year: 'Up to 17 December 1847 we have a *right* to the export, after that we have the President's *word*. Weigh that at £60,000!'[177] The episode reveals yet again the relative strength of the Peruvian government. Although very weak financially (guano returns still being low), its position as owner of the guano and as the party which could select who could and who could not participate in the trade had enabled it to tear up a formal agreement with little compunction and extract from the contractors a fresh loan of very considerable dimensions, forcing the latter to make new advances in order to protect old ones.

On the issue of prices, the earlier pages of this chapter reveal two important facts. First, that all the initiatives were taken in Britain rather than Peru; and second, that the policies pursued won the qualified approval of Gibbs's branch house in Lima. '*Price* must be left entirely to you and Myers', John Hayne had written in December 1843.[178] There were occasional disagreements between the London and Lima houses, but they reflected no lack of trust or sourness of relationship. 'Your management has been excellent', wrote Hayne in 1846.[179] Approval from the other parties in Lima was not so readily forthcoming. Initially the problem was a reflection of the conflicts between Gibbs and Myers in the early months of their association, the latter complaining to Lima that price reductions had been forced upon him'.[180] 'Now *you*', wrote Hayne to Gibbs in January 1844, 'have the credit of driving down the price. . . . There are too many interested in it for a correct judgement to be formed, and whoever advocates low prices will surely be blamed'.[181] Carlos Barroilhet, who had been party to the first and subsequent guano contracts and was active in the Bolivian trade, wrote to Gibbs in May 1844 that the way in which they were selling guano was shameful. 'That you have lost more than $500000 to the Huano speculation is too clear to need proof. I will only say that to gain your own evil ends you have sold guano at £10.'

[175] *Ibid.*, 16 April 1846.

[176] *Ibid.*, 7 February 1846.

[177] *Ibid.*, 26 August 1846. 'We shan't', he commented some months later, 'be allowed an hour beyond December 17'. 13 March 1847.

[178] *Ibid.*, 13 December 1843; also 13 December 1847.

[179] *Ibid.*, 13 May 1846.

[180] *Ibid.*, 18 January 1844; also 24 February, 24 April and 7 May 1844.

[181] *Ibid.*, 29 June 1844.

Gibbs, he wrote to another party, 'will listen to no reason... I need not try to show you the evils of their management, as they lie on the very face of it. A thousand experiments have proved that at £30[182] Huano is cheaper than any other manure, and even now there is not a farmer who would not prefer it at £15'.[183]

This sort of bickering over prices, sometimes ill-informed and highly intemperate, was a feature primarily of the first two or three years of the trade — an experimental period in which the various parties to the 1842 contract were finding it difficult to settle down together in harmonious joint enterprise. By the mid-1840s, when the scale and implications of the African competition became apparent to all, when a common enemy had to be faced, there was much more mutual understanding and goodwill. 'Government and Contractors highly pleased with total clearance at £10', reported Hayne in April 1845.[184] In 1846, the year of most acute competition, Hayne wrote in April: 'The advices from England drive the President (Castilla) *mad*',[185] but in the following month he indicated that one advantage arising from the bad market situation would be the checking of 'the illusory and absurd ideas of folks here'.[186] In June he observed: 'The President is in a better humour notwithstanding your disappointing advices. All the contractors are quite satisfied with you and are prepared to defend your course of action'.[187] In 1847 the question of prices was debated hardly at all between London and Lima. Taking the period up to 1847 as a whole, there was really surprisingly little fuss over marketing policy. The simple fact was that the moderate price scales adopted in Britain were broadly realistic, given the need to force sales in the first year or two of the trade and meet the challenge of competition in the period immediately following. And as time went by this fact gradually got through to the government and the guano contractors in Lima. Indeed, contrary to what Jonathan Levin's observations on the subject suggest, the consignees can be more easily faulted for keeping prices too high than for effecting unnecessary reductions. The decision to stick at the £10 level for about two and a half years after the African competition began almost certainly impaired sales. As Myers observed in September 1845, 'we didn't

[182]The handwriting is obscure at this point, and the figure may well be £50. It is certainly not £10 or £20.

[183]Both letters quoted in GGC, 17 October 1844. 'Barroilhet is working almost openly against you', wrote John Hayne to William Gibbs. 18 August 1844.

[184]*Ibid.*, 28 April 1845.

[185]*Ibid.*, 13 April 1846.

[186]*Ibid.*, 12 May 1846.

[187]*Ibid.*, 12 June 1846; also 12 July, 11 August, 7 and 11 September 1846.

choose to sell. . . .'[188] There were good reasons for this apparent obstinacy, as there usually were for almost any decision on prices. And such reasons, whether they applied to a price fall or a price rise, did not relate exclusively to the obvious and immediate interests of the consignees at the expense of those of merchants and government in Lima. There might *appear* to have been a possible conflict of interests in as much as the parties in Lima were concerned essentially with profits, while those in Britain were thinking about commissions. But the contractors and the consignees cannot be completely separated in this way, for the latter stood to gain from any successes achieved by their branch or associate houses in Lima, and, as the principal suppliers of credit to these branches, stood to lose if things went badly wrong. It was, moreover, in the interests of the consignees to secure good returns for the government in order to secure the loans that they had helped finance and to retain the goodwill of men who might otherwise seek to dispense with their services. Because of the loans, wrote William Gibbs in 1846, it was 'quite as much the interest of the contractors as of the Government that we should get a good price'.[189]

More serious as a source of conflict was the issue of intermediate costs. These can be divided into two categories: first, commission payments to Gibbs and Myers; second, payments for shipping, insurance, brokerage etc. to parties not directly involved in the guano contract. The former was the main source of trouble, largely because Gibbs and Myers, engaged in the difficult business of getting guano through to the farmers, had their own ideas as to what the appropriate level of reward should be. The two most awkward years were 1844 and 1846; in the first the main tussle was with the contractors in Lima, and in the second, with the Peruvian government.

The rate agreed at the start of the 1842 contract appears to have been 4 per cent, 2½ per cent of which represented a straight sales commission and 1½ per cent, delcredere guarantee.[190] The evidence available suggests that the aggregate figure of 4 per cent was simply applied to the gross proceeds of sales. There was also the question of brokerage payments — money paid out to shipping, insurance and commodity brokers at Gibbs's and Myers's own discretion. In December 1843 they were talking of rates of 1 per cent.[191] The principal disputes, however, centred on the general commission rate.

[188]See above, p. 65.
[189]GGC, 26 March 1846; also 22 and 24 April 1846.
[190]*Ibid.,* 13 May 1842 and 3 April 1843.
[191]*Ibid.,* 28, 29 and 30 December 1843.

It became a source of conflict because the trade got off to a bad start, this setting up two conflicting pressures. On the one hand the contractors wished to see payments to consignees reduced, thereby helping them marginally to enlarge their disturbingly low returns from guano sales; on the other hand the consignees, equally disappointed with their takings in a sluggish market, wished to see their commissions increased. In April 1843 Gibbs informed their Lima house (with whom, incidentally, they had proposed to share their commission earnings)[192] that they had agreed with Myers to charge 5 per cent for commissions and guarantees 'or 1% more than agreed with the Government because of the *urgente trabajo*'.[193] Such a high-handed decision was, not surprisingly, resented. John Hayne observed in December that it had caused 'endless discussions, and threatened a total break up'. His closest associates in the contract, Puymerol Poumarroux & Co., Montané, and Candamo 'look on you', he reported, 'as mere agents, and say you have run no risk but their solvency. They will not pay your charges, and propose 3% for Commission, Guarantee, Brokerage, Insurance and Charter, with 1½ more for foreign and outports'.[194] At about the same time Quiros Allier & Co. made similar proposals to Myers, offering, as the latter phrased it, to 'give us much trouble and little pay'.[195] In January 1844, however, Hayne wrote that the contractors had agreed that Myers and Gibbs should receive '2½% commission ½% guarantee ½% Brokerage but no Agency for outports.... For sales by direct cargoes in other markets you are to charge 1½ commission and ½% guarantee'.[196] These were slightly more generous arrangements than the ones lately mooted in Lima, but still represented a reduction from the rates established at the start of the contract. Gibbs and Myers remained adamant that they were being underpaid. 'Seeing that to sell £150000', Myers wrote to Gibbs in November, 'we have to incur £40, to £50,000 in charters and large sums in freights and advances — pay our establishment etc. and incur all risks; — and all for £4500,[197] I begin to feel my responsibility exceeding my reward, and that the business is not worth having'.[198] Some concessions, however, appear to have been made about this time by the contractors, although the details are not all that clear. In October 1844 Hayne observed that all

[192]*Ibid.*, 14 October 1843.

[193]*Ibid.*, 3 April 1843; also 13 December 1843, in which Hayne complains of a rate as high as 5.1/5 per cent in London and Liverpool.

[194]*Ibid.*, 13 December 1843; also 22 March 1844.

[195]*Ibid.*, 28 March 1844.

[196]*Ibid.*, 18 January 1844.

[197]i.e. 3 per cent of gross proceeds.

[198]GGC, 28 November; also 11 and 12 May, 1 July 1844.

was 'satisfactorily arranged about commissions for the present',[199] and in March 1845 Gibbs remarked to Myers: 'Contractors seem by Hayne's letters to have repented of their illiberality generally'.[200] In the same month they wrote to Lima that they were 'Glad the Commission question is settled by mutual concession'.[201] As the dispute between contractors and consignees was not revived we may assume that the rates finally agreed on were those which were cited in 1846 by the Peruvian minister in London: 4 per cent for commissions and guarantees (2½ per cent and 1½ per cent respectively), and a certain amount (presumably ½ or 1 per cent) for brokerage[202] — terms, it may be noted, more or less the same as those agreed on before the dispute began.

The year 1845 was quiet, but 1846 saw a revival of conflict, this time between the consignees and the Peruvian government. In April Hayne told the London house that Castilla was unhappy about the conduct of the business,[203] and in September he reported that Yterregui, the Peruvian minister in Britain, had 'been writing very improperly to the Government about your *Charges* asserting that he can get them done for *half,* and that your Overcharges must amount to $500000!'[204] Shortly after, Hayne and some of the other contractors were summoned before President Castilla who was, as Hayne reported, 'most violent about charges'.[205] On learning of the contents of Yterregui's letter from London on the subject, Hayne was surprised to discover that it in fact contained very little criticism of the consignees: 'It was plainly an answer to one from the President ordering him to investigate our charges'. Yterregui had found that the charges for delivery were the usual ones, that the 4 per cent commission was also normal, and that brokerage too was customary. Hayne asked Castilla if the minister 'had named any house who would do the business for half our charge. He *pretended* to read something of the kind which I am sure was not there', and then, somewhat paradoxically, went on to remark that Gibbs had always been deserving of the government's full confidence.[206] It would seem, therefore, that Castilla was either in a state of some confusion or was trying to bluff the merchants into agreeing to a cut in consignee

[199]*Ibid.,* 16 October 1844.
[200]*Ibid.,* 10 March 1845; also 10 January 1845.
[201]*Ibid.,* 15 March 1845.
[202]Quoted in *ibid.,* 10 October 1846; see also 10 January 1845.
[203]*Ibid.,* 13 April 1846.
[204]*Ibid.,* 11 September 1846.
[205]*Ibid.,* 10 October 1846.
[206]*Ibid.*

commissions. If he was attempting the latter, he failed. William Gibbs, in his reply to Hayne, observed that Yterregui had never raised the question of commissions with him, and that if he chose to in the future 'we shall of course be as firm as a Rock'.[207] He also reminded his colleague in Lima that the London house had 'charged no commission on Charters, as we were entitled to do'.[208] And there the matter appears to have rested. The only significant reference to the question in 1847 appears in a letter from John Hayne in August in which he remarked that Yterregui was still promising to send the government a scale of charges at which certain unnamed houses would be prepared to take the business, but that no-one was any longer paying much attention to him.[209]

As for the second category of payments, to people with no direct, long-term interests in the trade, the most important by far was freights. These, however, were never causes of dissension and there is no evidence whatever that the consignees went against government (and branch) interests by actively seeking higher rates in order to enlarge their commission earnings, as Levin implies they might have done.[210] They did not take commissions on freights, so the issue is hardly worth discussing. Rates rose and fell by quite considerable margins over the period and, of course, had a very major effect on net returns. During the 1844 season they were as low as £2 10.;[211] more commonly, however, they moved between £4 and £5.[212] The consignees quite naturally tried to charter at the lowest possible rates, sometimes running to excess in their pursuit of cheap shipping. 'Something must be done about charters', wrote Myers in November 1846. 'We are always just below the market, and can't get a ship at £4 4s'.[213] Another, and much lower, intermediate cost was insurance. Premiums of 3.5 or 4 per cent[214] were paid on valuations corresponding to net returns on each ton sold: £4, for example, in the summer of 1842, £6 in the 1844 and 1846 seasons, £4 again by the end of 1846.[215] The

[207]GGC, 16 December 1846; also 10 December 1846.

[208]*Ibid.,* 10 December 1846.

[209]*Ibid.,* 11 August 1847; also 14 September 1847.

[210]See above, p.5.

[211]GGC, 11 January and 8 June 1844.

[212]FO 61/81, Wilson to Palmerston, 22 December 1841; GGC, 26 August 1843, 10 and 14 March, 28 November, 4 and 16 December 1845, 25 March, 29 October and 2 November 1846.

[213]*Ibid.,* 12 November 1846.

[214]*Ibid.,* 13 May 1842, 1, 3 and 4 January 1844.

[215]*Ibid.,* 15 July and 1 August 1842, 16 January and 7 May 1844, 30 July, 12 and 16 November 1846.

Peruvian government, however, ordered a cessation of cargo insurance in 1846,[216] thereby enlarging risks but also securing marginally higher unit returns on the guano that arrived safely in the British market. Little information is available on other costs in the trade. Docking, warehousing and bagging charges are seldom mentioned in Gibbs's correspondence. In July 1842 they were paying storage rents of 2s. per ton per week for the first three months and 6d. a week thereafter.[217] In 1843 landing charges appear to have stood at between 3s. and 4s.[218] In September 1844 Gibbs informed Lima that they were doing all they could to get charges reduced.[219] By March 1845 they had lowered their weekly rate for 'general charges' from 1s. 6d. to 6d. per ton.[220] The principal point to be stressed at this stage is that although these various intermediate costs had a substantial bearing on the trade's profitability, they were, commissions apart, entirely non-controversial.

A further, relatively minor, problem concerned the role in the trade of the Peruvian minister in London. Should he or should he not have any say in its running? The question came to the fore in 1846. In the spring of that year, when Myers and Gibbs were preparing for a reduction in price, the latter at least seems to have considered discussing the matter with Yterregui.[221] However he certainly did not feel that he had any obligation so to do. In July, Hayne wrote that President Castilla, while approving of the price fall, 'hopes in such matters you always act d'accord with the Minister in England, and I have no doubt you did'.[222] 'I had no idea it was expected', Gibbs replied, 'and I should think the principle a bad one. I have always talked over matters with Yterregui who is a judicious person and has always agreed; but if he did not I should be obliged to act on my own responsibility'.[223] The consignees would happily converse with him on their own terms at times of their own choosing, but sensitive of their status, they would not accept that a diplomatic representative be allowed to exercise substantial authority in matters of commerce. 'I have carefully avoided', Gibbs wrote, 'admitting the right of the Government to give us orders (which may be absurd and impracticable)

[216]*Ibid.*, 10 December 1846.

[217]*Ibid.*, 15 July 1842.

[218]*Ibid.*, 25 July 1843.

[219]*Ibid.*, 25 September 1844; also 1 July 1844.

[220]*Ibid.*, 8 March 1845.

[221]See *ibid.*, 27 April 1846.

[222]*Ibid.*, 12 July 1846; also 8 November 1846.

[223]*Ibid.*, 15 September 1846.

through their Ministers'.[224] Myers appears to have agreed: in the same month he wrote that he disliked receiving instructions on insurance rates from Yterregui.[225] The practice of occasionally discussing matters with him continued,[226] however, and relations between consignees and minister appear to have been reasonably cordial,[227] although the fuss over charges must be taken as evidence of some degree of mutual tension and suspicion.

Given this quite wide range of disputes, and the difficulties encountered by Gibbs and Myers in their efforts to sell guano in the British and European markets, it is not surprising that the two houses sometimes expressed disenchantment with the business. Myers, as we have seen, toyed with the idea of abandoning the trade in 1844 when the contractors were proving troublesome.[228] During the same year, as the threat from African guano grew, William Gibbs commented that there were probably no other merchants who would be willing to bear the sorts of responsibilities which he and Myers were obliged to carry.[229] In May 1845, a black month in the guano market, Gibbs expressed the desire to be 'free from this harassing and risky business!'[230] In Lima, John Hayne was hardly any more enthusiastic: he was 'disgusted with the business' in February 1845.[231] A year or so later, in January 1846, when it seemed that no extension of the 1842 contract was going to be allowed, he commented that he would be more than happy if the trade and all its attendant difficulties were placed in other hands.[232] Later in the same year Acqilles Allier was apparently afraid to tell the consignees in Britain about the government's anger over commission rates lest they decided to abandon the business completely.[233]

By 1847, however, with better prospects in the market and most of the conflicts with Lima resolved, both Gibbs and Myers were taking up their separate positions for control of the trade after the old contract expired in December. Unhappy memories of the past were being rapidly obscured by brightening hopes for the future.

[224]*Ibid.*, 16 November 1846.

[225]*Ibid.*, 12 November 1846.

[226]See, for example, *ibid.*, 21, 23, 26 and 28 December 1846.

[227]See *ibid.*, 15 January 1847.

[228]See above, p.74; also GGC, 20 May 1844.

[229]GGC, 29 June 1844.

[230]*Ibid.*, 16 May 1845.

[231]*Ibid.*, 7 February 1845.

[232]*Ibid.*, 31 January 1846.

[233]*Ibid.*, 11 September 1846.

NEW CONTRACTS, 1847

In February 1847 William Gibbs expressed the suspicion that Myers, working through parties in London who were in touch with the Peruvian minister, was in treaty for a fresh contract,[234] and a month or so later Yterregui informed him that he had in fact concluded a contract, although it would have to be approved by Congress in Lima before it could become operational. There is no indication that Yterregui had sought Gibbs's participation. He appears to have been in league with certain financial groups in the City (no doubt anticipating some monetary rewards for himself),[235] a relationship which may help explain his attack on Gibbs over charges. 'He tells me', wrote William Gibbs, 'the Contractors are Cotesworth & Co. (Myers's friends) Schneider & Co. and other monied men. I dare say Myers and Bland have a share'. The stipulations, he noted, were that 200,000 tons be exported in 1846 and 1849, that £2 10s. be paid to the Peruvian government for each ton (representing, in effect, direct sale in Peru), that £180,000 be paid to the government more or less right away, that a further £320,000 be handed over in instalments in the second year of the contract, and that £120,000 of this total be used for dividend payments if any settlement was reached with the British bondholders. 'A very Bold Purchase!' commented Gibbs. Ratification could not arrive from Lima until October or November — 'too late for charters to load in January or February. . . . What a freight they will have to pay!' And the quantity of guano contracted for, was, he felt, too great for two year's consumption. 'Now *I* would have nothing to do with a purchase on such terms as above'. He expected the contract to be shelved in Peru 'and a higher price asked'.[236] He was right: the government regarded a return of £2 10s. per ton as insufficient and in June Hayne reported that the contract had indeed been rejected. Myers, he indicated, had definitely been party to it. 'I saw a letter which showed he was[237] — and that he was alarmed now and hoped it would be rejected.[238] In my opinion their only error was in the quantity. Half would do *well*'.[239] The Cotesworth group, however, did retain certain modest claims on guano. The Peruvian government

---

[234] *Ibid.*, 16 February 1847.

[235] See *ibid.*, 15 June 1847.

[236] *Ibid.*, 16 April 1847; also 15 May 1847.

[237] *Ibid.*, 11 June 1847. Myers's involvement is confirmed by Henry Gibbs, who inserts a note in this letter to the effect that two different parties had informed him in 1856 of Myers's activities. See also Levin, p. 64.

[238] So also, apparently, did Cotesworth and his friends. GGC, 14 October 1847. This concern, as we shall see shortly, was the result of crisis in the London money market.

[239] *Ibid.*, 11 June 1847; also 14 October 1847.

allowed them to take enough to cover a loan which they had already advanced through Yterregui: £20,000 worth, according to John Hayne, to be shipped after the expiry of the 1842 contract.[240]

The background to the Cotesworth arrangement was, as ever, the government's pursuit of fresh loans. Castilla had been worrying about Juan José Flores's preparations in Ireland for an expedition against Ecuador which, if successful, might help to re-establish Spanish power in the continent.[241] 'With the independence of Peru manifestly threatened by the expeditonary preparations being made in Europe by General Flores,' reported del Rio, the finance minister, 'the Government sought permission from the Council of State for the raising of a loan to protect the nation against such dangers. The Council authorized the Executive to borrow 900,000 pesos. . . .'[242] Thus the instructions to Yterregui, who was only able to raise money through guano sales to London merchants. With the rejection of the Cotesworth agreement the government then tried to raise funds from Peruvian traders, but without success owing to 'the lack of ready capital in our national commerce . . .'.[243] The solution, not surprisingly, lay with the current guano contractors.

Gibbs had been giving some thought to the conditions on which they would continue in the trade after the expiry of their contract. In December 1846 William Gibbs wrote that he would accept 'no new contract on worse terms than the present'.[244] Two months later he made reference to news from Lima that the Peruvian government was thinking of selling guano at the islands for a fixed price — a notion embodied in the Cotesworth contract — and to his objections to any such reorganization of the trade.[245] But in April, having remarked on the audacity of Cotesworth and his associates and on the likelihood of the new contract being scrapped, he observed that 'if any Lima folk will join the Government to send Guano to our care, fixing a certain Net Proceeds and the excess to be divided[246], I should not object even on

[240]*Ibid.*, 11 June 1847. For full details see *Anales,* IV, pp. 24-8. Cotesworth had taken 9,133 register tons by June 1st 1849 — judged to be more than sufficient for reimbursement.

[241]Jorge Basadre, *Historia de la República del Perú* (Lima, 3rd edn., 1946), 1, pp. 220-2.

[242]*Anales,* IV, p. 111.

[243]*Ibid.*

[244]*GGC,* 16 December 1846.

[245]*Ibid.*, 16 February 1847.

[246]As in the 1842 contract.

Modified rates of Commission'.[247] And in June Hayne wrote that with the London agreement annulled, the government, despite various other offers in Lima, would almost certainly turn to Gibbs Crawley in the end.[248] He had calculated correctly, although somewhat narrowly.

On 10 July the Lima house (now restyled William Gibbs & Company)[249] reported that they had succeeded in securing a contract for the sale of 40,000 tons[250] of guano.[251] They were not alone, however, as Hayne had hoped they might be. Quiros Allier & Co. and Montané were also party to the arrangement, and Myers once again was to be the former's consignee at the English end, the role being one he now accepted with reluctance.[252] There was to be an advance of 700,000 pesos (100,000 in debt certificates),[253] and ¾ of the sales proceeds were to be paid in cash and ¼ in bonds. The selling area excluded the United States, and the stipulated period was only six months, running up to June 18th 1848.[254] Castilla and del Río, without committing themselves very far into the future, thus managed to get the money they wanted to defend 'the national honour'. Funds were required not only to prepare for the Flores threat but to place 'the army on a war footing as demanded by the state of our relations with Bolivia'.[255]

[247]GGC, 16 April 1847.

[248]Ibid., 11 June 1847.

[249]As from 1 May 1847. See Maude, p. 124.

[250]It must be noted that the quantities cited in the contracts were usually in tons register: the aggregate official tonnage of the carrying vessels. This was something less than the weight of the guano itself: tons effective. Faivre, using British import figures (tons effective), has estimated that the ratio of effective to register was 4:3, i.e. an effective ton was one third more than a register ton. 'Guano', p. 125. The correctness of this calculation is confirmed in a Myers letter, dated September 1847, in which he twice converts a register figure into an effective figure by a 3:4 ratio. GGC, 22 September 1847. Likewise John Hayne in 1849. Ibid., 17 February 1849. The 40,000 tons cited in the contract, therefore, represented over 53,000 tons of guano. The contractors, it may be observed, had to account for the sale of the effective amount. There were no hidden profits in the differential.

[251]Ibid., 10 July 1847.

[252]'I must limit my liabilities by my means', Myers wrote to Gibbs in September 1847. 'The late engagements in Lima (40000 Tons) made without my consent, having given me enough to do, my Lima friends must be content with the way in which I do it'. Ibid., 22 September 1847.

[253]The margin for profit which this allowed served as interest on the loan. Anales, IV, p. 113.

[254]Ibid., IV, pp. 28-9, 113; FO 177/68, Sulivan to Clarendon, 12 May 1857; GGC, 11 August 1847.

[255]Anales, IV, p. 113

The government's achievement was quite considerable: a large loan in return for very modest exporting rights. As late as June, Gibbs's Lima house had thought that they might gain a new contract on their own for an advance of only 100,000 pesos.[256] The financial weakness of the Castilla administration does not appear to have impaired its negotiating strength. As owner of the commodity it enjoyed very substantial powers of patronage. It was, moreover, now going to take all the profits of the trade, with the contractors acting exclusively on a commission basis (although likely to retain the bulk of the proceeds for loan reimbursement). The level of commission payments is not indicated, but it can be assumed from the fact that William Gibbs gave his approval to the new arrangement[257] that the rates at the market end were not significantly different from those prevailing in the later stages of the old contract.

Additional funds were raised against guano from José Canevaro of Lima and Pedro Blanco & Co. of New York. The Canevaro arrangement was dated February 6th 1847 and involved a loan of 72,000 pesos (half in cash, half in bonds) to enable the government to purchase the Austrian warship *Jiovanna:* again with Flores very much in mind. Canevaro was to take guano in repayment after the 1842 Gibbs-Quiros contract had expired. He apparently began exporting in February 1846, and in the course of a year or so removed 5,134 register tons.[258] He was assisted in his enterprise by the Gibbs house. 'You are to Charter for Canevaro, and act for him as for us', John Hayne told William Gibbs in August 1847.[259] The Blanco agreement, arranged by the Peruvian minister in the United States, was dated 10th June 1847. Some 5,000 register tons were given for the purchase of the steamship *Rimac.*[260]

Thanks to the six-month contract of July 1847, Myers was entitled to continue as a consignee with Gibbs until at least the middle of 1848, despite the failure of his bid with Cotesworth. He would receive his portion of the guano exported under the new agreement, and no doubt was also given the task of handling the cargoes due to Cotesworth. But he had lost all enthusiasm for staying in the trade. Hayne suggested that the reason was 'the state of the money market

[256]GGC, 11 June 1847.

[257]*Ibid.,* 14 September 1847.

[258]*Anales,* IV, pp. 23-4, 112-3.

[259]GGC, 11 August 1847.

[260]*Anales,* IV, p. 28; Basadre, *Historia* (1969), p. 154.

and his purse'.[261] Gibbs could, therefore, look forward to a future in which they alone controlled sales in the United Kingdom. Their position in this respect was finally confirmed, for the time immediately ahead at least, in a contract of December 1847. So also was the government's determination to take all the profits of the trade. John Hayne reported in September that there were many men of influence who favoured direct public sales, with Gibbs as the sole buyer for Britain. This did not greatly appeal to him. 'We should make extraordinary exertion to retain it as a Commission business', he wrote, 'but I will run no imprudent race for it. . . .'[262] In December he reported that Castilla was having fantasies about raising $6 million in London at 6 per cent for the consignment. 'I bide my time', he wrote,[263] clearly confident that things would turn his way before very long. His firm, clearly, was not thrusting itself on the government. One factor here was the persisting crisis in the London money market, and Gibbs's confidence in their own relative financial security. 'Mr. Gibbs', wrote George Davy in October 1847, 'thinks that in these times you will have few competitors for a *New* Contract'.[264] He went on to spell out William Gibbs's conditions for involvement in any fresh arrangement. He would not submit to having his firm's assets examined by any agent of the Peruvian government. He wished that all charges be clearly defined. He objected to any joint agency 'as hindering the good management of the business'. And his position was inflexible. 'Unless these matters be arranged to his satisfaction he would rather be without the business'.[265]

Both Hayne and Gibbs got their way. The government badly needed money, other sources of cash were proving inadequate, and the only remedy available was 'to submit to the conditions which the contractors might think proper to impose'.[266] A contract was arranged on a commission basis on December 22nd and Gibbs were to be the sole British importers. It was negotiated in the company of Pedro de

---

[261]GGC, 11 November 1847. Henry Gibbs adds confirmation here. At this point in his extract from Hayne's letter he inserts the remark, 'so he told me, 1856'. See also *ibid.,* 14 January 1848, in which George Davy writes: 'Myers tells us the business was too heavy for him'.

[262]*Ibid.,* 11 September 1847; also 11 October 1847.

[263]*Ibid.,* 13 December 1847.

[264]*Ibid.,* 15 October 1847; also 13 November 1847.

[265]*Ibid.,* 15 October 1847.

[266]Witt Diaries, IV, 23 December 1847.

Candamo and Montané & Co.,[267] their shares being 33 per cent and 25 per cent respectively, Gibbs taking the remaining 42 per cent.[268] The agreement was to export 100,000 register tons[269] to all markets between June 18th 1848 and December 18th 1849[270] (i.e. the 18 months following the expiry of the six-month contract signed in the summer of 1847). Of this total 85,000 tons were designated for Britain.[271] There was to be an advance of 400,000 pesos down, and 450,000 in nine-monthly instalments, these loans carrying interest rates of 1 per cent per month and being intended for the provision of funds for the Civil List.[272] Commission rates were to be a generous 5 per cent in aggregate, and proceeds were to be paid to the government ¼ in debt paper and ¾ in cash.[273] If 100,000 tons were insufficient for the reimbursement of the contractors, more guano could be shipped to bring proceeds up to the required level.[274] Antony Gibbs & Sons and the Montané establishment in France were to be the sole consignees, operating within their own separate territories, and sales were to be made 'for account of government at best possible price in the judgement of the consignees, as has been the practice hitherto'. The contract was approved unanimously by the Senate, and carried on a division in the Chamber of Deputies.[275] The general response in London was enthusiastic. 'Bravo Hayne!', wrote George Davy.[276] Hayne himself, however, was just a little uneasy about the size of the new loan.[277]

And so departed the men who had begun the trade back in 1840. Without Myers's support, Quiros Allier & Co. could do little else but

[267]By the late 1840s this had become the largest of the French commercial establishments in Lima. For some comments on Montané, see Faivre, 'Guano', p. 121. He had, it seems, a low opinion of Quiros Allier & Co. (see GGC, 16 February 1847), so may have been disinclined to form any further associations with them. Information is lacking on the position of Puymerol Poumarroux & Co. at this juncture, but it is possible that some Puymerol money lay behind Montané's bid. The intimacy of their association is indicated by the establishment in Lima in 1845 of a house styled Puymerol Montané & Co. See Faivre, *loc. cit.*

[268]Witt Diaries, IV, 23 December 1847.

[269]i.e. over 130,000 effective tons.

[270]GGC, 7 and 16 January 1848.

[271]*Ibid.*, 17 February 1849.

[272]FO 61/118, Barton to Palmerston, 13 January 1848.

[273]*Ibid.* The contract is reproduced in full in *Anales*, IV, pp. 30-3.

[274]GGC, 7 January 1848.

[275]Henry Witt notes that it was 'violently discussed' in the Chamber. Witt Diaries, IV, 23rd December 1847.

[276]GGC, 16 March 1848.

[277]*Ibid.*, 10 January 1848.

witness the painful spectacle of guano passing entirely into the hands of those whose incursions they had tried so hard to resist in 1841-2. Partial displacement in 1842: total displacement in 1847. Myers's functions as a consignee, however, did not end overnight. He was, as we shall observe shortly, still selling Peruvian guano in 1849, and it was only towards the close of that year that his regular correspondence with Gibbs in London ceased. There are indications too that he remained active in the Bolivian trade — presumably less onerous financially.[278] There was not much of a future here, however. In the five-year period 1846-50 the annual average quantity of Bolivian guano imported into Britain amounted to no more than 1,742 tons.[279]

In consequence of the December 1847 contract, Gibbs were firmly settled in the Peruvian business on more or less their own terms until the end of the 1840s. This outcome appears to have been the product of at least four separate factors; the financial troubles of the Peruvian government, the monetary difficulties encountered by Gibbs's potential rivals, the strength of Gibbs themselves, and the confidence that the Peruvians placed in the London firm and its branch in Lima. The government's financial problems were acute in 1847.[280] In Peru's first biennial budget, for the years 1846-7, it was estimated that receipts would total only 8,383,600 pesos compared with expenditures of 11,926,722 pesos.[281] In such circumstances, short-term considerations made it highly desirable to come by fresh loans against current and future guano proceeds. Loans of the size required could only be had relatively quickly and cheaply from houses with substantial drawing rights on Europe.

The second factor, the financial difficulties experienced by Gibbs's rivals, was, as noted, the product of crisis in the London money market. This, clearly, had not developed sufficiently in the early part of the year (despite a double rise of discount rate and a rationing of bill acceptance by the Bank of England)[282] to deter Myers and his associates from tendering for an ambitious new contract. By the late summer and early autumn, however, the rush for liquidity had become intense, and doubts were growing about the Bank's capacity

[278]*Ibid.,* 12 October 1848; also 24 September 1849.

[279]*PP,* 1851, LIII, p. 309.

[280]See Bonilla, p. 214; Levin, pp. 60-1.

[281]MacQueen, p. 36.

[282]C. N. Ward-Perkins, 'The Commercial Crisis of 1847', in E. M. Carus-Wilson (ed.), *Essays in Economic History,* III (London, 1962), p. 265.

to act effectively as lender of last resort.[283] This appears to have been sufficient to scare off most of Gibbs's real or potential rivals.[284] Their own position appears to have been quite secure. They were not dependent, as Myers appears to have been, on financial assistance from other parties. And the form of their business in 1847 — commission trading, self-liquidating credit, and hardly any speculative activity in commodity or financial transactions[285] — meant that they were relatively unharmed by the crisis in the money market. It was in moments such as this that a house like Gibbs discovered the rewards of past caution. Their profit and loss accounts showed a positive balance of £28,188 for 1847, compared with an average of £26,202 for the five-year period 1845-9.[286] In a position of such obvious strength Gibbs accordingly were obliged to do nothing rash to stay in the trade, and could coolly state their own terms for continuing participation.

Finally, there is the fact that the Peruvian government clearly had confidence in Gibbs. The disputes between the two parties in the past had not been all that acute, and had been short-lived. They had, moreover, been based more on frustration, bluff and misinformation than on any real conflict of interests. Gibbs's price policies for the British market had, quite clearly, been realistic, especialy in the first years of the trade, and a lot of good, persuasive, propagandizing work for the firm appears to have been done by John Hayne in Lima. Furthermore, they had had six years' experience in the trade and had in the process built up a complex network of relationships with agents, brokers, dealers and shippers which could be of great service for the future. 'The Government', Hayne told the London house, 'trusts *entirely* to your good management'.[287]

---

[283]*Ibid.,* p. 266; Tooke, pp. 330-4.

[284]Monetary crisis, however, did not dispose of every competitor. James Jack, a British merchant involved in Peruvian trade (there was a firm by the name of Jack Brothers & Co. operating in Arequipa — the branch of a Liverpool merchant house: see FO 61/137, Jack Brothers to Granville, 23 January 1852), arrived in Lima on January 10th 1848 claiming that he had been granted drawing rights of £200,000 by 10 parties in England interested in guano. He was, according to Samuel Went (who had just taken over the management of the Gibbs Lima house), 'Much chagrined . . . to find the door closed'. (GGC, 12 January 1848). The trough of the crisis had in fact been passed by the beginning of November 1847. There had been a quite sudden increase of confidence in financial and commercial circles associated with the publication on October 27th of a letter from the Treasury authorizing a strengthening of the Bank of England's lending powers. (See Ward-Perkins, p. 266). As far as new guano contracts were concerned, however, recovery had come just a little too late in the year.

[285]The guano business, itself, of course, being the main exception to this.

[286]LGL, first ser., 12.

[287]GGC, 7 January 1848. See also del Río's remarks to Congress in 1847. *Anales,* IV, p. 107.

SALES, PRICES, AND POLICIES, 1848-9

In 1848 and 1849 British guano imports from Peru were estimated at 134,622 tons. Only 20,230 tons came from other sources. The five years since 1845 had witnessed steady growth, the successive tonnages being 14,101, 22,410, 57,762, 61,055 and 73,567.[288] A portion of the imports in the late 1840s represented guano from the contract that expired in December 1847. At the Peruvian end, however, all the old guano had been cleared by that month,[289] and the last shipments connected with the 1842 agreement arrived in Britain in the early months of 1848. The rest of the guano sold in 1848 and 1849 was handled under the 40,000 and 100,000 ton contracts[290] arranged in 1847, by which the merchants were operating exclusively on a commission basis and the Peruvian government was taking all the profits.

The year 1848 was an uneventful one in the trade. There was no dramatic acceleration in tempo, but the relatively large quantity taken was disposed of with little difficulty and harmony appears to have prevailed among all the participating parties. Sales proceeded sluggishly at the very start of the year,[291] but they did not take long to pick up.[292] 'Our sales this year', Gibbs remarked in the middle of May, 'highly satisfactory as to quantity, and all for actual consumption'.[293] By the end of the season they had hardly any supplies left[294] and total consumption over the six months had amounted to about 54,000 tons.[295] During the remainder of the year a further 23,000 tons were sold.[296] Farmers, in short, had spent over three-quarters of a million pounds on Peruvian guano. The issue of price policy, not surprisingly, lay more or less dormant throughout 1848. Towards the end of the year Liverpool dealers asked for a reduction in the price for lots of over 30 tons, but this Gibbs resisted: a reaction which Myers, who transmitted the request, did not challenge.[297] As for competition, Gibbs appear to have been correct in their calculation of the previous

[288] *PP*, 1851, LIII, p. 309.

[289] GGC, 13 December 1847.

[290] Also the small amount due to Cotesworth. See preceding section.

[291] GGC, 15 January 1848.

[292] *Ibid.*, 16 February 1848.

[293] *Ibid.*, 16 May 1848; also 16 June 1848.

[294] *Ibid.*, 14 July 1848.

[295] *Ibid.*, 17 February 1849.

[296] *Ibid.*

[297] GGC, 23 October and 2 November 1848.

September that 'second-hand' stocks would quickly disappear and that 'inferiors' would be easily absorbed.[298] A small importation from Africa was remarked on in October[299] and some notice was taken of the opinion held by 'many influential people' that superphosphate of lime was a better fertilizer than guano for root crops:[300] only a small cloud in 1848, but one that was to darken the sky during the 1850s.

If 1848 was unnaturally peaceful and free of problems, 1849 saw what one might describe as a return to normality. In particular, an active and somewhat acrimonious debate was resumed over price policy. Myers, whose life as a Peruvian consignee was due to expire with the completion of sales under the 40,000 ton contract of 1847, was now eager to sell off his diminishing stocks at the highest possible price, thereby maximizing his commission earnings in his last months in the trade. Gibbs, on the other hand, anticipating the arrival of guano under the 100,000 ton contract, were strongly of the opinion that prices ought to be left where they were. There was also the very immediate problem in the spring and early summer of a seriously under-supplied market,[301] a consequence, it would seem, of loading delays at the Chincha islands[302] rather than of mercantile miscalculation. A lot of guano certainly arrived in Britain in 1849, much more than in 1848, but a great deal of it came in too late in the year. Myers, with only 700 tons in hand in late March, was taking the view that the minimum price ought to be raised from £9, where it had stood since late 1847, to £10.[303] Gibbs thought this a thoroughly bad idea. 'We could get it for our small stock on hand but should prejudice the sale of the large stock we are expecting'.[304]

Myers replied bluntly that he was determined to get as much money as he could for his guano, and that he would approach the market by auction.[305] Gibbs sympathised, but only up to a point: 'If we

---

[298]See above, p. 69.

[299]GGC, 16 October 1848. In 1848, in fact, only 10,359 tons came in from non-Peruvian sources (of which almost a third was Bolivian). Peru, therefore, supplied 86 per cent of total guano imports by weight. (The percentage by value, if this could be worked out exactly, would be even higher). *PP*, 1851, LIII, p. 309.

[300]GGC, 16 May 1848.

[301]*Ibid.*, 31 March, 2 and 5 April, 17 May, 12 June 1849.

[302]See, for example, *ibid.*, 15 March, 16 August and 16 November 1850. For general comment, see W. M. Mathew, 'A Primitive Export Sector: Guano Production in Mid-Nineteenth Century Peru', *JLAS*, 9, I (1977), pp. 48-51.

[303]GGC, 31 March 1849.

[304]*Ibid.*

[305]*Ibid.*, 2 April 1849.

could be *sure* of getting £10 for stock and arrivals, it may be worth the experiment, but *your* reasons in 1847 for lowering, seem conclusive against raising'.[306] Myers, however, was not prepared to see his old arguments turned against him. The situation in 1847, he pointed out, had been quite different. The market had been glutted with guano in that year; now it was virtually bare. 'Hereafter', he demanded, 'you will sell all at £10!'[307] 'You are resolved, and I need say no more', Gibbs wrote with resignation on 5 April.[308] They had, as they saw it, no choice but to follow suit, even though it meant an undesirable 'change from our *steady* practice', and they instructed William Gibbs & Co. to 'keep down . . . any hope that the high price can be sustained'.[309] Between mid-April and mid-May the consignees opted for selling a lot of what guano they had by auction.[310] Prices ranged between £9 5s. and £11.[311] After a week or two, however, the market began to appear unresponsive, no doubt giving Gibbs some small satisfaction as to the correctness of their judgement: 'The fluctuation has shaken the confidence of the farmers and turning them to other manures, to which they were too addicted even when the price of Peruvian was £9 — especially 'Superphosphate of Lime' '.[312] Purchasers were taking a long time to collect the guano they had bought 'showing *their* buyers did not come in freely at new prices'.[313] No attempt was made, certainly on Myers's side, to wind up the long and hitherto fairly friendly relationship in a spirit of gentlemanly accord. Both argued rigidly to the last in terms of their own self-interest, and both managed to give weight to their arguments with displays of pious concern for the well-being of the Peruvian government. Gibbs only followed Myers because he had to. And Myers expounded his policy to Gibbs in tones which were frequently impatient and sarcastic.

Happily for Gibbs, Myers was in the process of selling off his last stocks of guano. Towards the end of the season the London firm could begin to formulate their own independent policy. In this, two things served as guides: their own experience of the effects of auction sales; and the recent publication of an essay by Professor J.T. Way, the

[306]*Ibid.,* 3 April 1849.

[307]*Ibid.,* 4 April 1849.

[308]*Ibid.,* 5 April 1849.

[309]*Ibid.,* 16 April 1849.

[310]*Ibid.,* 4 and 16 April 1849.

[311]*Ibid.,* 18 and 30 April, 3, 7, 16 and 18 May 1849.

[312]*Ibid.,* 16 May 1849; also 30 April and 7 May 1849 for mention of 'flat' market.

[313]*Ibid.,* 17 May 1849.

Royal Agricultural Society's consulting chemist, on the money value of guano's components. As for the former, Gibbs's conviction that a fixed and steady price suited the market best had been greatly strengthened during the spring. In essence, their case for steady prices rested on the fact that these had been fairly firm in the past, being held at certain fixed levels for quite long periods of time. This had been possible under the system of monopoly sales, and it meant, of course, that dealers and other purchasers had developed quite legitimate expectations about price constancy. Any sudden movement, upwards or downwards, was bound to confuse them and perhaps compromise their goodwill. If the price was to be fixed, though, it had to be set at a moderate and competitive level. Gibbs were very much aware of the dangers likely to materialize from the growing production of artificial fertilizers in Britain.[314] Theirs, they believed, was the best and (in terms of its content) the cheapest manure in the country,[315] and they wished to keep it that way. 'We now shall at last have to fix the price at £9 5s.', wrote Gibbs in May 1849.[316] This was the level at which their most recent auction sales had been made. And thereafter, it seems, they put an end to public sales, despite Myers' apparent intention to continue with them.[317] There was also scientific guidance on the optimum price. 'Way's pamphlet [Gibbs wrote to Lima in August] 'exhibits 1st, superiority of Peruvian and quantity of ammonia therein — in which chiefly consists the fertlizing value: 2nd that such quantity fully justifies the price of £9 to £9 10s.; for the phosphate and potash being worth £1 13s. and 14s. 6d. respectively, the Ammonia alone was worth £9 14s. It would be a mistake to suppose that therefore Huano should be worth £12; for Ammonia being food for some crops, and phosphates for others it is the former for which Peruvian Huano is bought; for the latter they take inferior guanos which have more phosphates.[318] After mature consideration therefore we think it would be unsafe to raise the price above £9 5s. to £9 10s., thus giving an *inducement* to the farmer to buy *it* rather than its component parts at the same value'.[319]

[314]See *ibid.*, 16 April, 16 May, 16 and 17 August 1849.

[315]*Ibid.*, 16 January 1850.

[316]*Ibid.*, 16 May 1849.

[317]*Ibid.*, 16 June 1849.

[318]Hardly so. More Peruvian guano in fact appears to have been used for turnips (which needed phosphate) than for wheat (which needed ammonia). (See chapter 3). Turnip crops would have been poorly served by phosphatic guano, for imports of these totalled less than 10,000 tons in 1849, compared with 73,567 tons of Peruvian. (*PP*, 1851, LIII, p. 309).

[319]GGC, 16 August 1849; also 17 August 1849.

In fact £9 5s. was to remain the principal wholesale price of guano in Britain until January 1854. In establishing it, Gibbs had little difficulty in persuading the other interested parties that their judgement was sound. Both Osma, the Peruvian plenipotentiary in London, and Cotesworth had disapproved of Myers's recent pursuit of higher prices.[320] So did William Gibbs & Co. in Lima.[321] Another of the contractors, Dutez, viewed with disapproval the abusive language which Myers was apparently using about Gibbs in his correspondence with Lima.[322] 'By endeavouring to prevent the highest price being obtained', Gibbs wrote, 'we give a handle to persons unacquainted with the working of the business, to impugn our motives.'[323] It seems they need not have worried. Samuel Went, now the manager in Lima, observed in June that their views on auction sales were likely to win the approval of Montané, Candamo, and the Peruvian government. President Castilla, he commented, was 'always an advocate for selling low to increase consumption'.[324] If there was any disagreement, it was more the result of the government wanting a price level even lower than that suggested by Gibbs. 'I believe Government would welcome even a reduction from the £9 5s. price', wrote Went in November 1849, 'if you could hold out a prospect of an increase of consumption to an extent which would compensate for it'.[325] A desire to augment income from guano, in a year when Peru had earmarked one half of sales proceeds for the repayment of British bondholders, was probably one factor here.[326] Another may have been British diplomatic intervention.[327] The British chargé d'affaires, William Pitt Adams, had been instructed by Lord Palmerston, then foreign secretary, to argue the case with the Peruvians for a freeing of the trade, on the assumption that if the monopoly-contract system of export were brought to an end guano could be sold more cheaply in Britain. Castilla refused to consider any such change,[328] but the episode did make him think about the benefits which Peru might gain

---

[320] *Ibid.*, 16 April and 17 May 1849.

[321] *Ibid.*, 12 June 1849.

[322] *Ibid.*, 11 June 1849.

[323] *Ibid.*, 16 April 1849.

[324] *Ibid.*, 11 June 1849; also 13 October 1849 and FO 61/130, Adams to Palmerston, 20 November 1851.

[325] GGC, 3 November 1849; also 16 January 1850.

[326] See Mathew, 'Debt', pp. 95-6; also below, chapter 3.

[327] See GGC, 3 November 1849.

[328] See W. M. Mathew, 'The Imperialism of Free Trade: Peru, 1820-70', *EHR*, 2nd ser., 21, no. 3 (1968), pp. 571-2; also below, chapter 3.

from a fall in prices and the possibility of satisfying at one and the same time both the needs of his own treasury and the wishes of the British government. Gibbs's advice was firm: 'we can't conscientiously say that it would be a gain to Peru that we should go lower'.[329]

It no doubt gave the government pleasure to learn that the British consignees had such confidence in guano. A source of further satisfaction, we may assume, was the news that reductions had been effected in certain small intermediate costs. 'We think the extent of the Business may warrant a reduction in the Charges', wrote Gibbs in August 1849, 'and we are occupied in the endeavour to attain this'.[330] By mid-October they were able to report success. They had placed all their business in the hands of the West India Dock Company. Charges on overside deliveries were to come down from 2s. to 1s. per ton and deliveries from the warehouses were to cost 3s. 9d. instead of 5s. Storage rentals were to be reduced from 6d. to 1d. a week and bags were now to be bought by contract, at half a million a time, costing 4.1/3d. each instead of 5¼d.[331] 'We think all the expenses are now reduced to the lowest possible point', remarked John Hayne.[332] 'Very glad', wrote Went.[333]

Sales during the 1849 season were slightly down on those for 1848: 52,000 tons or so,[334] compared with about 54,000 tons the year before. The main factors were temporary dearth in the spring, an increase in price over the last month or two of the season, and a continuing fall in wheat prices. By 1849 they had sunk to their lowest level in England and Wales since 1835.[335] Gibbs referred to this in March as the principal problem[336] and in April wrote to Myers of the foolishness of pushing up guano prices 'when ruin is staring the farmers in the face'.[337] This, however, did not make them too pessimistic about the future. Competition from other guanos had, for one thing, faded away. Peru was now the only important source for the British market, imports totalling over 73,000 tons in 1849. The next three most important suppliers were Chile, West Africa, and Patagonia,

[329]GGC, 16 January 1850.

[330]Ibid., 17 August 1849.

[331]Ibid., 16 October 1849.

[332]Ibid., 16 January 1850. Hayne was now back working in the London house.

[333]Ibid., 12 December 1850.

[334]Calculated from figures in ibid., 17 February and 16 July 1849.

[335]See Fairlie, p. 97.

[336]GGC, 16 March 1849.

[337]Ibid., 5 April 1849; also 16 April 1849.

imports from these areas being estimated at 4,311, 2,345, and 1,945 tons respectively.[338] In September, Gibbs were able to report that their recent sales had been larger than those for the same off-season weeks in 1848, and that they expected 'a brisk demand next season',[339] this despite the failure of wheat prices to recover. 'Demand springing up', they noted in October.[340] This was reassuring, for large quantities of guano were arriving from the 100,000 ton contract. Gibbs had made their first sales under this arrangement in June.[341] By November, less than 3,000 tons remained to be shipped.[342]

And so the 1840s came to an end. Myers had left the trade[343] and Gibbs stood alone in the British market. Despite all the troubles, the decade had been a tolerably successful one. The contractors, although not making any large profits, had at least averted loss and retrieved their advances. And the farming community in Britain had demonstrated very clearly as the years passed its satisfaction with guano and its willingness to spend large sums of money on the new fertilizer.

THE GROWTH OF GUANO CONSUMPTION

The progressive establishment of guano as the most important commodity in the British fertilizer market was the product of at least four factors: its evident efficacy, the policies and activities of the consignees, the receptiveness of British farmers, and the African trade.

Guano was attractive not only through its varied chemical composition and its relatively high solubility but also because it was a concentrated light-weight manure, capable of being carried at little expense on to the most remote and hilly fields, many of which had formerly lain beyond the reach of the dung cart. In the chorus of acclaim which had been singing guano's praises since it first arrived in the market there were few dissonant voices. One or two people wrote in agricultural journals that farmers ought to stick with their own yard manure and forget about new appliances 'bearing attractive titles',[344]

[338]*PP*, 1851, LIII, p. 309.

[339]*Ibid.*, 15 September 1849.

[340]*Ibid.*, 16 October 1849.

[341]*Ibid.*, 16 June 1849.

[342]*Ibid.*, 3 November 1849.

[343]He had only 'a few hundred ton left' in September 1849, and could anticipate no fresh arrivals. *Ibid.*, 24 September 1849.

[344]*JA* (October 1843), p. 142.

but almost all the sceptics remained silent. There was still no comprehensive, scientific case that could be formulated against guano. Danger threatened in 1845, but it came to nothing. Gibbs noted in September of that year that some newspapers were attributing the potato failure to the use of guano.[345] There was in fact a school of thought which, in seeking to explain the sudden and disastrous blight, saw the new fertilizer as a likely cause.[346] There is no indication, however, that serious doubts concerning guano spread very far or that its consumption was affected. The vast bulk of the potato crop was, for one thing, grown without it. James Johnston made a study of the disease in Scotland by sending questionnaires to some 85 farmers. One of the questions read: 'Has the kind of manure applied any influence on the appearance or fatality of the disease?' Only about half a dozen blamed the failure on liberal manuring, and only one, an Ayrshire farmer, cited guano specifically. Some advocated its use as a preventive measure. The great majority were of the opinion that manures had had no effect one way or the other.[347]

As for the activities of Gibbs and Myers, price alterations apart, William Gibbs had stated in 1842 that he would leave no stone unturned to extend the consumption of guano, and this promise he appears to have fulfilled. Notices were placed in journals and newspapers, and in 1843 a 36-page pamphlet was published by the firm, documenting a mass of successful experiments.[348] This was followed in 1844 by a 95-page booklet, packed with good reports.[349] Other parties also contributed: at the very start of the African trade merchants could only vaunt their wares by citing the successes of the Pacific fertilizer. In 1843, for example, W. & B. Brooke, intending importers of Ichaboe guano, brought out a pamphlet detailing a list of experiments with Peruvian.[350] Such publications, in the manner of the day, usually contained glowing testimonials from one or more

[345] GGC, 16 September 1845.

[346] See Cecil Woodham-Smith, *The Great Hunger, Ireland 1845-9* (London, 1962), p. 47.

[347] James F. W. Johnston (ed.), *The Potato Disease in Scotland* (Edinburgh, 1845), *passim.*

[348] Gibbs, *Guano.*

[349] Antony Gibbs & Sons and William Joseph Myers & Co., *Peruvian and Bolivian Guano: Its Nature, Properties and Results* (London, 1844).

[350] W. & B. Brooke, *Guano: Description of the Nature and Properties of Guano Manure* (London, 1843). See also J. H. Sheppard, *A Practical Treatise on the Use of Peruvian and Ichaboe African Guano* (London, 1844); Anon., *Hints to Farmers on the Nature, Purchase, and Application of Peruvian, Bolivian, and African Guano* (Liverpool and London, 1844).

chemists of repute. The energy with which the consignees pursued an enlargement of sales was probably due in no small measure to their anxieties over the terms of the 1842 contract. Large quantities of guano had to be forced on the British market before there could be any certainty that the loans granted to the government would be repaid. As the 1840s progressed, Gibbs and Myers were aided by the rapid extension of the railway network from London, Liverpool and other major ports. This helped minimise the difference between wholesale and retail prices, and made it feasible for increasing numbers of farmers to buy directly from the importers.[351]

Thirdly, there is the factor of receptivity among the farmers, these absorbing the huge quantities of guano coming in from all quarters of the world. There can be little doubt that the interest in agricultural chemistry was growing in Britain. All the main farming journals carried articles on the subject in every issue. A stream of books, large and small, ragged and systematic, poured from the publishing houses. Liebig's *Organic Chemistry* appeared in a rapidly growing number of editions.[352] Much of the new writing was stimulated by the success of guano and the wish to compare it with other manures, animal and artificial. Experimentation fed the agricultural chemists and commentators with a growing mass of new information to be lodged in their theoretical schemes and practical recommendations. John Bennet Lawes was working in rigorous scientific fashion at Rothamsted and concentrating most of his attention on the conditions regulating the fertility of the soil and the growth of crops.[353] The Royal Agricultural Society appointed a consulting chemist shortly after its foundation in 1838,[354] and encouraged farmers to carry out and record experiments with new manures.[355] In 1845 the Royal Agricultural College at Cirencester, founded by some members of the Society, received its royal charter.[356] In 1843 the Highland

[351]In 1845 M. M. Milburn published a prize-winning report on experiments with guano. In it, he cited prices paid by farmers in various parts of the country, mostly in 1843 and 1844 when the minimum wholesale price of Peruvian stood at £10 in London and Liverpool and £10 10s. to £11 in other ports. These (in the dozen cases where the quotation is *per ton*) range from £10 to £12, the average being £11 1s. 10½d. M. M. Milburn, 'Report on Experiments with Guano', *FM,* 2nd ser., 11 (1845), pp. 222-30.

[352]See Charles A. Browne, *A Source Book of Agricultural Chemistry* (Waltham, Mass., 1944), p. 239.

[353]C. M. Aikman, *Sixty Years of Agricultural Science* (Edinburgh, 1896), p. 11.

[354]Dr. Lyon Playfair, succeeded by Prof. J. T. Way in 1847.

[355]J. A. Scott Watson, *The History of the Royal Agricultural Society of England 1839-1939* (London, 1939), pp. 36, 118-9.

[356]*Ibid.,* p. 136.

and Agricultural Society of Scotland appointed its first chemist.[357] In the same year a group of Lothian farmers, with the help of the Highland Society, set up the Agricultural Chemistry Association in Edinburgh.[358] A number of Scottish farmers also came together in 1843 to publish details of their recent and highly successful experiments. The result, according to Andrew Aitken, 'was to establish for the information of farmers, the great value of nitrogenous and phosphatic manures'.[359] A lot, in short, was happening in the world of empirical and theoretical chemistry. And the whole process was self-reinforcing. Realistic prices encouraged sales; sales boosted experimentation; experimentation stirred people to write and publish; and books and articles, by giving much free publicity to guano, yielded a further boost to sales.

Paradoxical as it might seem, the African trade also strengthened Peruvian guano's position in the market. In the short term, of course, it greatly impaired the extension of Peruvian sales, but in the long run, by introducing many of the less wealthy and less scientific farmers to the new fertilizer, it must have served to widen the farming community's familiarity with and knowledge of guano. Of the thousands of new guano purchasers who came to the market when cheap African supplies were available, a large portion seem to have turned, when these supplies ran out, to the more potent and more versatile Peruvian variety. The African traders exploited the embryonic guano market developed by Gibbs and Myers and, in a very short space of time, gave it much larger dimensions. 'The discovery of guano on the coast of Africa', declared the Peruvian finance minister, Manuel del Río, in 1847, 'brought about an inevitable paralysation of the sale of our own. But the many speculations that took place effectively contributed to spreading the use of the fertilizer, providing it for farmers at very low prices, thereby . . . bringing guano into consumption and giving it a positive commercial value.'[360] Relative cheapness was one factor. Another was the preponderance of ships of a comparatively low carrying capacity in the Ichaboe trade, many of them chartered or owned by very small-scale speculators.[361] This meant that guano

---

[357] Prof. J. W. Johnston, succeeded by Dr. Thomas Anderson in 1849. Alexander Ramsay, *History of the Highland and Agricultural Society of Scotland* (Edinburgh and London, 1879), p. 453.

[358] Andrew P. Aitken, *Report on the Present State of the Agriculture of Scotland* (Edinburgh, 1878), p. 213.

[359] *Ibid.*

[360] *Anales,* IV, p. 107.

[361] See GGC, 15 April 1845.

could be landed in numerous little ports where the shallowness of the water precluded the entry of the generally larger vessels from Peru.[362] The wide geographical spread of such importations no doubt helped develop a familiarity with guano in regions of the country remote from the major ports.

Given such favourable circumstances, Gibbs, we may assume, looked to the future with much optimism at the end of the decade, anticipating a substantially enlarged trade and a commensurately increased income. There is no evidence from their correspondence that they were particularly concerned about two ominous developments that were shortly to darken their prospects: the growing desire of merchants in Lima to dislodge them and move into the buoyant British trade themselves, and the intensifying competition at home from manufactured fertilizers.

[362]See chapter 3. I am grateful to Robert Craig of University College London for communicating this information to me.

3

THE BRITISH TRADE, 1850-61:
BOOM YEARS AND SLUMP

'I rise, Sir, to answer the question which has been put by the honourable and gallant Gentleman [Colonel Blair], and I can assure him and the House that I entirely agree with him in the opinion that there is no matter upon which the agricultural interest of the United Kingdom is more dependent than an enlargement in the supply of guano, the great source of which is at the present moment a monopoly in the hands of the Peruvian Government. I am afraid that no argument which the British Government can address to that of Peru will prevail, so long as they possess that exclusive monopoly. At all events, they will continue to exact the largest possible price for the article. The real remedy lies in enlarging the sources of supply. . . .'

Sir James Graham, First Lord of the Admiralty, addressing the
House of Commons, 14 February 1854.

CONTRACTS FOR THE 1850s

Gibbs retained their position as the dominant mercantile body in the guano trade throughout the 1850s,[1] their lien upon the fertilizer finally expiring in the early 1860s. Their role as contractors for the British and most other markets officially came to an end on 18 December 1861, although in reality the terminal date was somewhat blurred. Loading and shipping did not suddenly stop on that day and stock clearance went on into 1862 and well beyond.[2] Despite this overlap, the transfer to other parties represented a fairly abrupt upset. There had been no whittling away of Gibbs's position towards the end of their contract period, no gradual change in control prior to the final break. Indeed, in their last years in the trade the physical spread of

---

[1] Figures available for 1854-7 show that seven different contractors were sending guano to a variety of world markets. A total of 1,506,930 register tons was exported, of which 969,524 (64 per cent) were despatched by Gibbs. The equivalent percentage for the late 1850s would have been substantially higher, for by then Gibbs had added France and Spain to their monopoly area. Archives Nationales de France (hereinafter ANF), sér. F 12, dossier 6860. Guiroy to Chemin Dupintes, 5 May 1858.

[2] English stocks were estimated at 108,210 tons on 21 March 1862, with a further 23,000 due to arrive. At the end of 1863 Gibbs still had around 30,000 tons in their hands. Antony Gibbs & Sons, Ltd., Business archives. Out-letter books (private) of Henry Hucks Gibbs, 1845-1882 [hereinafter HHGC (Henry Hucks Gibbs Correspondence), 3, Henry Gibbs to William Gibbs, 23 March 1862 and 14 December 1863.

their business was wider and the scale of their financial operations larger than they had ever been. They exercised control over almost the entire European market, and were also selling in the West Indies, Africa, the Indian Ocean and Australia. In March 1860, when they took one of their periodic stock tallies, the trading centres and areas cited were London, Liverpool, Bristol, Hamburg, Rotterdam, Belgium, Dunkirk, le Havre, Nantes, Bordeaux, Spain, Genoa, Barbados, Martinique, Guadeloupe, Réunion, Melbourne and Sydney.[3] It was out of this very large commercial network of well-used and supple lines of contact that Gibbs were finally prised a year or two later and into which a variety of new, often inexperienced, merchants were inserted.

A decade or so earlier, the threat to Gibbs's contract position was only just beginning to materialize, and they were able to make fresh arrangements with Peru in an almost casual manner, as though it was the most natural thing in the world that they and the government in Lima should continue to do business together. Two contracts, one drawn up in January 1849 and the other in May 1850, guaranteed the continuation of their territorial monopoly from December 1849 to December 1855. Both were arranged in London, not in Lima as before. It was the Peruvian government's wish to connect new guano contracts with provision for the repayment of its British bondholding creditors, and to employ Gibbs as both consignee and financial agent.[4]

In the early 1820s Peru had borrowed £1,816,000[5] in the London money market. The government of the new republic, however, lacked the capacity for regular servicing of this modest sum, and on 15 October 1825 payments were suspended on the entire state debt. Incapable of exercising any power of their own, and unable to win more than unofficial support from the government in London,[6] the bondholders had the choice of either selling off their paper at greatly depreciated prices or waiting until Peru found the means and the will to recommence payment and settle arrears. The means came with guano, and the will sprang from the Peruvian government's desire to restore its credit on the London money market.[7] Towards the end of

[3]HHGC, 2, Henry Gibbs to 'Don Juan' (probably John Hayne), 19 March 1860.

[4]GGC, 13 January and 12 February 1849.

[5]This was the nominal figure. The actual sum realised was substantially lower: £1,491,480. J. Fred Rippy, *British Investments in Latin America, 1822-1949* (Minneapolis, 1959), p. 20.

[6]Mathew, 'Debt', *passim*.

[7]See, for example, *Mensage que el Presidente de La República del Perú Dirige a las Camaras Lejislativas de 1847* (Lima, 1847), p. 18. Copy in FO 61/115.

1848 General Joaquín de Osma arrived in London as Peruvian plenipotentiary entrusted with the task of ending a dispute which had lasted close on a quarter of a century.[8]   On 21 December he wrote a formal note to the bondholders' committee outlining the Peruvian proposals,[9] and a few days later agreed to certain modifications. On 4 January 1849 the bondholders met in the London Tavern and declared their unanimous acceptance of the offer.[10] By this time Osma had drafted the terms of a new guano contract with Gibbs, to take effect after 18 December 1849, whereby the importers agreed to earmark half of the proceeds from the guano they sold in Britain under the contract for the payment of dividends, and from their current receipts to pay, through an agent, the first of the new half-yearly interest payments due on 1 October 1849.[11] This system had its conveniences, both for the Peruvian government and for the bond-holders. For the government it had the advantage of making unnecessary any possibly awkward transfers across the exchanges. For the latter, the fact that the funds due were accumulating in the hands of a respectable British trading house seemed to confer an attractive degree of security.

The contract was signed on 4 January 1849. In March it was approved by Castilla;[12] later in the year it won congressional ratification.[13] It was in the first instance a one-year arrangement, but by agreeing some months later to provide funds for bond payments in April 1850 as well as in October 1849 Gibbs were accorded, by the terms of an additional article postscripted on the January agreement, a two-year run.[14] This new commitment to the trade was something they appear to have taken on without serious reservation. They were awarded the entire European market excluding France and the quantity of guano to be taken in the first year was to be '70000 Register Tons or more or less, as may be agreed'.[15] For the second

---

[8]Some attempts at a settlement had already been made over the preceding two or three years, but these had come to nothing. Mathew, 'Debt', pp. 87-94.

[9]*The Times,* 5 January 1849, p. 6.

[10]For details, see Mathew, 'Debt', p. 95.

[11]*Ibid.; Correspondence betwen Great Britain and Foreign Powers and Commun-ications from the British Government to Claimants, Relative to Loans made by British Subjects, 1847-1853, PP,* 1854, LXIX (hereinafter *PP (British Loans)*), p. 137.

[12]GGC, 13 March 1849.

[13]*Ibid.,* 12 October 1849; *PP (British Loans),* pp. 183-9.

[14]GGC, 17 January and 14 September 1849: *PP (British Loans),* p. 138.

[15]GGC, 1 and 17 January 1849. The contract states 60,000 tons, but that apparently was in relation to the British market only. *Anales,* IV, p. 37.

year, no quantity was specified. Gibbs were not required to make a large initial loan in the normal fashion. Instead, there was the cash they were required to supply in advance of guano sales for the first two bond payments: £72,000 in all, carrying an interest rate of 5 per cent. Quite apart from these specific advances to the Peruvian government's financial agent, Gibbs were asked to hand over half of the net proceeds of guano sold in Britain (or in Europe, if re-exported) under the contract to the same agent, and hold the other half and the produce of guano exported directly to Europe to the order of the minister of finance. For importing and selling the guano they were entitled to 4 per cent commission and guarantee, 1 per cent brokerage and 2½ per cent for chartering. All advances for freights and other charges were to carry a 5 per cent interest rate.[16] The arrangement in some respects differed quite markedly from the previous contract: the 2½ per cent on charters represented an additional and quite major source of income. The money due to the Peruvian government, on the other hand, was all to be paid in cash and not, as before, partly in debt paper;[17] and the loan involved was different in form, lower-yielding in interest, and smaller in amount. The curtailment of lending opportunities, however, was more than offset by a new loan arranged in October 1849 between the Peruvian government and William Gibbs & Co. in Lima, involving substantial drafts on London. This appears to have been independent of any guano contracts (although would be repaid from guano money). 'We are to advance $400000 without interest', reported Samuel Went, 'by paying 18% in paper;[18] from which, and from the Exchange we shall get some 9 or 10%. Montané takes ¼ share'.[19] A couple of days later he wrote that Candamo, the Chilean merchant, had also become party to the transaction, taking a one-eighth share.[20] Gibbs's part of the loan, therefore, amounted to $295,000.[21]

---

[16]GGC, 17 January 1849; *PP (British Loans)*, p. 137; *Anales*, IV, pp. 37-8.

[17]Bonilla, p. 221.

[18]This in fact was an extra 18 per cent (rather than a portion of $400,000) giving a total loan of $472,000. Peruvian Government Huano Loan Account, 30 April 1841, in Antony Gibbs & Sons, Ltd. Lima Branch Accounts, File 3, 1847-62. See also *Anales*, IV, pp. 43-8.

[19]GGC, 10 October 1849.

[20]*Ibid.*, 12 October 1849.

[21]See Peruvian Government Huano Loan Account, 30 April 1851, in Lima Branch Accounts, File 3, 1847-62. The same account suggests that they may have incurred some rather irregular expenditures for the privilege of lending to the government. One of the items entered was 'Gratification: £13,022'. The Castilla regime wanted the loan 'exclusively for the purpose of making payments to government employees and pensioners in the capital. . . .' *Anales*, IV, p. 46.

It is interesting to note that Antony Gibbs & Sons did not, as one might have expected and the Peruvian government hoped, themselves assume full responsibility for paying the bondholders out of guano proceeds. 'Barreda[22] has sounded us about the Conversion, as to what we could cede out of our Commission to him Osma and Rivero. We said if we had to charge ½, ¼; but it must be explained to Government. We would make no simulated charge'.[23] The Peruvians in London who had the power to place the agency clearly wished to turn the affair to their personal advantage. Gibbs, high-minded as ever, rejected Barreda's advances. 'He went away and has arranged with Murrieta'.[24] In appointing Murrieta (a Spanish establishment) as financial agent on 9 April, at a commission rate of ½ per cent, Osma and Barreda pre-empted a Lima decree of four days later naming Barings as the agents.[25] The matter, Osma wrote in his own defence, had been an urgent one; there had been no time for delay and he had not known of the Peruvian government's wish to come to an arrangement with Barings. Osma, however, as he admitted, had ignored a presidential resolution of October 1848 which stated that the affair be placed in the hands of a firm named by the president himself which had the requisite knowledge, experience, and familiarity with the London money market. He countered rather weakly by describing the Murrieta house as 'one of the most respectable in this city'.[26] The matter appears not to have been disputed in Lima, despite suspicions of malpractice,[27] and the finance minister accorded the arrangement his approval on 13 July.[28]

There was little in all this to concern Gibbs. 'We pay the Dividends to Murrieta', wrote Henry Gibbs some time later, 'but

---

[22] Osma's companion on the debt-settlement mission to London; later a guano contractor for the United States market, and in the 1860s party to the British contract.

[23] GGC, 16 April 1849.

[24] *Ibid.*

[25] *Ibid.*, p. 142; also GGC, 15 September 1849. This was probably issued just after the government heard that Gibbs, their first choice for the job, were not interested.

[26] *PP (British Loans)*, p. 141.

[27] See GGC, 11 February 1850. For further instances of shady practice at the time, see Mathew, 'Debt', pp. 96-8.

[28] *PP (British Loans)*, pp. 140-2; *Anales,* IV, p. 40. GGC, 15 September 1849. Gibbs, despite their earlier reservations, did agree to become the Peruvian government's financial agents some time in the mid-1850s. FO 61/170, Rivero to Gibbs, 27 April 1857. This function survived Gibbs's expulsion from the trade. They were still performing the role in 1863, although Henry Gibbs did record in December that the government was proposing to hand it over to the new British consignees, Thomson Bonar & Co. HHGC, 3, Henry Gibbs to William Gibbs, 22 December 1863, *et seq.*

don't enquire what he does with the money'.[29] If they had any cause for worry, it lay in the terms of the congressional ratification of their contract. In a letter to Castilla dated 6 November 1849, Congress expressed approval of the consignment. It urged, however, that much greater efforts should be made in the future, through the stimulation of competitive bidding, to secure contracts that were 'more economical' and 'more beneficial for the Nation', and that in the selection of contractors preference should always be given to native Peruvians (*hijos del Perú*).[30] The same sentiments were expressed in a law passed on November 10th.[31]

There is no evidence, however, that this sting in the tail made any impression on Gibbs. Nor, it would seem, did it greatly inhibit Castilla himself, for only six months later a further contract, this time for a considerably longer period, was arranged with the Gibbs house. Once again the government was in urgent need of ready cash.[32] It may be significant though, in the light of congressional sensitivities, that in some important respects the terms of the agreement were less favourable to Gibbs than those of the 1849-51 contract. 'Castilla has desired Osma to propose to you to lower your Commissions', wrote the Lima house in February 1850, 'and the latter has answered that as they are stipulated in the Contract, of course you would not, but for future business he thought you would'.[33] In February Antony Gibbs

---

[29]Antony Gibbs & Sons, Ltd., Business archives. Copy-book of *in*-letters addressed to William Gibbs, 1854-1855 (hereinafter WGC (William Gibbs Correspondence), Henry Gibbs to William Gibbs, 5 May 1854. In the summer of 1851 (to give an instance of what they did do) the agents received half the guano sales proceeds from Gibbs: £107,200 in all. They retained £42,650 for the October dividend. The remainder, £64,550, was used for the purchase of Peruvian debt paper: £53,100 of Peruvian actives and £36,700 of deferreds (face value). FO 61/132, Alderman David Salomons to Palmerston, 19 July 1851.

[30]Cited in *El Peruano,* 28 March 1861.

[31]*Dictamen de la Comisión Especial sobre la nulidad de las prórrogas de consignación del huano* (Lima, 1856), p.3.

[32]The background to the new contract was sketched out as early as July 1849 by the British minister in Lima. The minister of finance had presented a memorial to Congress lamenting the shortage of public funds and answering charges of malversation. This document, Adams pointed out, made no suggestion as to how revenue might be increased or expenditure decreased, but confined itself 'to pointing out the necessity of raising an immediate loan on guano to the amount of 6-800,000 dollars, with which view instructions were forwarded to the Peruvian Minister in England in the month of March last, which the government does not anticipate any difficulty in obtaining; but as there will be a delay of three or four months and the wants of the Government are urgent, it is proposed to obtain a loan in Lima of 2 or 300,000 dollars to meet a part of the claims on the public Exchequer'. The memorial, Adams continued, put forward no 'statesmanlike proposition for meeting the financial difficulties of the Country' and did nothing to still feelings of disquiet over alleged incapacity and corruption in government. FO 61/121, Adams to Palmerston, 12 July 1849.

[33]GGC, 11 February 1850.

& Sons reported that Osma was 'throwing out feelers as to future business'.[34] Three months later it was all settled: a fresh contract was formally arranged on 16 May 1850. Other parties presumably could not supply what was asked of them, and the instructions which Osma received from Lima in the spring[35] very probably indicated Castilla's preference for Gibbs over any possible alternative merchant groups. It would seem, however, that Osma also took good note of his earlier directive from Castilla to get consignee commissions lowered. Gibbs, aware of the somewhat tougher mood in Lima, appear to have accepted poorer terms without any fuss. They were, no doubt, more than happy to extend their tenure by as much as four years. The precise duration was to be 19 December 1851 to 18 December 1855.[36] Territorially, the contract excluded France and the United States as before, and also took away Gibbs's right to sell in the Spanish market.[37] As for commission earnings, the former general rate of 4 per cent for sales and guarantee was brought down to 3½ per cent (of gross proceeds), this embracing brokerage as well (previously 1 per cent). And the 2½ per cent commission for chartering was scrapped altogether.[38] Imagining an annual importation of 100,000 tons at freights of £3 and prices of £9 5s. — under the first Osma contract Gibbs would earn £7,500 on charters and £46,250 on other commissions, giving £53,750 in all; under the second they would earn a straight £32,375. Their claim on the government for all commissions, therefore, would fall from about 10s. 10d. to 6s. 7d. per ton: a drop of close on 40 per cent.[39] To get matters in true perspective, however, it ought to be remembered that the terms of the 1850 contract were more normal, by 1840s standards, than were those of the 1849 arrangement. Moreover, Gibbs were required to make a large and therefore potentially very remunerative loan to the government: for £800,000 at 5 per cent interest, half the sum having to

[34]*Ibid.*, 16 February 1840; also March 1850.

[35]See *ibid.*, 16 March 1850.

[36]WGC, Henry Gibbs to William Gibbs, 24 March 1854. The government appears not to have been very eager to publicize the drawing up of yet another contract with Gibbs. Dancuart is unable to give details, for, as he notes, the text 'was never published in any newspaper or official document, nor can it be found in the archive of the Ministry of Finance'. *Anales,* V, p. 22.

[37]GGC, 16 and 23 May 1850. All these markets, and others, were offered to a group of Peruvian merchants. In the event, however, they were only able to take on the U.S. trade. France went to Montané, Spain to Murrieta. *Anales,* V, pp. 23-4. See also below, chapter 4.

[38]GGC, 16 and 23 May, 12 July and 17 September 1850; FO 177/68, Sulivan to Clarendon, 12 May 1857.

[39]If freights stood higher than £3 (as they did for most of the second contract period), then the fall in percentage terms would, of course, be even greater.

be paid on 1 October 1850 — well over a year before the contract term actually began.[40] An outlay of this order can be regarded in two quite opposite ways: either as a large payment straining the liquidity of the house and supplied under duress to an uncertain debtor in Lima; or as a splendid investment opportunity, its safety guaranteed by the system of self-repayment from guano proceeds. The latter view is almost certainly the correct one in the circumstances of 1850: Gibbs made no complaints about liquidity problems, the guano market looked as secure as it had ever done, the diversion of guano money to the bondholders caused no misgivings, and Castilla was seen as a man to be trusted. On the credit side there was also the relatively long duration of the contract, and the fact that no specific limits were set on the amount to be exported.[41]

Once again loans in London were accompanied by loans in Lima. These were all part of the guano business, although apparently not a conditional element in the new contracts. In October 1849, as we have seen, William Gibbs & Co. took a ⅝ share in a $472,000 loan. On 3 May 1850 they paid out a further $240,000 in cash as their portion of a $384,000 advance.[42] Montané supplied the rest.[43] The interest rate was to be 6 per cent,[44] and it was arranged that the money would be paid back in eight months or less. If, for some reason, it was not repaid after this time, the interest rate on the balance would rise to 1 per cent per month. The security for the loan, as always, lay in guano, and the funds which were to be used for reimbursement were to come from the Gibbs London loan:[45] 'you have to hold our $384,000 at our disposal out of the $4000000 you have to furnish October 1 next', the Lima house wrote London in July.[46] The loan clearly was not so much an additional item of borrowing from Gibbs as a means of bringing forward the date when the government, hungry as ever, could get some cash out of the new contract.

In 1853, Gibbs achieved their most dramatic coup yet. On 21 March they were awarded a six-year extension on their 1850 contract. Their monopoly, instead of expiring in December 1855, was

[40]GGC, 16 and 23 May, 27 July 1850. There was also a stipulation that Gibbs supplied funds for the October 1850 and April 1851 bond dividends. *Ibid.*, 16 and 23 May 1850.

[41]HHGC, 2, Henry Gibbs to William Gibbs, 5 December 1860.

[42]Peruvian Government Huano Loan Account, 30 April 1851, in Lima Branch Accounts, File 3, 1847-62.

[43]*Anales*, V, pp. 21-2; also FO 61/126, Adams to Palmerston, 25 May 1850.

[44]GGC, 12 May 1850.

[45]FO 61/126, Adams to Palmerston, 25 May 1850.

[46]GGC, 13 July 1850.

now to run until December 1861.[47] The *prórroga* was arranged in Lima[48] between William Gibbs & Co. and the government of General José Rufino Echenique, which had replaced that of Castilla by peaceful constitutional process in March 1851. It was a curious arrangement, according Gibbs dominance of the main axis of the trade for so many years at a time when indigenous commercial groups in Peru were becoming increasingly hostile to foreign participation in the guano business, and coming as it did from a government that had shown itself generally eager to please and reward these groups.[49] In seeking an explanation one finds little of relevance in the Gibbs correspondence: Henry Gibbs abstracted very few letters for 1853, and the original correspondence available for 1854 and after contains no retrospective remarks of much value. A large loan was certainly involved, although its exact size is difficult to determine. A congressional commission in 1856 gave a figure of $1,000,000.[50] A memorandum written at the British mission in Lima in 1857 indicated a sum of $2,000,000.[51] The finance ministry archives show that between March and December 1853 Gibbs were requested to hand over a total of $1,460,000 specifically in connection with the *prórroga:* 960,000 in eight monthly stipends of 120,000 each, the remaining 500,000 in 18 different payments ranging from $5,000 to $200,000. The lending appears to have stopped at the end of the year.[52] Gibbs's large liquid assets, combined with the insatiable financial appetite of the Peruvian government, probably were the essence of the matter. Added to this were the government's wish to avoid any disruption of the trade when Gibbs's contract for 1851-5 came to an end and their approval of the way the British firm had conducted themselves as consignees.[53] 'This measure', the Peruvian finance minister, Nicolás de Piérola[54] told Congress in 1853, referring to the *prórroga,* 'accords with justice and with our own

[47]WGC, Henry Gibbs to William Gibbs, 24 March 1854: FO 177/68, Sulivan to Clarendon, 12 May 1857.

[48]See GGC, 16 May 1853.

[49]See, e.g., Bonilla, pp. 257-69.

[50]*Dictamen,* p. 6; also Basadre (1946), I, p. 229.

[51]Enclosed in FO 177/68, Sulivan to Clarendon, 12 May 1857. See also *DBCR,* 16 (1854), p. 460.

[52]Hac Arch, Correspond. ᵃ con los Consignat.ˢ del Huano y Gobor. de las Islas de Chincha, Año de 1853 letters from Piérɔla, Saco, Paz Soldán and others to William Gibbs & Co. and Antony Gibbs & Sons, 26 March; 19, 25, 29 April; 2, 9, 11, 12, 28, 30 May; 25, 27 June; 15, 20, 26 July; 3, 4, 6, 10, 18 August; 1, 3, 16, 29 September; 4, 25 October; 3 November; 21 December 1853.

[53]*Dictamen,* pp. 5-6.

[54]Father of the future president of the same name.

recognized interests, since it is beyond question that this house, with its capital, its good sense, and its constant effort, has contributed greatly to the extension of guano's consumption and has publicized the qualities that give this article its value. . . . Further weighty influences affecting the Government's inclination to act in this way are the solid guarantees offered by Gibbs & Sons, and the ease of reaching an understanding with them, since the head of the branch in this city has been given sufficient independence to deal with every eventuality that may arise'.[55] Congress was given this information some considerable time after the *prórroga* was arranged. The whole affair had, in fact, been shrouded in secrecy. Dancuart notes that the terms of the contract were probably never published and that there is no copy in the archives.[56] Echenique avoided all reference to the matter in his two messages to Congress in 1853.[57]

No change was made to the terms of the contract: Gibbs were, as before, barred from the French, Spanish and United States markets; commission earnings stayed at 3½ per cent of gross sales proceeds (with nothing for charters); the interest on advances was still 5 per cent; and half the British returns remained hypothecated to the bondholders.[58] No restrictions were placed on the amount to be exported: 'if we can carry away the islands bodily before the 18 December '61', commented Henry Gibbs, 'we have strictly the right to do so'.[59] In May 1853 the London house conveyed to its Lima branch its satisfaction with the arrangement.[60] Their position, however, was not quite as secure as it looked on paper. The new agreement was offensive to vociferous Peruvian mercantile groups. And the government they were currently dealing with had committed major financial irregularities which could easily cause its downfall and replacement by another administration unwilling to honour inherited obligations of dubious origin.[61] People in high office,

[55] Quoted in Dávalos y Lissón, *La Primera Centuria* (Lima, 1926), IV, p. 64.

[56] *Anales,* V, p. 42.

[57] P. Emilio Dancuart, *Crónica Parlamentaria del Perú*, IV, 1851 á 1857 (Lima, 1910), pp. 152-5, 158-60. See also *Dictamen,* pp. 4, 7, 12. (I have also examined *El Comercio* for the two months following the *prórroga* and found no references to it therein).

[58] FO 177/68, Sulivan to Clarendon, 12 May 1857.

[59] HHGC, 2, Henry Gibbs to William Gibbs, 3 February 1860.

[60] GGC, 16 May 1853. In 1861, and presumably throughout the term of the contract, the firm regarded 1 per cent of the total as delcredere guarantee, all of which went to the London house. The remaining 2½ per cent was treated as pure commission and was split evenly between London and Lima. HHGC, 2, Henry Gibbs to William Gibbs, 4 January 1861.

[61] See Pike, *Peru,* p. 100; Levin, pp. 80-1; Mathew, 'Imperialism', pp. 575-6.

reported a British consul in 1852, having fought an expensive election in 1850-1, had since been busy 'reimbursing themselves at the expense of the nation'. There had occurred a 'most unprecedented prodigality, extravagance, and dilapidation . . . in the disposal of the Public Money . . .'.[62]

Gibbs's trading area was enlarged yet further in 1854 with a contract for Australia and the British West Indies. In the letter in which Henry Gibbs outlined the terms of this arrangement[63] he took note of the growing military effort of ex-President Castilla and others to displace the incumbent government.[64] Once again, this time because of rebellion, there was an urgent need for cash. Gibbs, still the best source of funds around, were, according to the British chargé d'affaires, asked for a loan and agreed to give it on condition that they were accorded extra trading rights.[65] The contract was arranged by the Lima house, but was drawn up in the name of Antony Gibbs & Sons. The latter were to be the controlling party and all the returns had to be channelled back to Peru through London. The monopoly was to last until 1861. The contractors could choose their own agents in the new markets, and the distribution of sales commission, brokerage and guarantee was to be 4 per cent to the latter and 2 per cent to Gibbs.[66] As for the crucial matter of loans to the government, the sums involved were very large, considering the size of the markets. The security, realistically, lay in guano sold in Europe rather than in whatever was disposed of in the new contract areas. 'We to advance through William Gibbs & Co. £100000 down', wrote Henry Gibbs, 'and charge the same in our account against the European Huano according to the original article. . . . Went has had some talk with Echenique about mesadas to be allowed to the Government and gives us calculations to show that he may safely and properly advance them some $200000 monthly'.[67] These regular stipends seem to have been additional to the original £100,000 (or $500,000), given that the latter had to be advanced at once in a single lump. The contract was embraced with very limited enthusiasm. The West Indian sugar

[62]FO 61/138, Crompton to Malmesbury, 2 December 1852.

[63]Dancuart makes no mention of this contract in his *Anales*, which suggests that the arrangement, like the previous two to which Gibbs had been party, was not one which the government wished to publicize.

[64]WGC, Henry Gibbs to William Gibbs, 31 August 1854; also 23 September 1854.

[65]FO 61/147, Sulivan to Clarendon, 11 July 1854; also FO 61/148, Sulivan to Clarendon, 10 October 1854.

[66]WGC, Henry Gibbs to William Gibbs, 31 August 1854.

[67]*Ibid.*

plantations represented a modestly attractive market, but Australia was regarded with some scepticism. 'At Melbourne they[68] think great things of what the business will be; but they have perhaps taken the Sanguine view of Colonists . . .'.[69] It was later confessed that Australia was 'a useless market. Le jeu ne vaut pas la chandelle . . .'.[70] William Gibbs, the head of the London house and now in semi-retirement, was very dubious about the affair, and his nephew, Henry Gibbs, now in control of daily business, did not take much trouble to reassure him. 'We quite agree in your view of the New Contract', he wrote, ' — only as the Government would have it, it was better in our hands than another's: it is very bad policy for Peru!'[71]

In January 1855 Echenique was overthrown. Shortly after, Ramón Castilla once again assumed the presidency. Gibbs, although relieved that political uncertainties had for the meantime been resolved,[72] looked to the future with some anxiety. In April 1855 Henry Gibbs thought it was still too early to 'count upon our proroga being respected',[73] and a year or so later Congress asked for the liquidation of all the existing guano contracts, appointing a commission to look into the question.[74] The latter's report in October of the same year argued that Gibbs's 1853 extension had been illegal and that it might be a source of contention if not subjected to some reform.[75] It was a very qualified and restrained indictment, however, and in May 1857 the Peruvian finance minister told the British chargé d'affaires that, despite pressure from local interests, it was not the intention of his government to make any alterations to the Gibbs contracts.[76] Indeed, far from having their wings clipped, Gibbs were given extra space for flight. In 1858 they were awarded the French and French colonial markets. Michel Montané was forced to quit his French territory as a result of what the Peruvian government judged to be inexcusable malpractice. The 1856 congressional commission had

---

[68]The associate house of Bright Bros. & Co., set up in Melbourne on 1 July 1853.

[69]WGC, Henry Gibbs to William Gibbs, 3 February 1855.

[70]HHGC, 2, Henry Gibbs to William Gibbs, 16 November 1861.

[71]WGC, Henry Gibbs to William Gibbs, 8 September 1854.

[72]*Ibid.,* 20 February 1855.

[73]*Ibid.,* 27 April 1855.

[74]FO 61/170, Sulivan to Clarendon, 12 May 1856.

[75]*Dictamen,* pp. 10, 26-7; see also HHGC, 2, Henry Gibbs to William Gibbs, 11 October 1846.

[76]FO 61/173, Zevallos to Sulivan, 22 May 1857; also *ibid.,* 61/173, Sulivan to Clarendon, 26 May 1857.

upheld the legality of the Montané contract,[77] but dissatisfaction and concern had been growing in Peru over the way in which the French consignee was handling the business.[78] He was accused of accounting to the Peruvian government in the normal way for guano sold at wholesale prices, while cashing in secretly on sales at higher prices by agents and retailers. He also appears to have had dealings with known adulterators.[79] Murrieta's activities in the Spanish market were creating similar problems. Both contractors, wrote Gibbs, 'have indeed made a great mess of the business'.[80] In the autumn of 1857 Henry Gibbs heard confidentially that Tomás de Vivero was being sent to France by the Peruvian government to investigate 'the abuses committed by Montané'. At this point, Gibbs could hardly have anticipated any new favours for his own firm, for another emissary was coming to London to examine the business in Bishopsgate.[81] Within a few months, however, Lima was to reveal, enquiries notwithstanding, its continuing confidence in Gibbs by handing it the French business. It was also, of course, manifesting its need for more cash from Gibbs. The contract was dated 26 January 1858 and was to run for four years. It required a loan of 300,000 pesos. The inheritance from Montané included not only France, but the French colonies as well, including Martinique and Guadeloupe in the West Indies, Algeria and Senegal in Africa, and Réunion in the Indian Ocean.[82] The contract appears to have had no specially distinctive features, except that it did reserve to the Peruvian government the right to determine how much guano should be shipped[83] and required the consignees to send their accounts to Peruvian diplomatic staff in France for inspection.[84]

The Spanish business was also transferred to Gibbs around this time. Information on the handover is very scanty, but there is just enough to show that the English house took charge of Spain between Murrieta's demise and the arrangement of a fresh contract with the

[77] *Dictamen,* pp. 15-8.

[78] See, for example, remarks by the minister of finance and others at the *Convención Nacional,* 7 September 1857, reported in *El Comercio,* 9 September 1857 and discussed in MAE, Lima/12, Huet to Walewski, 11 September 1857. See also *Anales,* VI, pp. 26-7.

[79] WGC, Henry Gibbs to 'Don Juan', 20 September 1855.

[80] *Ibid.,* Henry Gibbs to William Gibbs, 10 October 1855.

[81] HHGC, 2, Henry Gibbs to William Gibbs, 19 October 1857.

[82] *Ibid.,* Henry Gibbs to William Gibbs, early December 1858 and Henry Gibbs to 'Don Juan', 19 March 1860; *Anales,* VI, pp. 35-9.

[83] HHGC, 2, Henry Gibbs to William Gibbs, 8 November 1860.

[84] *Ibid.,* 3, Henry Gibbs to William Gibbs, 4 March 1862.

Peruvian firm of Zaracondegui in November 1859[85] (which probably took some time to come into operation). By the late 1850s the only important trading areas that lay outside Gibbs's control were the United States, Asia, parts of the Caribbean, Central America and Mauritius, most of which were attended to by Peruvian contractors.

The Peruvian treasury, as the then finance minister, Zevallos, freely admitted, was in very difficult straits in 1858. Among other things, he cited the rebellion led by ex-President Vivanco in 1856-7[86] which, as he expressed it, had 'depleted the Treasury'.[87] There had been a massive increase in outlay on the armed forces over the preceding years,[88] a great expansion of the internal and external bonded debts,[89] and the payment of large compensatory sums of money to ex-slaveowners after the abolition of slavery in 1854.[90] Many traditional sources of state revenue — like the Indian tribute — had lately been abandoned, and other taxes reduced,[91] thereby greatly increasing the government's dependence on guano. Hunt's figures for 1846, 1847, 1851, 1852 and 1861, converted into percentages, show the contribution from customs as 26.3, 40.0, 29.1, 35.8 and 15.3 respectively; from guano, 8.4, 0, 28.7, 37.9 and 79.6; and from all other sources, 65.3, 60.0, 42.1, 26.3 and 5.0.[92] The government, therefore, especially in periods of enlarged expenditure, had to lean even more heavily on Gibbs for support — and reward

[85]*Anales*, VI, pp. 45-9; HHGC, 2, Henry Gibbs to William Gibbs, early December 1858; *ibid.*, Henry Gibbs to 'Don Juan', 19 March 1860; *ibid.*, Henry Gibbs to William Gibbs, 20 October and 15 November 1858, 14 and 15 January 1859, 3 February and 12 December 1860, 18 October 1861. Manuel Basagoitia indicated that the transfer to Gibbs occurred in December 1857. *Oficio informativo que por conducto del Ministro de Hacienda eleva al Supremo Gobierno del Perú el cuidadano Manuel Mariano Basagoitia, Apoderado fiscal . . .* (Paris, 1858). See also 'The Trade in Guano', *FM*, 3rd ser., 15, no. 4 (April 1859), p. 313, and *Minutes of Evidence Taken Before the Royal Commission on Unseaworthy Ships, PP*, 1873, XXXVI, p. 48.

[86]See Pike, *Peru*, pp. 107-8.

[87] Dávalos y Lissón, IV, p. 120.

[88]Pike, *Peru*, p. 113. This was also the product of external frictions with Ecuador and Bolivia. See *ibid.*, p. 111; Marett, p. 110; Maiguashca, p. 65. Bonilla writes, 'the "revolution" of 1854 cost 13 million pesos; that of 1856, 41 million pesos, while the expedition against Ecuador cost more than 50 million pesos. If one considers that over the whole of this second period (1854-62) the profits from guano amounted to about 100 million pesos one can state that virtually all the earnings were absorbed by war expenses'. Pp. 282-3.

[89]Levin, pp. 80-1; Bonilla, pp. 255-61; MacQueen, pp. 37-8, 85-6; Emilio Romero, *Historia Económica Del Perú* (Buenos Aires, 1949), pp. 376-7; *Anales*, VI, pp. 57-68. See also below, pp.237-40.

[90]Pike, *Peru*, p. 112.

[91]Levin, pp. 93-4; Romero, pp. 365-7.

[92]Hunt, 'Guano', p. 70.

them with fresh trading privileges. Despite this, Gibbs were still moving on thin ice. The undercurrent of dissatisfaction over their involvement in the trade continued to flow steadily in commercial and congressional circles. Some of the hostility was finding eloquent expression, in particular in the writings of Carlos Barroilhet.[93] A legal question-mark hung over their 1853 *prórroga.* And the ways of government, blown from one expediency to another, were quite unpredictable. The security of Gibbs's position, which the events of 1853, 1854 and 1858 might suggest was very considerable, was thrown into bleak perspective by their total ejection from the trade in the early 1860s. The background to this dramatic change, and the somewhat confused circumstances of the transfer, will be examined in detail in the next chapter.

One further matter of importance remains to be considered here: the lending activities of Gibbs *additional* to the big London loans arranged when contracts were drawn up. This, so far, has been only partially examined. There was, for one thing, the discounting of bills in Lima drawn by the Peruvian government (and others) against the overseas guano balances. It did not always follow that a bill on Antony Gibbs & Sons was discounted at William Gibbs & Co.; there were a number of cross currents in the bill market. But a very large portion of discount work does appear to have gone Gibbs's way. It was 1862 before a full-fledged commercial bank appeared in Lima[94] and 1863 before the first British-owned bank was established in the city.[95] Competition, therefore, was not acute. They may indeed have come close to monopolizing the field in the 1850s. When Henry Gibbs wrote to his uncle William about the desirability of having the contract for the United States, he cited as one of the advantages the fact that Gibbs would then be in complete control of the guano-bill market.[96]

Note has already been taken of William Gibbs & Co.'s loans of $295,000 in 1849 and $240,000 in 1850. The account giving details of these advances also cites the following as 'sundry loans': $95,000 on 31 August 1850, $86,000 on 31 October, $34,000 on 30 November, $93,000 on 31 December, $30,000 on 31 January 1851, $60,000 on 28 February, $30,000 on 31 March and $80,000 on 30

[93] For discussion of the attacks of Barroilhet and others, see chapter 4.

[94] Levin, p. 83; Romero, p. 383.

[95] Romero, p. 383; David Joslin, *A Century of Banking in Latin America* (London, 1963), pp. 87-8.

[96] WGC, Henry Gibbs to William Gibbs, 20 February 1855.

April.[97] 'The Government are squeezing Went for further supplies of money which he was resisting at the date of his last [letter]', wrote Henry Gibbs in May 1854.[98] He appears to have yielded when the West Indian and Australian contract was drawn up, for in August 1854, as has been observed, Gibbs reported Went's willingness to supply the government with regular monthly stipends of $200,000 for an unspecified period. The interest rate is not indicated, but in late October Gibbs remarked that Went was able to put out London money in Lima on good security at 6 per cent at the lowest, and possibly at as high a rate as 10 per cent. Went, indeed, had written that the London house had provided him with more funds than he could use.[99] Clearly government borrowing caused no strains on liquidity. Gibbs in London were happy to provide funds through their Lima house. 'Money is rather easy just now', Henry Gibbs wrote in the autumn of 1854, 'and people with difficulty get 4½% for their spare cash'.[100]

By the end of 1854, however, political uncertainties were causing William Gibbs & Co. to proceed more cautiously. 'Went does not deliver money to the Government faster than he can avoid though he knows that we lose interest in consequence, because he wishes discreetly to keep back for fear of a change in the Government, which now appears to be inevitable when Castilla chooses to attack Lima'.[101] By the time Henry Gibbs wrote these words, in February 1855, Castilla had already won his decisive battle against the Echenique government not many miles from the capital. Castilla saw Went almost immediately after, and later authorized one of his ministers to say how, in Gibbs's words 'he was gratified to find that the income from the Huano had not been more forestalled. Went agreed to give him $500000 for which we shall have the order by the next packet'. The fact that the firm had plenty of money to spare 'delighted Don Ramon's heart exceedingly'.[102]

Money was still abundant in London in the spring of 1855 and Gibbs were eagerly looking around the money market for ways of

[97]Peruvian Government Huano Loan Account, 30 April 1851, in Lima Branch Accounts, 1847-62.

[98]WGC, Henry Gibbs to William Gibbs, 18 May 1854. Went had also been complaining to the Government about drafts which they had issued on the London Gibbs 'without the permission or cognizance of William Gibbs & Co'. Ibid.

[99]Ibid., 27 October 1854.

[100]Ibid.

[101]WGC, 5 February 1855.

[102]Ibid., 20 February 1855.

finding employment for their surplus funds.[103] By late summer, however, the situation had changed quite radically. Guano sales had fallen short of what had been expected and Gibbs had to contact their bankers for assistance.[104] Large drafts were coming in from the new government, which clearly was taking the fullest advantage of Gibbs's professions of liberality, and to meet these, financial help was requested from the associate house of Gibbs Bright & Co. in Liverpool.[105] The Castilla regime, activated by its finance minister Domingo Elías, was, in Gibbs's view, exhausting its credit.[106] Their lack of funds, Henry Gibbs complained in December, was 'an *exceeding* inconvenience'.[107] The crisis soon passed, however, and the years ahead were relatively trouble-free. Manuel Ortiz de Zevallos took over as finance minister and in 1858 told Congress that the time had come for 'the great task of systematizing the Treasury'.[108] Gibbs asked him not to run to any excesses in bill drawing, and to this request he apparently responded; he had, Henry Gibbs noted in December, become 'very particular' about drafts.[109] The government, nevertheless, was at that point operating very close to its credit margins. By the end of December 1858, Gibbs surmised, 'Stubbs [Charles Edward Stubbs, Went's successor as head of the Lima house] will have delivered every farthing they can hope to realise from sales of Huano up to June 30 [1859], on a liberal computation of our sales; on the English contract, that is . . .'.[110] But Gibbs now had plenty of cash in hand, so they displayed none of the alarm they had manifested three years earlier. 'Estimates made by the controllers of the public credit at the end of December 1858', announced Juan José Salcedo, Zevallos's successor, in 1860, 'show that the balance in favour of the guano consigning houses amounts to 6,969,798 pesos 2½ reales. For bills yet to mature and for cash loans made to the Treasury, 1,768,914 pesos 1 real. Total debit balance, 8,738,712

[103]*Ibid.*, 21 April 1855.

[104]*Ibid.*, 23 August and 21 December 1855.

[105]*Ibid.*, John Hayne to Samuel Bright, 5 and 9 September 1855; Henry Gibbs to William Gibbs, 11 and 12 September 1855; Henry Gibbs to Samuel Bright, 15 September, 12 and 15 October 1855; Henry Gibbs to William Gibbs, 18 and 22 October 1855; Henry Gibbs to Tyndall Bright, 18 and 20 December 1855; Henry Gibbs to William Gibbs, 20 and 28 December 1855. HHGC, 2, Henry Gibbs to William Gibbs, 2 January 1856; Henry Gibbs to Tyndall Bright, 8 and 11 January, 24 and 30 April 1856.

[106]WGC, Henry Gibbs to 'Don Juan', 20 September 1855.

[107]*Ibid.*, Henry Gibbs to Tyndall Bright, 18 December 1855.

[108]Dávalos y Lissón, IV, p. 121.

[109]HHGC, 2, Henry Gibbs to William Gibbs, 22 December 1858.

[110]HHGC, 2, Henry Gibbs to William Gibbs, 6 January 1859.

3½ reales'. He went on to list other debts and expenditures, and generally to expand on the grave state of the treasury when he took over in January 1859. The solution lay, apparently, in further loans from the contractors. There was clearly no will to break from old habits. 'The heads of these houses deserve honourable mention here for their willingness to supply me, in such distressing circumstances, with the monthly help that I required, in so far as their present reserves would allow . . . . In the midst of the troubles that encircled me . . . I decided to accept loans at an agreed rate of 5 per cent. . . '.[111]

Towards the end of 1860, however, Gibbs noted a slackening off in government borrowing, which they attributed to promised advances from the new contractors who had appeared on the scene.[112] In November 1861, when they had reason to believe that they might stay on in the trade after all, they wrote of 'continuing to feed the Government poco a poco as heretofore', but with somewhat less liberality than formerly.[113] They did not, in the event, win any new contract, but do appear to have continued short-term lending in 1862, 1863 and 1864, well after their tenure of office had officially expired.[114] And in December 1863 Henry Gibbs made a strangely casual reference to a very large advance of $4,000,000 which his firm had forwarded some considerable time before.[115] Quite clearly there had developed, during the 1850s, a very thick and complex tissue of financial relations between Gibbs and the Peruvian government. When this was ripped apart in the 1860s, major problems of readjustment were posed for both parties.

SHIPPING AND DISTRIBUTION

The main functions of the English merchants were commercial and financial, and one or two largely organizational aspects of these can

[111]Dávalos y Lissón, IV, pp. 121-2. 'Under the present system of contracting with mercantile houses for the sale of guano [commented a North American journal] the government can obtain an advance of money at any time it may be required, without the trouble of negotiating a loan in the manner adopted by other nations. This is found to be very convenient, as the government applies to the consignees for the sum it needs, the agents furnish the money, and render a semi-annual account of their sales and advances'.*DBCR*, 16 (1854), p. 461.

[112]HHGC, 2, Henry Gibbs to Francisco de Rivero, 18 December 1860.

[113]*Ibid.,* Henry Gibbs to William Gibbs, 1 November 1861.

[114]See, for example, *ibid.,* 3, Henry Gibbs to William Gibbs, 16 May 1862 and 14 December 1863; Hac Arch, Año 1864, Tesorería Principal, Loan of 1 October 1864.

[115]HHGC, 3, Henry Gibbs to William Gibbs, 14 December 1863.

conveniently be examined at this point. A good deal of information is available for the 1850s and this has substantial bearing on issues considered later in the chapter and on the overall judgement we shall attempt to formulate at the end of the book on Gibbs's performance in the guano trade.

In common with the other contractors, they had little direct involvement with the digging and loading of guano at the Chincha islands. They attended to this mainly through intermediaries in the 1840s. After 1849 even that very detached responsibility was shed. Loading contracts were awarded by the government, sequentially, to two Peruvians, Domingo Elías and Andrés Alvarez Calderón and the exporters' responsibilities thereafter normally commenced with the chartering of vessels to pick up guano at the islands. In January 1855 Gibbs were given charge of loading, after Elías had fallen foul of the incumbent Echenique government, and attended to it, again through agents, on a commission basis (¾ real per register ton). This arrangement, however, lasted little more than a year.[116] It ought also to be mentioned in passing that the workers who dug and loaded the guano, performing the first crucial tasks necessary before the merchants could earn any commissions or the government any profits, operated within a mixed system of slave (up to 1854), convict, indentured and free labour, and were treated in a way that appalled a good many contemporary observers. The acquisition of guano, in the words of a British journal, entailed 'an amount of misery and suffering on a portion of our fellow creatures, the relation of which, if not respectably attested, would be treated as a fiction'.[117] There are important questions here, but these have been dealt with in some detail elsewhere[118] and are of only marginal relevance to the main issues of this book: exports, trading monopolies and contractor-government relations.

Of more direct importance is the fact that the labour force (principally indentured Chinese by the 1850s) was frequently very inadequate numerically, with consequent delays in loading and shortfalls in supply. Even by the late 1850s, when the trade had assumed very large dimensions, the work-force was well under 1,000-strong, operating with virtually no mechanical assistance. Guano was dug with picks and shovels, carried in bags, wheeled in barrows or rolled along rails in trucks, deposited in large enclosures on the cliff tops, and dropped through canvas shoots into the holds of

[116]Mathew, 'Primitive Export Sector', *passim*.

[117]'The Chincha Islands', *NM* (April 1856), p. 181.

[118]Mathew, 'Primitive Export Sector', *passim*.

ships waiting below or into small feeder launches.[119] The tempo of production, therefore, bore a fairly direct relation to the number of workers. In November 1850 Gibbs in London complained to their Lima house of a 'want of power of loading at the islands'.[120] Lima acknowledged the problem, placing their hopes for improvement on the fact that 'the Government have bought new launches for the purpose of aiding the loading'.[121] According to Nicolás de Piérola in 1853, however, there was still an insufficiency of small boats in service: only 31, and most of them in a bad state of repair. At least 50 were required, he reckoned.[122] Piérola's biggest concern was 'the shortage of labourers'. The work force, he suggested, ought to be doubled.[123] James Caird, the British agricultural writer, alleged in 1853 that loading facilities were no better than they had been some seven years before when the trade was only about one-tenth of its current size. There was no good reason, as he saw it, why a ship should spend any more than one week lying off the islands. A vessel of 1,000 tons, he contended, could be loaded in two days through the shoots; a shortage of loading places, however, meant that 'a numerous fleet . . . are constantly in succession waiting their turn . . .'. Delays could be in the order of two to three months.[124] As many as 100 vessels were waiting at the north island when a British naval officer went there in 1853.[125]

There was not much that Gibbs could do about the problem by themselves, even during the year or so when they were in charge. 'They are at present despatching at the Islands 40,000 Tons a month for all nations', wrote Henry Gibbs in May 1854. The Lima house anticipated that this would be 'raised to 60,000 when the Rails Launches etc. which have been ordered arrive out'.[126] No such improvement in fact occurred. The average monthly clearance over the whole of 1854 had been as low as 33,028 tons. In 1855 this

[119]*Ibid.*, pp. 48-9.

[120]GGC, 16 November 1850.

[121]*Ibid.*, 9 October 1850.

[122]Nicolás de Piérola, *Informe sobre el estado del carguío de huano en las Islas de Chincha, y sobre el cumplimiento del contrato celebrado con D. Domingo Elías* (Lima, 1853), p. 9.

[123]*Ibid.*, pp. 11, 18-9.

[124]*The Times,* 26 November 1853, p. 18 and 16 February 1854, p. 7.

[125]*Ibid.*, 7 December 1853, p. 12; also FO 61/144, Clarendon to Sulivan, 13 April 1854 and FO 61/146, Sulivan to Clarendon, 25 June 1854.

[126]WGC, Henry Gibbs to William Gibbs, 18 May 1854; also Hac Arch, Islas Chincha, Mendiburu to Governor of Chincha, 4 November 1854; Gálvez to Governor of Chincha, 25 January 1855.

increased only marginally, to 33,813 tons. In 1856 it slumped to 17,849. In 1857 there was a sharp recovery, the average rising to 40,888[127] — but this was no higher than the figure cited by Gibbs in May 1854. In March 1857 there were as many as 128 ships at the island: 188,804 register tons in all,[128] capable of carrying about 160,000 tons of guano, a quantity that would take a good four months to load. In November 1860 Henry Gibbs noted that since June of that year only 20,000 had been cleared each month, and that 'the carguío has been unwontedly bad'.[129] As late as 1866 Thomson Bonar &Co., Gibbs's successors as consignees in Britain, observed that any one ship had usually to wait 70 or 80 days at the islands, and that there was always a queue of 90 or 100 vessels.[130] Charles Stubbs was asked by the Royal Commission on Unseaworthy Ships in London twenty years or so later about the 'common report that the vessels rather what is called "shied"' at the guano trade. He agreed that there had been a problem. 'They had', he replied, 'long lay days at the islands, as many vessels arrived at once, and demurrage occurred. ... The quantity was 10 tons a day,[131] and the lay days were never fewer than 30 nor more than 80 days, according to charter party'.[132]

Ships in fact were beset by a host of problems, which must have made it difficult for Gibbs to charter in sufficient quantity when employment conditions in the British and American shipping industries were fairly buoyant. Guano, usually loaded unbagged, was an awkward cargo: 'any cargo which you put into a ship which forms a mass . . .', commented George Reid, a surveyor employed by the Gibbs house in Lima, 'is always trying, there is no spring in it'.[133] Ships had usually to be loaded under cliffs, often in heavy surf,[134] and this caused a number of obvious dangers and inconveniences. There were also some awkward institutional procedures to be observed. In the 1840s, early and late 1850s, and 1860s vessels on a guano run were required by the Peruvian government to call twice at Callao and twice at Pisco to

[127]ANF, sér. F12, dossier 6860, Guiroy to Chemin Dupintes, 5 May 1858.

[128]FO 61/172, Sulivan to Clarendon, 12 March 1857.

[129]HHGC, 2, Henry Gibbs to William Gibbs, 8 November 1860.

[130]The Times, 10 December 1866, p. 7.

[131]i.e. the amount given free as compensation, in lieu of demurrage payments in money.

[132]Minutes of Evidence Taken Before the Royal Commission on Unseaworthy Ships. PP, 1873, XXXVI (hereinafter RCUS), p. 51.

[133]Ibid.

[134]WGC, Henry Gibbs to William Gibbs, 20 February and 5 April 1855; Piérola, p.6.

observe various commercial formalities[135] — 'a great annoyance to all masters of ships visiting Peru, and a source of additional expense to English ship-owners and charterers', in the words of one mariner. 'Over this battledore duty a ship often wastes nearly a month, besides generally losing some of her hands from desertion in Callao'.[136] After 1854 vessels had also to undergo a sea-worthiness survey by the Gibbs office in Callao. There had been a large casualty rate on the high seas lately and the inspections, both before and after loading, were intended to reduce this.[137] According to Charles Stubbs, mass inspection was 'initiated with some difficulty'. When ship-masters came to Gibbs for a charter and were told that they must submit to a survey, 'some went away and took the ship to another place. . . '.[138]

In the period 5 April 1850 to 30 April 1851 as many as 196 vessels were chartered for guano in Lima, Valparaiso and San Francisco.[139] This represented the bulk of the guano fleet at that time. West Coast chartering, however, appears to have diminished in importance later in the decade. 'The principal part of the shipping which loaded the guano', Stubbs recalled in 1873, 'was chartered in Europe before it went out, and it was only a few vessels that we picked up in Callao . . . some few were taken up in Australia, and some few in California, but the majority were chartered in England'.[140] Most of the European chartering was effected by Gibbs in London. Agents in the British and continental ports also did a good deal of business, although probably under clear instructions from Gibbs as to quantity and rate,

---

[135]FO 61/134, Adams to Malmesbury, 25 June 1852; FO 61/174, Sulivan to Clarendon, 12 October 1857; Hac Arch, Correspond.ᵃ con el General Gob.ʳ de las Islas de Chincha, Mendiburu to Governor of Chincha, 9 January 1854; *Informe Circunstanciado que la Comisión de Delegados Fiscales eleva al Congreso, en cumplimiento del Artículo 8 de la Ley de 28 de enero de 1869* (London, 1872[?]), p. xxxi.

[136]'The Guano Diggings', *HW*, 6, no. 131 (25 September 1852), pp. 42-3; also FO 61/131, Memorial from masters of 30 vessels to Captain Frederick, 2 August 1851; *ibid.*, Captain Frederick to Adams, 2 August 1850; FO 61/134, Adams to Palmerston, 8 February 1852; *ibid.*, Adams to Malmesbury, 25 June 1852.

[137]*RCUS*, pp. 32, 35, 36, 37, 49, 51, 53.

[138]*Ibid.*, p. 32. This measure seems to have had a distinct effect on the casualty rate. The average for 1850-4 had been 23 vessels and 11,868 register tons per year. For 1855-60, with a much larger carrying capacity at work, the rate was 14 vessels and 9,722 register tons. *Ibid.*, Appendix X, pp. 502-3.

[139]Statement of Freights on Vessels Chartered on the Coast Belonging to 1st Consignment Account to 30 April 1851. Lima Branch Accounts, File 3, 1847-62.

[140]*RCUS*, pp. 48-9. Of 35,420 tons ordered in April 1854, for example, 28,495 were acquired in Britain and Europe. WGC, Henry Gibbs to William Gibbs, 18 May 1854; also *ibid.*, 3 February 1855.

and with a good deal of financial assistance as well.[141] When a sufficient quantity of ships was available in Britain and when their own funds were ample Gibbs preferred to do most of the business themselves.[142] Brokerage returns were no doubt a consideration here. But the ability to pick up extra capacity through Callao, San Francisco, Sydney and Melbourne (where the associate houses of Bright Brothers & Co. had been set up in 1853) was very useful when the market got tight. Australian and Californian gold had been attracting great numbers of migrants, and vessels frequently found it difficult to fill up with return cargoes from such virgin economies.[143] A lot of ships lay idle in Melbourne and San Francisco,[144] and agents of the guano merchants could make easy pickings. Vessels would usually sail to Callao in ballast from these ports, and on the long hot run across the Pacific from Australia ships 'flying light' often suffered considerable physical deterioration, necessitating the rigorous inspections and repairs in Peru mentioned earlier. A great many of the ships chartered in Britain also reached Chincha by way of Melbourne and Sydney.[145] Henry Gibbs noted at the end of 1858 that ships currently being hired in England could not normally be expected back home before February 1860, given the large proportion of the total 'bound for Australia'.[146] Looking at the pre-guano voyages of a sample 38 vessels entering British ports with Peruvian fertilizer in 1852,[147] one finds that 12 went to Australia first, two to California and four to other parts of North America. One had been to the Mediterranean and 15 made an initial trip to Central and South American countries other than Peru. Only four of the 38 went straight to Callao and Chincha to fetch their guano.[148]

[141]See WGC, Henry Gibbs to William Gibbs, 22 October 1855; HHGC, 2, Henry Gibbs to Böhl, 11 September 1858; *ibid.*, Henry Gibbs to 'Ferdinand', 1 October 1858. Gibbs's accounts show, for example, that in the last weeks of 1858 Feldmann Böhl, the agents in Hamburg, drew on Gibbs for over £6,000. LGL, first ser., 15.

[142]See WGC, 3 February and 27 April 1855; HHGC, 2, Henry Gibbs to Bright, 14 April 1859.

[143]See, for example, Edward Shann, *An Economic History of Australia* (Cambridge, 1930), pp. 169-85.

[144]*The Times,* 26 March 1852, p. 8; T. W. Buller's letter to *ibid.,* dated 14 April 1852, in FO 61/137.

[145]*RCUS,* pp. 48-9, 50.

[146]HHGC, 2, Henry Gibbs to William Gibbs, 28 December 1858; also GGC, 1 February 1852.

[147]*Lloyd's Register of Shipping* (hereinafter *LRS*), volumes for 1851, 1852 and 1853. The number represents about half of all ships coming in with guano in that year. These are the ones where the pre-guano voyages can be established with reasonable certainty.

[148]One factor here was Britain's very large import surplus with Peru. See figures in D. C. M. Platt, *Latin America and British Trade 1806-1914* (London, 1972), pp. 316-7, 320-1. Also below, pp. 235-6.

Even when Gibbs did not employ circumnavigators, ships could take many months to bring home a cargo. The most direct trip to Chincha and back meant two trips round Cape Horn and involved many delays, both physical and institutional, as we have seen, on the Peruvian coast. In 1857, 40 guano-laden vessels sailing back from Callao to Liverpool took an average of 18 weeks to complete the homeward journey.[149] Such long time-lapses between the chartering of a vessel and the arrival of guano on the European market posed awkward problems of judgement for the consignees. They had to make forecasts of consumption a year or more ahead and charter accordingly, hoping all the while that they would not be seriously overstocked or undersupplied. Errors were very common, with shortages a recurrent and damaging problem on the British market in the 1850s. A memorial to the Board of Trade from shipowners and others of Liverpool in 1853, complaining about the way in which the trade was organised, cited recent years of scarcity as proof of the fact that Gibbs alone were incapable 'of meeting the varied requirements of so extended a trade. . . .'.[150] Had a large number of merchants been operating, it was probably assumed, mistakes would to a degree have cancelled each other out. In September 1854 Gibbs were chartering 'at a great rate' for the 1856 season.[151] In the months of October, November and December 1855 they paid out freights for vessels which were not expected to arrive at the Chinchas until late in 1856.[152] Charters, they observed in November 1858, involved 'looking forward for 13 months: on an average'.[153] In February 1860 they were writing of the need to start providing for the 1862 season.[154]

Some freights appear to have been paid before the vessels left Europe[155] and as the money could not be reclaimed from the shipowner in the event of the cargo being lost Gibbs insured these advances.[156] Payments to shippers before cargoes were sold were treated as loans to the Peruvian government and as such carried a handsome 5 per cent interest rate. Most of these loans, however, were very short term, for the bulk of freight payments were made not before the voyage but after the ship had docked in Europe. On 301,464 tons

[149]*Liverpool Customs Bills of Entry.* A similar average is indicated in HHGC, 2, Henry Gibbs to William Gibbs, 12 December 1860.

[150]*The Times,* 26 November 1853, p. 8.

[151]WGC, John Hayne to William Gibbs, 23 September 1854.

[152]*Ibid.,* Henry Gibbs to William Gibbs, 4 October 1855.

[153]HHGC, 2, Henry Gibbs to William Gibbs, 20 November 1858.

[154]*Ibid.,* 3 February 1860; also 3, Henry Gibbs to William Gibbs, 4 March 1862.

[155]See, for example, WGC, Henry Gibbs to William Gibbs, 4 October 1855.

[156]*RCUS,* pp. 32, 36-7, 50; also Mesones, pp. 115, 119.

sold in the mid-1850s Gibbs earned only £9,509 2s. 6d. for interest on advances connected with the trade[157] (or about 7½d. per ton of guano). Even if all these were for freights, the average time-lapse between payments and sale indicated by the figures is only about two months. Generally these outlays were effected without causing Gibbs any very serious problems. The proceeds from the old guano financed the movement of the new. In October 1854 Henry Gibbs noted that their liabilities on freights amounted to about £200,000, but that such sums could be 'continually met by our sales, so that the actual working capital this business *at present* requires is not all that great'.[158] There was, however, a danger that heavy outlays on freights might have to be made at a time when, for one reason or another, guano sales were proceeding slowly and when, perhaps, other calls on guano funds were mounting. There was, as we have already seen, a temporary disequilibrium in Gibbs's financial affairs in the second half of 1855. Heavy government drawing on London was one factor, but the principal cause of the difficulty, in Henry Gibbs's view, was an excessive outlay on shipping. 'We chartered too much and are feeling the inconvenience'.[159]

TABLE I: Guano vessels despatched from Peru under Gibbs's consignment, 1850-60.

	Number of Vessels	Aggregate Register Tonnage
1850	215	101,795
1851	305	140,595
1852	117	53,406
1853	276	146,056
1854	408	214,827
1855	478	275,358
1856	169	106,254
1857	477	357,147
1858	257	201,604
1859	118	77,303
1860	231	199,285
Total	3051	1,873,630
Annual average	277	170,330

1 Source: *RCUS,* Appendix X, pp. 502-3.

[157]Basagoitia, statistical appendix.

[158]WGC, Henry Gibbs to William Gibbs, 13 October 1854.

[159]WGC, Henry Gibbs to William Gibbs, 20 December 1855; also *ibid.,* Henry Gibbs to William Gibbs, 25 September, 10 and 18 October, 3, 18, 20, 22 and 28 December 1855; Henry Gibbs to Bright, 12 and 15 October, 18 and 20 December 1855.

Comparing 1850-4 with 1855-9, we can see that there was no great increase in the number of ships employed. The annual average for the first half of the decade was 264 vessels; for the second half, 300. The ships, however, were tending to increase in size, so that the register tonnage figures show a somewhat more marked increase: from an average of 131,336 in 1850-4 to 203,533 in 1855-9. In 1858, the year of maximum guano importations into Britain, the average size of all vessels arriving from Peru was 714 tons.[160] The great majority of them were carrying guano. The largest ships of all entering Britain came from the United States, averaging 921 tons, followed by Australia and New Zealand (828) and the East Indies, Ceylon and Singapore (782). Peru ranked fourth, and well ahead of any other Latin American country. Ships from Chile averaged only 409 tons and from Ecuador, 341.[161] These figures show that by the late 1850s, if not before, guano was attracting some of the largest ships then operating in world commerce.[162] This growing utilization of large-scale shipping had a number of possible advantages for the consignees and the Peruvian government. In the first place it made chartering easier. It was much less troublesome to employ 100 vessels of 1,000 tons each to carry 133,000 tons of guano than to take on 400 vessels of 250 tons each to carry the same amount. Secondly, the larger a ship the greater tended to be its productivity. This did not mean that freight rates always fell in step with declining unit costs. Rather it meant that margins of profitability widened for shipowners. These wider margins probably made it easier for owners to sail at low rates in periods of surplus capacity and to put up with some of the inconveniences and delays of the trade. The largest single cost for a sailing ship lay in wages and provisions for crews, and one can get a crude measure of productivity by dividing the tonnage of a vessel by its crew number. A ship's earning capacity tended to rise faster than its size. The cost of operating it, however, rose less quickly than its size. In 1842 one man was required for 20.9 register tons of ship in the British guano trade. By 1847 this had increased to 26.6 tons, and by 1852 to 34.3. In 1857 the figure was 38.2 and in 1862 it stood as high as 47.2. Productivity, thus measured, rose by 126 per cent over the 20-year period.[163]

On the question of freight rates, there is, for the 1850s, as for the 1840s, no evidence of the sort of regular upward trend that Jonathan

[160] As distinct from the 784-ton average for the vessels cited by Stubbs that *left* Peru in that year.

[161] Calculated from figures in *PP*, 1859, XXVIII, p. 389.

[162] It may also have activated some of the building. 'The large yearly imports of guano', commented the *Farmer's Magazine* in 1859, 'called into existence a considerable portion of the large-sized ships'. 'The Trade in Guano', *loc. cit.*

[163] Calculated from data in *LRS*.

Levin and others have suggested took place.[164] Only one of the contracts held by Gibbs during the decade — that for December 1849 to December 1851 — awarded commissions for charters, so there were no incentives here for the contractors to go for high rates. The pattern over the period was certainly not a regular one. Broadly, however, one can detect a sharp rise between 1852 and 1854,[165] a substantial fall between 1855 and 1858-9,[166] and another increase, this time fairly gentle, between 1859 and 1861.[167] The 1852-4 rise was quite steep and had, as we shall see later, a considerable effect on the price of guano in the European market. In 1851-2 rates generally fluctuated within limits fairly close to £3. By February 1853, however, the demand for shipping arising from the Crimean War had pushed the guano rate up to £4, and some difficulty was experienced in finding enough vessels even at that price. The situation worsened in 1854: 'we are in a complete fix with regard to Ships', wrote Henry Gibbs in March, 'and we have no confidence that an increase to £5 will at all better our position'.[168] They in fact went up to £5 at the end of the month, did fairly well, and were obliged to hold there for most of the remainder of the year. Thereafter the shipping industry gradually moved back into its normal mid-century condition of overcapacity, and rates came down. As for overall trends during the decade, one finds that whereas in 1849-53 Gibbs had taken up only one vessel at £2 10s. or less, in 1853-60 they came by as many as 134 at such very low levels. At rates of £3 and under, the numbers were 195 ships in 1849-53 and 378 in 1853-60.[169] Figures such as these make nonsense of any contention that freight rates were steadily rising under the contract system of exporting. Guano shipping costs reached their lowest point ever in 1858-9.

[164]Levin, pp. 68-9; Bonilla, pp. 76-7; Pásara, p. 15.

[165]GGC, 1 March, 16 July and 1 December 1852; WGC, Henry Gibbs to William Gibbs, 24 March, 13 April, 5 May and 13 October 1854; HHGC, 2, Henry Gibbs to William Gibbs, 5 November 1860; Statement of Freights, *loc. cit.*; FO 61/137, Wilson to Malmesbury, 9 June 1852; FO 61/148, Sulivan to Clarendon, 10 October 1854; MAE, Lima/11, Ratti-Menton to Baroche, 8 September 1851; *The Times*, 25 August 1853, p. 7.

[166]WGC, Henry Gibbs to William Gibbs, 3 February and 21 September 1855; HHGC, 2, Henry Gibbs to William Gibbs, 18 November, 28 and 30 December 1858, 6 and 26 January 1859; *HMM*, 37, no. 5 (November 1857), p. 574; 'The Trade in Guano', *FM*, 3rd ser., 15, no. 4 (April 1859), p. 60.

[167]HHGC, 2, Henry Gibbs to William Gibbs, 5 and 8 November, 5 December 1860; Henry Gibbs to Francisco de Rivero, 18 December 1860; 3, Henry Gibbs to William Gibbs, 4 March 1862; FO 61/198, Jerningham to Russell, 13 May 1861; FO 61/201, Kernaghan to Russell, 16 March 1861; 'The Manure Trade of the Past Year', *FM*, 3rd ser., 29, no. 2 (February 1861), p. 159.

[168]WGC, Henry Gibbs to William Gibbs, 24 March 1854.

[169]HHGC, 2, Henry Gibbs to William Gibbs, 5 November 1860.

No one at the time related freight problems in the guano trade to any pressure from the English consignees for higher intermediate costs: not even their harshest critics. In 1853 *El Comercio* complained that the rates Gibbs were offering were unnecessarily *low* and that this was making it difficult to obtain a sufficient capacity of shipping to keep the European market stocked. The English firm, they alleged, were behaving in a 'niggardly' manner and were failing to show 'a proper liberality in regard to freights' and their policy had 'shaken all confidence in future supplies'.[170] In 1857 the British chargé d'affaires offered the view that the monopolistic organization of the trade, with only one bidder for shipping for any single market, kept freights lower than they would be under a more competitive system, and noted that a party of American shipowners, with just that point in mind, had been proposing the abolition of the present consignment system to the Peruvian government.[171] A few years earlier British shippers had expressed a similar desire.[172] Gibbs reckoned in 1860 that if, after they had left the trade, their European monopoly was broken up into smaller territorial segments, competition between half a dozen or more contractors would raise freights 10s. or 20s. higher than they would otherwise be.[173] The same view was taken by the *Farmer's Magazine* in 1861. 'By the centralizing which has existed, tonnage has been obtained upon the most favourable terms, all competition being destroyed, but by the new arrangements which divided the business between six different firms, the shipping interest is likely to profit considerably at the expense of the Peruvian Government'.[174] Monopoly power, Gibbs argued some years earlier, had also brought economies in other areas of intermediate cost: 'the charges here, of Rent, bagging, etc. have been reduced by us lower than individuals competing with one another would reduce them'.[175]

From the end of 1851 until the close of their contract period Gibbs earned no commissions from the government on charters. They appear, however, to have found ways of compensating themselves for this loss, and in this respect did lay themselves open to well-founded criticism. 'The British agents of the Peruvian Government', wrote a shipbroker, 'to carry out more completely the principle of enriching

[170]Quoted in *The Times,* 25 August 1853, p. 7.

[171]FO 61/173, Sulivan to Clarendon, 12 May 1857.

[172]See section below on 'Guano Question'.

[173]HHGC, 2, Henry Gibbs to Francisco de Rivero, 18 December 1860; also Henry Gibbs to William Gibbs, 8 November 1860.

[174]'The Manure Trade of the Past Year', *loc. cit.*; also *HMM,* 36 (June 1857), p. 686.

[175]GGC, 16 July 1852.

themselves, insist upon a full moiety of the broker's commission, and demand, before signing any charter, that the broker shall endorse upon every charter-party for a ship an obligation to pay to them half his brokerage for the privilege of giving them a ship'. The brokerage was paid in the first instance by the shipowner, and brokers, wishing to hold on to the full payment themselves, were naturally disinclined to deal with Gibbs. 'I, for instance, never take a ship to them unless their rate of freight requires me conscientiously to do so . .'.[176] Such arrangements may well have exerted small upward pressures on guano freights. Equally, they may have served to aggravate problems of acquiring shipping in periods of under-capacity. But the practice was probably more a reflection of strength than a cause of weakness. With hundreds of thousands of tons of guano at their command, Gibbs were very major figures in world shipping markets. Their powers of patronage, indeed, must have been among the greatest in Western Europe. In charging a brokerage commission they were exploiting this situation to the full. The *prórroga* commission of 1856 noted that 'a business as large as that of guano must draw all the shipowners towards the house of Gibbs, relieving the consignees of all effort in this respect'.[177] 'The Gibbs firm', observed José Ulloa in 1859, 'do not need to run around to find ships to hire'.[178]

The full brokerage commission, according to Carlos Barroilhet's somewhat confused account of the matter in 1857, amounted to 5 per cent.[179] Gibbs's share, accordingly, came to 2½ per cent: the same as the freight commission formerly paid to them by the Peruvian government. In Ulloa's treatment of the question a couple of years later we read of a straight 2½ per cent being paid directly to Gibbs by the shipowner.[180] There is also a reference to this in Gibbs's correspondence in 1852.[181] It no doubt made sense for brokers to be dispensed with whenever possible, given the costs involved and the fact that the transactions were not particularly complicated. 'The masters of vessels or shipowners themselves go to the office of the consignees', and if there was agreement on rates matters could be

---

[176]Quoted in *The Times,* 22 February 1854, p. 10.

[177]*Dictamen,* p. 14.

[178]Ulloa, p. 58.

[179]Barroilhet, *Opúsculo,* pp. 65-6.

[180]Ulloa, pp. 51-9.

[181]GGC, 1 May 1852. It seems that when chartering was done in Lima the charge may have been as much as 7½ per cent, 2½ per cent coming back to Gibbs in London and the rest being held by William Gibbs & Co. Henry Gibbs advised that these charges were excessive and, in the light of complaints on the subject in 1856, suggested that William Gibbs & Co. take only 2½ per cent and that the 2½ per cent due to London be waived if objections persisted. HHGC, 2, Henry Gibbs to William Gibbs, 21 August 1856.

settled 'in a couple of words'.[182] The practice of charging such a commission found official acceptance of a sort in Gibbs's French contract of 1858, in which a maximum of 2½ per cent was laid down for foreign shipowners (with exemption for Peruvian vessels), assuming that this was no higher than normal brokerage rates in the places where the ships were chartered.[183]

The fact that these commissions were levied as a percentage of freight costs meant of course that any increase in shipping expenses would enlarge Gibbs's earnings from that source. The incentive to raise freight rates was therefore still there, but the evidence cited above indicates that it was not acted upon. The main effect, as suggested by contemporaries, was to cause shipowners to raise their rates in compensation for the commissions they were obliged to pay.[184] If this happened (and it is unlikely that it did all that much when shippers were competing for guano freights in normal times of underemployment) the cost, of course, was ultimately borne by the government. The only people clearly gaining were Gibbs themselves, and for very little effort.[185]

Turning now to questions of distribution, the merchants quite clearly had major problems in determining, for a particular season, how much guano each country, region or port was going to require. Aggregate calculations were awkward enough. The fact that these had to be broken down into a number of territorial components added extra difficulty. The simple solution was to bring all the guano to London first, then look at the pattern of demand and distribute accordingly. But this was a somewhat cumbersome way of proceeding. Henry Gibbs did think it desirable to sell a lot of the guano for the British market from London. On the other hand, he confessed to a 'strong prejudice' in favour of 'direct cargoes', since these meant cheaper guano[186] for provincial consumers and a substantially enlarged demand.[187] This prejudice was not much reflected in

[182]Ulloa, p. 58.

[183]*Anales*, VI, pp. 36-7.

[184]This was asserted rather than demonstrated. See Barroilhet, *Opúsculo*, pp.65-6; Ulloa, pp. 54, 57; *Dictamen*, pp. 14-5.

[185]For comment, see Mesones, p. 119. Gibbs were additionally accused of charging excessive agency fees to ships arriving in Peru, to meet costs connected with customs, health regulations, harbour dues, provisions, ballast and the like at Callao and Chincha. The fee was 150 pesos per vessel. Luis Mesones asserted, although without documentary proof, that 100 pesos represented clear profit for Gibbs and that on an exportation of 250,000 tons of guano they could expect to make 35,000 pesos or £7,000. He also accused Gibbs of lending money to ships' captains at an unfavourable rate of exchange. *Ibid.*, p. 116, 119; also Barroilhet, *Opúsculo*, pp. 64-5 and Ulloa, p. 52.

[186]Through lower internal transport costs from port to purchaser.

[187]HHGC, 2, Henry Gibbs to William Gibbs, 30 December 1858; also 8 November 1860.

128

practice. The available statistics show that the great majority of guano
vessels coming into Britain in the 1850s docked at London: a fact
which bore no relation to the geography of consumption, the south-
east of England being relatively inconsequential as a guano-using
region. Customs bills, covering the five major English ports, show that
in 1847 31 ships docked at Liverpool, 24 at London, 3 at Bristol and 3
at Hull. In 1852, with Myers gone, 59 ships came into London and
only 13 went to Liverpool; Bristol took the remaining three. In 1857
135 went to London, 43 to Liverpool and 10 to Bristol,[188] Liverpool
and Bristol being the ports where Gibbs's two main associate firms
(Gibbs Bright & Co.) resided. Examining another source, which
provides import figures for all the ports of Britain, one finds that in
1858 (the peak importing year) 243,957 of the 353,541 tons of
guano[189] brought in came through London: almost 70 per cent.
Liverpool took 51,524 tons, Bristol 20,120; Glasgow 8,756; Leith
6,984; Aberdeen 3,423; Dublin 2,643; Hull 1,888; Plymouth 1,215;
Dundee 1,029. All the other guano ports took less than 1,000 tons
each.[190]

This sort of distribution posed problems for the marketing of a
commodity like guano, considering that it was bulky and therefore
quite costly to transport. Scotland, for example, was a much more
important area of consumption than the Home Counties. Scottish
imports in 1858, however, were only one-tenth of London's. Gibbs
were taken to task for this by José Ulloa. 'The contractors' system in
this market has been to do the selling themselves. For this purpose
they have reduced to four the places where sales are effected; namely:
London, Liverpool, Glasgow and Aberdeen'. He rejected Gibbs's
argument that the purpose of such concentration was the prevention of
adulteration.[191] This may not have been entirely fair, since adulteration
was a serious problem and the channelling of a high proportion of
imports through Antony Gibbs and Gibbs Bright obviously facilitated
direct controls and checks, but it does seem rather unlikely that the
presumably reliable agents whom Gibbs were already employing in
ports around the coast could only be trusted with small dribbles of

[188]*Bills A. Customs, London. Ships Reports.* (I am indebted to David Williams of
Leicester University for drawing my attention to this valuable source).

[189]The figures are for *all* guano imports (of which roughly 85 per cent was Peruvian).

[190]*Annual Statement of the Trade and Navigation of the United Kingdom with
Foreign Countries and British Possessions in the Year 1858* (London, 1859), pp.
124-5, 128, 130.

[191]Ulloa, p. 17. The situation was, of course, worse than Ulloa indicated. A fair
distribution between these four ports would have been much healthier for the trade than
the system that in fact prevailed.

guano. There was of course the possible additional factor of wishing to get the guano in first, and distributing it later once regional demand had been confidently assessed. It could, however, be well argued that such flexibility did not have to be London-based: that the guesses could be made at the time of chartering, the regional imports effected, and imbalance then corrected by redistribution from Leith, or Hull, or wherever Ships, moreover, could be redirected prior to unloading.[192] Yet another consideration may have been ship size and harbour facilities. Some of the smaller ports certainly would have been unable to receive the big ships which were becoming increasingly conspicuous in the trade. This may explain why Gloucester, Montrose and Limerick took no guano in 1858. It does not, however, explain why London took five times as much as Liverpool, 12 times as much as Bristol, 28 times as much as Glasgow, and 72 times as much as Aberdeen.

A major factor may well have been Gibbs's wish to maximize their income. The inflated retail prices that resulted from the prevailing system are irrelevant, as the consignee's commissions were levied on fixed wholesale prices. The channelling of the bulk of the trade through London did, however, mean that Gibbs did not have to do much commission splitting. As Ulloa asserted, Gibbs were affected by 'the desire to take the entire sales commission . . . without sharing it with their appointed agents'.[193] In the 1840s the consignees appear to have kept the full commission on every ton sold in Britain, with agents being paid from the returns on appropriately increased outport prices.[194] This way of working the business lapsed in the 1850s. Outport prices were the same as in London. Gibbs Bright & Co. received 1¾ per cent on sales in Liverpool and Bristol; Gibbs in London took the remainder.[195] In 1862 Gibbs Bright asked if they could sell from London stocks when they ran short.[196] The London house's answer is not recorded, but Henry Gibbs wrote to William Gibbs saying that it was difficult to come to a decision: to do what Gibbs Bright wanted would foment sales; on the other hand London would lose commissions.[197] Gibbs's pen as well as his practice reveals that he was quite prepared to set the interests of his house above those of the business. It is notable too that the only proper depots outside

[192]See *The Times,* 26 November 1853, p. 8.

[193]Ulloa, pp. 17-8.

[194]See references to higher outport prices in chapter 2.

[195]HHGC, 2, Henry Gibbs to Tyndall Bright, 30 April 1856.

[196]See HHGC, 3, Henry Gibbs to William Gibbs, 19 February 1862.

[197]*Ibid.*

London were in the two ports where an associate firm was operating. Antony Gibbs & Sons were reluctant to share; when they did, they did so mainly with sister houses. The volume of sales, as Gibbs acknowledged, was almost certainly reduced in consequence.[198]

As for distribution in Europe, the evidence to hand is very confusing. Gibbs's ledgers show that they had a large number of European clients in the 1850s. Unfortunately, the precise location of a great many of them is not given. The business they were doing with Gibbs is also obscure, for the commodities they received are usually not specified; the words 'sales' and 'shipments' are used, but one cannot tell in most individual cases whether the items in question included guano. There is no way either of knowing from Gibbs's accounts whether such goods came to European clients directly or by way of London. Some clues, however, can be gleaned from other sources. If we examine the destinations of a sample 354 vessels under the Gibbs consignment, we find that 226 unloaded their guano in Britain and 97 made for European ports. A further 31 ships unloaded some in Britain and some in Europe. The number of cargoes going wholly or partly to Europe, therefore, was 128 — or 36 per cent of the total. This might be taken as evidence that continental markets got most of their guano directly from Peru. However, if we look at the European ports receiving the guano we discover that more than half of the vessels went to Antwerp, and most of the rest to Hamburg and Rotterdam.[199] Some of the guano required by Italy, S.E. Europe, the Scandinavian countries, Russia and other areas around the Baltic may of course have been redistributed (at considerable extra cost) from these ports, but a lot of it almost certainly came from Britain. British commercial statistics show that there was a substantial re-export trade in guano in the 1850s.[200] Between 1855 and 1859, for example, 69,308 tons were exported to German and Hanse ports, 14,775 to Spain and the Canaries, 8,898 to Scandinavian countries, 5,734 to France, and 4,649 to Italy.[201] 'Other' areas in Europe received 9,711 tons. And despite the direct cargoes to Antwerp and Rotterdam, Belgium took 42,100 tons of re-exported guano and Holland, 15,787. These figures apply to *all* sorts of guano, but

[198]For a comment on the undersupplying of the Scottish market, see L. Marchand,'Les engrais artificiels en Angleterre et en Ecosse', *AP*, 2nd ser., 3 (October 1861-September 1862), p. 229.

[199]Basagoitia, statistical appendix.

[200]*PP*, 1854-5, L, pp. 312-3; 1856, LVI, p. 126; 1857, XXXV, p. 583; 1857-8, LIV, p. 160; 1859, XXVIII, p. 164; 1860, LXIV, pp. 32, 166.

[201]These are minimum estimates. The geographical categories change somewhat from year to year. When figures for a particular area are not specified it is likely that they form part of the category labelled 'other countries'.

probably most of it was Peruvian.[202] If Gibbs brought guano to London and then sold it from there to European importers they could take their full 3½ per cent commission. This was the system they were presumably referring to when they wrote in 1858: 'we ourselves have sent guano to 14 houses in Gothenburg, Christiansand and Nortdkjoping, which have place direct orders with us . . . .'.[203] It no doubt meant a very high price by the time it reached the continental farmer. When designated agents received their guano directly, however — Dankaerts of Antwerp, Böhl of Hamburg, Trenor of Valencia, Quesnel of le Havre, Santa Coloma of Bordeaux[204] — they took their portion of the sales commission. Under Gibbs' French contract of 1858, Quesnel and Santa Coloma earned 1 per cent each of gross proceeds from guano sold through their houses. The total commission paid by the government was 3 per cent, and Gibbs pocketed the difference.[205]

There were not very many guano depots, with individual agents, around the coast of Europe. In 1858 Gibbs cited stocks in Hamburg, Rotterdam, Antwerp, Dunkirk, le Havre, Nantes, Bordeaux, Valencia and Genoa.[206] Antwerp and le Havre seem to have been the principal continental ports, the latter (with the other French centres) coming within Gibbs's orbit in the last years of the 1850s. In 1858, according to Ulloa, le Havre alone held almost two-thirds of French guano stocks. To reach the main areas of consumption, he pointed out, 'it is necessary to traverse great distances and undertake difficult and costly journeys'.[207] Luis Mesones also suggested that guano contractors such as Gibbs, with enormous territorial responsibilities, were ineffective in pushing sales throughout the full extent of their markets. Such complaints echo official sentiments of some years earlier. In 1852 Manuel Mendiburu arrived as Peruvian plenipotentiary in London with instructions from his government to do something about

[202]There are frequent references to re-exports of Peruvian guano in farming journals and newspapers and in the Gibbs correspondence. The 'computed real value' of the re-exports also indicates that most of the guano was the expensive, i.e. Chincha, variety.

[203]Antony Gibbs & Sons, *Contestación de la Casa Gibbs a los cargos sobre el huano* (London, 1858), p. 26. There is also reference here to nine agents buying guano in London for shipment to Scandinavian markets.

[204]The last three ports do not feature in the figures given above for vessel distribution since in the mid-1850s Gibbs did not serve either the French or the Spanish markets.

[205]Mesones, p. 112; *Anales,* VI, p. 39.

[206]HHGC, 2, Henry Gibbs to William Gibbs, ? December 1858; also Henry Gibbs to 'Don Juan', 19 March 1860.

[207]Ulloa, p. 14. Of 42 guano vessels leaving Peru for France in 1858, as many as 27 were making for le Havre; of the remainder, 7 were bound for Dunkirk, 4 for Nantes, and 4 for Bordeaux. ANF, sér. F 12, dossier 6860, Guiroy to Chemin Dupintes, 5 May 1858.

poor European sales. 'The reason for such paralysis', he reported, 'lies in the contract with the house of Gibbs. While it is undeniable that the business is well discharged in England, in the rest of Europe there is no evidence of effort on their part to propagate guano's name or stimulate its consumption.... In particular I draw your attention to Germany and Russia, whose exhausted lands are much in need of guano, but where up to now it is entirely unknown'.[208]

Consumption in Europe is rather difficult to estimate with confidence, for although Rivero provides sales figures for the different countries,[209] it may well be that these exclude guano sold in London for shipment to the continent. One still gains the strong impression, however, that the European market was badly served. In 1856, the peak sales year in Britain and Europe, the British figure of 214,707 tons was more than twice the figure for Gibbs's European territories (then excluding France and Spain). Over half of the continental sales, moreover, were concentrated in just one very small country, Belgium. Sales in Britain and Belgium together amounted to 269,694 tons. In the vast expanse of Europe to the east of the Rhine they came to less than 50,000 tons.

Reference has been made to direct and indirect imports. The latter gave flexibility (at a cost) to the trade, and helped maximize Gibbs's earnings. Some extra flexibility was lent by the so-called 'continental clause' which Gibbs inserted in their charter parties, enabling them to redirect vessels to certain European ports if the demand pattern nearer the time seemed to warrant it.[210] In 1858 they wrote of possible increases in French consumption and of the need for appropriate shipping arrangements. If, however, the French marked proved weak, then vessels hired to supply it could be diverted to Ostend or Hamburg.[211] In the autumn of 1861 they sent large cargoes to Antwerp where demand seemed buoyant, kept guano away from ports like Rotterdam and Hamburg which did not require fresh supplies, and discussed the need to divert British-bound vessels to replenish the understocked market in Bordeaux. Shippers, unquestionably, did not like the uncertainties and extra voyage time that the system entailed.[212] The fact that they usually went along with it is further evidence of the power Gibbs enjoyed in the shipping market when there was excess

[208]Quoted in Francisco de Rivero, *Ojeada Sobre El Huano* (Paris, 1860), p. 28.

[209]*Ibid.*, Appendix: Estado Comparativo de las Ventas de Huano desde 1° de Julio de 1849, hasta 1860 inclusivo.

[210]See, for example, HHGC, 2, Henry Gibbs to William Gibbs, 18 and 20 November 1858; 3, Henry Gibbs to William Gibbs, 23 March 1862.

[211]*Ibid.*, 2, Henry Gibbs to William Gibbs, 30 December 1858.

[212]See, for example, *ibid.*

capacity. Henry Gibbs wrote in 1860 that he would refuse to give a Liverpool vessel a charter without the continental clause: he would accept 'no compromise that will prevent me from sending the *Palatine* to the most disagreeable place in France if the necessity should arise'.[213]

The distribution system overall, therefore, was both costly and pliant, involving as it did a confusing but not senseless mixture of direct chartering, internal redistribution, diverted shipments and re-exports. Its flaws resulted from over-centralisation and the reluctance of the consignees to delegate responsibility and split their earnings.

Finally, a few details can be presented on the techniques of distribution within the British market and the return of sales proceeds to the Peruvian government. When guano arrived in the ports it was weighed by Customs House officials. Certificates were given to the consignees and these were sent back to the government in Lima with details of sales.[214] This made it impossible for the importers to engage in fraudulent dealings by bringing in more than they accounted for, or by taking irregular profits out of the ton-register/ton-effective differential. The fertilizer was then stored in dock warehouses prior to internal distribution. Gibbs appear to have had no stores of their own.[215] Buyers made their own arrangements for carriage from the ports. Payment was made by cash or cheque rather than by bill. This led Mesones to wonder why it was that Gibbs were still being paid delcredere commission.[216] Their 3½ per cent (and their 4 per cent in 1850-1) was officially designated as a fee for sales and guarantee. This, of course, may have been just a slightly wordy way of saying 'sales commision'. But if Gibbs had in fact got a compound commission in which a sales fee and a delcredere fee had been added together,[217] then they were being paid for a service that they were not usually required to perform. Since guano was mainly sold for cash, no risk attached to the transaction and delcredere was irrelevant.[218]

[213]*Ibid.*, Henry Gibbs to Tyndall Bright, 15 December 1860.

[214]Rivero, p. 216.

[215]In 1852 they listed their dock charges as follows: 5s. 9d. per ton for unloading, moving to warehouses, and delivery from same; and 1 d. per ton per week for store rents. They also cited 'Bags 4d. each'. A good deal of the guano was bagged at the ports, most of it being imported in bulk. GGC, 16 July 1852; also Basagoitia, p. 17.

[216]Mesones, p. 110.

[217]See above, pp. 96-9, HHGC, 2, Henry Gibbs to Tyndall Bright, 30 April 1856.

[218]Cash payment was also favoured by the Barredas in the United States. In 1852 a major Baltimore dealer advertised as follows: 'We solicit orders for Guano. We buy direct from the agents of the Peruvian Government . . . but as they require *cash down,* we require either a permission to draw a sight draft or cash in hand . . .'. Prices Current, Baltimore, 1852, 1858. (From collection of materials on produce prices in the Baker Library, Graduate School of Business Administration, Harvard University).

Funds from agents in Britain and Europe did arrive, needless to say, mainly in the form of London bills,[219] but these, in normal circumstances, could be easily and quickly exchanged for cash.

The establishment in London, arranging the sales and receiving the proceeds, consisted of the management plus a few dozen employees in the late 1850s.[220] One of their additional tasks was to make a report to the Peruvian government every 15 days on the progress of the business.[221] And then, of course, the Peruvian government would claim its returns. Half of the net proceeds were earmarked for the British bondholders. And from the gross proceeds the consignees retained what was owing to them for freights and freight interest, other intermediate costs, loans and loan interest. The remainder was available for the government. A lot of the money went on further disbursements in England.[222] In taking its funds it was also able to give assistance to Peruvian importers who required foreign exchange and some extra earning power to William Gibbs & Co. of Lima as well. Luis Mesones gives the following description:

> The merchants who find themselves pressed by the maturing of their debts procure hides, iron, cochineal, cotton, wool, bark, silver bars, etc. for despatch to Europe; these articles are not sufficient to make up the sums owing, for exports unfortunately do not measure up to imports, so they have recourse to the house of Gibbs for bills. . . . The Gibbs firm makes all the profits from guano in London available to the Government; but that money only enters the national coffers by virtue of bills drawn in favour of the merchants who pay in Peruvian, or better still, Bolivian currency in Lima. The Gibbs agents sign drafts at 42 or 43 pence per peso; 48 pence represent par; and as a penny makes two centavos, it follows that the merchants lose 5 or 6 pence and the Government gains 10 or 12 per cent on the exchange. The agents award themselves a halfpenny for the service of issuing bills against funds belonging to the State. . .[223]

Everyone presumably was fairly happy. The government got much of the local currency it required directly, and profitably, from

[219]LGL, first ser., 13-20.

[220]Rivero, p. 182.

[221]*Ibid.*

[222]See, for example, Huano Consignment Contract no. 1, 1852-53, in LGL, first ser., 13b. This account shows that in 1852 the Peruvian government used much of its money to make payments to a variety of people in London, a great many of them connected with the purchase and equipping of the custom-built steam frigate *Amazonas.* See also FO 61/137, Hay to Stanley, 9 June 1852.

[223]Mesones, pp. 116-7. The Huano Consignment Contract no. 1 account (*loc. cit.*) shows bills in the name of Marcó del Pont (a substantial Peruvian merchant) alone totalling over £16,000 in 1853.

merchants in Peru. The merchants, at some cost, found the foreign exchange they needed. And Gibbs, without much effort, won a further small commission.

EXPANDING SALES AND RISING PRICES, 1850-6.

The first half of the 1850s constituted probably the happiest period in the guano trade. Sales increased rapidly, each year registering an improvement on the one preceding. Prices also rose, partly through increased costs but partly too because a growing trade gave the Peruvian government and its agents added confidence in the market-ability of the product. Sales and prices both arrived at their peak in 1856. In that year Gibbs disposed of 211,647 tons in Britain,[224] a figure substantially in excess of any over the remaining years of their contract. In December 1856 the minimum wholesale price reached £13, at which level it remained until the summer of 1858.[225] In the early 1850s guano achieved its greatest relative importance as an aid to British farmers. It occupied a dominant and commanding position in the fertilizer market, and was widely acknowledged to have become a vital element in British agricultural advance. At the very start of the decade it could be described as 'the commonest kind of artificial manure'.[226] It was, in the view of one observer in 1851, 'to the farmer what insurance is to the merchant — it guarantees to him the profit of his labours'.[227] The London Farmers' Club drew attention in 1852 to its great reliability, 'the cases in which it is reported that guano has failed to be productive of benefit being perfectly exceptional'.[228] An 1853 study of East Lothian, one of Britain's most advanced agricultural regions, documented its importance for wheat, oats, beans, turnips and potatoes, and its very clear ascendancy over all other purchased manures; it was 'now all but the indispensable fertilizer'.[229] According to James Caird, guano had 'become like a necessary of life to us, with

[224]W. M. Mathew, 'Peru and the British Guano Market, 1840-1870', *EHR*, 2nd ser., 23, no.1 (1970), p. 118.

[225]*Ibid.*, p. 117.

[226]Thomas Anderson, 'Economy of Manures', *FM*, 2nd ser., 22, no. 3 (September 1850), p. 226.

[227]*The Times*, 16 May 1851, p. 6.

[228]'Guano; Its Application, Supply, and Adulteration', *FM*, 3rd ser., 1, no. 3 (March 1852), p. 207.

[229]Charles Stevenson, 'On the Farming of East Lothian', *JRAS*, 16 (1853), pp. 277-304.

our narrow boundaries and worn out cornfields, with no tracts of rich unbroken soil for our increasing population to fall back upon . . . '.[230] The need for further increases in consumption was, he considered, 'a matter of vast importance'.[231] The *Farmer's Magazine* endowed it with almost magical qualities: 'If ever a philosopher's stone, the elixir of life, the infallible catholicism, the universal solvent, or the perpetual motion were discovered, it is the application of guano in agriculture'.[232] By 1856 it had become Britain's 'staff of life'[233] and 'a treasure far more valuable to this country than that of the goldfields of Australia. . . '.[234]

Farmers themselves, of course, generally took a sober, practical line. Whatever enthusiasm they displayed for guano was very much a function of its price, its supply, its superiority over the available alternatives, and their own capacity to buy. Its command of the market would last roughly as long as it made economic sense to employ it, and the advantages that it held over its rivals were much narrower and more susceptible to change than one might imagine from some of the literary eulogies. Briefly, one may observe that guano's success in the early 1850s was the product of three basic factors: increased supply, limited competition, and rising food prices. The first arose mainly from enlarged inputs of labour. There were severe and very frequent short-term irregularities in supply but the secular trend was markedly expansive. The second resulted from the failure of commercial speculators to discover any deposits of guano comparable in size and value to the Peruvian *huaneras* and to the still fairly modest bearing of British fertilizer manufacturing. The third was partly related to the Crimean War: British wheat imports fell for a year or two after 1853, the home acreage expanded, and wheat prices rose from a trough in 1851 to their highest point for almost 40 years in 1855.[235] There was also much buoyancy in prices for livestock products.[236]

[230] *The Times,* 22 December 1853, p. 7.

[231] *Ibid.,* 10 September 1853, p. 8; also *ibid.,* 16 February 1854, p. 7.

[232] 'Guano', *FM,* 3rd ser., 5, no. 4 (April 1854), p. 314.

[233] 'Proposed Sales of the Chincha Guano Islands', *ibid.,* 9, no. 2 (February 1856), p. 109.

[234] 'Guano', *ibid.,* 10, no. 1 (July 1856), p. 42.

[235] Fairlie, p. 100; Tooke, VI, pp. 487-8; B. R. Mitchell with Phyllis Deane, *Abstract of British Historical Statistics* (Cambridge, 1971), p. 488.

[236] E. L. Jones, 'The Changing Basis of English Agricultural Prosperity, 1853-73', *Ag HR,* 10 (1962), part II, *passim;* J. D. Chambers and G. E. Mingay, *The Agricultural Revolution 1750-1880* (London, 1966), pp. 177-8.

TABLE 2: Gibbs's Sales of Peruvian Guano in Europe, 1849-56 (tons)

	Britain			Continental Europe, less France and Spain	
July 1 1849— June 30 1850	77,098	⎱ +25%		8,326	⎱ +114%
1850-1	96,145	⎱ +17%		17,846	⎱ + 58%
1851-2	112,638	⎱ + 5%		28,193	⎱ + 18%
1852-3	118,286	⎱ +15%		33,144	⎱ + 88%
1853-4	135,524	⎱ +31%		62,385	⎱ + 14%
1854-5	177,500	⎱ +21%		71,167	⎱ + 48%
1855-6	214,707			105,019	
Total	931,898			326,080	
Annual average	133,128			46,583	

Source: Rivero, *Estado de las ventas.*

Table 2 shows the increasing scale of the guano business in the early 1850s. Sales in Britain in 1855-6 were 178 per cent up on those for 1849-50. If the continental trade is added, the expansion is of the order of 274 per cent. Prices also rose steadily: from £9 5s. to £10 in January 1854; to £11 in July 1854; to £12 in July 1856; and to £13 in December 1856. This rise in the cost of guano to farmers was in many respects the most important feature of the trade in the 1850s and for that reason must be carefully analysed. Initially it combined with growing consumption to augment greatly the income of the Peruvian government and the guano consignees. Its longer-run consequences, however, were much less happy. It served to energize Peru's competitors and bring about a marked transfer of preference away from guano in the late 1850s — a loss of ground that was never fully recovered. The 1850s present a picture of rapid success followed by sudden and dramatic decline. Increasing prices reflected the first and helped cause the second. The issue of prices, moreover (as we shall see in the next chapter), lay at the heart of much contemporary Peruvian criticism of Gibbs. Throughout the discussion that follows it will be as well to bear in mind again that the English consignees were (and are) widely accused of holding prices at unnecessarily low levels and of lacking faith in guano as a marketable commodity.

The minimum wholesale price of £9 5s.,[237] inherited from 1849, persisted for the first four years of the 1850s. The question of its alteration did, however, arise periodically. Castilla apparently favoured an increase in the autumn of 1850, and wished to know Gibbs's opinion on the matter.[238] Their view was fairly decisive: 'At a time when the Abolition of the Corn Laws has terrified the farmers . . . a rise in price would be very inopportune and would greatly risk the popularity of Huano. . .'.[239] Gibbs reiterated their plea for caution in 1851 and got support from the Peruvian minister in London.[240] They adduced the danger of competition, the opinion among many farmers that guano was already too expensive, and 'the present price of Agricultural produce'.[241] in 1851 wheat prices fell to their lowest point since 1780.[242] There were no notable retorts from Lima. There was, in the circumstances, probably some satisfaction that British sales totalled as much as 96,145 tons over the year 1850-1.[243] The government's approach was reflected in a pamphlet published in 1851: 'every rational monopolist takes advantage of his privilege as modestly as possible so as to place his products within reach of the largest number of consumers, knowing that even if the profit from each sale is only moderate, the total returns will increasingly make up for it'.[244]

British farmers did not let low produce-prices stop them buying guano. A great many were eager to employ it as a means of cutting unit costs.[245] Agricultural depression both stimulated the desire to use guano and impaired the capacity to buy it. The resulting frustrations grew after the 1851 harvest and came to a head in the main guano-purchasing season in 1852.[246] Complaints over high prices were widely and vigorously expressed, as were demands that the British

[237]The maximum for small amounts was £10 15s. See FO 61/173, Sulivan to Clarendon, 12 May 1857.

[238] GGC, 8 and 9 October 1850.

[239]*Ibid.*, 16 December 1850; also 17 December 1850.

[240]*Ibid.*, 16 January 1851.

[241]*Ibid.*, 16 January and 16 October 1851.

[242]Oats and barley were also low: see Mitchell and Deane, p. 488.

[243]Rivero, Estado de las ventas.

[244]*L.E.S., Estudios Sobre El Huano* (Lima, 1851), p. 32. In a letter to the British foreign secretary, Lord Malmesbury, dated 4 May 1852, Francisco de Rivero observed that this had been published under the auspices of the Ministry of Finance. *PP*, 1852, LIV, p. 172.

[245]There had for some time been a large body of farmers 'able by high investment in more productive techniques to meet the fall in prices by a higher output produced at lower unit costs'. Jones, *English Agriculture*, p. 14.

[246]See section on 'Guano Question'.

government take remedial action. This clearly was not the time for thoughts about price increases. On the other hand, it was not considered appropriate to lower either.[247] Protest became most intense in the early summer. Gibbs judged, however, that any reduction in prices would 'appear like a weak concession'.[248] The current level was 'not only fair but more than liberal'.[249] By the end of the year the crisis had passed. 112,638 tons of guano had been sold in Britain,[250] and grain prices were starting to pick up after a wet summer and a below-average harvest.[251]

Given the recency of the farming agitation, the modesty of the produce-price recovery, and their past tendency to argue for caution in price policy, it is surprising to discover Gibbs advocating a rise from the long-established level of £9 5s. in the spring of 1853 and equally surprising, perhaps, to find the government counselling against it:[252] for 'reasons of State', as Gibbs expressed it.[253] These may have had something to do with concern in Lima over the way in which the British and United States governments had taken up the issues of guano prices and monopoly trading on behalf of their farmers, merchants and shipowners.[254] As for Gibbs's reasons for wanting a price increase, they record simply that they had thought 'the moment had perhaps now come to effect a rise'.[255] They may have been heartened to see how well guano had weathered the recent storm. Shortage of stocks may also have been an influence. 'At this time of year', wrote the *Farmer's Magazine* in January 1853, 'the imports of guano are usually large; but this season they have been unusally small'.[256] In April supplies were 'much reduced'.[257] In June, the last month of the season, guano was still 'very scarce' and selling retail at up to £12 a ton.[258]

[247]GGC, 16 February 1852.

[248]*Ibid.,* 16 June 1852; also 16 August 1851 and 16 September 1852.

[249]*Ibid.,* 16 July 1852; also Gibbs, *Contestación,* pp. 10-1.

[250]Rivero, *Estado de las ventas.*

[251]Tooke, VI, p. 487; Fairlie, p. 97.

[252]Gibbs, *Contestación,* p. 11.

[253]*Ibid.*

[254]See section on 'Guano Question'.

[255]Gibbs, *Contestación,* p. 11.

[256]Agricultural Report for January 1853, *FM.* (These reports, quite frequently cited below, usually appeared in the number for the month following the one discussed).

[257]*Ibid.* for April 1853; also May 1853.

[258]*Ibid.* for June 1853.

In the meantime, the government in Lima was reviewing the matter. An important new factor had come into play. 'In view of the fact that there is a shortage of shipping for carrying guano overseas'; wrote the Peruvian finance minister on 24 November 1853, 'that the freight which has to be paid to the shippers has risen to 20 pesos per ton; that farmers can afford to pay a bit more for guano than the price. . . fixed for the purpose of making it known and spreading its consumption, it is resolved: that henceforth the consignees shall set the sales price for amounts of thirty tons and more . . . at £10. . . .'.[259] Gibbs implemented the directive immediately after completing their current orders, at the same time abandoning their 2½ per cent discount.[260] The effective rise in prices, therefore, was just under £1 per ton. The Peruvian government's main concern, it would appear, was that shipping costs were rising and biting into profits. Gibbs's proposals earlier in the year, however, must have given them the necessary confidence to risk a price change.[261]

There was a continuing scarcity of guano in the British market during most of the 1854 season. Shipping problems were the main factor, aggravated by Gibbs's reluctance to advance rates sufficiently during the preceding year.[262] 'The agents of the Peruvian government', it was reported for February 1854, '. . . have given notice that they are unable to supply the public'.[263] James Caird asserted that the guano market was in effect closed, and wrote of 'the utter inadequacy of any single house of agency attempting to regulate the supply to the ever-varying demands of a whole nation'.[264] No notable improvement had occurred by the spring: 'orders for several thousand tons are yet unfulfilled', it was reported in April.[265] Once again the government considered the possibility of a price increase. Farmers were clearly willing to pay handsomely for guano if they could get hold of it. Wheat prices had continued their ascent after the worst harvest for many years in 1853 and the war-induced reduction in imports.[266] By April

[259]Paz Soldán to William Gibbs & Co., 24 November 1853. (In Rivero, pp. 137-8). See also GGC, 12 December 1853.

[260]Gibbs, *Contestación,* p. 12.

[261]See Paz Soldán to Sulivan, 5 December 1853. (In Rivero, pp. 230-5).

[262]GGC, 1 March 1853; *The Times,* 25 August 1853, p. 7 and 26 November 1853, p. 8.

[263]Agricultural Report for February 1854, *FM*.

[264]*The Times,* 9 February 1854, p. 8.

[265]Agricultural Report for April 1854, *FM;* see also *ibid.* for May 1854.

[266]Tooke, VI, p. 487; Fairlie, p. 97.

1854, moreover, guano freights had risen to £5.[267] Bags too were becoming more expensive, manufactured as they were from imported jute.[268] Less than four months after ordering the increase to £10 the Peruvian government wrote to Gibbs asking for a further rise. As before, the objective was to prevent the erosion of profits.[269] The instructions, dated March 18th,[270] crossed a note that Gibbs had sent to Lima on April 29th about 'the need for a further price rise' to compensate for rising costs.[271] The tenor of the exchange suggests that what was wanted was an increase equivalent to the increased expenses and no more: something in the order of £1. On 18 July the price was advanced to £11.[272] This ended the phase of essentially cost-related increases. The next two rises, to £12 and £13, came in July and December 1856. By that time freights were falling again.

By the end of 1854 Gibbs had sold 154,271 tons in Britain,[273] only 9,000 or so more than they had disposed of in 1852. Considering that prices had risen quite substantially, however, the government and the consignees were probably fairly content with that figure. The £11 price came fully into effect with the start of the main selling season in the early weeks of 1855. The year began with Gibbs in a confident mood. January sales almost doubled those of the same period in 1854.[274] The main problem once again appears to have been periodic shortage rather than expense. 'Very few imports have taken place', was the complaint in February.[275] 'Very small imports continue to arrive', it was reported in May.[276] In the off-season months demand also began to contract more than usual and dissatisfaction over sales featured on and off in Gibbs's correspondence until the end of the year.[277] 1855 registered a sale of 161,852 tons in Britain, only a small advance on the year preceding.[278]

[267]See above, p. 124.

[268]Antony Gibbs & Sons to William Gibbs & Co., 29 April 1854. (In Rivero, p. 139.)

[269]WGC, Henry Gibbs to William Gibbs, 5 May 1854.

[270]GGC, Peruvian Government to Antony Gibbs & Sons, 18 March 1854.

[271]Antony Gibbs & Sons to William Gibbs & Co., 29 April 1854. (In Rivero, p. 139.)

[272]GGC, 1 August 1854; also Rivero, p. 140.

[273]Antony Gibbs & Sons to Rodulfo, cited in *Fenn's Compendium of the English and Foreign Funds* (London, 9th edn., 1867), pp. 377-8. For some monthly figures, see WGC, Henry Gibbs to William Gibbs, 23 August and 4 October 1855.

[274]See *ibid.*, 3 and 20 February 1855.

[275]Agricultural Report for February 1855, *FM*.

[276]*Ibid.*, May 1855; also June 1855.

[277]WGC, Henry Gibbs to William Gibbs, 23 August, ?, 25, 28 September and 3 December 1855; Henry Gibbs to 'Don Juan', 3 October 1855.

[278]Gibbs to Rodulfo, *loc. cit.* If we compare agricultural years (1 July to 30 June), however, 1854-5 showed a very marked advance on 1853-4. See figures given near the beginning of this section.

142

Gibbs, however, seemed quite happy to leave prices where they were. Not so the Peruvian government. On 20 April 1855 it issued one of the most significant documents of the guano trade. This was a circular to consignees signed by the finance minister of the new Castilla regime, Domingo Elías: 'I inform you of the supreme resolution that the net product accruing to the Nation from guano sales shall be thirty pesos . . .'.[279] In his report to the *Convención Nacional* in the summer Elías made it clear that the government was dissatisfied with current net proceeds of around 20 pesos.[280] The directive to the contractors was a bid for a 50 per cent increase in unit returns. Rising costs were not a factor. The background to the move lay in the financial difficulties of the new administration, attempting to consolidate its position after the 1854-5 revolution.[281] By some odd oversight the government omitted to send details of its new policy to Gibbs.[282] It was the beginning of October before the Peruvian minister in London supplied them with the necessary instructions and their reaction was highly critical. 'The Government have sent Rivero an oficio to be communicated to us ordering the price so to be regulated as to produce *never less* than $30!! This is impossible but we may have to raise the price, which would be a very serious matter in itself. What are we to do? It is a dodge of Elías's which Rivero thinks as absurd as we do'.[283] An increase, they warned, 'is always an experiment which can have grave and ruinous consequences for the Government . . .',[284] but it seems to have been the timing rather than the rise itself that mainly concerned them.[285] An important consideration here may have been the state of their own purse. Gibbs, as already noted, experienced a rare crisis of liquidity towards the end of 1855. Any check to sales, they wrote on 6 October, would cause them much financial inconvenience.[286] The market was already less buoyant than they would have wished. 'To Went I shall write to say again that any such orders as may curtail the sales must of course materially tend to curtail our advances to the Government'.[287] Concern over their own

[279]Cited in Rivero, p. 340.

[280]FO 61/155, Sulivan to Clarendon, 25 August 1855.

[281]See *Crónica Parlamentaria,* IV, p. 219.

[282]See note by Salvador Soyer (*oficial archivero*), 22 May 1855, cited in Rivero, p. 341.

[283]WGC, Henry Gibbs to William Gibbs, 4 October 1855; also GGC, Rivero to Antony Gibbs & Sons, 5 October 1855; Gibbs, *Contestación,* p. 13.

[284]Antony Gibbs & Sons to Rivero, 12 October 1855, *loc. cit.*

[285]See WGC, Henry Gibbs to William Gibbs, 10 October 1855.

[286]*Ibid.,* 6 October 1855.

[287]*Ibid.,* Henry Gibbs to 'Don Juan', 8 (?) October 1855.

strained resources was obviously tied in very closely with fears of a decrease in guano consumption. But they were also very confused as to what the most likely effects of a price rise would be — 'I am not *fully* convinced by my own *argument* in the matter',[288] wrote Henry Gibbs. The main point really is that they felt in no condition to run any risks.

The combination of reason and threat appears to have worked with the Peruvians. There was in fact a very good argument to be made out for caution, for the challenge from other fertilizers was growing all the time. J. C. Nesbit warned Gibbs in December that any further increase was bound to alienate British farmers.[289] The Peruvian minister in London expressed himself in agreement with Gibbs's opinion on the matter,[290] and on 14 October wrote to his government advising them to take serious account of consignee reservations.[291] Gibbs had already accepted that it might be possible to raise the price at the end of the main selling season in 1856,[292] and along with Rivero proposed to keep a careful eye on the receptivity of the market. They had in fact entered their best season ever. In 1855-6 they achieved record sales of 214,707 tons in Britain and 105,019 in their European markets.[293] Rivero sent home favourable reports and optimistic forecasts in the spring, and with British agricultural prices running high[294] and farmers eagerly mopping up the available guano at minimum wholesale prices of £11 and retail prices of around £12 10s.,[295] a further increase of £1 did not now seem unduly risky. In April 1856 the government requested that Gibbs 'raise the price . . . by as high a margin as possible . . . '.[296] The consignees complied on 1 July, putting the price up to £12.[297] Their financial troubles had eased and they expressed no reservations about the increase.

[288]*Ibid.,* Henry Gibbs to William Gibbs, 10 October 1855.

[289]J. C. Nesbit to Antony Gibbs & Sons, 3 December 1855. (In Rivero, pp. 274-6).

[290]WGC, Henry Gibbs to William Gibbs, 6 October 1855.

[291]Rivero to Peruvian foreign minister, 14 October 1855. (In Rivero, pp. 122-3); also Rivero to Antony Gibbs & Sons, 8 January 1856 (*ibid.,* pp. 126-7); Gibbs, *Contestación,* pp. 6-7; GGC, 8 and 15 January 1856.

[292]WGC, Henry Gibbs to William Gibbs, 10 October 1855.

[293]Rivero, Estado de las ventas.

[294]Took, VI, p. 48; Mitchell and Deane, p. 488.

[295]J. C. Nesbit to Antony Gibbs & Sons, 3 December 1855, *loc. cit.*

[296]Melgar to Peruvian foreign minister, 27 April 1856. (In Rivero, p. 258). Also GGC, Peruvian government to Antony Gibbs & Sons, 5 May 1856; Gibbs, *Contestación,* p. 14; Melgar to Peruvian foreign minister, 2 June 1856. (In Rivero, pp. 266-7).

[297]Gibbs, *Contestación,* p. 14; GGC, 30 June 1856.

It had been two years since the last price rise, and well over a year since the Elías circular asking for net proceeds of 30 pesos had been issued. Elías had wanted a 10 peso increase in income per ton. Given current freight rates, a further rise of around £1 was still required.[298] Rivero asked Gibbs in June to watch the progress of consumption and consider the possibility of an additional increase.[299] The Peruvian government, however, was not yet pressing matters. Indeed it showed some signs of concern over the possibility of diminished consumption at £12.[300] But the instructions were, so to speak, on the table and 'as there came into our hands a circular dated 5 May 1856 from the Minister of Finance in Lima, D. José Melgar, ordering us to increase the price gradually, we naturally concluded that the wish and intention of the Government was to effect, if possible, a further increase . . .'.[301] Gibbs's only available comment came in October, and it hardly represented a decisive viewpoint; 'it occurs to me', wrote Henry Gibbs, 'that after all we have said about the danger of disturbing the price in the middle of a season and the difficulty of making a correct judgement of the brisk season from the consumption of the slack one, I hope we shall be very shy of raising the price in December. Still there may be paramount reasons of course'.[302]

Such paramount reasons must have materialized in the next month or two. The price went up to £13 at the end of the year, and Gibbs seems to have taken the initiative. An important factor was the recurrence of supply problems.[303] On 30 December 1856 Rivero wrote to Lima that 'the consigning house of Antony Gibbs & Sons have come to the conclusion that they ought to raise the price of guano to £13 . . . . Some of the present problems would not have arisen if the pace of loading at the islands had been accelerated'. He went on to praise 'the zeal of our consignees' in advocating a price rise the instant that circumstances seemed to warrant it.[304] 'We beg to inform you', Gibbs politely told their customers on 24 December 1856, 'that our price for guano was advanced last evening to £13 per ton for 30 tons

[298]See Rivero to Antony Gibbs & Sons, 21 June 1856. (In Rivero, pp. 134-5).

[299]*Ibid., loc. cit.*

[300]See Rivero, p. 135; Melgar to Peruvian foreign minister, 12 August 1856. (In *ibid.*, p. 272).

[301]Gibbs, *Contestación*, p. 14.

[302]HHGC, 2, Henry Gibbs to William Gibbs, 3 October 1856.

[303]Gibbs, *Contestación*, p. 14.

[304]Rivero to Peruvian foreign minister, 30 December 1856. (In Rivero, pp. 64-5). See also Gibbs, *Contestación*, p. 14.

and upwards; £14 5s. for 1 ton up to 30 tons. All other conditions of sale remaining unaltered'.[305] This short circular marks the high water mark of the guano business in Britain. The tide of prosperity in the trade started receding almost at once. If Gibbs thought another guano shortage offered the best opportunity for fulfilling the government's instructions, then they made a most serious error. An inadequate supply was bad enough; higher prices into the bargain were more than farmers were prepared to tolerate. Offences against customers were compounded and the guano trade passed its peak.

In bidding for wider profit margins the Peruvian government may well have been responding to more than mere opportunity. Two other important factors may have had a bearing on the matter: the desire to preserve a wasting asset and the compelling need for increased income to help alleviate mounting financial difficulties. Of these, the latter was almost certainly the more powerful. Peru's debt commitments had been greatly enlarged. Guano profits had enabled the country to arrange for the settlement of old external debts in 1848, 1849 and 1853, and fresh borrowings had begun again in 1853.[306] There had also occurred in the early 1850s a massive and fraudulent expansion of the internal debt, accompanied by irregular operations converting a portion of this new paper into external bonds with a large guano hypothecation.[307] And, of course, under the prevailing guano export system, substantial anticipatory advances could be raised from contractors. With such varied and growing debt accumulations, a good deal of guano earnings went directly to creditors. And in 1855-6, during the last phase of the price increases, no large new alleviating loans were contracted with either merchants or bondholders. These problems of indebtedness were compounded, as noted above, by massive increases in government expenditure and the progressive erosion of the old internal tax structure. In circumstances such as these a government was likely to grasp eagerly at the possibility of increased revenues from the guano trade.

The point about slowing down the depletion of a wasting asset is of lesser importance. There certainly was a strong long-term case for decelerating the trade and taking the highest possible unit returns, assuming that prices were not inflated to a point at which the market withered into insignificance. But long-term considerations could

---

[305] Circular reproduced in Rivero, p. 81.

[306] See Romero, p. 376; Mathew, 'Debt', *passim; ibid.*, 'Anglo-Peruvian Commercial and Financial Relations, 1820-65' (unpublished Ph.D. thesis, London University, 1964), pp. 277-309.

[307] See chapter 4.

hardly have had much influence on governments in Lima in the 1850s, struggling with immediate and pressing financial difficulties, eager to seize the spoils of office, and unlikely to be in power for very many years. This is not to say that there was no awareness of the exhaustibility problem and its implications. 'It is quite true', wrote the Peruvian finance minister, José Paz Soldán in 1853, 'that with all products whose quantity can be increased through labour and manufacturing, price reductions bring their own reward . . . but it is also the case that the principle is inapplicable to commodities whose supply is finite. Each ton of guano that is consumed represents an irreversible diminution: this resource cannot be reproduced through labour or manufacturing; every reduction in its price means a loss of capital'.[308] This was a little exaggerated, considering that there were labourers in the sky and raw materials in the sea, but the statement did underline the fact that what was an appropriate economic philosophy for a manufacturing country was not of equal relevance for one trading off manure heaps. Peruvian thinking, therefore, was not unsophisticated on the matter, but such notions probably had little impact on policy. We have already made the point about short-term pressures. To this might be added the fact that guano exhaustibility did not appear as a problem of any immediacy in the mid-1850s. In 1851 it was observed, semi-officially, that at current exporting rates the estimated deposits of over 26 million tons would last until the year 2112.[309] Taking a more modest view of the future, the British chargé d'affaires wrote in 1854 that it would take almost 40 years to exhaust the Chincha islands alone, and that the mass of other deposits might be regarded as virtually inexhaustible.[310] In 1859 an American commercial journal cited a figure of 27 million tons for the Chincha and other deposits.[311] Three years later it was estimated that Chincha had 9 million tons; enough for 23 years at an exporting rate of 400,000 tons annually.[312] The bleakest calculation was one mentioned by Sulivan in 1857 which gave Chincha only 6-8 million tons.[313] Even this last figure, however, hardly brought the day of clearance close enough to alarm the short-tenure ministers of finance in Lima, beset as always by a host of immediate budgetary difficulties. When such men wrote to

[308]Paz Soldán to Sulivan, 5 December 1853. (In Rivero, pp. 230-5).

[309]L.E.S., pp. 45-6.

[310]FO 61/146, Sulivan to Clarendon, 11 June 1854.

[311]*DBCR*, 41 (1859), p. 645.

[312]*HMM*, 46 (1862), p. 86.

[313]FO 61/172, Sulivan to Clarendon, 12 March 1857.

London of the need to advance prices, they never once mentioned depletion as a relevant consideration.

THE 'GUANO QUESTION' OF 1851-2

The most dramatic expression of discontent among farmers over what were held to be excessively high guano prices came in 1851 and 1852. In these years the agricultural community, in league with shipping and mercantile interests, attempted to alleviate the problem through political action. The object of attack was not merely the £9 5s. price but the whole monopoly-import system which made high and rigid prices possible. As already suggested, the timing of the farmers' agitation owed much to the serious slump in produce prices. (The shipping interest too was greatly concerned over low freight rates). Beyond that, the trouble might be viewed in two ways, from which differing conclusions can be drawn. On the one hand it might be taken to represent the enormous importance which British farmers attached to guano consumption. Their pain was that of dependence. On the other hand, it might be regarded as the first big storm signal, indicating the possibility of severe consumer resistance if further offence were given to a sensitive purchasing public. Gibbs and the Peruvian government clearly took the first view, although the consignees did recognise that ill-will had been generated and that it might recur in the future. Peru's critics in 1852 expressed more than mere dissatisfaction; they revealed a good deal of chauvinistic hostility and self-righteousness as well. When their cause failed, as it did, they resorted to other and quieter approaches to the problem. Allegiance was transferred, at first very gradually, and then very rapidly, to other fertilizers. In the early 1850s the method had been dramatic and the achievement modest. In the late 1850s it was the other way round. In between, by displaying such an interest in guano, the farmers were giving Peru the rope to hang herself with. It was not, of course, a deliberate plot, but it was not any the less effective for that. When the day of reckoning appeared to have arrived for Peru there was little sympathy to be had. 'Like a pig swimming, monopoly going too fast a-head will only end by cutting its own throat'.[314]

The agitation was most in evidence in 1852. It had, however, been building up for some years. In July 1849 Sir Robert Peel sent a memorandum to Lord Palmerston, then foreign secretary, advising him that the system of guano importing, and the high prices ensuing from it, were injuring the agricultural interest. Peel had retired from active politics and had assumed the role of improving landlord on his

[314]'The Guano Crisis', *FM,* 3rd ser., 11, no. 3 (March 1857), p. 267.

family's estates in the Midlands.[315] He alleged that excessive mercantile profits were the reason for guano's costliness and that if the Gibbs monopoly were scrapped prices could fall to £6 and consumption greatly expand. 'It is difficult', he wrote, 'to estimate the advantages to agriculture of a reduction in the Price of Guano to the extent of one third'.[316] Palmerston immediately sent an account of Peel's views to the British chargé d'affaires in Lima, William Pitt Adams, instructing him to contact the Peruvian government and 'point out to them that their Interests . . . are much injured by the Monopoly which now exists'.[317] Adams noticed, however, that Peel and Palmerston were misinformed on a number of points: Gibbs certainly had a monopoly in sales, but the more basic monopoly — that of ownership — was in the hands of the government. There was, nonetheless, an argument to be made out for lower prices and he decided to present this verbally to the Peruvian authorities. Discovering 'that the Ministers of Foreign Affairs and of Finance were but slightly acquainted with the subject' he sought an interview with Castilla, 'who has made this subject his particular study . . .'.[318] The president, as it turned out, proved quite inflexible. His objective, he indicated, was the establishment of Peru's credit on a firm basis, and for that purpose present sales policies and systems seemed the most appropriate. Guano could, of course, be sold for a fixed sum to private speculators at the islands, but as such men would want higher returns than those Gibbs earned from their commissions and as freight rates would probably rise as different merchants competed for the available shipping, such a change would only serve to increase guano prices in Britain. It would also mean the accumulation of funds in Lima rather than London and offer increased temptations to the many revolutionary aspirants in Peru. Castilla said that this was his biggest worry and that he was glad to have the chance to talk about it since it could not be mentioned in any public

---

[315] There were many who wrote and spoke on the issue of guano prices and supplies, and the briefest descriptive details will be given for most of them. These are based on a wide variety of sources, and it is unnecessary to cite them individually. Much use was made of volumes in the splendid English Local History Collection in the Library of Leicester University. A number of standard biographies and books on the British peerage and landed classes generally were also consulted, as were the volumes on Cambridge, Glasgow, and Oxford undergraduates edited by J. and J. A. Venn, W. Innes Addison and Joseph Foster respectively. Another importance source was the *Dictionary of National Biography*.

[316] FO 61/124, Peel to Palmerston, 12 July 1849 ('Observations respecting the Monopoly given by the Peruvian Government to Messrs Gibbs & Myers of supply to the Market of their Country of Peruvian Guano').

[317] FO 61/121, Palmerston to Adams, 16 July 1849.

[318] FO 61/122, Adams to Palmerston, 12 October 1849.

declaration or document. Adams thought the political argument a strong one and observed further that 'the Bondholders would have a very doubtful security if their funds passed through Lima'. Peru, he noted, was bound to make the most of her natural monopoly in nitrogenous guano. The best hope for overcoming the price problem, he suggested, lay in the discovery of fresh deposits elsewhere or in the processing of cheap and effective alternatives.[319] Palmerston did not argue the matter further and sent Sir Robert Peel a full abstract of Adam's report.[320] Peel, however, died only a few months later, and the debate was taken up by others.

A copy of the report was also sent in July to Sir Robert Clive,[321] a Shropshire M.P. and friend and near-neighbour of Peel's, who had expressed an interest in the matter. Another was despatched to the Royal Agricultural Society in November,[322] this being part of a more general exchange of views between the Foreign Office and the Society towards the end of 1850. This most powerful of all the farmers' organisations had been becoming increasingly interested in the subject of guano prices, and delegated the task of treating with the government to the Duke of Richmond.[323] Richmond was one of the founders of the Society and was also active in the Royal Highland and Agricultural Society of Scotland. He was one of the country's biggest landowners, holding very large estates in North-Eastern Scotland and in Sussex, and had been a vigorous opponent of Corn Law Repeal. He continued to be an active defender of the agricultural interest. Farmers, he had commented earlier in the year, were 'seeing ruin stare them in the face'; they would not 'patiently submit to an injury'.[324] Greville describes him variously as 'coarse', 'violent', 'furious', 'talkative', and 'clamouring'.[325] Clearly he had good credentials for leading the guano lobby. Gibbs noted in July 1851 that Richmond had been in conference with Palmerston on the subject of cheaper and more plentiful guano, and accordingly anticipated further moves by

[319]*Ibid.;* also GGC, 13 March 1850.

[320]FO 61/128, Palmerston to Peel, 11 January 1850.

[321]*Ibid.,* Palmerston to Clive, 21 July 1850; see also later exchanges with George Traill, M.P. for Caithness, in FO 61/132.

[322]FO 61/128, Palmerston to Royal Agricultural Society, 13 November 1850.

[323]Thomas Wentworth Buller, *The Hare and Many Friends. Remarks on the Monopoly of Guano* (London, 1852), pp. 6-7.

[324]Hansard, *Parliamentary Debates,* 3rd ser. (hereinafter *Parl Debs),* CVIII, 31 January 1850, col. 38.

[325]Lytton Strachey and Roger Fulford (eds.), *The Greville Memoirs, 1814-1860* (London, 1938), V, p. 336; VI, pp. 196, 270.

the British government on the matter.[326] Richmond also took the government to task in May for permitting the local colonial authorities to impose a £2 per ton export charge on a small guano deposit in Western Australia. This seemed to him inexcusable at a time when British farmers were experiencing such hardship from falling produce prices.[327]

A new and, in the event, more influential voice was added to the debate in the spring of 1851: that of Thomas Wentworth Buller, a formal naval officer, a governor of the Royal Agricultural Society, and one of the Tithe and Enclosure Commissioners for England and Wales. Like Richmond he was a convinced protectionist, having many years earlier written a challenge to David Ricardo's advocacy of free trade in grain.[328] His stake in the land, however, was much more modest. He was lord of the manors of Whimple, Strete, Raleigh and Cobdon in the parish of Whimple in Devon. His main role in the guano agitation was to introduce the issue of ownership of the Lobos islands into the debate: the issue that was to generate much of the heat in 1852. In the spring of 1851 he visited the library of the Royal Geographical Society and examined the book that had activated the Ichaboe trade in the 1840s: Benjamin Morrell's *A Narrative of Four Voyages*.[329] In it he read of Morrell's call at the Lobos islands, off northern Peru, in September 1823 where he observed 'dung of aquatic birds . . . sufficient to load thousands of ships, having been accumulating for untold ages'.[330] On 18 April Buller wrote to Palmerston citing Morrell and suggesting that Peru could hardly have legitimate claims over such 'desert islands' well off her coast.[331] He asked for a warship to be sent to check that they were in fact unoccupied and to protect British merchant vessels which, skirting the Chincha monopoly, might wish to load guano at Lobos. 'If, as an agriculturist, I submit to all the disadvantages of Free Trade, it is but just and reasonable that I should expect a share of its advantages, the greatest of which would be the obtaining of this most valuable manure at a moderate price . . .'.[332] This was to become a common theme of the protesting agriculturists and shippers: since they both had had to

[326]GGC, 16 January 1851.

[327]*Parl Debs,* CXVI, 23 May 1851, cols. 1315-6.

[328]Thomas Wentworth Buller, *A Reply to a Pamphlet, published by David Ricardo, Esq. M.P., on Protection to Agriculture* (London, 1822).

[329]See Buller, *Hare and Many Friends,* pp. 13-4; Buller to Palmerston, 18 April 1851, in *Correspondence Respecting the Guano Islands of Lobos De Tierra & Lobos de Afuera, 1833-1852, PP,* 1852, LIV (hereinafter *Lob Corr*), pp. 157-8.

[330]*Lob Corr,* p. 121.

[331]The Lobos de Tierra group was about 12 miles from the mainland, and Lobos de Afuera roughly 40 miles distant.

[332]Buller to Palmerston, 18 April 1851 (*Lob Corr.* pp. 157-8).

swallow the liberal philosophies of the Corn Law and Navigation Law repealers they could demand consistency and propose a like removal of restrictions from the guano trade. Palmerston, however, was unimpressed. He directed his under-secretary, Lord Stanley, to reply that Peru seemed to have 'a *prima facie* claim' to Lobos for reasons of proximity and that there was 'no ground upon which the British Government would be justified in claiming for British subjects the right to appropriate at their pleasure the guano to be found on those islands'.[333] A few weeks later he sent off another despatch to Adams instructing him to urge on the Peruvian government the necessity of supplying Britain with larger quantities of guano at lower prices, thereby, it was suggested, increasing its own revenues at the same time as pleasing the British consumer. Lobos was not mentioned.[334] Adams replied, as before, that there seemed little chance of persuading Peru to change her policies except through competition in the market with other manures.[335]

Later in the month the question of guano prices and supplies was first raised in Parliament. Thomas Alcock, the member for East Surrey and a small landowner in that county, asked for decisive action to break the monopoly and lower the price, and suggested the possible imposition 'of very high customs duties . . . to bring the Government of Peru to its senses'.[336] Palmerston's answer was that a tariff would probably do more harm to the farmers than to the Peruvians.[337] A few days later Alcock again received fairly cursory dismissal, this time from Henry Labouchère, the president of the Board of Trade.[338] The high price of guano was the subject of a letter received at the Foreign Office in mid-July from Alderman David Salomons, who represented Greenwich in the Commons and held land in Kent. He was also a City man and was able to inform Palmerston of some of the financial aspects of the trade.[339]

Despite Alcock's failure to set the issue alight, the Peruvian minister in London, Francisco de Rivero, felt a little uneasy that exchanges on the question had taken place at all in one of the highest chambers in the land and that everyone seemed to assume Peru was in the wrong. At his own request he had a meeting with Palmerston at the beginning of August. The discussion was not particularly reassuring.

[333] Stanley to Buller, 10 May 1851 (*ibid.,* pp. 158-9).

[334] FO 61/129, Palmerston to Adams, 1 July 1851.

[335] FO 61/130, Adams to Palmerston, 8 September 1851.

[336] *Parl Debs,* CXVIII, 17 July 1851, col. 966.

[337] *Ibid.,* cols. 966-7.

[338] See Rivero to Peruvian foreign minister, 9 August 1851. (In Rivero, pp. 225-9).

[339] FO 61/132, Salomons to Palmerston, 19 July 1851.

The foreign secretary asserted, in Rivero's words, that Peru 'ought not to speculate in the nourishment of the human race thereby alienating the goodwill of friendly countries . . .'.[340] Making use of what he had learnt from Salomons he asserted that 'the profits were enormous', and that Peru was 'only emptying the pockets of the farmers to fill those of the bondholders. . . .'[341] Rivero in reply gave a stout defence of his country's right to do as it chose, but pointed out in his report of the occasion to Lima that 'the desire to procure the fertilizer at the lowest possible price is a vehement one . . .'. Palmerston, like all his colleagues in the Cabinet, 'wishes to help alleviate the sufferings of the farming classes . . .'.[342] A week after seeing Rivero, Palmerston sent off yet another despatch to Adams, setting out the familiar argument that lower prices would bring larger sales, insisting that this could do Peru no harm since the deposits were inexhaustible, and pointing out that a continuation of high prices would stimulate competition to a degree that might prove very damaging to guano.[343] Adams duly got in touch with the Peruvian government and received what he described as 'a courteous but evasive' reply.[344] British pretensions, in fact, were always handled with much patience. 'I have', reported Adams, 'used the arguments with which Your Lordship has supplied me in favour of the diminution of the price of Guano on every occasion but am generally reminded of the irresistible law of supply and demand which England has so amply developed, and I have little reason to think Peru will ever be persuaded to forego the full advantage of the monopoly with which Nature has endowed her except in obedience to that law and by open competition with such other discoveries or inventions as may supplant her in the Market'.[345]

In February 1852 there occurred a political change which the farmers initially hoped would be greatly to their benefit. The anti-protectionist Whig government of Lord John Russell resigned and an administration was formed by the Earl of Derby, leader of the anti-Peelite protectionist rump of the Tory party. 'The farmers' friends' had come to power. Derby had frequently pronounced on the need for a revived corn tariff. He immediately sowed doubt and disappointment among his supporters when he became prime minister, however, by declaring that he would only restore protection when public opinion

[340]Rivero, p. 22.

[341]Rivero to Peruvian foreign minister, 9 August 1851, loc. cit.

[342]Ibid.

[343]FO 61/130, Palmerston to Adams, 11 August 1851.

[344]Ibid., Adams to Palmerston, 20 November 1851.

[345]Ibid.

had expressed itself emphatically in its favour.[346] He could carry no parliamentary majority for it and needed an election to help resolve the issue. Many of the farmers who were soon to press Derby for action on guano were asking not so much for support from a sympathetic friend as compensation from a man who was seeming to betray them. Much of the anger directed against Peru was generated by the fear that protection had perhaps become a lost cause. 'The most valuable Protectionist figures', *Punch* commented, 'are those that are stationed in corn-fields to frighten the birds away, as they at least consist of genuine rags and real straw, and do actually serve the purpose of protection to agriculture'.[347] As the *Edinburgh Review* saw it, the farmer had been deluded and misled over recent years. 'Instead of telling him the plain truth, that the Corn Law settlement cannot be disturbed, they have inflated his mind with false hopes, and soured it with vain regrets . . . '.[348]

In March Thomas Wentworth Buller wrote to Lord Malmesbury, the new foreign secretary, in the hope that he would prove more amenable than Palmerston on the matter of the Lobos islands. He wanted the Law Officers of the Crown to consider the view of Mr. Wingrove Cooke, a lawyer, who believed that since Peru had not occupied the islands they were 'still *juris gentium*, and . . . may by occupancy become the property of any sovereign State'.[349] But the Foreign Office could see no good reason to change its policy. Lord Malmesbury, it was stated, agreed entirely with the views already expressed by Lord Palmerston.[350] The Lobos issue, however, was gradually seeping out into the arena of public discussion. In March Gibbs took note of the 'new discovery' in the Pacific.[351] Towards the end of the month reports on Lobos guano appeared in the *Shipping and Mercantile Gazette*. Application was made to the Admiralty by interested parties for naval protection, but this was refused.[352] A similar request came in mid-April from the powerful Liverpool Shipowners' Association. Its chairman, Robert Rankin, said that several ships were being sent out from Liverpool and their owners needed to know what sort of assistance they could expect against

---

[346]*Parl Debs,* CXIX, 27 February 1852, cols. 898-9, 905.

[347]*Punch,* 8 May 1852, p. 195.

[348]'Lord Derby's Ministry and Protection', *ER,* 95 (April 1852), p. 581.

[349]Buller to Malmesbury, 24 March 1852 (*Lob Corr,* pp. 159-60).

[350]Addington to Buller (*ibid.,* p. 160).

[351]GGC, 16 March 1852; also 1 April 1852.

[352]See *The Times,* 26 March 1852, p. 8, and 3 April 1852, p. 8.

'interference by Peru'.[353] The answer was that legal commerce would be protected, but that no special directives had been issued on guano loading.[354] Not discouraged, Rankin made later approaches to both the foreign secretary[355] and the prime minister. 'I need not impress upon your Lordship', he wrote to Derby, 'the great value the guano on these islands would be to this nation, as affording vast employment to our shipping, now so greatly depressed . . . .'.[356] The possibility of taking guano from Lobos and by-passing the Peruvian monopoly was set most clearly before the public by Thomas Wentworth Buller on 17 April. *The Times* published a long letter from him which was a clear call to action and opened the way to much more intense agitation. Buller reiterated the legal case, as he saw it, for occupation, arguing that Peru could have no claim to the islands and was operating a guano monopoly 'injurious to the whole civilized world', in particular to British farmers and shippers. Such parties, he wrote, 'must feel, that whoever may be Minister, they are equally doomed to suffer all the disadvantages of free trade. It will be their own fault if they do not obtain some of the advantages'.[357]

The Peruvian Legation immediately countered by stating very clearly, in a brief document published in *The Times* on 22 April, what its government's claims were. The islands had been part of the Spanish Vice-Royalty; they had been visited for centuries by fishermen from Lambayeque province; they came under the jurisdiction of the Libertad department; and their guano had been surveyed and measured by the government in the 1840s. Naval vessels already patrolled the waters nearby to prevent both foreigners and Peruvians from removing the guano, and any foreign ships found loading there would be seized.[358] This warning was followed up by a meeting between Rivero and Malmesbury on 3 May, and on 4 May the foreign secretary was sent a letter and some documents proving that Lobos was occupied by Peru and that the quantity of guano there[359] was much smaller than commonly supposed: only 742,576 tons, according to an 1847 survey.[360] Malmesbury did not trouble to acknowledge the letter.

[353]Rankin to the lords commissioners of the Admiralty, 13 April 1852 (*Lob Corr*, pp. 168-9).

[354]Hamilton to Rankin, 14 April 1852 (*ibid.*, p. 169).

[355]Rankin to Malmesbury, 27 April 1852 (*ibid.*, p. 170).

[356]Rankin to Derby, 21 April 1852 (*ibid.*, p. 168); also GGC, 1 May 1852.

[357]*The Times*, 17 April 1852, p. 8.

[358]*Ibid.*, 22 April 1852, p. 6.

[359]There were six small islands in all — Lobos de Afuera and five in the Lobos de Tierra group. See Rivero to Malmesbury, 4 May 1852 (*Lob Corr*, p. 173).

[360]*Ibid.*, p. 199.

If it was intended to put an end to the unrest, the Peruvian Legation's statement was quite ineffectual. On 4 May, John Rae, an Aberdeen merchant, wrote to the Admiralty asking whether he could expect naval protection for vessels he wished to send to Lobos.[361] On 5 May there was a public meeting of shipowners in Dundee, who sent a memorial to Malmesbury requesting either British possession of Lobos or government action to secure free access there. Erosion of the Gibbs monopoly would benefit them through 'open competition for British shipping in the trade'.[362] Malmesbury answered through H. V. Addington that the government was not 'at present' prepared to protect British vessels loading at Lobos.[363] It was not the firmest of replies, and combined with Malmesbury's silence over Rivero's letter, suggests that the government had not clearly determined its policy.

Meanwhile the farmers were also becoming more active and there was much concern over the government's passivity. As one man saw it, agriculture was being asked to pay the interest on the Peruvian debt and had been thrown 'overboard for the sake of the bondholders'.[364] A Shropshire landlord implored *The Times* to use all its influence 'to hasten the abolition of this shameless monopoly'.[365] The farming newspaper *Mark Lane Express* commented that since free trade in corn now seemed to be 'un fait accompli,' we consider that all parties concurring it its propriety are more especially bound to advocate free trade in guano'. The Lobos islands ought to be occupied by Britain: 'we do say that the present ministers of this country are bound by the most imperative sense of duty to consider not merely what may be generous towards Peru, but what may be just towards the English agriculturists and shipowners'.[366] In the middle of May Gibbs reported 'great agitation about Lobos, and the Huano trade in general'.[367] On 7 May there had occurred the first of many public meetings of farmers demanding action. It took place in Inverness, and the local member of parliament, Charles Lennox Cumming-Bruce, was asked to urge on the government 'the necessity of a speedy attention to the very important subject of free and more extended trade

[361]FO 61/137, Rae to Pakington, 4 May 1852.

[362]Memorial of the Shipowners of Dundee Unto the . . . Earl of Malmesbury, 5 May 1852 (*Lob Corr,* pp. 200-1).

[363]Addington to Clarke, 11 May 1852 (*ibid.,* p. 201).

[364]*The Times,* 4 May 1852, p. 8.

[365]*Ibid.,* 5 May 1852, p. 6.

[366]*MLE,* 10 May 1852, p. 8.

[367]GGC, 16 May 1852.

in guano'.[368] This he did, and received a reply virtually identical to that delivered to the Dundee shippers.[369] Later in the month a signed memorial was sent to Malmesbury from the farmers, shipowners and merchants of Inverness-shire and Ross-shire.[370] On 18 May a similar document, with 48 signatures, was despatched by the farmers of Northamptonshire through the agency of Thomas Maunsell, a local M.P. and landlord.[371] On 24 May 164 farmers attending the Edinburgh corn market forwarded a memorial through Sir John Hope, the member for Midlothian.[372] A few days later the farmers of the Doncaster area in Yorkshire sent in their demands.[373]

The question, clearly, was becoming something very much more than the sporadic complaints and solicitations of a few disgruntled individuals and the Royal Agricultural Society. At the end of May it once again came before Parliament. Peru's claims to Lobos were queried by William Bagge, a substantial East Anglian landowner and the member for West Norfolk.[374] He was answered by Lord Stanley, the under-secretary at the Foreign Office, who stressed the continuity of policy between his government and its predecessor and, after alluding to the claims of both Peru and the would-be Lobos-seizers, stated that Britain did not intend to challenge Peru or send any warships to the islands.[375] Sir Francis Baring, the first lord of the Admiralty in the previous administration, said he had heard directly from the Pacific that a warship was on its way to protect British traders at Lobos,[376] but Stanley informed him that the vessel was Guayaquil-bound and had simply been asked to look in at the islands when passing and make a report.[377] These remarks, it seems, were not well received. 'Nothing', reported *The Times,* 'could have been more perplexing or unsatisfactory than the effect produced in the House of Commons last night regarding the guano question and the Lobos islands'. The government, it suggested, had not proved the full

---

[368]Dallas to Bruce, 10 May 1852 (*Lob Corr*, pp. 201-2).

[369]Addington to Bruce, 17 May 1852 (*ibid.*, p. 203).

[370]FO 61/137, Memorial to the Right Hon. Her Majesty's Secretary of State for the Foreign Department . . . , 29 May 1852. See also *Lob Corr*, p. 202.

[371]Memorial from Owners and Occupiers of Land in Northampton, 18 May 1852 (*Lob Corr*, pp. 203-4).

[372]FO 61/137, Hope to Malmesbury, 24 May 1852.

[373]*Ibid.*, Fenton to Malmesbury, 29 May 1852.

[374]*Parl Debs*, CXXI, 27 May 1852, col. 1199.

[375]*Ibid.*, cols. 1199-1201.

[376]*Ibid.*, col. 1201.

[377]*Ibid.*, 28 May 1852, col. 1293.

validity of Peruvian claims and in default of that could not just sit back and allow Peru to bring Lobos within the orbit of her 'baneful monopoly' and treat British traders 'as common robbers'. The least that could be done was to refer the matter to the Law Officers of the Crown, and then resolve the uncertainty one way or another with 'an unequivocal statement'.[378] Two days later the *Mark Lane Express* wrote that if it was to be accepted that Lobos was Peruvian, then the British government should find ways to *compel* Peru to sell guano at a lower price.[379]

At the end of May the Peruvian minister in London was again in touch with Malmesbury, seeing him on the 27th, and writing him a formal note on the 28th. Rivero complained that his letter of 4 May had still not been answered. He was a little unsettled by a remark of Malmesbury's that Lobos was Peruvian 'according to appearances'. This seemed less than unambiguous acknowledgement of Peruvian rights. In his letter of the following day Rivero added a fresh item of information in the hope of finally settling the issue. The Peruvian government, he had just heard, had prohibited foreign ships from sealing at Lobos back in the 1830s, and this assertion of Peruvian sovereignty had been accepted by the then British minister in Lima, Belford Wilson. He pointed out to Malmesbury that Wilson, now the minister in Venezuela, was presently in London and could therefore be easily consulted on the matter.[380] Malmesbury was willing to give Rivero some clear satisfaction right away. He produced a statement on 31 May declaring that no warships could be sent to Lobos to protect any illegal British traders there, and gave the Peruvian minister authority the day after to publish this.[381] The document, however, queried Peru's claims to the islands, and Rivero sent it back to the foreign secretary expressing dissatisfaction with the persisting ambiguity.[382] Malmesbury was not prepared to say outright that Britain accepted the claims, but agreed to remove remarks implying that the claims were questionable.[383] He also followed up Rivero's suggestion about contacting Belford Wilson. There had, indeed, he discovered, been a Lima government decree, dated 6 September 1833, prohibiting foreign vessels from fishing off the Peruvian coast.[384] In March 1834 Wilson had received a complaint from

[378]*The Times,* 29 May 1852, p. 6.

[379]*MLE,* 31 May 1852, p. 8.

[380]Rivero to Malmesbury, 28 May 1852 (*Lob Corr,* p. 205).

[381]FO 61/136, Malmesbury to Rivero, 1 June 1852.

[382]*Ibid.,* Rivero to Malmesbury, 2 June 1852.

[383]*Ibid.,* Malmesbury to Rivero, 7 June 1852.

[384]See enclosure in Wilson to Bidwell, 23 September 1833 (*Lob Corr,* p. 125).

the Peruvian foreign ministry that a British schooner had violated the law by killing seals at the Lobos islands.[385] Wilson had been disinclined to rebut this complaint, but had taken the precaution of writing to Palmerston, then foreign secretary, for advice.[386] 'Lord Palmerston stated to me in reply, that there did not appear to be any grounds for disputing the right of Peru to the possession of the islands in question'.[387] A precedent therefore had been set. Wilson wrote to Malmesbury of his conviction 'that it would neither redound to the honour or well-understood interest of Great Britain as a State, to put forth or to uphold pretensions, on the part of British subjects, that are not founded in justice or supported by international rights...'. He also sent him extracts from eighteenth-century books citing Lobos as part of the Spanish Vice-Royalty of Peru: it was, he asserted, 'too late in the day' to challenge Peru's rights in the matter.[388]

Malmesbury's problem, of course, was that large numbers of aggrieved British subjects were still clamouring for some effective action over guano prices, and were already disillusioned over the government's failure to act on other issues affecting their livelihood. 'The Lobos controversy still rages', Gibbs reported at the beginning of June.[389] There had, they wrote, been many public meetings and an 'extraordinary excitement'.[390] The statements in the House of Commons had in no way quietened the storm. The *Glasgow Herald,* in no mood for legal niceties, insisted that even if Lobos did belong to Peru, 'it is never to be conceived that the Government of that country is to be allowed to keep under lock and key deposits of such immense importance to the universal human family...'.[391] On 2 June around 200 farmers and merchants assembled in the Court House in Dumfries and signed a long memorial declaring that Britain would become a land of plenty if only she could acquire more guano at a lower price. If Peru proved obstinate, the government should apply 'vigorous and sincere remonstrances'. The message was entrusted to a powerful deputation who arranged a meeting with Lord Malmesbury a few days later.[392] This was led by the Duke of Buccleuch, a past

---

[385]Corbacho to Wilson, 28 March 1834 (*ibid,* p. 126).

[386]Wilson to Palmerston, 1 April 1834 (*ibid,* p. 126).

[387]Wilson to Malmesbury, 7 June 1852 (*ibid,* p. 206).

[388]*Ibid.,* pp. 206-7.

[389]GGC, 1 June 1852.

[390]*Ibid.*

[391]*GH,* 7 June 1852 (cutting in FO 61/137).

[392]FO 61/137, The Memorial of the Landholders, Farmers, and Merchants of the County of Dumfries ..., 2 June 1852.

president of the Highland and Agricultural Society and Britain's biggest landowner. Other memorials were produced shortly after by Kircudbright farmers[393] and by landlords and tenants in Kincardine-shire.[394] The Scotch, it appears, were the most active agitators. On June 8th the farmers of Ayrshire presented their requests to the government through Lord James Stuart,[395] the member of parliament for Ayr Burghs. The day after, the farmers and shipowners of the county of Nairn followed suit.[396]

The campaign reached its peak on 11 June when 'a deputation of the most influential character' met the prime minister, Lord Derby, to impress on him 'the great importance of using every possible means to obtain a cheap and abundant supply of guano' and to raise once again the specific question of the Lobos islands.[397] Thomas Wentworth Buller represented the Royal Agricultural Society of England and the Duke of Buccleuch spoke for the Highland and Agricultural Society of Scotland. The Duke of Richmond brought a memorial from Banffshire. John Hudson of Castleacre in Norfolk was the represent-ative of the tenant farmers of England. Robert Hildyard, the protectionist M.P. for Whitehaven, was there on behalf of the shipping interest. A number of other individuals representing local farming and shipping associations also presented memorials. All the well-practised arguments were produced: some spoke in moderate terms, others more vehemently. John Hudson asserted that guano at £6 would give more benefit to the farmers than any fair duty that might be placed on corn imports. This, according to *The Times,* 'was received with loud cries of "hear" ', and 'produced a marked sensation'.[398] Derby listened and then gave the deputation an account of the history and organisation of the trade and of British negotiations with Peru on guano. Clearly influenced by Belford Wilson's observa-tions, he insisted that Peru was the sole and rightful owner of the Lobos islands and that this had been accepted by a Law Officer of the Crown as far back as 1834. The British, whether they liked it or not, were entirely in Peru's hands as far as guano was concerned: she exercised a monopoly and knew that farmers were still eager to buy

[393]*Ibid.,* Memorial dated 7 June 1852.

[394]*Ibid.,* 8 June 1852.

[395]*Ibid.*

[396]*Ibid.,* 9 June 1852.

[397]*The Times,* 12 June 1852, p. 8.

[398]*Ibid. Punch* made the same point in a poem which began:

'Tis all up wi' Protection; so let's be content,
It wasn't much good but to bolster up Rent;
A ton of cheap guano'd be werth more to we,
Than all the Protection as ever could be'.

('The Substitute for Protection. Song for the Agricultural Society', 24 July 1852, p. 49).

the fertilizer, high prices notwithstanding. 'The attention of the Government would be devoted to impressing on the Government of Peru the advantages that must result from a largely increased demand, but he feared that it would be a difficult piece of diplomacy to convince them'. The deputation then withdrew, 'a good deal disappointed with the result of the interview'.[399] All the meetings and memorials, all the letters and the questions, it appeared, had been to no avail. Derby was telling the farmers and shippers that he had no intention whatever of meeting the Peruvian problem head on.

There was, however, one line of action that the government could pursue without any qualms. It was suggested only the day before the meeting with Derby in a letter from the Duke of Richmond to Lord Malmesbury. Richmond asked for searches to be undertaken for new guano deposits: 'the attention of all captains and officers employed in the tropical regions, or in surveys in different parts of the world, should be directed to the subject'. He enclosed a report naming the conditions under which guano might be found.[400] This was based in part on information supplied to him by Thomas Wentworth Buller 18 months earlier.[401] Malmesbury was glad to discover something he could do which might please the farmers. Naval surveys by under-employed vessels in different part of the world raised no legal or ethical difficulties, and the foreign secretary immediately passed on the Richmond report to the Admiralty and the Colonial Office, requesting that copies be forwarded to officers commanding British vessels in foreign stations and to governors of British colonies.[402] The Admiralty wrote back asking for 200 copies of the document.[403]

Memorials were still coming in: from Kent and Arbroath on 17 June, and from Wigtownshire on 23 June.[404] The issue was raised again in the House of Commons by Edward Cayley and Francis Scott, substantial landowners in Yorkshire and Berwickshire respectively. Answering them, Lord Stanley took the opportunity to cite the 1830s decision on Lobos and to inform the House that searches and surveys in the name of the British government were about to be undertaken for fresh deposits of guano as an alternative to a Peruvian confrontation.[405] Three days later Lord Malmesbury made a similar

[399]*The Times*, 12 June 1852, p. 8; also Buller, pp. 38-9.

[400]FO 61/137, Rivero to Malmesbury, 10 July 1852.

[401]See Buller, p. 11.

[402]See FO 61/137, Malmesbury to Richmond, 14 June 1852.

[403]FO 61/138, Stafford to Addington, 16 June 1852.

[404]In FO 61/137.

[405]*Parl Debs*, CXXII, 18 June 1852, cols. 935-6.

statement in the House of Lords, in answer to a petition from Devon farmers presented by one of the great magnates of the south-west, Earl Fortescue.[406] At the end of the month the government laid before Parliament a large body of documents pertaining to Lobos.[407]

With an abundance of official declarations now making it clear that no coercive action was going to be taken against Peru, and with the close of the purchasing season at the end of June, it was obvious that the affair was over. On July 1st the last memorial was submitted to the Foreign Office: from the Hawick Farmers' Club.[408] Parliament was dissolved and members prepared to fight an autumn election. The Lobos controversy, Gibbs wrote in mid-July, was 'now calming down'.[409] In Francisco de Rivero's view the publication of the Lobos papers and the prime minister's remarks to the deputation in June were sufficient to prove that Britain accepted Peru's sovereignty over the islands.[410] At the end of July Gibbs observed that the agitation had now ceased altogether.[411] It was about this time that Thomas Wentworth Buller published his summary of the events that he had had such a major part in shaping. It was a bitter piece of invective against the Russell and Derby governments — the latter in particular. 'The farmers' friends' had abandoned the protectionist cause, and had made no effort to give any other assistance to agriculture by way of compensation. The stance taken on the issue of guano prices and Lobos had been ineffectual in the extreme. 'I contend', wrote Buller, 'that it is of no use to ask a man to reduce his price, and at the same time to tell him as Lord Palmerston, and Lord Derby tell the Peruvian Government, that they are prepared to give whatever he asks'.[412] Britain had acted decisively on the Pacifico affair, an issue of the greatest inconsequence, but would do nothing of significance on the vital question of fertilizer supply. 'Truly it is difficult to see by what rule of proportion the affairs of this world are managed.'[413] As for the legal arguments presented by the government to justify its restraint, these Buller dismissed with an imperialist's contempt. 'There is in fact no law of nations. The laws of nations are decided by three or four of the most powerful statesmen of the three or four most powerful nations in the world.'[414]

[406]*Ibid.,* 21 June 1852, cols. 994-5.

[407]*Lob Corr;* see also GGC, 30 June 1852.

[408]In FO 61/137.

[409]GGC, 16 July 1852.

[410]Rivero to Peruvian foreign minister, 27 September 1852. (In Rivero, p. 237).

[411]GGC, 31 July 1852.

[412]Buller, p. 21.

[413]*Ibid.,* pp. 29-30.

[414]*Ibid.,* p. 30.

Before the year was out, Buller was dead.[415] With his death the guano lobby lost its most eloquent and pugilistic spokesman. Had he survived, however, it is unlikely that he would have had any success in budging the British government from its commitment to propriety. 'Every day', wrote the formerly aggressive *Mark Lane Express* in September, 'brings forth fresh proof of the sovereignty of Peru over the Lobos islands'.[416] In the same month Francisco de Rivero noted how 'the very newspapers that previously challenged our rights, now defend them. . . .'[417]

The episode had been a revealing one. It had shown that farmers attached very great importance to acquiring large quantities of low-priced guano, and that in a time of acute depression they were prepared to agitate vigorously for this objective. They carried the support of some of the most powerful representatives of landed society in Britain and managed to cause considerable embarrassment to the government. They, and those who joined the battle with them, manifested much arrogant ill-feeling towards Peru. The British government, although it refused to employ coercive measures, itself tended to speak portentously to Peru as a nation that had strayed far from the paths of liberal righteousness.

The restraint characterizing British policy is of considerable interest, given the internal political pressures. One or two people at the time ascribed this to some scheme of priorities in which greater importance was attached to financial than to agrarian interests. High guano prices suited the Peruvian bondholders, and a government that was reluctant to bring about a reduction in these prices must have had the well-being of City men at heart. This view also appears in modern interpretations, by Levin and Bonilla.[418] It is almost certainly a mistaken one. Power was undoubtedly shifting slowly out of agriculture and into industry and finance, but it was no sudden movement and the political weight of farming men was still very considerable. The repeal of the Corn Laws was a response to new pressures within society, but it was also an act of self-preservation on the part of the landed classes.[419] As for the Derby government of 1852, it was about the last that could be described as representative of some new, middle class

---

[415]Obituary in *The Times*, 3 November 1852, p. 6.

[416]*MLE*, 13 September 1852, p. 8; also *NQ*, 9 October 1852 and 23 October 1852.

[417]Rivero to Peruvian foreign minister, 27 September 1852. (In Rivero, pp. 235-8).

[418]Levin, p. 76; Bonilla, p. 236.

[419]See G. Kitson Clark, 'The Repeal of the Corn Laws and the Politics of the Forties', *EHR*, 2nd ser., 4, no. 1 (1951), p. 13; F.M.L. Thompson, *English Landed Society in the Nineteenth Century* (London, 1963), p. 186.

order. The Cabinet comprised a duke, a marquess, four earls, two barons, a baronet and only four commoners. Many of them owned vast tracts of land. Using estimates made in the 1870s[420] (the only ones available) for the size and value of the holdings of these individuals or their descendants, it can be calculated that the average property in the Cabinet extended to about 35,000 acres, yielding a gross average annual income of over £45,000. Even the four commoners, Spencer Walpole, Benjamin Disraeli, J. C. Herries and J. W. Henley, owned four to five thousand acres between them. 'It would really seem as if the Ministry had been compounded out of that "Old Nobility"', commented *Punch,* 'for which his Lordship [Derby] prayed that Wealth, Commerce, and everything in the country might die first, sooner that it should be taken away from us!'[421] Men such as these were hardly likely to be more sympathetic to a handful of financial speculators in the City of London than to the great and sturdy body of British farmers. And it ought to be remembered as well that the pressure group on guano did not exist exclusively of agriculturalists: shipowners and merchants had also been much aroused. The fact that such people already felt damaged by past government policy, in 1846 and 1849, made it all the more awkward to refuse their pleas. Why, then, were they turned away?

In the first place, Derby's was a weak administration. The only thing that lent it distinctiveness, apart from the bucolic obscurity of its members,[422] was its supposed belief in agricultural protection. This it was unable to implement, partly because some of the enthusiasm had worn thin, but mainly because no majority could be found in Parliament to support it. And so the government laid itself wide open to accusations of timidity and betrayal from its erstwhile supporters and to the contempt and ridicule of its opponents. By the end of the year it was out of office. It manifestly lacked the confidence and security necessary for pursuing bold lines of policy and engaging in foreign adventures. A second factor may have been Derby's own distaste for aggressive, bullying behaviour. In 1850 he had made a three-hour speech in the House of Lords vigorously denouncing Palmerston's policy in the Pacifico affair: acts of injustice and violence had been committed against 'a weak friendly foreign State the very weakness of which State should have been the strongest

[420]John Bateman, *The Great Landowners of Great Britain and Ireland* (London, 1878), *passim.*

[421]*Punch,* 13 March 1852, p. 112.

[422]Known as the 'Who? Who?' ministry because of the Duke of Wellington's queries when told the names of the individual appointees in February. Wilbur Devereux Jones, *Lord Derby and Victorian Conservatism* (Oxford, 1956), p. 161.

inducement upon our part to exercise the greatest forbearance . . .'.[423] In 1857 he adopted the same line over Palmerston's China policy. He was, he declared, 'an advocate for weakness against power', for 'feeble defencelessness . . . against the overpowering might of Great Britain'.[424] And whereas British governments could give some sort of legalistic gloss to their blustering activities in Greece and China, it would have been very difficult to find any justification in international law or treaty agreements for coercing Peru on the issue of guano prices. In pursuing such a policy Derby would have had to abandon the moderation that even Palmerston had adopted and dramatically betrayed his own declared notions as to the proper international behaviour of powerful states.[425]

Expressions of discontent over the high price and irregular supply of guano continued in Britain throughout the 1850s. A host of people, some very eminent, others less well-known, wrote letters to the press and asked questions in Parliament. Government spokesmen included a prime minister, two foreign secretaries, two colonial secretaries, two first lords of the Admiralty and one president of the Board of Trade.[426] And from time to time the British government made its customary pleas to the Peruvian government, all invariably quite ineffectual.[427] The heat of 1852, however, was never regenerated, and all demands for a tough, aggressive approach to the problem were dropped. Further instructions for guano surveys were sent out from the Colonial Office and the Admiralty in 1853 and 1857, but no discoveries were made that could have any significant impact on the Peruvian monopoly.[428] In 1854 Britain took possession of the Kooria Mooria islands off the coast of

[423]*Parl Debs,* CVIII, 4 February 1850, col. 258.

[424]*Ibid.,* CXLIV, 24 February 1857, cols. 1155, 1159.

[425]Belligerence, moreover, would not necessarily have won rewards. The United States adopted an aggressive line on the guano problem for a time, but without success. See *The Times,* 6 October 1852, p. 4; *Crónica Parlamentaria,* IV, p. 144; Claude Moore Fuess, *Daniel Webster* (Boston, 1930), II, p. 265.

[426]*Parl Debs,* CXXX, 14 February 1854, cols. 690-1; CXXXVII, 23 April 1855, col. 1625; CXLIV, 20 February 1857, col. 935; 23 February 1857, cols. 1032-4, 1058-9; 6 March 1857, cols. 1952-3; 16 March 1857, col. 2367; CXLV, 14 May 1857, cols. 261-2; CXLVI, 6 July 1857, col. 969; CLI, 2 July 1858, col. 931; CLV, 22 July 1859, col. 278; CLXII, 12 April 1861, col. 506; CLXIV, 23 July 1861, col. 1378. A glance at the backgrounds of these men shows how discussions on the subject in fact represented the landed interest talking to itself. The critics and questioners were members of the aristocracy and county squirearchy. The proponents and defenders of government policies likewise stood firmly on the soil.

[427]See, for example, FO 61/197, Russell to Jerningham, 10 July 1861.

[428]See, for example, naval reports in *PP,* 1857, XXXVIII, pp. 307-34.

Arabia after guano had been found there by a private trader.[429] 'I trust', wrote James Caird in 1857, 'that the Peruvian monopoly has been foiled at last'.[430] But he was being grossly over-optimistic. The deposits were low-grade and not particularly abundant, and the British government incurred a good deal of ill-feeling from farmers by permitting the establishment of a private monopoly for their exploitation. It was, commented Lord Berners, a major Leicestershire landowner and a man prominent in the Royal Agricultural Society, 'somewhat contradictory that while the Government were endeavouring to put an end to the monopoly in regard to Peruvian guano, they should be actually encouraging monopoly in regard to the supply of the same article from another part of the world'.[431] The events of the 1850s had revealed very clearly to farmers that there was unlikely to be any political solution to their problem.

THE DAMAGED MARKET, 1857-62

In December 1856 the minimum wholesale price of Peruvian guano was raised to £13 per ton. 'With one wave of his baton', wrote the *Farmer's Magazine* shortly after, 'the mighty Jullien[432] stills his audience and commands the anxious attention of his hundreds of fiddlers. With one dash of the pen do the Messrs. Gibbs achieve as grand an effect. Without even the gradual warning of an overture, we come at once to the crash. . . . Audience or musicians, customers or agents, are alike aghast.'[433] In 1856 Gibbs had sold 211,647 tons of guano in Britain. In 1857 they disposed of little more than half of that quantity: 110,490 tons. There had never been such a reverse in the history of the trade.

Although, as table 3 shows, there was some recovery in the years that followed, sales totals in the period of the Gibbs contracts never again came close to the 1856 level. The best year, 1861, was more

---

[429]For most of the relevant official documents, see *Copies or Extracts of Correspondence with the Colonial Office, respecting a Grant made by the Crown to raise and take away Guano from the Islands of Jibleca, Huskie, and Ghwrzoad, on the South Coast of Arabia; and, of the Licence under which the Grant has been made, PP*, 1857, XXXVIII. For fuller accounts of the episode see R. Coupland, *East Africa and its Invaders* (Oxford, 1938), pp. 523-44; Mathew, 'Anglo-Peruvian Relations', pp. 406-18.

[430]*The Times,* 13 March 1857, p. 9.

[431]*Parl Debs,* CXLIV, 20 February 1857, cols. 1033-4.

[432]Louis-Antoine Jullien, a flamboyant and histrionic French conductor of the mid-19th century.

[433]'The Present Price of Guano', *FM*, 3rd ser., 11, no. 2 (February 1857), p. 148.

TABLE 3: Imports and Sales of Peruvian Guano (tons): Britain, 1856-62

	Imports	Sales
1856	177,016	211,647
1857	264,230	110,490
1858	302,207	122,819
1859	49,064	132,082
1860	122,459	146,145
1861	161,566	161,707
1862	69,390	not available
Total (to 1861)	1,076,542	884,890
Annual average (to 1861)	179,423	147,482

Source: Gibbs to Rodulfo, *loc, cit., PP,* 1860, LXIV, p. 337; 1865, LII, p. 314.

than 30 per cent short of 1856, and the average for the five years 1857-61 was 36 per cent down on the 1856 figure.[434] Sales estimates are not available for the years after 1861, but other evidence suggests that 1856 may well have been the all-time peak for guano selling in Britain. Imports, for which we do have a complete series, reached their highest point in 1858 and then slumped dramatically to their lowest level since 1846, when the African competition was in full force. The trade revived somewhat in 1860 and 1861, but in 1862 it was at a level lower than that for 1849. Despite these two very poor years, however, imports exceeded sales by almost 200,000 tons between 1856 and 1861.

The European situation was not much happier. Sales on the continent (excluding France and Spain) grew from 33,144 tons in 1852-3 to 62,385 in 1853-4, 71,167 tons in 1854-5, and 105,019 tons in 1855-6. There was a slide backwards to 86,348 tons in 1856-7 and 70,179 in 1857-8. A small recovery in 1858-9 pulled the figure up to 84,808 tons.[435] There clearly was no calamitous fall in sales, and

[434]It is possible, although there is no confirmation on the point, that Gibbs included the sales they made to European clients from London in their figures. Even if this was so, and if *all* the guano exported from Britain in these years was *Peruvian* guano which Gibbs had sold to continental buyers, 1856 still remains a peak for specifically British consumption (although the measure of recovery achieved by the last year of the period becomes more marked). *PP,* 1860, LXIV, 32 and 337; 1865, LII, 33 and 314; 1870, LXIII, p. 305 and LXVIII, p. 81.

[435]Rivero, Estado de las ventas. Sales in British colonial markets reveal no very clear trend. Gibbs's sales peak came in 1859 when 7,847 tons were disposed of. Figures for 1854-61 were, in sequence, 1,021; 696; 1,950; 7,099; 6,999; 7,847; 5,238; and 5,044 tons. *Ibid.*

of course the figures for the late 1850s were very much higher than those for the early 1850s. Even for Britain itself, one can exaggerate the problem. Sales in 1860, for example, were higher than they had been in 1852; sales in 1861 were almost identical to those of 1855. As for gross proceeds, these were much higher in the late 1850s than they had been a few years earlier. Obviously we are not discussing any terrible crisis for the Peruvian treasury. What is beyond doubt, however, is that in volume terms Peru's guano trade with Britain had reached and passed its peak. A phase of rapid acceleration had very abruptly come to an end. Guano had entered a period of decline only a decade and a half after the trade had begun. Annual average imports into Britain in 1855-9 had stood at 209,610 tons (£2,546,744). In 1860-4 they were at 132,641 tons (£1,617,254); in 1865-9 at 167,785 (£2,055,940); in 1870-4 at 133,088 (£1,753,177); in 1875-9 at 105,376 (£1,272,000).[436] Peruvian gross earnings from guano sold in Britain were halved between the late 1850s and the late 1870s. The last years of our period, then, cover a very notable turning point in the trade.

The year 1857 was a very bad one. The rise to £13, Rivero reported home in January, 'has not failed to produce the complaints that were anticipated from the farmers'. There had been much press comment 'attacking the house of Gibbs and threatening that the use of Peruvian guano would be abandoned'.[437] Towards the end of a quite disastrous season he was advising of the need for a reduction in price.[438] Gibbs's retrospective view, however, was that the December rise 'made sense at the time, considering the inadequate stock replenishment we were anticipating during the first six months of the year, thanks to the delays that occurred in the loading of vessels at the Islands . . . '.[439] Supply was in fact the crucial problem in 1857. Shortages materialized right at the beginning of the year. Ideally, the bulk of guano imports came into the country just before and during the main consuming season.[440] In 1857, however, the quarterly sequence was 9,241; 50,417; 53,716; 174,988.[441] The importation in the first quarter in particular was grotesquely inadequate. This resulted from a massive slump in Gibbs's guano clearance rate at the Chincha islands

---

[436]*PP*, 1860, LXIV, p. 337; 1865, LII, p. 314; 1870, LXIII, p. 305; 1875, LXXIII, p. 217; 1880, LXXI, p. 215.

[437]Rivero to Peruvian foreign minister, 15 January 1857. (In Rivero, pp. 65-6).

[438]Rivero to Peruvian foreign minister, 16 May 1857. (In *ibid.,* pp. 69-70).

[439]Gibbs, *Contestación,* p. 14; also above, pp. 116-8.

[440]See *PP*, 1857, XXXVIII, pp. 4, 34, 62, 90, 120, 148, 176, 206.

[441]*Ibid.,* 1857-8, LIII, pp. 4, 36, 62, 94.

in 1856. In 1854 they had despatched on average 16,810 tons per month. In 1855 this had risen to 23,480, and in 1857 it was as high as 31,500. In 1856, however, it fell to the astonishingly low level of 9,004 tons. The quarterly rates over the year were, in sequence, 9,621; 9,021; 5,331; and 11,786.[442] Why did this happen? A brief occupation of the Chinchas by the rebellious forces of ex-President Vivanco towards the end of 1856 is irrelevant here.[443] Gibbs's loading rate in fact rose during this period.[444] Among other possible explanations, one is labour shortage at the islands; another is that Gibbs did not charter a sufficient number of ships to carry guano in 1856. There was indeed a chronic problem of labour shortage and inadequate loading facilities at the islands, as already noted, but there is no evidence that this became notably worse in 1856. Barreda's exports to the United States decreased only slightly, from 64,293 tons in 1855 to 61,197 in 1856; and Montané found it possible to raise his exports to France to 42,131 tons, compared with only 13,961 in 1855 and 15,105 in 1854. Of the principal contractors Gibbs were alone in greatly reducing the scale of their trade: 108,046 tons removed in 1856, compared with 281,761 tons the year before.[445]

Inadequate chartering seems to have been the main problem and relates in part to Gibbs's reading of supply and demand in 1855, for it was then that most of the shipping was taken up. Sales in Britain in 1855 had registered very little advance on those of 1854, and shipping was still expensive. In late 1855 payments on earlier charters were falling due and causing the house considerable financial strain. These circumstances alone probably induced a highly cautious policy. An additional factor had been the diversion to the British market in 1855 of substantial quantities of guano from the glutted United States market.[446] According to the French chargé d'affaires in Lima, this in fact had been the main reason for Gibbs's reduced exports in 1856.[447] He exaggerated, however. Although guano imports into Britain from the United States were unusually high in 1855 — 38,082 tons, compared with 1,502 in 1854 and 1,267 in 1856[448] — the quantity

[442]ANF, sér. F 12, dossier 6860, Guiroy to Chemin Dupintes, 5 May 1858.

[443]Both Gibbs and Rivero cited it as an explanatory factor. Gibbs, *Contestación*, p. 14. Rivero to Peruvian foreign minister, 16 May 1857. (In Rivero, pp. 69-70).

[444]ANF, sér. F 12, dossier 6860, Guiroy to Chemin Dupintes, 5 May 1858.

[445]*Ibid.*

[446]See below, chapter 4, p. 190.

[447]MAE, Lima/12, Huet to Walewski, 10 September 1856.

[448]*PP.* 1854-5, L, p. 415; 1860, LXIV, p.323.

was hardly sufficient by itself to cause any drastic cut in chartering. Whatever the relative weight of these different factors, the point remains that Gibbs underestimated the amount of guano it would be appropriate to bring in for the 1857 season, and stood guilty of costly miscalculation.

At the beginning of 1857 both Gibbs and Rivero were greatly concerned at the prospect of a bare market.[449] So were many farmers, high prices notwithstanding. 'We are just now at the very height of our guano difficulty', wrote the *Farmer's Magazine*. 'That is to say, this is the season — a most favourable season, too — when above all others we need it; and there is none to be had . ..'. The British farmer, faced with excessively high prices and inexcusable shortages, was now 'in open rebellion' against Peru.[450] Mr. Baker of the Central Farmers' Club suggested that with the fact of guano scarcity 'put palpably before him', the farmer now 'saw the necessity of placing himself in a condition to be able to do without it hereafter'.[451] Francis Scott complained in the House of Commons that there had never been a period 'when the imports of that article had fallen off so much as during the last year'.[452] British farmers, he insisted, 'felt the importance of this question quite as much as the affairs in Canton'.[453]

The situation eased later in the season. By this time, of course, the market was very inactive, so most of the guano was dead-weight in the consignees' hands. And quite heavy imports continued through the late summer and autumn. The problem of guano shortage was giving way rapidly to one of glut. The market in fact remained overstocked for all the remaining years of Gibbs's contract. The focus of complaint by farmers now moved exclusively on to prices.

'The stock of Peruvian guano in London is now very large', reported the *Mark Lane Express* in May 1858: 'consumers will not take it at the present extreme price'.[454] It was also noted at about this time that there was a discrepancy between prices in Britain and in the United States: in the latter country guano was selling at £11 7s. — 33s.

[449]Rivero to Peruvian foreign minister, 30 January and 15 February 1857. (In Rivero, pp. 66-8).

[450]'The Guano Crisis', *FM*, 3rd ser., 11, no. 3 (March 1857), p. 266.

[451]'The Manure Difficulty and its Solution', *ibid.,* p. 261; also 'The Supply of Guano', *ibid.,* no.4 (April 1857), p.356.

[452]*Parl Debs,* CXLIV, 6 March 1857, col. 1951; also 'The Supply of Guano', *loc. cit.;* 'The Supply of Guano', *FM,* 3rd ser., 11, no. 4 (March 1857), p. 226; 'Liquefied Manures', *loc. cit.*

[453]A reference to current British belligerence on the China coast.

[454]*MLE,* 3 May 1858, p. 13; also 28 June 1858, p. 11.

cheaper than in the British market.[455] The under-secretary at the Foreign Office, Seymour Fitzgerald, was in communication with Gibbs about it[456] and James Caird raised the matter in the House of Commons.[457] Gibbs pointed out that a decision had already been taken to bring the British price down from £13 to £12 and to raise the United States price to the same figure.[458] The British reduction had apparently been ordered by the Peruvian government because of the low consumption in the 1858 season.[459] In 1857 they could blame bad sales on short supplies. In 1858, with very adequate stocks available, it became clear that high prices were having a powerful independent effect. Farmers, moreover, were suffering again from falling wheat prices in a period of domestic overproduction.[460] They were, according to one observer, 'unwilling to part with their money throughout the year'.[461] In 1858 sales had registered only a marginal improvement on 1857, and the overall picture was still one of diminished consumption. 'The sale of guano has much declined during the last few years in consequence of its high price', wrote Clare Sewell Read in a report on Norfolk. Farmers would 'leave off buying guano at £15[462] per ton as long as they continue to sell wheat at 5s. per bushel'.[463] The quantity bought by Scottish farmers had also 'considerably diminished', according to Thomas Anderson, as preference grew for other, cheaper applications.[464]

The reduction by £1 in July was generally regarded as inadequate. With poor wheat prices, wrote James Caird, there was 'no margin of profit to induce the farmer to buy guano'. Former customers were being 'driven to find substitutes or to do without, and in either case the guano remains unsold . . .'.[465] The same message was being delivered in Lima by S.H.Sulivan's successor as British chargé, Thomas Jerningham; the government, he considered, 'must be compelled to lower in spite of themselves'.[466] Henry Gibbs's conclusion too was that a further reduction had become essential: to £11, or possibly £10 10s., at the

[455] FO 61/184, Caird to Fitzgerald, 22 June 1858; Scott to Fitzgerald, 25 June 1858.

[456] See Parl Debs, CLI, 2 July 1858, col. 874.

[457] Ibid., cols. 873-4; also FO 61/184, Memorial from Kelso Farmers' Club, 2 July 1858.

[458] FO 61/184, Gibbs to Fitzgerald, 1 July 1858.

[459] Rivero, p. 169; also FO 61/190, Osma to Malmesbury, 24 March 1859.

[460] Fairlie, pp. 97, 100.

[461] John Keen, 'Review of the Trade in Manures and Oilcakes during 1858', FM, 3rd ser., 15, no. 2 (February 1859), p. 172.

[462] Retail price.

[463] Clare Sewell Read, 'Recent Improvements in Norfolk Farming', JRAS, 29 (1858), pp. 278-9.

[464] Thomas Anderson, 'On the Composition of Some Kinds of Guano now in the Market', THAS, new ser., 16 (July 1858), p. 351.

[465] FO 61/184, Caird to Fitzgerald, 9 July 1858.

[466] See FO 61/181, Jerningham to Malmesbury, 11 September 1858; also Keen, loc. cit.

beginning of 1859.[467] 'I don't think the Consumers are *at all* satisfied with £12', he wrote. 'On the contrary I know that many are totally abstaining from guano in consequence . . .'.[468] In the autumn he received authority from Lima to lower the price if he judged it appropriate. But by now he was having second thoughts. Sales of floating cargoes were picking up quite fast and it was felt that 'perhaps the £12 price under the adverse circumstances of the Corn market had not had a full trial . . .'. The reduction, he suggested, could now be delayed until June 1859 at the earliest.[469]

It was a curious judgement, for the task of stock clearance was a massive one. In early December 1858 459,805 tons of guano lay unsold in Gibbs's various depots around the world. 315,962 tons were in London, Liverpool and Bristol (with over a quarter of a million tons in London alone), 39,780 in le Havre, 37,443 in Valencia, 17,070 in Antwerp, 13,795 in Genoa — and so on, down to 499 tons in Sydney.[470] By the turn of the year British stocks amounted to over 320,000.[471] Business was slow in January: slower indeed than at the start of either 1857 or 1858.[472] Gibbs's expectation, however, was that the 1859 season would be better than its immediate predecessors.[473] They anticipated correctly, but the recovery over the year as a whole was a very modest one. As a result of guano's high price, it was reported in February, 'the consumption has, in almost every district, fallen short of that of former years'. The cost of purchase was still much too high in relation to current farm incomes.[474] *The Journal of Agriculture* noted in March that high guano prices had made people more sparing in their use of the Peruvian fertilizer.[475] In James Caird's opinion guano was piling up quite unnecessarily at the docks. In any normal business, he told Parliament, these stocks would come on to the market at reduced prices. But the guano trade, as currently organized, was highly abnormal. 'There was at present lying in the Victoria Docks guano enough to fill the Crystal Palace . . .'.[476]

[467]HHGC, 2, Henry Gibbs to William Gibbs, 14 September 1858.

[468]*Ibid.,* 15 October 1858; also 15 November 1858.

[469]HHGC, 2, Henry Gibbs to William Gibbs, 20 November 1858; also 15 January 1859.

[470]*Ibid.,* undated but apparently between 4 and 14 December 1858.

[471]*Ibid.,* 14 January 1859.

[472]*Ibid.*

[473]*Ibid.,* 30 December 1858.

[474]Keen, p. 172.

[475]*JA* (March 1858), p. 322.

[476]*Parl Debs,* CLII, 18 February 1859, cols. 511-2.

There is little evidence of serious concern on the part of either the consignees or the government. The feeling may well have been that low farm produce prices were the cause of the trouble and that it would be sensible to hold fast until they recovered. In May Jerningham advised in Lima once more of the need for a price reduction, but created little impression.[477] In November he reported that there were still no grounds for expecting a decrease from the Peruvian government.[478] Back in England, however, W. H. Gregory, the member for County Galway, was telling the Commons that farmers were very much disinclined to buy guano at its present price and that much ingenuity was being applied by manufacturing men to the provision of cheap alternatives.[479] The foreign secretary, Russell, estimated that 300,000 tons were still lying unsold in different parts of the country and warned that Peru might not be able to sell this off at the prices demanded since 'there were so many artificial manures in use' now.[480] The feeling of frustrating dependence on Peru, so much in evidence in the early 1850s, was passing. The farmer could come on to the market in a discriminating frame of mind and make a judicious selection from an ever-widening range of applications.

At the beginning of 1860, after some very slow sales, Gibbs started worrying again about the price level. 'I begin to doubt whether the falling off is not *real*, and whether the Government won't have to lower price in July!'[481] There was little comfort to be got from the agricultural journals. Alexander Simpson, a Scottish farmer, wrote in the *Farmer's Magazine*: 'the extravagant price put upon guano has much limited my use of it. If sold at £10 to £11 per ton, I would use it to the extent of 4/5ths of my expenditure . . .'.[482] John Keen, in his annual review of the fertilizer trade in the same journal, declared that the price of guano was 'much above its real value compared with other artificial manures' and that large accumulations were still lying unsold in the ports.[483] Gibbs calculated in mid-March that their total stocks amounted to 258,266 tons.[484] This was a considerable improvement

[477]FO 61/186, Jerningham to Malmesbury, 11 May 1859.

[478]FO 61/188, Jerningham to Russell, 26 November 1859.

[479]*Parl Debs,* CLV, 22 July 1859, cols. 277-8.

[480]*Ibid.,* col. 278.

[481]HHGC, 2, Henry Gibbs to William Gibbs, 10 February 1860.

[482]Alexander Simpson, 'High Farming with Profit', *FM,* 3rd ser., 17, no. 2 (February 1860), p. 241.

[483]John Keen, 'Review of the Artificial Manure and Oilcake Trade During the Past Year', *ibid.,* no. 3 (March 1860), p. 160.

[484]HHGC, 2, Henry Gibbs to 'Don Juan', 19 March 1860.

on the situation of a year or so earlier and had been helped by the very low importations of 1859, but with expected arrivals in Britain and the other markets of 299,126 tons.[485] and with little more than three months of the season left, it was clear that the excess-supply problem (with warehousing costs nibbling into profits) was going to persist for a good while to come. Sales in the early months of 1860 showed a small improvement on those of the same period in 1859[486] but there were no signs whatever of major recovery. Taken as a whole 1860 was a little better than 1859.[487] By December stocks in all markets amounted to 267,944 tons, with an estimated 254,000 tons on the way.[488]

It was beginning to seem likely, but by no means certain, that the Gibbs contract would not be renewed.[489] Accordingly, the house's main interest now lay in importing as much guano as it could and selling this fairly slowly at high prices. Henry Gibbs claimed that they had the right to take all the guano that could be exported during their contract period, and that since freights were still low it would be to Peru's advantage, as well as their own, to move the maximum possible quantity. It was clear, though, whose interests he was more concerned about: 'We must take whatever hard earned advantage our contract gives us — not take unfair advantage, indeed, of any man, but not throw away any privilege or vantage ground we may have acquired'.[490] These sentiments, first expressed in January 1860, and still held at the end of the year, activated a policy of fairly energetic chartering. A quarter of a million tons were expected after the end of 1860, despite the fact that the consignees and their agents held stocks of roughly that amount already.[491] William Gibbs and John Hayne (as well as others in Lima)[492] did not approve of the policy, and Henry Gibbs agreed at the end of 1860 that he had been in error. He had examined the contract, had found his case to be a bad one, and had accepted that he had the right only to export enough to satisfy the consumption up to the end of the contract.[493] By this time, of course, he had already made sure that he would be offering guano to farmers

[485]*Ibid.*

[486]*Ibid.*

[487]See *ibid.*, Henry Gibbs to William Gibbs, 12 December 1860, and consumption figures cited earlier.

[488]*Ibid.*, 2, Henry Gibbs to 'Don Juan', 12 December 1860.

[489]See chapter 4.

[490]See HHGC, 23 February 1860.

[491]*Ibid.*, 2, Henry Gibbs to 'Don Juan', 12 December 1860.

[492]See chapter 4.

[493]HHGC, 2, Henry Gibbs to William Gibbs, 12 December 1860.

for some considerable time after the expiry, but his late conversion to propriety probably put a brake on chartering in 1861. His concern was that the government might prevent his ships loading at the Chincha islands[494] or place a total ban on further chartering, but there did not seem to be all that much to worry about now: 'exclusive of any charters we may yet make, we shall have stock for the whole of the season of '62 and some to spare for the Autumn — their diligence comes too late'.[495] Such confidence was well-founded. In November 1861, just a few weeks before the contract was due to end, stocks were calculated at 230,000 tons,[496] with a lot more due to come.[497] The questionable legality of this had also been partially resolved by the government granting to Gibbs the right to supply all their old markets until the late summer of 1862.[498] This simply represented a recognition of realities.

Gibbs had no more interest in the longer-term problems of the guano trade. The case for lowering prices was one they had totally abandoned. And yet the market for guano, while continuing to recover a little each year, was still in an unhealthy condition. Agricultural dissatisfaction came before Parliament again in July 1861,[499] and it was noted in a report on farming in Yorkshire that guano was 'not so extensively used . . . as it was a few years ago, principally on account of its present high price . . .'.[500] In early 1862 Gibbs suggested that this price ought to be raised again. The transfer of control in the trade was going to cause a shortage of guano and this seemed to be a situation worth exploiting.[501] Advice was sent to Lima and instructions awaited.[502] The Peruvian government reacted promptly, ordering Gibbs to raise in all markets at their discretion.[503] The increase, to £13, was brought into effect in June 1862.[504] The likelihood of coming shortages was underlined by the fact that over the year as a whole only 69,390 tons of guano were imported from Peru. The Peruvian govern-

[494]*Ibid.*, 3 December 1860; 3, 12 December 1861.

[495]HHGC, 2, Henry Gibbs to Francisco de Rivero, 18 December 1860.

[496]*Ibid.*, Henry Gibbs to William Gibbs, 1 November 1861.

[497]See *ibid.*, 3, Henry Gibbs to William Gibbs, 4 March 1862.

[498]*Ibid.*, 2, Henry Gibbs to William Gibbs, 15 October and 16 November 1861.

[499]*Parl Debs*, CLXIV, 23 July 1861, cols. 1378 and 1402.

[500]William Wright, 'On the Improvements in the Farming of Yorkshire . . .', *JRAS*, 22 (1861), p. 109.

[501]HHGC, 3, Henry Gibbs to William Gibbs, 4 March 1862.

[502]*Ibid.*, 27 March 1862.

[503]See FO 61/206, Russell to Kernaghan, 23 September 1862.

[504]*Ibid.*, Kernaghan to Russell, 14 June 1862.

ment, for its part, was no doubt persuaded by the impending-scarcity argument. They may also have been influenced now in some measure by fears that the best Chincha guano might be depleted before the end of the decade.[505]

The price prevailed, however, for less than a year. It was brought back to £12 by Gibbs's successors early in 1863 (a year of quite heavy importations, as it turned out)[506] and remained at that level for most of the remainder of the 1860s. The new men, with their quite different, long-term perspectives, feared that allowing the £13 minimum to persist might halt and reverse the modest recovery in consumption that had been in evidence since the black year of 1857.[507] 'We are glad', the new Lima contractors wrote to their British consignees in February 1863, 'to see an end to the crisis which the rise in the price of guano caused in the English market in the last five months of the past year, and we trust that the return to the former price of £12 will enable you to maximise your returns from the sale of guano. . .'.[508] No great increase in sales, however, could be seriously expected. Too much ground had already been lost, and a good deal of it at the very price to which the contractors were now returning. The past tense was creeping into a lot of the accounts of guano's functions in British agriculture. The heyday of the trade, without question, had passed.

It might be argued that this was inevitable.[509] Low produce prices in the short run and increased competition in the long run were sufficiently powerful factors to ensure that the rapid advances of the late 1840s and early 1850s would be checked. It is very doubtful, however, if the check would have come so early and so decisively if guano prices had not risen, or risen less steeply. For one thing, the higher the price of guano the more ample the cover under which factory producers and other competitors could find the shade needed for their early growth. For another, high prices, added to irregular supplies, served to give added offence to British farmers, whose sense

[505]See *ibid.*, Russell to Kernaghan, 23 September 1862.

[506]196,704 tons: almost treble the 1862 figure. *PP*, 1865, LII, p. 314.

[507]For discussion on prices prior to the decrease, see Pardo to Thomson Bonar & Co., 28 August, 13 September, 12 and 28 November, 12 and 27 December 1862; 27 January and 12 February 1863. *Correspondencia de los Signatorios del Contrato de Consignación para la Venta del Guano en la Gran Bretaña y sus Colonias, Dirigida á los SS. J. Thomson, T. Bonar y Compañia* (Lima, 1877), pp. 16, 19, 24, 26, 27-8, 30-1.

[508]Pardo to Thomson Bonar & Co., 12 February 1863, *ibid.*, p. 31.

[509]A substantial portion of the material for the last pages of this section has already been used in the author's article, already cited, 'Peru and the British Guano Market, 1840-1870', pp. 115-6, 119-25.

of grievance against Peru had been firmly established and powerfully articulated in 1852. Peru could ill afford to intensify the hostility of the consumers in her main market, especially now that there were growing quantities of alternative applications to which they could easily transfer their loyalties. The main threat came from manufactured manures. Competition from other guanos was not a serious problem,[510] and imports of nitrate of soda reached only 15,486 tons by 1856,[511] possibly a half or more of this being used for industrial rather than agricultural purposes.[512] Superphosphate, however, was coming onto the market in ever-increasing quantities. It was described by Gibbs as 'very formidable' as early as 1850,[513] and in 1854 they wrote of 'the importance of not driving farmers to the phosphates'.[514] The rise to £11 in July 1854, they judged, had 'managed to give an extraordinary boost to the manufactures of these manures'.[515] J.C. Nesbit, the agricultural chemist, told Gibbs at the end of 1855 that every increase in the price of guano 'offers a premium to the local manufactures with whom one has to compete . . . Before the rise in the price of guano the manufacture of fertilizers here was in comparatively few hands and was a very modest business. After the rise, the increase in the numbers of factories producing manures has been extraordinary and the quantities manufactured and sold have taken on massive proportions'.[516]

---

[510]Between 1850 and 1856 Gibbs made an abundance of references, sometimes casual, sometimes concerned, to real or alleged guano discoveries overseas and to arrivals of shiploads from places other than Peru. There was not, as it happened, a great deal to worry about. Most of the other deposits were small and located in parts of the world where precipitation had removed much of the nitrogenous content of the fertilizer. Henry Gibbs had achieved a mirthful complacency by 1855 after so many alarms over external dangers. 'I don't think much of the new discoveries', he wrote. 'I 'hear of none where the rain does not fall — and as long as *their* Rain continues our Reign will also. So we will sing "Long to rain over them!" '. WGC, Henry Gibbs to William Gibbs, 9 February 1855; also GGC, 16 October and 16 November 1850, 16 January, 12 and 15 February, 15 March, 16 April, 16 May 1851; 30 July 1853; HHGC, 2, Henry Gibbs to Tyndall Bright, 2 May 1856; *The Times,* 27 November 1850, p. 6; 6 May 1851, p. 6; 12 May 1851, p. 6; 16 May 1851, p. 6; 3 July 1852, p. 3; 17 August 1853, p. 9; 18 August 1853, p. 9; 22 November 1853, p. 8; 19 June 1854, p. 10; 13 September 1854, p. 5; 19 October 1854, p. 8; 18 December 1856, p. 8; Rivero, p. 22; Antony Gibbs & Sons to Rivero, 12 October 1855 (in *ibid,* pp. 118-21); Rivero to Peruvian foreign minister, 31 May and 16 June 1856 (in *ibid.,* pp. 267-9 and 270-1); Melgar to Peruvian foreign minister, 2 June and 12 July 1856 (in *ibid.,* pp. 266-7 and 269).

[511]*PP,* 1860, LXIV, p. 16.

[512]See Anderson, 'Instructions', p. 432.

[513]GGC, 16 December 1850.

[514]WGC, Henry Gibbs to William Gibbs, 18 May 1854.

[515]Antony Gibbs & Sons to Rivero, 12 October 1855, *loc. cit.*

[516]Nesbit to Antony Gibbs & Sons, 3 December 1855, *loc. cit.*

The commanding position of Peruvian guano in the British fertilizer market in the 1840s and 1850s was in fact much more precariously based than either the government or the agents seem to have realised. Vulnerability lay principally in the widespread use of guano for turnips, the great improving crop in British agriculture. Turnips, as it happened, required a phosphatic rather than a nitrogenous manure. Guano served well in as much as it did contain a substantial proportion of phosphatic materials, but its high nitrogen content was of only limited benefit to the turnip. Cheaper fertilizers with much less nitrogen usually did just as well for turnips. Their use was only limited by the fact that they were initially in less abundant supply and by agricultural predisposition towards using the tried and tested Peruvian fertilizer while it remained moderately priced.

The most successful manure in commercial terms was likely to be the one most popular with turnip growers. Such a popularity, once secured, should have been jealously guarded. Under the four-course rotation, observed the *Farmer's Magazine* in May 1850, 'they only manure the crop once in the four years — the turnips'.[517] In the words of a German writer in the same year: 'The turnip crop is that to which these [purchased] manures have been most extensively and most successfully applied'.[518] Thomas Rowlandson voiced his approval in 1852 of the system followed in the most advanced agricultural districts: 'that of applying the manure to the first, or, as is commonly called, the green crop, rather than dividing the manure into portions and appropriating it separately to each crop'.[519] The prevalence of this system is very amply revealed in James Caird's regional surveys of English farming in 1850 and 1851.[520] 'The English farmers', wrote Léonce de Lavergne in 1855, 'spare no pains upon the turnip crop; for it they reserve almost all their manures'.[521] There were at least three very sound reasons for this. In the first place, roots were vital crops in mixed farming, especially in the drier parts of the country where it was often difficult to get a good growth of fodder grass. Large turnip crops could increase the livestock-carrying capacity of a farm and, by the same token, assist other crops in a rotation through the augmentation

---

[517]'The Proper Time of Applying Manure', *FM*, 2nd ser., 21, no. 5 (May 1850), p.459.

[518]'The History of Artificial Manures' (from the German), *JA* (July 1849), p.426.

[519]Thomas Rowlandson, 'The Science of Manuring', *FM*, 3rd ser., 2, no. 3 (September 1852), p. 198.

[520]James Caird, *English Agriculture in 1850-51* (London, 1852), pp. 13, 35, 61, 92, 101, 108, 120, 160, 195, 203, 227, 247, 324, 333, 337, 341-2, 356, 362-3, 376, 381, 384, 456.

[521]Léonce de Lavergne, *The Rural Economy of England, Scotland, and Ireland* (Edinburgh and London, 1855), p. 58.

of supplies of animal manure. Secondly, the turnip was very demanding nutritionally. Experiments were showing very clearly that root yields on unmanured land, unlike those of corn, could sink to extremely low levels.[522] Thirdly, concentrated fertilizers like guano were effective (much more so than farmyard manure) in stimulating the early growth of the plant. In the case of the turnip, rapid development in the first weeks helped it to resist the potentially ruinous attacks of the turnip fly.[523]

All this, of course, relates to fertilizers in general. It would seem to follow, however, that as guano was the main manure purchased by British farmers over most of our period it was to a very considerable extent directed towards roots.[524] The attention of people who published details of their experiments with guano in the 1840s and early 1850s certainly seems to have been heavily focused on the turnip crop. This sort of emphasis, the evidence would suggest, was equally apparent in farming practice. The farmers of Dumfriesshire, in their memorial to the Foreign Office in 1852, observed: 'In the production more especially of Green or Root Crops, which form in a great degree the basis of successful agriculture, guano has been an almost essential element'.[525] The farmers of Hawick in the same year wrote that guano had been used mainly 'for the profitable cultivation of Turnips and other root crops'.[526] In his 1850-1 survey, James Caird recorded the use of guano for turnips in 14 of the English counties he visited; only in five, however, did he mention its use for grass, only in four for wheat, and only in one for potatoes.[527] 'The larger proportion of the Peruvian guano at present imported', he wrote in 1853, 'is believed to be applied to green crops'.[528] 'The first large-scale

[522]J. B. Lawes, 'Turnip Culture (part I)', *FM*, 2nd ser., 17, no. 4 (April 1848), pp. 323, 340; Morton, 11, p. 1009.

[523]'The Turnip Fly', *FM*, 3rd ser., 2, no. 1 (July 1852), p. 34.

[524]Such a consumption pattern does not invalidate the frequent reference to wheat prices when explaining rises and falls in the demand for guano. Farmers who grew turnips usually produced grain as well, and cereal sales were a major determinant of their income levels and, therefore, fertilizer-purchasing capacity.

[525]FO 61/137, Memorial of 2 June 1852.

[526]*Ibid.*, Memorial of 1 July 1852. Scotland was the principal source of memorials in 1852 and it may be no coincidence that turnip growing was widely practised there, especially in the southern and eastern counties: 'turnip cultivation', wrote John Haxton in 1855, 'has found a greater development in Scotland than in any other country on the face of the globe'. (In Morton, IX, p. 1008.).

[527]Caird, *passim*.

[528]Letter to *The Times*, quoted in *FM*, 3rd ser., 4, no. 6 (December 1853), p. 552. See also Augustus Voelcker, 'On the Comparative Value of Different Aritificial Manures for raising a crop of Swedes', *JRAS*, 16 (1855), p. 90.

applications of guano were exclusively for the growth of turnips and other roots', observed J. C. Nesbit in 1855, 'and even although its use for wheat has increased, and continues to increase, the greater part is still taken for turnips'.[529]

Guano, it is clear, was being used principally for a crop to which other fertilizers were better suited. In buying guano, farmers were obtaining phosphate, which was very useful for the turnip, but they were also paying for nitrogen, which they could largely do without. This fact was pointed out with increasing frequency by the agricultural writers of the day. The most economical application for turnips, they contended, was not guano but the cheaper and more phosphatic manures such as ground or dissolved bones and manufactured superphosphate.[530] Many farmers were already using these to good effect, especially in some of the southern and eastern counties of England.[531] Many more, it was believed, should be doing likewise. Most corn crops, however *did* require nitrogenous manure, and it was to these, the experts argued, that Peruvian guano could best be applied.[532] All the available evidence indicates that such crops were receiving relatively little guano in the 1840s and early 1850s. Where corn was grown in a turnip rotation, turnips usually got the artificials and corn gained from the increased supply of animal manure that resulted. To apply artificials to roots and corn alike was an extravagance which, as Caird's study reveals, very few farmers could afford. Even on the heavy lands, where roots were not extensively grown, few farmers used guano for their wheat. Fertilizer consumption in general was low in such areas. In the words of one observer, 'the farming of strong clays has hardly taken a step in advance since the days of our grandfathers. The application of artificial[533] manures of every kind to cereals has hitherto been a complete failure, so far as superseding farmyard manure on strong clay lands is concerned'.[534]

[529]Nesbit to Antony Gibbs & Sons, 3 December 1855, *loc. cit.* See also 'Plan for reducing the price of guano twenty-five per cent', *JA* (July 1846), p. 386.

[530]See J.B. Lawes and J.H.Gilbert, 'On Agricultural Chemistry', *JRAS,* 12 (1851), p. 33; J.C. Nesbit, *Lecture on the Application of Chemistry to Agriculture* (London, 1849), p. 8; 'Importance of Artificial Manures', *F M,* 3rd ser., 1, no. 4 (April 1852), p. 329; W.C. Spooner, *On the Most Economic and Profitable Method of Growing and Consuming Root Crops* (London, 1854), pp. 14-5.

[531]Caird, pp. 92, 101, 104, 444, 456.

[532]Nesbit, *loc. cit.;* Spooner, *loc. cit.;* Caird, p. 461.

[533]This term, incidentally, was normally applied to guano as well as manufactured fertilizers. It was a synonym for 'purchased'.

[534]A Farmer, 'Chemistry Applied to Agriculture', *FM,* 2nd ser., 21, no. 5 (May 1850), p. 413; also E. J. T. Collins and E. L. Jones, 'Sectoral Advance in English Agriculture, 1850-80', *AgHR,* 15 (1967), pp. 74-5.

Guano's position was tolerably secure so long as the supply of phosphatic alternatives was limited and the price differential between them and guano was not too wide. We have already seen, however, how rapidly superphosphate manufacture was extending in the early 1850s. The expansion continued in the second half of the decade. Demand was becoming increasingly lively as cost and supply problems intensified in the guano trade. 'The high price farmers had been getting for their produce', wrote John Keen, 'together with the scarcity of guano, led them to use artificial manures during 1857 to an enormous extent, and the demand for all kinds of fertilizers in that year was quite unprecedented . . . .'.[535] Lower produce prices later in the 1850s caused farmers to set a premium on cheapness when buying manures. In 1860 it was reported that there had been a 'great increase of local makers all over the kingdom' in superphosphate production.[536] 'Manure manufactories are now spread over the length and breadth of the country', wrote Professor Voelcker, 'and in all these works the staple product, under whatsoever name it may be sent out, is in reality, in nine cases out of ten, superphosphate of lime'.[537] In 1862 he reported that the fertilizer industry had assumed 'gigantic dimensions . . . during the past few years'.[538] There was, observed the *Farmer's Magazine* in 1863, 'a manure manufactory in almost every town'.[539]

The two basic materials required for superphosphate production were sulphuric acid and animal or mineral phosphate. In the 1840s the main source of phosphate had been bones, acquired domestically and also imported from the Baltic and South America. Suffolk coprolites too were used to a limited extent. Both became increasingly available during the 1850s. Bone and bone-ash imports, valued at £139,766 in 1849 and £129,192 in 1850, had risen to £421,207 by 1859 and £306,765 by 1860,[540] and coprolite workings were extended from Suffolk to a number of other counties in the south and east of England.[541] The late 1850s also saw the start of phosphate imports from abroad, as well as a continuing importation of cheap phosphatic

[535]Keen, report for 1858, p. 172.

[536]Keen, report for 1859, p. 160.

[537]Quoted in Cuthbert Johnson, 'Phosphate of Lime', *FM*, 3rd ser., 19, no. 6 (June 1861), p. 425; see also Sir W. G. Armstrong *et al.* (eds.), *The Industrial Resources of the District of the Three Northern Rivers* (London and Newcastle, 1864), p. 173.

[538]Augustus Voelcker, 'On the Commercial Value of Artificial Manures', *JRAS*, 23 (1862), p. 278.

[539]'Artificial Manures', *FM*, 3rd ser., 23, no. 3 (March 1863), pp. 270-1.

[540]*PP*, 1854-5, LI, p. 8; 1860, LIX, p. 15; 1865, LII, p. 14.

[541]See A. N. Gray, *Phosphates and Superphosphates* (London, 1930), p. 11.

guanos that could be used in fertilizer manufacture.[542] Sulphuric acid too was coming onto the market in increasing quantities, thanks to technological advances in production.[543] In consequence of such developments the output of superphosphate in Britain rose, according to a variety of estimates, from 30,000 tons in 1854[544] to 182,000 tons in 1860,[545] to between 150,000 and 200,000 tons in 1862,[546] and to 250,000 tons in 1866.[547] In Rivero's view, superphosphate consumption by the end of the 1850s was already in advance of that of Peruvian guano.[548] The change in the relative commercial stature of the two manures had been startlingly rapid. As for other applications, bones and coprolites were both fertilizers in their own right,[549] and supplies, as noted, were increasing. Imports of nitrate of soda, the most popular nitrogenous fertilizer after guano, also grew fairly steadily in the 1850s and 1860s. Annual average imports increased from 19,869 tons in 1855-9 to 32,627 tons in 1860-4.[550] What is very clear is that the sluggishness of guano sales was not the result of any general stagnation in the demand for manures. The evidence from other branches of the fertilizer trade suggests that the market was expanding rapidly.

Not only were superphosphate and other applications becoming available in increasing abundance: the price differential between them and guano was also tending to widen. The rise in prices noted for guano was not characteristic of the manure market as a whole. London dealers' prices[551] show that between 1852 and 1862 the cost of guano increased by 39.2 per cent, whereas superphosphate went up by

[542]*Ibid.*, pp. 11. 187; A. Voelcker, 'On the Chemical Composition and Commercial Value of Norwegian Apatite, Spanish Phosphate, Coprolites', *JRAS,* 21 (1860), pp. 350-81.

[543]'On the Manufacture of Sulphuric Acid', *FM,* 3rd ser., 11, no. 2 (February 1857), p. 129.

[544]Gray, p. 50.

[545]Anderson, 'Instructions', pp. 431-2.

[546]C. M. Aikman, *Manures and the Principles of Manuring* (Edinburgh, 1894), p. 382.

[547]W. Wallace Fyfe, 'Artificial Manures', *JA* (April 1866), p. 596.

[548]Rivero, p. 46.

[549]Anderson suggested in 1860 that 30 per cent of the available bone supply was used directly as fertilizer, 55 per cent went to the superphosphate manufacturers, and 15 per cent was taken for non-agricultural purposes. 'Instructions', pp. 431-2.

[550]*PP,* 1860, LXIV, p. 16; 1865, LII, p. 15. The nitrate was applied in generally smaller quantities per acre than guano.

[551]As supplied in most issues of the *Farmer's Magazine.*

only 2.9 per cent, coprolites by 3.7 per cent, sulphate of ammonia by 4.1 per cent,[552] and half-inch bones by 23.9 per cent.[553] The price of nitrate of soda came down by 3.7 per cent.[554] 'The relatively high price of Chincha guano at £12', wrote Rivero in 1860, 'when compared with superphosphate at £6, and other cheaper guanos with a higher phosphate content, stands as a very difficult, if not insuperable, obstacle to be overcome'.[555]

We can, therefore, move away from hazy generalisations about costly guano and growing competition, and offer a very specific explanation of guano's decline. The main factor was the loss of a large portion of the enormously important turnip market to superphosphate. This happened, first because superphosphate was generally a more suitable fertilizer for the turnip, secondly because it was becoming more abundant (and regularly so, contrasting with the periodic inadequacy of guano supplies), and thirdly because it was becoming relatively much cheaper than guano, its price remaining fairly steady while that of guano rose steeply. Superphosphate, observed one farming journal in 1858, had 'risen greatly in favour as a manure for turnips'.[556] John Keen, in his review of the manure business for the same year, suggested that any future fall in guano prices would have little effect on the growth of the superphosphate trade; 'the superiority of superphosphate over guano for root crops', he wrote, was 'now pretty generally acknowledged'.[557] In 1864 *The Economist* commented that guano 'year by year is being superseded by the higher class of manufactured manures;' for root crops, it noted, 'it is now quite a settled point that superphosphate of lime . . . is by far the most effective and economical manure than can be used; this article therefore has largely increased in consumption'.[558]

Unhappily for guano, root crops appear to have remained the main recipients of bought fertilizers. The farmer had 'found by experience', wrote Professor Voelcker in 1861, 'that in most cases in which it is deemed desirable to make up a deficiency of yard-manure, it pays

---

[552]The figure is for the period 1853-62, there being no quotations for 1852.

[553]The figure is for the period 1852-61, there being no quotations for 1862.

[554]For illustration of yearly price movements, see graph in Mathew, 'Guano Market', p. 120.

[555]Rivero, p. 45.

[556]'Guano and Superphosphate', *JA* (March 1858), p. 322.

[557]Keen, report for 1858, p. 172; also Anderson, 'Composition of Guano', p. 351.

[558]*The Economist*, 11 March 1864, p. 17.

better to purchase superphosphate and similar manures for the root-crop than to buy nitrogenous manures for the white crop'.[559] On the clay lands, where roots were not widely cultivated, the situation was no brighter. In this generally backward and depressed sector of British agriculture the use of fertilizers was still uncommon. There were, moreover, special problems connected with wheat's rather uncertain response to manuring. Many people were of the opinion that farmyard manure was the only safe application. Concentrated nitrogenous manures, it was widely held, produced an excessive quantity of straw and rendered the crop more liable to flattening in adverse weather conditions.[560] The availability of good farmyard manure was growing with the increase of green crop yields,[561] the spread of cake feeding,[562] and the gradual improvement in methods of dung collection and storage.[563] In addition, the manure requirements of corn could be substantially reduced if it was preceded in a rotation by nitrogen-fixing leguminous plants. And even if the farmer did decide to purchase fertilizers for his corn, he did not necessarily choose guano. Nitrate of soda and sulphate of ammonia, both nitrogenous manures, were becoming increasingly available and competitive in the late 1850s and early 1860s. It was observed in 1858 of Holkham Park, one of the most celebrated seats of advanced agriculture, that for wheat 'nitrate of soda is greatly preferred as a top-dressing to guano'.[564]

It would be the grossest exaggeration, however, to imply that corn offered no market whatever for guano. Grain crops, after all, occupied more than half the total arable land in England and Wales as late as 1870. It was not a buoyant sector but it was a very extensive one. There were without question many farmers who were prepared to purchase manure for their corn as well as for their roots, and quite a number too in the depressed clay lands who used guano to overcome

[559]Voelcker, 'Norwegian Apatite', p. 351.

[560]Morton, 11, p. 1141; J. C. Nesbit, 'The Relative Values of Artificial Manures', *FM*, 3rd ser., 9, no. 5 (May 1856), p. 420; 'Is it Profitable to Apply Portable Manure as Top-Dressings to Cereal Crops?', *ibid.*, 12, no. 4 (October 1857), pp. 316-7.

[561]Resulting in part, ironically, from the application of guano.

[562]See Jones, 'English Agricultural Prosperity', pp. 104, 107; Thompson, 'Second Agricultural Revolution', pp. 66-8, 73-7.

[563]See 'The Progress of British Agriculture During the Last Century', *FM*, 3rd ser., II, no. 2 (February 1857), p. 123; 'The Most Judicious Management and Application of Farmyard and Artificial Manures', *ibid.*, no. 3 (March 1857), pp. 253-60. Thomas Anderson suggested in 1860 that around 60 million tons of farmyard manure (valued at £20 million) were applied to British crops each year. Anderson, 'Instructions', p. 433.

[564]Read, p. 275.

deficiencies in their supplies of farmyard manure. This is clear from discussions of the period in farming clubs all over the country. Guano, moreover, did not lose the turnip market in its entirety. Where roots were grown on fairly heavy soils, superphosphate was often found to be a less effective application than guano,[565] and in the northern parts of the country, where the growth limits of turnips tended to be higher than they were in the south, quite large quantities of nitrogen were normally required to achieve the high maximum yields possible.[566] Guano was also reckoned by some to be more useful in the wetter parts of the country.[567] Even in the dry, light-soil areas of the south and east superphosphate's rule was not absolute by the 1860s. All the chemists agreed that turnips needed *some* nitrogen and that quantities of ammoniacal fertilizer should be mixed in with the phosphatic applications.[568] In the south, too, mangels were growing in popularity as a hardy substitute for the vulnerable turnip, and these needed quite substantial quantities of ammoniacal matter to assist their growth.[569] Guano also remained a favourite fertilizer for the potato;[570] and for permanent meadow lands, Lawes and Gilbert concluded from experiments in 1858 that the most effective dressings were nitrogenous manures.[571]

So the guano business in Britain survived, and indeed came quite close to old peaks again in 1870.[572] But the advance of super-phosphate and the loss of the old commanding position in the roots market had dealt a severe blow to a once buoyant and growing trade. This was a development which perhaps was bound to have come some time, but it was unquestionably hastened by the rise in the price of guano and by the frequent and frustrating irregularities in its supply. It is noticeable that while the threat from competitors was continually

[565] Morton, II, p. 1024; also J. J. Mechi's remarks at April 1856 meeting of the Central Farmers' Club, *FM*, 3rd ser., 9, no. 5 (May 1856), p. 424.

[566] See Sir E. John Russell, *History of Agricultural Science* (London, 1966), p. 134.

[567] 'Guano, Its Application, Supply and Adulteration', *FM*, 3rd ser., 1, no. 3 (March 1852), p. 215; Fyfe, p. 594.

[568] See, for instance, Nesbit, 'Artificial Manures', pp. 420-1; W. C. Spooner, 'Influence of Nitrogen on Crops', *FM*, 3rd ser., 15, no. 4 (April 1859), p. 342.

[569] J. C. Nesbit, 'On Peruvian Guano', *FM*, 3rd ser., 9, no. 6 (June 1856), p. 512; Read, pp. 276, 279.

[570] Wright, p. 109; A Practical Farmer, 'The Cultivation and Growth of the Potato', *FM*, 3rd ser., 23, no. 5 (May 1863), p. 407.

[571] J. B. Lawes and J. H. Gilbert, 'Report of Experiments with Different Manures on Permanent Meadow Land', *JRAS*, 19 (1858), p. 573.

[572] See import figures in Appendix IV, Table I.

alluded to by the Peruvian government, by the Peruvian ministers in London, and in particular by Gibbs, it was never pulled right out into the centre of their deliberations and subjected to rigorous and detailed analysis. Gibbs's awareness of the perils facing the guano trade was of a highly generalized nature. Absurdly, they were accused by their critics not of that serious failing, but of exaggerating the problem of competition and, indeed, manifesting neurotic obsession over it.

4

THE REMOVAL OF GIBBS

The noble precepts of justice, the violated standards of commercial morality, and the clear interests of the Treasury point to the revocation and condemnation of the Gibbs contract.

El Comercio, 17 January 1861

THE LEGAL ISSUE

Gibbs's contract came to an end in December 1861 and was not renewed. Their European territories were divided up between a number of new contractors and the British market was awarded to a group of Peruvian merchants — Felipe Barreda, José Canevaro, Carlos Delgado, Felipe Gordillo, Manuel Pardo and Clemente de Villate — who employed the English firm of Thomson Bonar & Company as their consignees. Gibbs departed without a struggle but amid much confusion. They had found it difficult to decide whether they wished to remain in the trade, and accordingly had allowed themselves to drift into a condition of inert ambivalence. The government, for its part, had made no clear decision that Gibbs ought to go, and Castilla had apparently wished to retain them. The new Peruvian contractors, moreover, had a good deal of trouble finding the funds necessary to take over the British market. One contract, of October 1860, had to be scrapped. The one which actually came into operation was arranged in January 1862: more than a month after the Gibbs contract had officially expired. A further element of confusion arose from Gibbs's continued chartering and selling well after the end of their contract period.

The transfer of power may have been effected in a highly uncertain fashion, but that it did come about could not have surprised very many people at the time. Gibbs's position as contractors had been powerfully challenged in the 1850s: the legality of their contract had been questioned, their mercantile conduct had been criticized, and the capacity of indigenous merchants to displace them had notably improved. Their removal is of great interest in at least two important respects. First, because it revealed the authority of the Peruvian government: its ability to exclude a wealthy and powerful foreign firm from further self-enriching participation in a highly profitable trade. Second, because it occurred against a background of intensifying, if narrowly based, economic liberalism and economic nationalism. A good number of Peruvians wished to end what seemed a subordinative relationship. With the *colosales fortunas* that they had made out of the prevailing export system, in José Ulloa's view in 1859, the contractors had been able to exercise an offensive and ruinous *despotismo financial* over Peruvian affairs.[1]

On the question of contract legality, the principal issue was the validity of the 1853 arrangement whereby the Echenique government had granted Gibbs a six-year extension on the contract due to expire at the end of 1855.[2]   Reference has already been made to the congressional resolution of November 1849 calling for more competitive tenders, for better terms for Peru in any later contract, and for the government, in making its selection, always to give 'preference to native Peruvians'. The four-year contract of 1850 conformed to some degree with this resolution in as much as it was a more advantageous arrangement for the Peruvian government, and Gibbs were obliged to contend with at least the threat of competition. When this contract was extended in 1853, however, negotiations, as we have seen, were conducted in secret and there was never any question of local or any other capitalists being allowed to compete. The congressional resolution had in fact been largely ignored and Gibbs were entrenched until the end of 1861. The 1853 *prórroga,* commented the *Comisión Especial* set up by Congress in 1856 to examine all the extensions granted by the former government, 'contravenes the law [of 1849] because when it was drawn up there was no competitive bidding, as prescribed by that law; because it is not more economic than the contract of 1850, nor more profitable for the Nation; and because, being arranged in secret, it could not and did not give any preferences to native Peruvians . . .'.[3]   Given such clear condemnation, the resolution that followed was surprisingly mild: it was merely stated that the contract would 'prove contentious' if not adjusted 'in terms more advantageous to the Nation'.[4]   The matter, it was suggested, should be referred for judgement 'before competent tribunals'.[5]   The *Dictamen* was signed by Juan de Dios Calderón, Manuel de la Torre and Ignacio Escudero. Two other members of the commission, Pedro José Tordoya and J. Simeón Tejeda, believing that a stronger line should be taken, produced their own minority report. They considered that simply to threaten the reform of the Gibbs contract was quite insufficient in view of the declared illegality of the arrangement.

[1]Ulloa, p. 113.

[2]See chapter 3, pp. 105-8.

[3]*Dictamen,* p. 4.

[4]*Ibid.,* p. 26.

[5]*Ibid.;* also FO 61/165, Sulivan to Clarendon, 26 October 1856.

Annulment was more appropriate than adjustment.[6] Congress, more-over, would be shelving its own responsibilities if it placed a final decision on the matter before tribunals.[7].

The contract, in the event, was subject to no revisions whatever. Both the majority and minority reports, however, had insisted that the 1849 law be applied to all future arrangements,[8] and the deliberations of 1856 had unquestionably reminded Peruvian merchants of their rights and the Peruvian government of its duties. It was never a question of wholesale expulsion of foreigners, and their replacement by Peruvians: rather it was a matter of asserting that foreigners should only continue if they could offer notably better terms than Peruvians and that the uncompetitive system of extending existing contracts should be abandoned. The government's interpretation of its obliga-tions was shown in May 1860 when it invited proposals for new contracts, including the British, and declared that the authorities 'will, other things being equal, give preference to native Peruvians, in conformity with the above-mentioned law . . .'.[9] In August 1860 Congress resolved once again that contracts 'be drawn up in accordance with the provisions of the legislative resolution of 10 November 1849'.[10] In February 1861 it insisted that the resolution actually be inserted in the new guano contracts.[11]

Gibbs, clearly, were not precluded from continuing in the trade, but they could not look forward to any more secret *prórrogas*. If they were to retain hold of guano they would have to offer better contract terms than any Peruvian, or group of Peruvians, could. They would, moreover, have to struggle against a *mood*, of which the law and its restatement were mere symptoms: the feeling on the part of Peruvian legislators (if not of the government itself) that foreign predominance within the trade should be ended[12] and indigenous capitalists encour-aged to take over; the feeling too, perhaps, that Gibbs, in being allowed to continue operating a contract of challengeable legality, had already been treated with excessive indulgence by Peru.

[6]*Dictamen de la Minoría de la Comisión Especial sobre la nulidad de las prórrogas de consignación del huano* (Lima, 1856), p. 4.

[7]*Ibid.*, p. 5.

[8]*Dictamen*, p. 27; *Dictamen de la Minoría*, p. 14.

[9]Cited in *El Peruano*, 28 March 1861.

[10]*Ibid.*

[11]*Ibid.*

[12]For indication of Gibbs's awareness of this, see HHGC, 2, Henry Gibbs to William Gibbs, 16 November 1861.

THE INDIGENOUS MERCHANTS

The congressional desire to introduce a much larger national element to the trade was not mere wishful thinking. The local mercantile class had, by the early 1860s, considerably enlarged its capacity to compete for guano contracts. As far back as 1846 Castilla had threatened to expel Gibbs and replace them with Peruvian merchants, and even then the danger had been taken quite seriously by the English house.[13] Over the course of the intervening decade-and-a-half, two things had happened to make the challenge a considerably more ominous one. In the first place, Peruvians had been acquiring experience in guano trading with other markets. Secondly, certain financial manoeuvres by the Castilla and Echenique administrations in the early 1850s had placed large quantities of liquid wealth in the hands of the Peruvian middle and upper classes: wealth that could be used to facilitate entry into the guano trade.

Francisco de Quiros, it will be recalled, was prominent in the trade from its inception until the late 1840s. Pedro de Candamo, a Chilean by origin but a Peruvian by residence, was also conspicuous in the early days, being party to at least two contracts. In 1860 the British chargé described him as 'the Rothschild of Chile and Peru'.[14] There was also José Canevaro, who had begun his commercial life in Panama, moved on to Guayaquil, and then settled in Peru in 1832. By the 1840s, according to Witt, he had become 'one of the wealthiest men in Lima'.[15] In 1847, as observed earlier, he lent the government 72,000 pesos in exchange for guano-exporting rights, and went ahead to despatch 17 vessels carrying around 7,000 tons of the fertilizer.[16] In October 1850 the Peruvian government, doubtless influenced by the 1849 congressional resolution, made its most extravagant offer yet towards indigenous capitalists. Rejecting foreign tenders, it granted four local merchants, Felipe and Federico Barreda, Julián de Zaracondegui and Nicolás Rodrigo, a ten-year contract for the export of guano to North America, France, Spain, China, Brazil and the West Indies. Significantly, perhaps, no preliminary advance was required and remuneration was unusually generous, with sales commissions of 7½% and interest on disbursement for freights etc. of 6%.[17] Despite a clause enabling the merchants to invite the

---

[13] See chapter 2.

[14] FO 61/193, Jerningham to Russell, 13 October 1860.

[15] Witt Diaries, IV, entry for 1 to 8 September 1846.

[16] See chapter 2 and *Anales,* IV, pp. 23-4.

[17] Rivero, p. 26.

participation of other commercial men in Peru,[18] and their attempts to subcontract the business,[19] the responsibility of handling guano exports over such a wide range of markets proved too much and in August 1851 the Barredas and their associates sought and were granted a major adjustment of the contract, limiting their territory to the United States and the period to five years.[20] North America was, by itself, a fairly commodious market, taking as much as 42,000 tons in 1851.[21] An extension was granted in July 1853 similar to the one obtained by Gibbs a few months earlier.[22]

The American business, however, ran into considerable problems in the mid-1850s. 'The Barredas have been getting into an awful scrape', Gibbs reported in February 1855. They had chartered to ship far more guano for the United States than the market there could bear and were unable to meet freight charges out of current sales receipts: 'to all appearances it looks as if they had been trying to accumulate so large a stock in the U.S. as to prevent anybody competing for the business there at the expiration of their contract and before they knew that they would get the *prórroga*'. They had been forced, accordingly, to bring the price down to the equivalent of £10 per ton (compared with £11 in Britain), without any authority from Lima to do so. Gibbs were alarmed by this, since the difference left a margin for shipments to be profitably made to England: some guano, indeed, was already coming across the North Atlantic. They wrote to Felipe Barreda in Baltimore about it and got a reply pleading for help. The Peruvian president also asked Gibbs to provide assistance. This they were prepared to give, since it might help Barreda raise the price again and avoid the danger of 'the whole of the Huano in the States' being 'let loose upon us'. So they agreed to take 28,000 tons off his hands, allowing him to draw on London for the shipping costs, and also to arrange through William Gibbs & Co. in Lima for the transfer of some Barreda-chartered vessels to the British consignment.[23] Gibbs reckoned that bills drawn against them would give Barreda about £150,000. Another £200,000 had, apparently, been borrowed from Alsop & Co., agent for the Peruvian merchants in New York. Felipe Barreda in

[18]*Anales*, V, p. 25.

[19]*Ibid.*, p. 26; Levin, pp. 78-9.

[20]*Anales*, V, pp. 25, 27-8.

[21]*Ibid.*, p. 28.

[22]*Dictamen*, p. 26. Except for the article allowing them to share the contract with other parties, the arrangement was upheld by the *Comisión Especial* in its report of 1856, on the grounds that the 1849 law had been conceived exclusively in relation to Gibbs's contract. *Ibid.*, pp. 15-8, 26.

[23]WGC, Henry Gibbs to William Gibbs, 3 February 1855.

Lima was also in the habit of drawing quite heavily, even in normal times, on Murrieta of London.[24] Peruvian control over the United States trade, therefore, was not all that it might seem on contract paper. London and New York finance provided some very essential props. The Barredas and their colleagues weathered the storm, but were not to survive much longer in the trade. At the beginning of 1857 their contract was suspended by ex-President Vivanco during his short occupation of the Chincha islands.[25] Later in the year it was rescinded by the government in Lima after an official enquiry into their business conduct.[26]

A number of small contracts, none of which necessitated preliminary advances, were awarded to Peruvians in the 1850s for guano exports to Asia, Central America, Cuba and Puerto Rico[27] and in October 1857 a new contract for the United States was granted to Zaracondegui & Co. (who had been party to the 1850 arrangements) in association with Juan de Ugarte and José Vicente Oyague y hermano. (Proposals had also been received from a local group named *Sociedad Peruana,* from Canevaro & Co., and from Alsop & Co.). It was to run for four years, and it carried a 400,000 pesos loan at 5 per cent, to be delivered in four equal instalments.[28] Zaracondegui scored another success two years later when he won the Spanish contract. Murrieta had been dismissed from the trade for alleged malpractice, and Gibbs had taken temporary charge of it. The English house put in no bid for supplying Spain: most of the firms placing tenders seem to have been Peruvian — Zaracondegui, Pardo y Barrón, Ruiz Hermanos, José Antonio Garcia y Garcia,[29] and Andrés Alvarez Calderón[30] (acting 'both for himself and for a *sociedad anónima'.*[31]) Zaracondegui's main competitors were Alvarez Calderón and his friends. Both parties offered a loan of 1,000,000 pesos, but Zaracondegui had the edge by being prepared to give half of this at once, with the rest in two instalments of

[24] *Ibid.,* 5 February 1855.

[25] FO 61/172, Sulivan to Clarendon, 12 February 1857.

[26] *Anales,* VI, p. 31; *Informe Circunstanciado,* p. xix.

[27] *Anales,* V, pp. 35-8; VI, pp.29-30, 44-5.

[28] *Ibid.,* VI, pp. 31-2.

[29] The representative of 'fortes maisons espagnoles d'Europe'. MAE, Lima/12, Jion (?) to Walewski, 25 November 1859.

[30] Currently holder of the guano loading contract which, according to Witt, earned him 'several millions of dollars'. See Mathew, 'Primitive Export Sector', p. 39.

[31] *Anales,* VI, pp. 45-6.

250,000 pesos. Alvarez Calderón could only manage 300,000 down and a series of small instalments. He also wanted 5 per cent for sales in the Spanish colonies, whereas Zaracondegui asked for only 4 per cent and also felt able to throw in an offer to build a railway line between Pisco and Ica.[32]

Zaracondegui had twice been challenged by companies whose personnel, Alvarez Calderón apart, remains a mystery. His success, not surprisingly, was resented in Lima. He now held two important contracts, and one for Cuba and Puerto Rico as well.[33] The Spanish contract was forcibly attacked in the press, and allegations were made that the government could have secured better terms from other parties.[34] There appears to have been some suspicion that Zaracondegui was receiving undue favour. Some may also have wondered if he and his colleagues were not overstretching themselves in making large loans to the government and undertaking to supply markets in the West Indies, North America and Europe. One curiosity is that Zaracondegui had vanished (in name at least) from the guano scene by the early 1860s. His activities are, unquestionably, of the greatest interest to any student of the nascent Peruvian bourgeoisie. He was easily the most important of the indigenous guano merchants in the 1850s. How, precisely, he got his money, one cannot tell. He had a retail business in Lima in the 1840s, dealing mainly in foreign goods,[35] and certainly in time came to enjoy liberal bill-drawing rights with finance houses abroad. He also worked in league with rich Limeños like Oyague and Ugarte (as the United States contract reveals) and with Pedro de Candamo.[36] Another wealthy associate was Manuel de Argumaniz Muñoz, an energetic Peruvian promoter, speculator and financier with whom Zaracondegui had founded a company in 1849 to import European manufactures,[37] no doubt to facilitate his retailing activities.

[32]*Ibid.*, p. 46.

[33]*Ibid.*, p. 44.

[34]FO 61/188, Jerningham to Russell, 26 November 1859; also item 4219 in Jorge Basadre, *Introducción A Las Bases Documentales Para La Historia De La República Del Perú Con Algunas Reflexiones* (Lima, 1971), 1, p. 335; and MAE, Lima/12, Jion(?) to Walewski, 25 November 1859. (It was observed in the French despatch that as much as half of the new loan could be paid in bills drawn on Zaracondegui's associates in New York and reimbursed out of the proceeds of his North American sales).

[35]Memorias de Manuel de Argumaniz Muñoz, Libro 1, p. 3 (of typescript kindly given to me by Sr. Félix Denegri Luna. The original documents are in his possession).

[36]FO 61/193, Jerningham to Russell, 13 October 1860.

[37]Argumaniz Memorias, Libro 1, pp. 1, 31.

In 1858 Zaracondegui, with Argumaniz's assistance, tried to win the French (and French colonial) contract.[38] Montané had been removed from the French trade after an enquiry into his affairs had upheld charges of misconduct. New tenders were invited by the government. Apart from Zaracondegui, applications were received from Canevaro e hijos, Montés y Colombier, Thomas Lachambre & Co., the General Maritime Company of Paris, and Antony Gibbs & Sons. The contract, as noted earlier, was awarded to Gibbs, on 26 January 1858. It was to run for four years, and it required an advance of only 300,000 pesos.[39] Gibbs, clearly, did not succeed through any extravagant loan offer. Perhaps the relatively low commission asked for, 3 per cent, gave them an advantage. José Ulloa claimed, however, that their success was largely owing to the partiality which Zevallos, the finance minister, had always displayed towards them,[40] and that far too short a period had been allowed for the presentation of proposals, meaning that it was impossible to call in much competition from Europe.[41] 'I have', Castilla wrote to Zevallos with revealing casualness, 'received the copy of the contract celebrated with the house of Gibbs for the consignment of guano to France: I have not yet had time to examine it, but it seems to me right that this proposal has been adopted, since it was the best for us . . . .'.[42] Gibbs's success is interesting, for it shows that even as late as 1858 they could win a contract in competition with prominent Peruvian capitalists. There clearly was no inclination as yet on the part of the Castilla regime to give preference to local merchants over Gibbs if the latter could submit competitive tenders. Governments may have been more aware now of their obligations under the 1849 law, but they were certainly not going to become obsessive about them. The achievement of local merchants in certain branches of the trade had not been impressive. Gibbs no doubt could afford to feel more arrogantly self-assured when they recalled how they had had to salvage Barreda from his excesses in 1855. There was, however, no general conviction that the awarding of contracts to nationals had been mistaken. Whatever Barreda's difficulties in 1851 and 1855, the fact remained that a major market like the United States had been in Peruvian hands since 1850. Other markets were also being taken over. Valuable experience was

[38] *Ibid.,* Libro 5, p. 52.

[39] *Anales,* V, pp. 35-9.

[40] Ulloa, p. 83.

[41] *Ibid.,* p. 98. In fact, all but two of the interested parties were European.

[42] Castilla to Zevallos, 6 February 1858, in Instituto 'Libertador Ramón Castilla', *Archivo Castilla,* 111, p. 256; also MAE, Lima/12, Huet to Walewski, 11 September 1858.

being gained and money was being made. Men like the Barredas and Zaracondegui had now to be taken very seriously. The law, moreover, was on their side, and Congress had taken the trouble to remind the government of it in 1856 and again in 1860 and 1861. Such merchants could usually make use of European and North American funds to help consolidate their positions. It would be wrong to view such dependence on outside help exclusively as a sign of weakness. It certainly revealed the inadequacy of domestic funds of capital and reflected the periodic mistakes of Peruvians in the difficult business of international trade, but the fact that such problems could be overcome through help from abroad was a source of considerable strength in the struggles against the foreign guano merchants. One must not, in any case, exaggerate deficiencies in the supply of money in Peru. This, it would seem, had grown rapidly during the 1850s. If there was a problem it lay not so much in the quantity of cash in Peruvian hands, but in the reluctance of many wealthy men to use their money for productive ends and in the absence of institutions to facilitate the rapid transfer of funds to people in urgent need of credit.

The largest single causes of increased wealth in Peru in the 1850s were the debt consolidation and conversion operations of 1850-3. On 16 March 1850 the Castilla government approved a Law of Consolidation whereby it invited people holding claims against the government dating back to the war of independence to bring these forward to special tribunals. If found to be valid they would be converted into 6 per cent bonds of the internal debt. Obligations to foreign creditors had already been honoured; now it was the turn of the Peruvians themselves. The range of possible claims was very wide indeed[43] and the tribunals assessed them fairly uncritically. People not only brought forward their own entitlements, but those of others that had been purchased in the provinces, often for nominal sums.[44] Laxity on the part of those who adjudicated encouraged a great deal of fraudulent activity. 'In the drawing up of the claims', Henry Witt observed in his diary, 'the most frightful abuses were committed. . . . In one word, every description of deceit was practised. . .'.[45] When the Castilla administration came to an end in 1851 the consolidated internal debt amounted to just under five million pesos.[46] Greater excesses, however, were yet to follow. Echenique, succeeding Castilla in the presidency, released all the brakes and allowed the debt

[43] Bonilla, p. 256; Romero, p. 17.

[44] Levin, p. 80.

[45] Witt Diaries, VI, Residence in Lima from 28th October 1852 till 11 August 1854.

[46] Bonilla, p. 256.

to mount to over 23 million pesos.[47] According to Romero, almost every known local and foreign name in Peru at the time made its appearance in the official lists of bondholders.[48]

The bonds were, of course, less liquid than cash, and fetched prices much lower than their face value. There was the danger too that the irregularities manifested in their creation and the scale of the interest burden they imposed might cause some future administration to repudiate them. Since the principal object of the exercise had been to put money in people's pockets it was decided to convert a large portion of the new bonds into an external debt. By this, paper held by those in the regime's favour was redeemed at face value by foreign banking houses which then sold corresponding bonds in Britain and France. The conversion was carried out in secret, and the new bonds were backed by the proceeds of guano sales,[49] thereby ensuring that they would be purchased at a high price. According to one source, 11 million pesos were taken by the English house of Joseph Hegan (2 million) and the French firm of Uribarren (9 million) for conversion in Britain, and bonds to the value of 4 million were converted in France through the guano-trading house of Montané. All carried an interest rate of 4½ per cent: 1½ per cent lower than the former internal rate.[50] The conversion had come about partly through fears for the future of the new debt paper in Peru. Similar concern was now felt in London:[51] 'great exertions', it was reported in February 1855, were now being made 'to get these bonds into the hands of innocent third parties' owing to doubts about 'the permanence of the actual government of Peru, and the well grounded fear, that the conversion . . will be annulled by the succeeding government'.[52] The fear was indeed

[47] Echenique, 11, p. 199.

[48] Romero, p. 377.

[49] *Ibid.,* p. 258; Levin, p. 80.

[50] Around 3 million pesos worth of the new bonds were never issued, presumably being retained by the bankers and other parties privy to the conversion. Notice by Francisco de Rivero in *The Times* of 16 July 1855; also FO 61/161, Sulivan to Clarendon, 10 June 1855. Somewhat lower figures for the conversion are given in *Anales,* VI, p. 65 and VII, p. 106.

[51] The paper was deemed highly irregular by the London Stock Exchange and refused admission. The existing Anglo-Peruvian bondholders, to whom half the British guano proceeds had already been pledged, formed a committee in January 1854 to fight the issue. Richard Thornton was appointed chairman and later in the year expressed the view that admitting the Hegan and Uribarren bonds would involve 'a *principle* altogether inadmissible. A door would be opened for other Foreign States to follow the example without limit and render all Foreign Bonds insecure. It is a principle which will not therefore be recognised in the Stock Exchanges of Europe'. FO 61/147, Thornton to Sulivan, 31 July 1854; also FO 61/161, Sulivan to Clarendon, 10 April 1855; *The Times,* 16 April 1857 (letter from 'An Old Bondholder' referring to the events of 1854), p. 6.

[52] FO 61/161, Ward to Wodehouse, 15 February 1855.

justified. With Castilla's return to power, following a revolution which had gained a good deal of its heat from the consolidation and conversion abuses, a decree was issued cancelling all the bonds issued under the Echenique administration.[53] According to Sulivan, however, the very process of punishing fraud was itself fraudulent. 'The whole transaction has been in fact a most scandalous stock jobbing affair, for the Decree . . . was dated on the 26th of February, and was not published in the "Peruano" until the 3rd of April. By so doing, those who were in the secret, were enabled to transfer their bonds, and both General Castilla and his three Ministers have gained large sums of money'.[54] The issue was disputed for almost two years, with the British and French governments party to the discussions, and in February 1857 the Castilla regime finally agreed to let the entire debt stand and accept all the onerous obligations that this entailed.[55] The cancellation, in fact, had mainly affected foreign bondholders. Peruvians who had taken their money from the conversion were in no way harmed.

The consolidation and conversion operations, whatever abuses they may have entailed, represented a large cash injection into the economy, placing possibly as much as 15 million pesos in Peruvian pockets almost overnight. Those who held unconverted bonds could normally expect to receive interest and amortization payments; if they wished, of course, they could also get cash by selling the paper. Echenique, surveying in retrospect the financial events of 1853, believed that Peru had gained greatly: 'it was then', he wrote, 'that one could see a growth of trade and a vitalisation of industry; it was then that a thousand families, impoverished by the exactions of war, were released from their poverty . . .'.[56] Peru had suffered from shortage of capital in the past;[57] now something had been done to rectify the deficiency. In Maiguashca's view, Echenique had every right to claim the role of benefactor. He had been much more sensitive to economic issues than Castilla, and had sought to place funds in the hands of potential entrepreneurs.[58] Other historians, while taking a

---

[53] *Ibid.*, Sulivan to Clarendon, 10 April 1855.

[54] *Ibid.*

[55] FO 61/172, Sulivan to Clarendon, 26 February 1857; FO 61/173, 'Statement of the External Debt Recognised by the Republic of Peru . . .', 28 February 1857; also Neptali Benvenutto, *Crónica Parlamentaria Del Perú*, V, 1855-1857 (Lima, 1926), pp. 164-5. For a discussion of the dispute and an explanation of the settlement see Mathew, 'Imperialism', pp. 576-7.

[56] Echenique, 11, p. 200.

[57] *Ibid.*, p. 195.

[58] Maiguashca, pp. 53-63.

somewhat more sceptical view of Echenique's motives,[59] agree that some good came of his extravagances. Levin believes that the main result was price inflation, but also asserts that with an increased supply of capital in Peru 'one limitation upon the award of guano-export contracts to nationals was weakened'.[60] Yepes del Castillo writes that 'thanks to internal debt certificates . . . there formed in Lima a group of capitalists who, little by little, gained possession of new contracts as the old ones expired'.[61] Bonilla too claims that the great quantity of capital that came into the hands of the '*bourgeoisie foncière-commerciale*' gave them the economic power needed to attempt the removal of foreign merchant houses from the trade.[62]

It ought to be stressed that none of these authors has been able to prove that the people who were attempting to move into the guano trade had, individually, been notably enriched by the consolidation and the conversion. It may indeed be pure coincidence that Peruvian merchants became more assertive after these operations took place. It will be recalled too that Quiros, Canevaro, Candamo, Zaracondegui, Ugarte, Oyague and the Barreda brothers all became party to the guano business *prior* to the rapid expansion of the debt. The available Gibbs correspondence, moreover, contains no reference to these financial developments and any threat to their position which they might have posed. It does, nevertheless, seem reasonable to assume that a lot of the new wealth did come to men who would wish to use it to claim or consolidate positions in the trade. Commercial men were the sort of people who would be most alert to the financial opportunities opened up by the new policies and the best able, given their speculative talents and their location in Lima, to take full advantage of these. And with extra money in their pockets, they were likely to be attracted more to guano than to industry or mining or agriculture.[63] These other areas of economic activity normally required long-term investment and considerable entrepreneurial skill. They were each beset by a host of problems and held out little promise of quick and ample reward.[64] The guano trade, on the other hand, was a relatively simple affair and was manifestly remunerative. Returns came in

---

[59] As did many contemporaries. 'Honest he was not', wrote Witt, 'at least as a public functionary; he was covetous and at the same time extravagant . . .'. Witt Diaries, VI, Residence in Lima from 28th October till 11th August 1854.

[60] Levin, p. 83.

[61] Yepes, p. 68.

[62] Bonilla, pp. 261, 269; also his *Guano y Burguesía en el Perú* (Lima, 1974), p.33.

[63] See Bonilla, 'Aspects', p. 270.

[64] See, for example, Hunt, 'Guano', pp. 43-58, 97-107.

quickly after the initial investments had been made. To a merchant in Lima it probably seemed that all one needed to break into the business profitably was a good supply of ready cash to meet government loans and freight advances. And the more money a man had in Lima, the better able he would be to secure generous bill-drawing facilities from some finance house in Europe or the United States.

THE PAMPHLET WAR

Gibbs had frequently been under fire in the past. Some ill-feeling, as we have seen, had been generated by their price policies and their commission rates in the 1840s. Many of the harshest words had come from the pen of a fellow-contractor, Carlos Barroilhet.[65] Their very presence in the trade had been resented by some. In December their most recent contract was 'violently discussed in the Chamber of Deputies'.[66] Hitherto, however, the attacks had been ill-concerted and often badly reasoned, and they did little to disturb Gibbs' metropolitan composure. Their power lay essentially in government patronage, and there was no sign that administrations in Lima felt any general unease or concern over the activities of the English firm. In 1856, however, there began a period of vigorous, sustained and detailed criticism of the Gibbs house, ending only when it became clear that their contract was unlikely to be renewed. This had been one of the principal objectives of the critics. To what extent they had the further aim of advancing the cause of the national bourgeoisie[67] is more difficult to determine, but the timing of the attack alone is such as to suggest that the motives of the pamphleteers may not always have been disinterested. The literary assault was backed up by congressional debate and by the appointment of fiscal inspectors in 1857 to examine and report on the conduct of Gibbs and the other principal contractors.

In the late 1840s Carlos Barroilhet quit the guano trade which he had helped to set in motion and went off to spend three years in California.[68] From there he moved to Europe and took the opportunity to observe the progress of the business at the market end. By 1856, however, he was back in Peru, eager to publicise his view that the

[65] See chapter 2; also reference to criticism of the consignees in L.E.S., p. 31.

[66] Witt Diaries, IV, 23 December 1847.

[67] Bonilla has reservations about this term in relation to mid-19th century Peru, since the people involved were not employers of wage labour and, being heavily dependent on overseas financial assistance, were only nominally national. He suggests instead '*la clase comercial-terrateniente*'. *Guano*, pp. 43-4, 53 etc.

[68] Barroilhet, *Opúsculo*, p. 13.

trade was being badly managed. Castilla agreed to see him, but apparently was in no mood to listen, complaining of 'charlatans who make him lose his time and his patience over their preposterous schemes'.[69] Others, however, took a keener interest and asked him to give an account of his opinions to the *Convención Nacional.* A five-man commission was set up[70] and on February 22nd 1856 Barroilhet addressed them.[71] His remarks were published shortly after[72] and represent the first big blast in the war against Gibbs.

His essential message was that guano offered much greater opportunities for Peru than had generally been realised. The country's natural monopoly of guano ought to be exploited to the full through a more ambitious pricing policy and the returns would be sufficient to ensure a speedy clearance of the foreign debt. The Gibbs house, however, was standing in the way. 'His proverbial prudence', wrote Barroilhet of William Gibbs, 'is now close to monomania . . . His fevered imagination is set to work in a thousand different ways to spread alarm and implant terrors in the minds of the Peruvian agents and the Government, with the object of legitimising his scheme of price depreciation'.[73] His advice was that the price be increased from the present £11 to £15 and suggested indeed that £20 might be quite feasible.[74] As long as Gibbs had any say, however, such ambitious policies could never be implemented. They stood accused of 'monstrous mismanagement'. Their involvement in the guano trade had, for Peru, 'been a complete disaster, a public calamity'.[75]

It is difficult to believe that Barroilhet made the long voyage from France to Peru merely to offer advice for the pleasure of it or to indulge publicly some passionately held conviction concerning the value of guano. There is no evidence to hand suggesting that he was invited in by Peruvian merchants who had an interest in acquiring guano contracts — and who would of course welcome any attacks on the foreign firm. One certainly cannot dismiss this possibility, but it does seem quite likely that, initially at least, Barroilhet came to Peru

[69] *Ibid.,* pp. 14-5.

[70] Sres, Aráoz, Costas, Escudero, Roca and Tejeda. *Crónica Parlamentaria,* IV, p. 240. Escudero and Tejeda also sat on the commission that examined the guano contract *prórrogas.*

[71] Barroilhet, *Opúsculo,* pp. 15-6.

[72] Carlos Barroilhet, *Exposición que presenta a la Honorable comisión nombrada por la Convención Nacional* (Lima, 1856), (This is reproduced in *Opúsculo sobre el Huano,* pp. 16-48: thus the *Opúsculo* references below).

[73] *Opúsculo,* pp. 31-2.

[74] *Ibid.,* pp. 35, 45.

[75] *Ibid.,* pp. 41, 47.

for pecuniary motives of his own. It may have been his ambition to re-establish himself in the trade on the grounds that he would serve Peru better than Gibbs had done. He certainly hoped for some sort of reward. If the Government took his advice it could, he was saying, expect to make a lot more money out of the trade. In such circumstances he might be entitled to recompense, possibly in the form of 'a certain quantity of guano'.[76]

The initial impact of his discourse in Peru was slight. Congress was dissolved shortly after he spoke to the commission, and was reformed later with men largely unsympathetic to his opinions.[77] Castilla remained as implacable as ever, and refused to grant him any more interviews.[78] He left Peru a disappointed man at the end of April and arrived back in France the following June.[79] Later in the year the special congressional commission appointed to enquire into the contract *prórrogas* produced its report. The Gibbs extension was, as we have seen, held to be illegal; but the main object of criticism was not so much the merchant house as the former government and its irregular and clandestine proceedings. The commissioners declared that they respected Gibbs's overall probity and noted that one of the reasons for the *prórroga* had been 'the good service given the Nation' by the English house.[80] Gibbs gained further comfort from the literary efforts of the liberal politician Santiago Távara on their behalf.[81] In 1856 he published a number of pieces on guano, in one strongly defending them against Barroilhet's denunciations.[82]

This, however, stung Barroilhet into a further attack. He wrote to Gibbs from Paris in August warning that he intended going into print again. 'The lies of Barroilhet', commented Henry Gibbs, 'may produce an *emente* in Lima both against the Government and against our house, and it is impossible to say what might be the

---

[76] *Ibid.,* p. 15. Henry Gibbs's fear was that Barroilhet's main interest might be extortion. 'No doubt he is "open to conviction" or at least would be glad to seduce us into the false step of making an offer to him. Hayne says if he fails in the attempt to extort money, he is the man to go on to every extremity . . .'. HHGC, 2, Henry Gibbs to William Gibbs, 20 August 1856. There is no evidence that he in fact put any pressure of this sort on Gibbs.

[77] Barroilhet, *Opúsculo,* p. 50.

[78] *Ibid.,* p. 52.

[79] *Ibid.,* pp. 52-3.

[80] *Dictamen,* pp. 6, 10. Individuals assisting the country in this way, they asserted, should be rewarded with 'favours, medals, money, rewards', but not, as they considered Gibbs had been, with 'the administration of a branch of the Treasury'. *Ibid.,* p. 6.

[81] HHGC, 2, Henry Gibbs to William Gibbs, 15 September 1856.

[82] Basadre, *Bases Documentales,* 1, p. 354.

consequence. . . . Secure as we may feel in the consciousness of right, it is not a matter to be treated with indifference. . .'.[83] In addition to repeating his case for a more confident pricing policy Barroilhet now levelled some new and very specific accusations against Gibbs. He suggested, first, that a 150 peso fee charged to ships' captains in Callao for various expenses there and at the Chincha islands was excessive and that Gibbs were able to keep almost half the sum for themselves.[84] Second, he made critical reference to the freight commissions that shipowners were obliged to pay the consignees.[85] Third, he insisted that Gibbs's 3½ per cent sales and guarantee commission was 'scandalous'. There were, he suggested, a hundred respectable houses in Europe who would be happy to have the business at 1½ per cent or even 1 per cent.[86] His fourth accusation was that they had been guilty of fraudulent behaviour in 1845 when they had charged the government 7d. for sacks needed in the trade. Gibbs, he suggested, had probably been able to get them at about half that price, and had quietly pocketed the difference.[87] Unfortunately, as he saw it, there was no chance of the government taking any drastic action against the contractors.[88] A presidential election in fact might be the only way of resolving the issue.[89] The best immediate plan would be to send to Europe 'a Commission made up of people knowledgeable in mercantile matters' to enquire into sales, charters and other contentious questions.[90]

Samuel Went, who had returned to England, also believed that an official enquiry would be useful, as it would help clear the air. His firm, he believed, had nothing to hide. The time had arrived 'to take a high ground: we have been grossly accused' and indeed ought to 'demand that a commission should be nominated to enquire into our management of the business'.[91] A direct challenge to Barroilhet, answering all his charges, did not, however, seem appropriate. 'To enter the lists against such a scoundrel as Barroilhet', wrote Henry Gibbs, 'is to fight with a Chimney Sweep — you may conquer but you

[83]HHGC, 2, Henry Gibbs to William Gibbs, 20 August 1856.

[84]Barroilhet, Opúsculo, pp. 64-5.

[85]Ibid., pp. 65-7.

[86]Ibid., p. 97.

[87]Ibid., pp. 69-70.

[88]Ibid., p. 94.

[89]Ibid., p. 104.

[90]Ibid., p. 94.

[91]Remarks ascribed to Went in HHGC, 2, Henry Gibbs to William Gibbs, 23 August 1856.

come out grievously soiled from the encounter'. The government knew of their innocence, 'and I would rather have them see that we treat such charges with the contempt they deserve than that we suffered them to give us any uneasiness'.[92] Barroilhet, however, *had* managed to ruffle Gibbs. He was referred to variously as 'a convicted scoundrel', 'a rogue and a liar' and 'the Brute'.[93] They wished to dismiss him as a vulgar nuisance, but also realized that he was writing for an audience that might be able to exercise damaging influence in Peru. And over one of the charges, that concerning bag prices, they felt quite seriously worried. Henry Gibbs seemed unable to convince himself that no abuse had been committed, since the period in question predated his taking charge of the business, and responsibility in any case seemed to rest largely with the Liverpool house of Gibbs Bright & Co. and with W. J. Myers.[94] The latter proved reluctant to discuss the matter, so there was no reassurance to be gained there,[95] and Gibbs himself was unwilling to interrogate Gibbs Bright.[96] As for the London bag accounts, these had been examined and seemed regular on the whole,[97] although there was some uncertainty about a 2½ per cent discount that had been allowed to Gibbs but not passed on to the government and the consignees.[98] Henry Gibbs had certainly taken the task of finding the relevant invoices very seriously. 'I have', he wrote, 'eaten more dirt and dust than I hope to do for a long while in routing up the papers'.[99]

Barroilhet had written self-dramatising and self-pitying accounts, with much excess of language and inadequacy of documentation. His

[92] *Ibid.,* 9 October 1857.

[93] *Ibid.,* 22 August 1856, 13 and 24 October 1857.

[94] *Ibid.,* 20 August 1856, 24 and 28 October 1857.

[95] *Ibid.,* 9 October 1857.

[96] *Ibid.,* 24 October 1857.

[97] Through some faulty calculations Gibbs, apparently, had been *under*charging the government. *Ibid.,* 24 and 28 October 1857.

[98] *Ibid.,* 30 October 1857. There is also an interesting item in William Gibbs & Co.'s profit and loss account for 1852-3. $2,964 is entered as 'gain on Huano sacks'. This was described as 'being equal to a fair commission', a phraseology which suggests that the earnings were irregular. In the two profit and loss accounts that followed further gains of $3,842 and $1,210 were recorded. The principal abuses were perhaps being committed by the branch house rather than by the parent concern. Lima Branch Accounts, File 3, 1847-1862. There is also a letter of 1854 from the Peruvian finance minister to William Gibbs & Co., informing them that the government had agreed to buy 132,368 empty bags at 21 centimos each from Federico Pfeiffer and instructing them to pay for the bags at that price and make the appropriate entries in their guano accounts. This suggests some attempt at government control of the bag-buying transactions. Hac Arch, Correspond[a]. Con los Consignat[S]. del Huano y Gobor. de las Islas de Chincha, Año de 1853, Mendiburu to William Gibbs & Co., 3 July 1854.

[99] HHGC, 2, Henry Gibbs to William Gibbs, 24 October 1857.

case rested more on calumny, ridicule and emotional fervour than on reasoned and substantiated argument.[100] He wrote, however, with some force and appears to have commanded a sizable and influential readership in Lima. Having despaired of alienating the government from Gibbs, he was now including Castilla in his attacks and directing his appeal towards the Peruvian electorate and Congress. In September 1857 the *Convención Nacional* held a four day debate on his charges, at the instigation of the prominent liberal politician, José Gálvez.[101] At this 'clamorous and memorable discussion'[102] a strong defence of Gibbs was offered by Zevallos, the minister of finance. He concentrated his attention on price policy, and in a number of rather confused and wordy speeches insisted that there was no conflict of interests between Peru and Gibbs. Both sought the highest prices that the market would bear and the *Convención* would do well to ignore unsubstantiated charges levelled against them by a man whose motives in the affair invited only suspicion. He was willing to accept that Montané in France might be guilty of malpractice, but could find no evidence whatever that Gibbs could be similarly indicted, or that they had any sinister interest in the impoverishment of Peru.[103] The *Convención*, however, was not entirely persuaded and on September 9th passed a resolution requiring the executive to send commissioners to Britain, as well as to France and the United States, to see if guano *had* been sold there at unnecessarily low prices, to enquire into the causes of any depreciation that had occurred, to consider what the possibilities were for a rise in prices, and to check if the contractors had been working according to the precise terms of their contracts.[104] The government immediately complied and appointed Manuel Basagoitia to examine Gibbs and their various markets. This had been anticipated in London. Samuel Went had already asserted that a commission would be welcome. Henry Gibbs, however, believed otherwise. He thought it unlikely that he could 'beat into the brains' of any visiting Peruvians the fact 'that English merchants can manage a great business and yet be honourable men'. Even if they were given a clean report, people such as Barroilhet would insist 'that we had

---

[100]The style of his attack was described as 'virulent' by the French chargé d'affaires in 1856. It had, he observed, been composed 'in a spirit of vengeance against the consignatory houses'. MAE, Lima/12, Huet to Walewski, 1 May 1856.

[101]*Informe Circunstanciado*, p. xviii. Barroilhet had apparently sent a large number of copies of his *Opúsculo* to Lima. These, in the words of the French minister, had caused 'a great sensation', thereby precipitating the *Convención* debate. MAE, Lima/12, Huet to Walewski, 11 September 1857.

[102]*Informe Circunstanciado*, p. xviii.

[103]*El Comercio*, 6, 7 and 9 September 1857.

[104]*Crónica Parlamentaria*, V, pp. 203-4.

bought them as we have forsooth bought all the Ministers and apparently all the Governments hitherto'.[105] And he was certainly not going to put himself out to assist Basagoitia in his enquiries: 'if the Commissioner seeks to satisfy himself on any point, let him dirty his fingers himself. We wash our hands of it!'[106]

Meanwhile Barroilhet was scribbling again in Paris. Zevallos's remarks to the *Convención* had greatly annoyed him: his self-assumed role, it seemed, was that of 'lawyer for the calamitous house of Gibbs . . .'.[107] The Castilla administration in fact was 'blinded by its limitless confidence in the consignees . . .'.[108] The *Convención* also came in for attack, having been most ineffective in rebutting Zevallos's ill-informed and malign assertions.[109] The commissions set up to examine the contractors' affairs would, he insisted, be quite useless (despite having himself recommended such a course of action the year before). 'To undertake and bring to completion this difficult task, a battalion of clerks would be needed for each commissioner'.[110] He repeated his former charges on freight commissions, bags and prices, asserting that the recent price increases had not stimulated even an embryonic guano manufacturing industry in Britain.[111] Artificial manures, Barroilhet appears to have believed, could only threaten guano by imitating it. The danger from superphosphate he either ignored or failed to recognise. Free from Gibbs, and operating a sensible and confident policy of high prices, Peru, he proclaimed, would become 'the richest and happiest country in the world' — and if, some day, the country were to remember 'by a spontaneous gesture, the man who laboured so hard in serving them, oh, then his gratitude will be boundless and eternal!'[112]

Gibbs give no account of Basagoitia's visit to their premises. According to Luis Mesones, the *apoderado fiscal* began work around 11 or 12 November, and on the 13th sent a note back to Lima saying he considered Gibbs to be guiltless. He made a further dozen visits between mid-November and mid-December, each lasting no more than two hours, and on January 13th 1858 reported to Lima that his

[105]HHGC, 2, Henry Gibbs to William Gibbs, 13 October 1857.

[106]*Ibid.,* 24 October 1857.

[107]Carlos Barroilhet, *Contestación al Señor Ministro de Hacienda del Perú* (Paris, 1857), p. 7.

[108]*Ibid.,* p. 29.

[109]*Ibid.,* pp. 16, 34.

[110]*Ibid.,* pp. 35-6.

[111]*Ibid.,* p. 28.

[112]*Ibid.,* p. 38.

mission had been completed.[113] The notion that Basagoitia had been less than thorough was later challenged by Francisco de Rivero,[114] and by the *apoderado fiscal* himself.[115] While asserting that he had worked hard, however, Basagoitia admitted that he was ignorant of the English language, that he had to use assistants for studying the accounts, and that he had little knowledge or experience of commercial affairs.[116] He was also intimidated by the disadvantages besetting him in 'a nation so infamous for its power and superior ways' as a result of his lack of both title and reputation.[117] Whatever the adequacy of the enquiry, the important fact was that the government accepted that no charges of misconduct could be sustained against Gibbs.[118] This exoneration appeared in a resolution of January 11 1858 and was based, according to Ulloa, on Basagoitia's letter of November 13.[119] If this is correct, then the government was certainly acting with unseemly haste, appearing to confirm the widely-entertained belief that they were not prepared to accept even the possibility of wrong-doing on Gibbs's part.[120] They were, it seems, profoundly reluctant to disturb a relationship with a firm which could be so easily tapped for money, and with whom they had developed a relatively comfortable and harmonious association, operating by known and established procedures.

Later in 1858 Gibbs produced their own defence.[121] True to their earlier instincts, they chose to ignore Barroilhet, concentrating much of their attention instead on assertions by Mesones,[122] the interim Peruvian chargé in Paris, that they had been guilty of sending quantities of guano to the French market while it was a Montané preserve. Gibbs denied this, insisting that the guano had got into

[113]Mesones, pp. 102-6.

[114]Rivero, pp. 171-2.

[115]Basagoitia, p. 30.

[116]*Ibid.*, pp. 1, 3-4, 30.

[117]*Ibid.*, pp. 4-5.

[118]'Honour and rigour', Basagoitia wrote, 'do not consist of calumny, of giving way blindly and timidly to current rumours because they are popular; people have, in all good faith, been mistaken ... and are misled when they take notice of impassioned and, perhaps, interested reports, sent from afar and spread skilfully and deliberately, and when they form judgements without accurate knowledge of the business ...', *ibid.*, p. 29.

[119]Ulloa, p. 83.

[120]See *Informe Circunstanciado*, p. xix.

[121]Gibbs, *Contestación*. It was not, however, a normal commercial publication. The unbound copy in the Biblioteca Nacional in Lima carries the handwritten inscription: 'This *contestación* came into only very limited circulation'.

[122]In a letter to Basagoitia of 11 December 1857.

French hands without their knowledge through their agency in Antwerp.[123] They also presented a long account of their record on guano prices, arguing that they had always taken the fullest account of 'the Nation's interests, which the Supreme Government had trusted to our charge . . .'.[124] Their private sentiments, however, were a shade less pious. Discussing the case for a reduction in price in 1858, Henry Gibbs wrote that such a move might lead to disapproval in Peru, but that this was of no account: 'if the thing is *right*, and the Government see that it is, I don't care a straw for what the opposition say'.[125] The phraseology is interesting, confirming the impression one gets from Barroilhet's writings that discussion of guano policies in Lima had become polarized politically, and that their own future, as they saw it, depended on maintaining a good relationship with the incumbent administration. Meanwhile, Barroilhet was producing still more pamphlets,[126] all elaborating on familiar themes. He was being driven on, he told his readers, by 'an inner voice' which insistently cried, 'Behold the prodigious wealth of guano! It is the infallible panacea which God has granted Peru'. The voice, however, was not supplying him with fresh information and Gibbs had largely stopped worrying about his denunciations. These were now seldom discussed in their letters, and in December 1858 Henry Gibbs dismissed the most recent publication as 'much more an attack on Ministers than on us'.[128]

In 1859 two much weightier attacks were published; one by Luis Mesones, the other by José Ulloa. Mesones was by then the Peruvian minister in Rome, and his position no doubt gave added authority to his opinions. He aimed his fire at his government as well as at the English contractors. One of his principal concerns was to query the government's defence of Gibbs[129] and to question the worth of the Basagoitia report.[130] His own case against Gibbs, however, was not so much that they had acted deviously and fraudulently, but that they were foreign and that they were being paid far too much money for the services they were performing. He condemned their costly loans to ships' captains on the Peruvian coast, their charges for expenses at Callao and

[123]Gibbs, *Contestación*, pp. 21-5.

[124]*Ibid.*, pp. 9-15.

[125]HHGC, 2, Henry Gibbs to William Gibbs, 20 October 1858.

[126]Carlos Barroilhet, *Grandeza y Decadencia del Perú* (Paris, 1858); *Consider acionessobre la Riqueza del Perú* (Paris, 1859); *Ojeada sobre la Crisis Política y Financiera del Perú* (Paris, 1859).

[127]Barroilhet, *Crisis*, p. 1.

[128]HHGC, 2, Henry Gibbs to William Gibbs, 17 December 1858.

[129]Mesones, p. 1.

[130]*Ibid.*, pp. 102-6.

Chincha, their dominance of the guano bill market in Lima, their allegedly unearned income from sales in Europe through agent houses, and their excessively high interest rates of 5 per cent.[131] 'If it is declared that a foreign house offers a better guarantee of responsible action than Peruvian firms, I should reply in protest, with all the force that is in me, against the humiliating insult thus delivered to the Peruvian character . . . . The nation that, for want of suitable citizens, has to place its interests under the degrading tutelage of foreign and mercenary authority, is less a political entity than a horde of savages or knaves . . .'.[132] Gibbs, as usual, were contemptuous. Mesones exhibited a 'ridiculous ignorance of commercial matters'[133] and was described as 'personally hostile', and a source of 'lying attacks'.[134]

Ulloa, another Peruvian official in Europe,[135] also believed that Gibbs earned excessive commissions, that they had been responsible for a proliferation of unnecessary costs and charges, that they exerted undue pressure on the treasury and on national commerce, that they had engaged in irregular exporting to France in 1856-7, that they had been cleared erroneously by Basagoitia, and that they were defended in all their deeds far too readily by the Peruvian minister in London.[136] These were by now familiar charges. The most interesting features of Ulloa's long study are his discussion of the price issue, his assertion that the markets were being inadequately supplied, and his sharp criticism of government guano policies. Prices, he insisted, were too low[137] and consignees had been responsible for persistent depreciation. Contrary to what Zevallos had said there *was* a conflict of interest between Peru and the guano merchants. Lower prices meant bigger sales and higher commissions for the consignees. This, however, did not suit Peru, 'which has to sell, not the greatest possible quantity of guano at a debased price, but the smallest possible amount at the highest possible price'.[138] Ulloa did not acknowledge that the consignees

[131] *Ibid.,* pp. 109-20.

[132] *Ibid.,* p. 114.

[133] HHGC, 2, Henry Gibbs to Rivero, 10 March 1860.

[134] *Ibid.,* 3, Henry Gibbs to William Gibbs, 4 March 1862.

[135] Ulloa, *Huano.* The title page indicates that he was *Secretario de la Comisión Fiscal del Perú en Francia y sus Colonias* and that the pamphlet was published by special resolution of Congress. I am grateful to Dr. Jorge Basadre for drawing my attention to this interesting study. It is not discussed in the Gibbs correspondence and might easily have escaped my notice.

[136] *Ibid.,* pp. 43-59, 113-8, 131.

[137] *Ibid.,* pp. 5-7, 130.

[138] *Ibid.,* pp. 114-5.

might also gain from higher prices; nor did he draw any distinction between the Peruvian nation's long-term interests and the Peruvian government's short-term interests. He also levelled a very specific charge against Gibbs over prices: that they had inexcusably delayed the implementation of the instructions contained in the Elías circular of April 1855.[139] On the question of supplies, he believed that there was an insufficiency of depots in Europe.[140] The contractors, moreover, had displayed a 'lack of zeal in selling'.[141] His attack on the government was very much focused on Zevallos who, it was declared, had been responsible for 'the sacrifice of justice and the national interest on behalf of this house . . .'.[142] The absolution of Gibbs in August 1858 had been quite unjustified,[143] as had been the rushed decision to give them the new French contract.[144] The government, moreover, exercised no imagination or originality in the drawing up of contracts. The heavy hand of habit directed their every move and made them deaf to pleas for reform.[145] The financial aspects were a particular cause for national concern: consignees such as Gibbs imposed on the government 'the harshest possible conditions for loans; they can withhold them at will and, to put it briefly, enjoy the greatest possible despotism that a person or a family could exercise over a nation'.[146] Ulloa's solution was a simple one: private contractors should be swept from the business and replaced in the various markets around the world by Peruvian government officials.[147] Ownership of guano had been nationalized in the early 1840s; now the principle should be extended to the trade itself.

In 1860 Francisco de Rivero, the former Peruvian minister in London, took up the cudgels on Gibbs's behalf, confirming thereby the widely entertained belief that he was an over-enthusiastic apologist for the English contractors. One of Rivero's motives, of course, was to show that his admiration was well-founded. There can be no doubting, however, that he was intimate with the Gibbs house, more so perhaps than a public functionary and watchdog ought to have been. It is unlikely, however, that there was anything corrupt about the relation-

[139] *Ibid.*, p. 48.

[140] *Ibid.*, pp. 3, 13-9.

[141] *Ibid.*, p. 115.

[142] *Ibid.*, p. 83.

[143] *Ibid.*, pp. 83-97.

[144] *Ibid.*, pp. 98-102, 131.

[145] *Ibid.*, p. 106.

[146] *Ibid.*, p. 116.

[147] *Ibid.*, p. 132.

ship. If Rivero had been in Gibbs's pay he would probably not have been so fulsome in his praise. The defence would have been more subtle and less open to misinterpretation. It is more than probable that, for locational reasons alone, he viewed the trade with London rather than Lima perspectives. Rivero devoted much of his space to attacking his fellow diplomat, Luis Mesones: the latter's errors and personal imputations had, he claimed, been his principal reason for writing.[148] His work had been frivolous and his assertions unsubstantiated; he had lacked any knowledge of the background to official confidence in Gibbs; and he had unjustly maligned Basagoitia.[149] Zevallos, contrary to Mesones's suggestions, was a person of 'great ability'. Castilla too was a shrewd man who had always taken the closest interest in the guano trade and regularly sought out the latest information on its progress.[150] There were, he suggested, already 'enough scandals, enough spiteful quarrels' to sully the good name of Peru, without officials overseas engaging in such denigration of their superiors in Lima.[151] He also challenged Ulloa's contention that the trade would be better handled by the Peruvian bureaucracy. It was simply not practical or realistic to send out a large number of salaried officials from Lima and expect them to do a better job in the labyrinths of European commerce and finance than the professional merchants with their metropolitan experience and their funds of wealth and skill.[152] The present system yielded most generous returns to the government, and Gibbs's behaviour, in relation to what the government had asked of them, was quite beyond reproach. Their price policies had always been appropriate to market circumstances, and it was foolish to believe that one could still raise prices without damaging consumption.[153] The contractors worked hard at their job, and pursued only what returns were legally theirs.[154] Every Peruvian minister who had served in London arrived there 'cherishing, if not the most vulgar notions bred among us, at least some doubts as to their management of the business as honest men'. After closely observing the consignees at work, however, they were obliged 'to do full justice to the energy, integrity and probity with which the trade is run ....'.[155]

[148]Rivero, p. v.

[149]*Ibid.,* p. 145.

[150]*Ibid.,* p. 102.

[151]*Ibid.,* p. 185.

[152]*Ibid.,* pp. 207, 210, 214.

[153]*Ibid.,* p. 219.

[154]*Ibid.,* p. 182.

[155]*Ibid.,* p. 33.

Only ill-informed and mean-spirited men had taken a different view. Gibbs had been 'vilely, unjustly and crudely attacked by certain individuals full of rancour and envy . . .', by 'communists of a new species, enemies of their wealth . . .'.[156]

Mesones retaliated with a letter to *El Comercio,* which Rivero answered with a further pamphlet.[157] In 1860 and 1861 two more publications of Barroilhet's appeared.[158] The problems that guano had lately been encountering in the markets of Europe were of little concern to him: it was 'the most monstrous scandal that the house of Gibbs should sell guano in England for £12, causing Peru the loss of a colossal fortune . . .'.[159] Gibbs's motivation was not just the wish to increase their own income at Peru's expense, but their 'intense desire to curry favour with the powerful English aristocracy . . .'. Their involvement with agricultural intrigue was 'an extraordinary scandal'.[160]

An entirely new issue appeared in 1861 and was the subject of considerable newspaper and congressional discussion, namely Gibbs's decision to ship as much guano as they could in the last months of their contract, thereby extending the period during which they had fertilizer to sell (and hoping as well, perhaps, that stocking-up would improve their chances of winning the new contract). Such a policy, as noted in the previous chapter, appears only to have been pursued in 1860, and was checked from within the firm itself. But the timing was still such that largestocks could be guaranteed beyond December 1861. At the beginning of that year Juan José Salcedo, Zevallos' successor as finance minister, told Congress that the government had wished to limit Gibbs's exports of guano, but doubted if this could be put into effect and feared the possible consequences for the treasury of placing temporary brakes on the trade.[161] It would be difficult to judge precisely what sort of restriction to impose, and if it happened that the market was under-supplied this would damage national interests by further encouraging the use of alternative fertilizers. Salcedo's remarks, however, did not carry very much conviction and failed to persuade a number of members of Congress, who continued to insist that a major abuse had been committed.[162]

[156]*Ibid.,* p. 34.

[157]Francisco de Rivero, *Reflexiones Sobre Una Carta Del Doctor Luis Mesones* Lima, 1861).

[158]Carlos Barroilhet, *Examen Crítico De Un Opúsculo Sobre El Guano* (Paris, 1860); *Examen Crítico de Dos Publicaciones del Sr. Don Francisco Rivero* (Paris, 1861).

[159]Barroilhet, *Examen Crítico,* p. 26.

[160]*Ibid.,* pp. 30-1.

[161]*El Comercio,* 17 January 1861.

[162]See remarks of Irigoyen and Cornejo, *ibid.*

El Comercio developed the point in an editorial on 17 January. It repeated most of the accusations that the pamphleteers had levelled against Gibbs, and observed that since May of the previous year the English contractors had been carrying away excessively large quantities of guano. This had been a quite shameless and brazen breach of confidence. 'The house of Gibbs has thrown aside the veil of hypocrisy with which it has hitherto covered itself, and now has no scruples about appearing proud of its abuses, which menace Peru and which, *in law,* constitute a criminal offence . . .'.[163] The legal position was not clarified, but *El Comercio* was convinced that the contractors had now blatantly revealed, if further revelations were necessary, how unworthy they were of Peru's trust. What was additionally disturbing was the way in which both Congress and the government had in the past tended to turn blind eyes to the sins of the English merchants. Congress, it was admitted, had been critical, but ineffectively so. The government for its part had always bent over backwards to defend the foreigners. For the future there was only one honourable course. 'The noble precepts of justice, the violated standards of commercial morality, and the clear interests of the Treasury point to the revocation and condemnation of the Gibbs contract'.[164]

Whatever *El Comercio* may have suggested, Gibbs found it difficult to believe that they had many valuable friends left in Congress or in the government. In the early 1860s they saw themselves as beset by enemies on all sides. Just how the government had offended them is not made clear, but it appears to have had something to do with a willingness in the Finance Ministry to accept some of the criticisms levelled at Gibbs by Mesones and Ulloa (and perhaps also with some expressions of dismay over Gibbs's exporting policy). With the departure of Zevallos, Gibbs had lost their most enthusiastic apologist. It was no doubt becoming increasingly less opportune politically for the government to be seen as uncritical intimates of foreign merchants. 'You will see', Henry Gibbs wrote to Rivero early in 1860, 'that they have adopted Mesones for their mentor, and want to carry out his ideas!'[165] By the end of the year Salcedo was being described as a rascal and a liar. Even the old loyalist Castilla had 'shewn no little ingratitude to our House both here and in Lima who have served him so well'.[166] In the summer of

---

[163]'El Congreso, El Gobierno y La Casa de Gibbs', *ibid.*

[164]*Ibid.*

[165]HHGC, 2, Henry Gibbs to Rivero, 10 March 1860.

[166]*Ibid.*, Henry Gibbs to George Gibbs, 1 November 1860.

1861, by which time Salcedo had been replaced by José Fabio Melgar, Gibbs were asking the government to redeem itself with 'a public declaration that our conduct has been irreproachable'. Castilla and his colleagues 'ought to have known us long enough to be aware that we make no charge but what we actually pay . . .'.[167] As for recent criticism in Congress, this was little more than 'the chattering of individual scoundrels'[168] and the government could hardly be expected to declare disapproval of this. They had in any case expressed regret in private and told Gibbs not to take it too seriously.[169] The government's own public pronouncements, however, were another matter. 'We do complain, and have complained that Salcedo did not speak up for us, and tell the truth as he ought'.[170] Reparation from the Peruvian representative in London 'would go for nothing'; it had to come directly from Lima.[171] Towards the end of 1861 they received some satisfaction in the form of friendly and approving remarks from the finance minister,[172] although there is no indication that these were other than private. The contractors, clearly, would tolerate no criticism of their conduct. It was especially upsetting when it came from a government with whom their relations had always been so good, but which now seemed to be responding to political pressures and withdrawing some of the protection and favour which had always been such a vital element of their power in the past.

It is, perhaps, of no little significance that the pamphleteers laid down their pens after Gibbs left the trade. Was it that Gibbs were the principal sinners and that with their expulsion there was little need to pronounce further? This is unlikely, for the Peruvian merchants who moved into the British trade performed the same functions as Gibbs had done and were granted almost identical rewards for their labours.[173] Their business standards, moreover, were such as to provoke an official enquiry in the early 1870s which produced a highly unfavourable report.[174] Was it, then, simply that, with the trade now securely in Peruvian hands, there was no longer any important objective to be pursued — in short, that the pamphlet-writers and journalists had been energized more by opportunism and

[167]*Ibid.,* Henry Gibbs to William Gibbs, 14 August 1861.

[168]*Ibid.,* 1 November 1861. Congress spent quite a lot of time discussing the trade in late 1860 and early 1861. *Crónica Parlamentaria,* VI, pp. 185-225.

[169]HHGC, 2, Henry Gibbs to William Gibbs, 1 November 1861.

[170]*Ibid.,* 16 November 1861.

[171]*Ibid.,* 1 November 1861.

[172]*Ibid.,* 29 November 1861.

[173]See below, pp. 221-2.

[174]See below, pp. 241-2.

nationalism than by genuine moral indignation? There is no documentary evidence to hand to sustain such a conclusion, but it does seem very likely that most of Gibbs's critics were eager to see the trade taken from them and awarded to indigenous groups. What connections there were between the aspiring local merchants and the pamphleteers cannot be established here, although the issue does seem worth exploring, especially since the merchants themselves managed to maintain a dignified silence during all the heated exchanges. It would be unlikely, however, that close enquiry would show Gibbs's critics to be a co-ordinated body of like-minded men. Barroilhet, for instance, was probably motivated in the main by self-interest, and the hyperbolic, bombastic tenor of his arguments contrasts sharply with the sober, weighty, literate observations of men like Ulloa. Ulloa himself, it will be recalled, did not advocate a transfer to Peruvian merchants, but rather to government officials. So the issue of pamphleteers as a literary spearhead for the local bourgeoisie remains an open one.

Two other points ought to be stressed. First, that Gibbs were almost bound to attract criticism in the late 1850s from perceptive and questioning observers of the trade. They had been party to certain arrangements on which information had been withheld from the public; they had gained control over an enormously wide range of markets; they were involved in a system of exporting that was enmeshing the treasury in a tightening net of indebtedness; and, if the tone of their private correspondence is anything to go by, they were treating Peruvian sensitivities and aspirations beyond official circles with supercilious contempt. Second, they seem to have got tangled up unwittingly in the political turmoil of Castilla's last years in power. The attack on Gibbs was, as a number of the remarks quoted above suggest, to quite a substantial degree really part of a general attack on a man who, with one short break, had ruled Peru since 1845. Many of the men involved in questioning Gibbs's position in the trade were prominent and vociferous liberals, seeking social progress through, in Pike's words, 'freedom of competition and unfettered political and economic individualism'.[175] They had some success in forcing a moderately liberal constitution on an unsympathetic Castilla in 1856,[176] but the merits of this were hotly contested both in debate and in military revolt in the years that followed, and in 1860 the president succeeded in having a much more conservative constitution drawn up, an achievement deeply resented by liberals and resulting in two

[175] Pike, *Peru*, p. 104.

[176] *Ibid.*, pp. 106-7.

attempts on Castilla's life.[177] Among those exiled at the time were José Gálvez, who had instigated the *Convención Nacional* debate on Barroilhet's charges in 1857. Pike portrays him as dogmatic and aggressive: 'the epitome of Peru's revived liberalism'.[178] José Simeón Tejeda and Ignacio Escudero, who sat on the 1856 commissions to examine Barroilhet's initial declarations and the Echenique contract-extensions, were also very prominent within liberal groups, Tejeda in particular being dedicated to the principles of the free market.[179] Santiago Távara, of like mind,[180] supported Gibbs with a pamphlet in 1856, but after listening to Zevallos at the *Convención Nacional* in 1857 rose to say that official approval of the contractors had been carried too far, the minister's defence of Gibbs being 'a hundred times' more fulsome than his own.[181] *El Comercio,* which attacked Gibbs so vigorously in 1861, was usually on the liberal side of any social or political argument, and José Casimiro Ulloa, the most substantial of Gibbs's critics, is referred to by Bonilla as one of the *representantes ideológicos* of the rising bourgeoisie.[182] Basadre makes it clear that he was a man of some eminence within literary and liberal circles in Lima.[183]

In the assault on Gibbs, therefore, high-minded liberalism, political contention, genuine concern over the defects of the export system, desire (self-serving, nationalistic, or both) to see the trade transferred to Peruvians, dislike of the English firm, disquiet over the geographical range of their monopoly, spite, envy, and personal ambition were all at work. A lot of the assertions were ill-judged, as it happened, but the balance between truth and fiction was difficult to establish in Lima, at such a distance from the market. Gibbs knew this, and their normal posture was one of cynical resignation. 'We have got to tell the truth — which though it will always prevail with those who understand the subject matter, and I may say with honest men, yet it is no better than a lie with the majority of those whom our opponent [Barroilhet] addresses, and who are probably neither the one nor the other'.[184]

[177]*Ibid.,* pp. 107-9.

[178]*Ibid.,* pp. 104-5, 109.

[179]*Ibid.,* p. 105; also Bonilla, *Guano,* p. 51.

[180]Pike, *Peru,* p. 103.

[181]*El Comercio,* 6 September 1857.

[182]Bonilla, *Guano,* p. 51.

[183]Basadre, *Historia* (1946), I, pp. 159, 348, 363, 382; II, pp. 99-100.

[184]Remarks ascribed to Went in HHGC, 2, Henry Gibbs to William Gibbs, 23 August 1856.

THE TRANSFER OF CONTROL

It would have been most surprising, given the background thus described, if Gibbs had succeeded in winning further contracts for the 1860s. Even as late as 1861, however, their departure from the trade had by no means become a certainty. The expectation that they might continue as guano contractors was quite widely entertained, not least by Gibbs themselves. In his message to Congress in 1860 Castilla observed that the trade and its organization had lately been the subject of a lot of heated and irrational discussion, but that the government did not consider itself as yet sufficiently well-informed on all relevant matters to make up its own collective mind on possible changes.[185] According to Maiguashca, Castilla's inclination was probably to keep Gibbs in the trade if only because, as foreigners, they would have the virtue of political neutrality.[186] Jerningham, the British chargé, considered that economic realities alone might help preserve the status quo. Congress would make 'strenuous attempts . . . to change the present system and take it out of Foreign Hands, but whether the Government will agree to this, remains to be seen, as there are no native Houses who can afford to presume to take the Consignment of this Article on such favourable terms to the Peruvian Government as British Capitalists'.[187]

Henry Gibbs believed that his best tactic would be to offer a large advance rather than to agree to any cut in commissions, and there is evidence that a big sum had in fact been handed over around 1860.[188] Remuneration, he considered, was low enough already: 'we must be shy of embarking in the same boat with a set of thieves with neither money nor means, who provided they get a contract will take any commission however small, trusting to make 5 times as much by means which we will not use'. Big loans, made in the fairly near future, would have the advantage of tying the government's hands when the question of new contracts came to be discussed: 'it will be an unpleasant element in anybody else's contract to have to pay us half a million sterling, or to find money for the Government while we are repaying ourselves out of the Huano in our hands'.[189] A connected element in the plan was, of course, guano stockpiling: that would further complicate matters for any new contractors, and give Gibbs the security they needed for large loans.

[185] *Crónica Parlamentaria,* VI, p. LX.

[186] Maiguashca, p. 70.

[187] FO 61/193, Jerningham to Russell, 14 August 1860.

[188] See chapter 3, p. 115.

[189] HHGC, 2, Henry Gibbs to William Gibbs, 6 January 1869.

In October 1860, however, the government took the decisive and radical step of celebrating six new contracts, each for four years, which between them mopped up virtually all Gibbs's existing markets. Zaracondegui was awarded Britain, the British empire and the United States; Lachambre was given France; Witt y Schutte, Germany; Patrone, Italy; Valdeavellano, Belgium; Canevaro, Pardo y Barrón, Holland.[190] Britain, her colonies and the Low Countries were therefore added to the list of territories controlled by Peruvians. Zaracondegui's achievement was the most impressive. Gibbs had submitted a tender, 'but the terms not being so advantageous as those of Zaracondegui, it was therefore refused'.[191] The Peruvian firm was backed by Ugarte, Barreda, Oyague and Candamo, and appears to have won through by the surprising generosity of the loan offer: 4½ million pesos at 4 per cent. They also agreed to take only 2½ per cent for sales, guarantee and brokerage.[192] 'The temptation of immediate ready money', Jerningham reported, 'coupled with the fact of giving the new contract to a Native Firm, has no doubt induced the Government to break with the House of Gibbs which has served them honestly'. The government, he pointed out, badly needed cash after the 'immense' outlays that were currently being made on army and navy personnel, men 'who feed upon the public Prosperity'.[193] Henry Gibbs asked a visiting Peruvian in London how Zaracondegui had been able to raise the money. 'He has collected it from the capitalists of Lima', was the reply. On what, Gibbs asked further, would the government spend the loan? 'Rifles!' their caller answered.[194] Jerningham also mentioned another possible consideration. 'I have heard', he wrote, 'that the President was inclined to continue the Huano contract with this Firm [Gibbs], but was overruled by others, who scared him by saying that if he did not give it to a Native Firm, there would be a Revolution'.[195] Gibbs, he considered, would easily survive the transfer. The government still owed them large sums of money, but they had plenty of time left to dig whatever guano they needed to cover their advances.[196] Henry Gibbs certainly appeared unruffled. 'I shall

[190]*Anales*, VI, p. 49.

[191]FO 61/193, Jerningham to Russell, 13 October 1860; also HHGC, 2, Henry Gibbs to William Gibbs, 1 November 1860, where it is implied that there had been some irregularity and injustice in the selection. It was believed at the time that, after Zaracondegui's success, Gibbs intrigued to prevent the transfer from actually taking place. See MAE, Lima/12, De Lesseps to Thouvenel, 30 September 1860; De Lesseps to Walewski, 14 October 1860

[192]*Anales*, VI, p. 52.

[193]FO 61/193, Jerningham to Russell, 13 October 1860.

[194]HHGC, 2, Henry Gibbs to William Gibbs, 5 November 1860.

[195]FO 61/193, Jerningham to Russell, 13 October 1860.

[196]*Ibid*.

be quite satisfied that it would have brought more . . . kicks than halfpence, and certainly I should think the new people will find it so to their cost, tenfold more than we should if we continued it'.[197]

The matter, however, was still far from being settled. In conformity with their resolution of August 1860,[198] Congress had set up a committee to examine the new contracts.[199] In February 1861 this body advised, among other things, that Gibbs retain the right to sell guano in Britain until May 1862, and then transfer their stocks to the new consignees in return for compensation for freight and other charges already incurred, as well as interest due on these disbursements.[200] Zaracondegui and his colleagues, however, declared that this would involve 'enormous losses' and that it was, therefore, unacceptable.[201] The government insisted that Congress's decision could not be revoked and that, accordingly, the British and British colonial parts of the Zaracondegui contract must now be annulled.[202] Gibbs's guano stocks were bound, as the contractors had intended, to complicate the new business in its early months. And with such a large loan on offer and such a wide range of markets now his responsibility, Zaracondegui may well have felt he had taken on more than he could handle.[203] In March 1861 the government published a decree calling for new tenders for Britain, stating its conditions of acceptability.[204] (All the other contracts, incidentally, remained in force). Contractors would have to agree to official determination of quantities to be exported each year, as well as of prices, and remuneration on loans was not to exceed 4 per cent, and on sales 2½ per cent. The government would retain the power to suspend freights when it considered that enough guano had been shipped, and could revise the terms of the contract *after* it had been signed by both parties.[205]

[197]HHGC, 2, Henry Gibbs to George Gibbs, 1 November 1860.

[198]Cited in *El Peruano*, 28 March 1861.

[199]See HHGC, 2, Henry Gibbs to Tyndall Bright, 15 December 1860; Henry Gibbs to Rivero, 18 December 1860.

[200]*El Peruano*, 28 March 1861.

[201]*Ibid.*

[202]*Ibid.*

[203]His opponents in Lima also seem to have been making things more difficult for him. A later report on the guano trade, in a retrospective comment on these events, observed that Zaracondegui had been the victim of 'disgraceful chicanery'. The nature of the scheming was not specified. *Informe Circunstanciado*, p. xx.

[204]*El Peruano*, 28 March 1861; FO 61/198, Jerningham to Russell, 13 May 1861.

[205]*El Peruano*, 28 March 1861.

Tenders would be received up until the end of July 1861. No satisfactory offers, however, were forthcoming and the matter remained wide open.[206]

In the summer of 1861 Gibbs made it known in Lima that they did not want to submit any further bids,[207] and in October Henry Gibbs wrote that the finance minister had 'again received our refusal to undertake the business. . .'[208], the phraseology suggesting that they had received overtures.[209] Possibly despairing of a successful outcome in Lima, the government had instructed J. J. de Osma, now minister in Madrid and the author of Gibbs's 1849 and 1850 contracts, to try to come to some arrangement with a European house.[210] Osma contacted Gibbs in London,[211] and was told that if they did continue in the trade they would do so against their will, even on the present terms.[212] Henry Gibbs believed that not only would Peru have considerable difficulty finding someone to take the British market, but that the new contractors for the continent would soon run into money troubles and, after quarrelling with the government, be thrown out: 'then the Government will come to us "with cap in hand"' offering back all the old domains. He imagined what his imperious reply would be: 'if we take you again it is not to please ourselves but you. We much prefer that you should find another house to do your business —but if you can't, we will see what can be done'. He would ask for the retention of present commission levels 'and our hands perfectly unfettered . . . in the arrangement of the business.'[213] One reason for Gibbs's lack of interest was the government's decree of March 1861 stating its relatively harsh conditions for a new British contract.[214] Henry Gibbs said he would not care to do any business under it: it was clearly a law for rogues, for only they would be prepared to make the necessary circumventions.[215]

[206]The basis on which tenders would be admitted, Jerningham had commented, was such 'as to exclude all possibility of its leading to any bona fide business'. FO 61/198, Jerningham to Russell, 13 May 1861.

[207]HHGC, 2, Henry Gibbs to William Gibbs, 14 August 1861.

[208]*Ibid.*, 14 October 1861.

[209]See also FO 61/203, Barton to Layard, 29 January 1862.

[210]HHGC, 2, Henry Gibbs to William Gibbs, 15 October 1861.

[211]He also got in touch with Peabody & Co., who were not interested, considering the terms 'too low'. *Ibid.,* 18 October 1861

[212]*Ibid.,* 15 October 1861.

[213]*Ibid.*

[214]*Ibid.,* 16 November 1861.

[215]*Ibid.,* 29 November 1861.

A solution almost materialised in the autumn of 1861, the government agreeing to give a group of local capitalists the British contract in return for a loan of 4 to 5 million pesos. The terms, on the mercantile side, were to be more favourable than those presented in the March decree: 3 per cent for commissions and 5 per cent for interest. The merchants attempted to raise funds by public subscription, but receipts began to flag before 2 million had come in.[216] The target was never reached and the deal fell through.[217] In Europe, meanwhile, Osma was making unsuccessful approaches to the houses of Baring and Rothschild,[218] having abandoned the effort to catch Gibbs again. Other firms, though, did show considerable interest. Bids came in from Atherton Kelly and Joseph Hegan, each with a good deal of financial backing in London and Liverpool.[219]

Towards the end of 1861, however, a final settlement was at last taking shape in Lima. Gibbs considered the attempt to draw up contracts simultaneously in both Peru and Europe highly improper. There was the absurd possibility that two contracts might be arranged and signed at the same time.[220] Osma expressed his own objections in a letter to Lima.[221] But the Castilla government, understandably in the circumstances, had been seeking possible contractors wherever they could be found. Gibbs's contract had already run out, and the English house was showing indifference over a new arrangement. The matter could not be allowed to drift much longer.

'The best news I have to give you', Henry Gibbs wrote to his Uncle William in February 1862, 'is that Barreda [formerly of the U.S. trade] has expressed his willingness to take the English Contract. It is not quite settled, but I have great hopes it will be, and that we shall be free. . . '.[222] A month or so later he wrote that the matter had been definitely concluded: 'Much good may it do them'.[223] Henry Witt, a former Gibbs manager and now a guano contractor for Germany, had observed the proceedings with an expert's eye. Over the last two weeks of 1861, he noted in his diary, Felipe Barreda, his son-in-law

---

[216]*Ibid.*, 16 November 1861. (The names of the merchants are not given).

[217]*Ibid.*, early December 1861.

[218]*Ibid.*, 29 November 1861; 3, Henry Gibbs to William Gibbs, 23 January 1862.

[219]*Ibid.*, 3, Henry Gibbs to William Gibbs, 23 January 1862.

[220]*Ibid.*, 2, Henry Gibbs to William Gibbs, early December 1861; 3, Henry Gibbs to William Gibbs, 12 December 1861 and 8 February 1862.

[221]*Ibid.*, 3, Henry Gibbs to William Gibbs, 19 December 1861.

[222]*Ibid.*, 1 February 1862.

[223]*Ibid.*, 4 March 1862.

Manuel Pardo, José Canevaro[224] and his son José Canevaro Jr. had been negotiating with Castilla for the British market. The president had agreed to make an eight-year award, and allowed 3 per cent on sales and 5 per cent on interest. There was to be an advance of $1,000,000, showing how radically the Government's loan expectations had been modified. Even this relatively modest sum seemed likely to pose problems: 'now', wrote Witt, 'came the difficulty to raise this million. Candamo, Goyeneche, Felipe Gordillo, Clemente Villate and others were applied to; Candamo refused, Goyeneche wavered, and Gordillo and Villate were inclined to enter but unwilling to leave the management to young Pardo and young Canevaro, and at the same time the great difficulty consisted in bringing the money together, nevertheless negotiations always continued . . . . Now came on the 2ᵈ [January] this news of the possibility of a war between the United States and England which at once dampened the spirits of Gordillo and Villate; Barreda however was willing to go on if the others would, and thus on this date nobody knew how the affair really stood . . . it was also reported that Barreda would draw by the following steamer upon England which showed that he required funds'.[225] On January 8th there was a lot of fresh talking, and a decision was finally taken not to enter the business since the merchants 'considered that the present state of political affairs, with the war impending between England and the United States, was too precarious to be able to calculate with certainty upon assistance being obtained from European capitalists . . .'.[226] Clearly there had never been any question of Peruvians going it alone in the trade.

A week or so later the old contractors made a surprise reappearance. 'It became known that Gibbs would within a few days pay to the Government about $600,000, which sum would enable them to overcome their most pressing difficulties'.[227] This is further evidence of the confusions of the time and of the continuing adverse financial circumstances of the Peruvian government. It can hardly be taken as a tardy bid on Gibbs's part for a new contract, otherwise Witt would have mentioned the fact. It was simply a fresh and profitable loan, and possibly also a gesture of contempt on Gibbs's part towards the local merchants. By the end of the month, however, Barreda and his

---

[224]Pardo and Canevaro were, as noted earlier, already party to the Dutch contract. Pardo later became the first *Civilista* president of Peru (1872-6).

[225]Witt Diaries, VI, entry for 1 January 1862.

[226]*Ibid.*, entry for 8 January 1862.

[227]*Ibid.*, entry for 14 January 1862.

friends had reconsidered their position and agreed to take the contract after all. 'Those who had put their names to the proposal were: Clemente Ortiz de Villate, José Canevaro Sr., Carlos Delgado y Moreno, Felipe Gordillo, Manuel Pardo, and Felipe Barreda . . .'.[228] Their offer had been made on January 21st, and the arrangement was dated January 28th. The contract was to run for eight years. There was to be, as originally planned, a 1,000,000 peso loan at 5 per cent, the same interest rate being given on all other advance payments. Sales commissions were to be 3 per cent (and 5 per cent in colonial areas), and the merchants were given permission to charge a 2½ per cent commission to foreign shipowners. 1,000 peso shares to the aggregate value of 2,000,000 were to be offered to investors in Peru and abroad. The merchants had also wished to be allowed to make upward adjustments to the interest rate in the event of the Bank of England, in a possible war, raising its discount rate to a level higher than that stipulated for the contractors, but this was disallowed.[229] This sort of worry was clear indication of the merchants' intention to draw heavily on the London money market. The share provisions, too, show that considerable outside help was required. In the early spring Osma arranged in London for Thomson Bonar & Co. to be the consignees,[230] and Gibbs noted in May that this firm had just sent out a clerk to Lima to make arrangements for a loan.[231]

As a triumph for economic nationalism, then, the new contract was not quite as dramatic as it seemed. It showed, moreover, that what the pamphleteers had held to be the excessive remuneration granted Gibbs was not going to be suddenly corrected when they left the trade. The new contractors were allowed to make the same charges to shipowners, and given only ½ per cent less in sales commission. They were allowed ½d per peso as well for guano bills issued to other merchants against sales proceeds in London.[232] Gibbs had also taken this fee and had been vigorously attacked by Mesones for doing so. The terms, then, were very similar to Gibbs's terms. And they were, from the government's point of view, much worse than those agreed more than a year earlier with Zaracondegui, and for that matter with those of the other 1860 contracts now in operation. They also failed to measure up to the requirements of the government's own

[228]*Ibid.*, entry for 30 January 1862. Bonilla suggests, wrongly, that the revised contract went again to Zaracondegui and his friends. *Guano*, p. 42. Barreda was the only merchant involved in both groups.

[229]Witt Diaries, entry for 30 January 1862; *Anales*, VII, pp. 56-7.

[230]*The Times*, 23 April, p. 7; *Informe Circunstanciado*, p. xx.

[231]HHGC, 3, Henry Gibbs to William Gibbs, 2 May 1862; also Bonilla, 'Aspects', p. 274.

[232]Witt Diaries, VI, entry for 30 January 1862.

March 1861 declaration. That this was so showed just what a mess the British arrangements had been allowed to get into. The authors of the *Informe Circunstanciado* a decade later described the 1862 contract as being 'in shocking violation of the Law' and 'enormously damaging to the interests of the Treasury'. Excessively generous terms had been granted to men dealing with the market which not only was the largest and therefore the most remunerative one abroad, but also provided the best facilities for the recruitment of sub-agents.[233] The reasons for this are obscure. The government may, with the British contract, have been giving favoured treatment to its friends. On the other hand, it may simply have been making the best of a bad job, cutting its losses and bringing to an end as decisively as possible a long period of great confusion and uncertainty.

It is odd to find Gibbs giving the government a loan of 600,000 pesos at a time when the new contractors were finding it so difficult to organize their own advance. Perhaps this made it easier for the government to make do with only a modest sum from Barreda and his associates (half the 1860 advance for the French contract and smaller even than the advance for the Belgian contract). Gibbs may also have lent the much larger sum of 4,000,000 pesos some time before the Barreda contract was agreed,[234] and in 1864 they supplied a further 200,000 pesos on the security of damaged guano still in their possession.[235] With this sort of financial strength they could easily have improved on Barreda's offer for the British contract and retained part of their old market area without running foul of the 1849 law. They appear, however, not to have submitted a tender, nor to have been invited to do so in late 1861 and early 1862. The government now refrained from any gesture towards them, probably because of its awareness of local sensitivities and because past approaches had been met with chilly responses. Gibbs's own reluctance to stay in the trade is more difficult to understand, but it may have had something to do with the feeling that any future contract was bound to be troublesome, especially with the impending departure of Castilla from

[233] *Informe Circunstanciado*, p. xx; also Witt Diaries, VI, entry for 30 January 1862.

[234] See chapter 3, p. 115.

[235] Hac Arch, Año 1864, Tesoreria Principal, Loan of 1 October 1864. The new merchants were poor substitutes for Gibbs as sources of ready cash. When John Barton reported Gibbs's departure from the trade he also recorded that the government was 'very hard up' and that word had just got out that 'Melgar the late Minister for Foreign Affairs is to proceed shortly to England, with the object of raising a Loan'. FO 61/203, Barton to Layard, 29 January 1862. Later that year a £5,500,000 loan was in fact floated on the London money market. *Anales*, VII, pp. 96-101. For further comment on the government's financial predicament, see MAE, Lima/12, De Lesseps to Thouvenel, 11 August 1862.

the presidency and the now problematical condition of the market. They had far too many enemies in Lima, and a future government might be pressurized into upsetting their contract. They could continue to earn money by selling off old guano stocks, and by making further loans to the government at least for as long as they had the security of guano-in-hand.

Even more important, of course, they could recognise their capacity to move into totally different lines of business, as well as enlarging and widening their traditional trading work, by making use of the large funds of liquid capital that guano had brought them. And despite the inevitable inconveniences and uncertainties connected with what was bound, in sum, to be very major change, they may have looked forward to escaping from a trade in which ethical and political considerations were becoming increasingly intrusive to areas of activity where the raw profit motive could prevail unassailed.

GIBBS AFTER GUANO

Henry Gibbs looked to the future with confidence. 'With the capital that this business will set free', he wrote in 1860, 'other good business will no doubt come tumbling in as fast as we can welcome it. We must take care to separate the chaff from the wheat, and to grind the latter in a businesslike way'.[236] He later realized, though, that new work might involve some radical changes in the pattern of the firm's activities. It would be impossible, he noted in 1863, to find 'pure commission business to employ all our capital'. It appeared, therefore, 'that those classes of business which we should have been quite right formerly to reject, as not being in the range of *our* business, we should do quite well now to embrace, if they are in themselves legitimate'.[237] He saw that the London establishment was now standing at a major turning-point in its history. Guano had lifted a fairly obscure commission house into one of the wealthiest firms in the City of London. The Peruvian trade had been the chrysalis: now they could take flight into the elevated world of merchant banking. Henceforward operations of an exclusively financial nature were to take up a good deal of their time and their capital.

In the 1860s they engaged on a hitherto unprecedented scale in the hazardous business of Stock Exchange investment and speculation.[238] Prior to the 1850s they had held only small quantities of paper, mainly

[236]HHGC, 2, Henry Gibbs to George Gibbs, 1 November 1860.

[237]*Ibid.*, 3, Henry Gibbs to William Gibbs, 16 September 1863.

[238]The remainder of this section is largely based on data in LGL, first ser., 5-29.

shares of the Great Western Railway and the Pacific Steam Navigation Company. From the mid-1850s on they became increasingly interested in home, imperial and foreign government bonds (including Peruvian and other South American paper). In the early 1860s this sort of business rapidly expanded. In the course of the decade large speculations were made in Indian, Turkish, Egyptian, Russian, Danish, Brazilian and Chilean stocks. To a lesser extent they invested in railways, especially in Indian, North American, Cuban and Mexican lines. Entries in their profit and loss accounts show that government bond buying was successful on balance over the 1860s as a whole, with a net gain of £77,739. The main problems arose with Brazilian and Chilean paper, and to a smaller degree with Spanish and Danish. Turkey, Egypt and Russia yielded the largest rewards. Railways on the other hand brought losses totalling £151,173, the worst failures coming from speculations in the Imperial Mexican (£122,236) and Mid-Wales (£22,500) lines. Most of their Cuban investments also proved unprofitable. Gibbs money found its way as well into the City of Moscow Gas Company, the Atlantic Telegraph Company, the East Greenland Expedition, the Metropolitan Sewage and Essex Reclamation Company, and the International Finance Company. That much of their effort, whether with governments or companies, was speculative is suggested by the great amount of stock selling which they engaged in. Trading, needless to say, was not neglected. Taking 1865 as a sample year, we find that Gibbs had large accounts with a couple of Far Eastern commercial houses: Wallace & Co. of Bombay, from whom they received wool, cotton and a number of other Indian exports, and Wilson Ritchie & Co. of Colombo who sent them coffee, coconut oil, cotton and coir yarn. Corkling of Alexandria was also consigning cotton, Bright Brothers of Melbourne sent wool, Avelino Aramayo of Buenos Aires, piña, and Burling of Philadelphia, furs. There were still dozens of clients on the West Coast and in Central America supplying, among other things, copper and silver ores, nitrate, wool, cotton and bark. And for a lot of these people Gibbs not only sold goods on commission but purchased on order as well. With their European correspondents, however, they tended to have a largely financial relationship, attending to the buying and selling of bonds, the collection of dividends, and the provision of acceptance credits. Despite all the commercial activity, which kept the firm active in traditional fashion in a variety of commodity markets, one can see from a glance at their 1865 profit and loss account, quite typical of the decade as a whole, that financial dealings had now become their principal preoccupation. Entries relating to company and government investment added up to 67 and 60 per cent of their debit and credit totals respectively.

This shift of focus is not at all surprising, although it does show how far the firm had moved since the early 1840s when business had been so heavily based on agency trade and when such a premium had been set on commercial caution. Lending to the Peruvian government had clearly helped remove many of the old inhibitions. The quickest way for Gibbs to employ idle capital after they had left the guano trade was to place it on the Stock Exchange. In that fashion surpluses could be disposed of in a matter of hours. And in the early 1860s the opportunities for new investment were rapidly increasing. British company law had recently been reformed to permit easier recourse to the investing public. A great many foreign governments were borrowing in London. Railway companies were sprouting fast around the world and coming to England for money. It was Gibbs's misfortune to get sucked into this whirlpool of financial activity at a time when the London money market was moving towards its greatest crisis yet: the Overend and Gurney collapse of 1866. In that year — their first in the red since 1834 — they recorded a net loss of £60,798. In 1867 they did even worse, with a net loss of £71,105. In the 1870s losses were registered in as many as four different years.

In the 1830s Gibbs had recorded an annual average profit level of £11,480. In the 1840s this rose to £26,828. In the 1850s, when the guano trade had its greatest impact on their fortunes, the figure reached £91,984. Deviation from the old norms, however, pulled the average down to £60,984 in the 1860s and in the 1870s the figure of £15,892 brought Gibbs's net earnings back to almost pre-guano levels. There was to be no retreat, however, from the new areas of activity. In the long run, diversification brought expansion and substantial success. By the end of the century the firm was still engaged in a wide range of commission trading, but had also become a major issuing house, an important source of acceptance credits, and a major participant, both as producer and trader, in the Chilean (formerly Peruvian) nitrate industry.[239] They were strong enough in 1890 to be included in the syndicate arranged by the Bank of England to support the money market during the Baring crisis.[240] Henry Gibbs had served as a director of the Bank since 1853, as its governor between 1875 and 1877, and as member of parliament for the City of London in 1891-2. In 1896 he was elevated to the peerage as

[239] See, *inter alia*, Maude pp. 29-33; Rory M. Miller and Robert G. Greenhill, 'The Peruvian Government and the Nitrate Trade, 1873-1879', *JLAS*, 5, I (1973); Harold Blakemore, *British Nitrates and Chilean Politics, 1886-1896* (London, 1974).

[240] Maude, p. 33.

Baron Aldenham.[241] Guano had become a distant memory[242] and the Lima branch was closed down in 1880. One rhymer, however, made sure that their past should not fade entirely from recall. They were referred to in the City as

> The House of Gibbs that made their dibs
> By selling turds of foreign birds.[243]

[241] *Dictionary of National Biography. Supplement, 1901-1911* (London, 1912), pp. 101-3. See also obituary in *Proceedings of the Society of Antiquaries of London,* 2nd ser., 22 (1907-1909), pp. 284-5.

[242] They were briefly involved again in 1881-3 during the War of the Pacific when Chile temporarily took charge of the business, but only very small quantities were handled. See Maude, pp. 29-30.

[243] According to the present Lord Aldenham.

CONCLUSIONS

'The tenor of these letters [from Gibbs] displays the most exact scrupulousness in securing, through all difficulties, the reputation of the fertilizer and the highest possible price — nor could it be otherwise, since their interests are at one with those of the Nation'.
Manuel Ortiz de Zevallos,
Peruvian finance minister, 1857.

'the present consignment system is vicious, the charges are exorbitant, and the losses caused to the national Treasury unquestionable'.
Luis Mesones, 1859

We can now attempt a general assessment of Gibbs's record in the trade,[1] and in the process specify the principal items of profit and loss for merchants and government within the monopoly-contract system. In particular, answers will be attempted to the various questions set out at the beginning of the book. To start with, we shall consider the most serious and widely sustained charge levelled against Gibbs, namely that they sold guano at excessively low prices, thereby narrowing the profit margins of the Peruvian government and maximizing their own commission earnings. Such a conflict of interests, it would seem, is largely mythical. Two things are particularly worth stressing: first, that Gibbs had more interest in high prices than has usually been made out; second, that the government understood the case for moderation in price policy and on occasions wanted lower levels than Gibbs thought appropriate.

It is a gross over-simplification to suggest that all Gibbs's energies in pricing were directed towards a cheapening of guano. In 1844-6 they insisted on maintaining the £10 level, and even went above it briefly, despite the pressures of African competition. They argued against Myers's pleas for a reduction in the autumn of 1847. They advised the Peruvian government against a price fall in 1850, and presented a case for holding steady during the farmers' agitation in 1851-2. They wanted a price rise in the spring of 1853, which the government refused to sanction. They argued again for an increase in the spring of 1854 and in the winter of 1856. In November 1858, despite having government authority to lower from £12, they decided against a reduction and in the early 1860s successfully argued for a return to £13. There certainly were times, most notably in the first year or two of the trade and in the months following the receipt of the Elías instructions of April 1855, when Gibbs exercised considerable

[1] As this is a summarizing chapter, references will only be given for new quotations and fresh points of information.

downward or restraining pressures, but it would be difficult to fault them then in relation to market circumstances: inconsequential demand in 1842; growing competition in 1855.

No high-minded altruism or self-sacrifice attached to such behaviour. Gibbs had a number of reasons — some permanent, some temporary — for pursuing higher prices or resisting falls. At the simplest level, of course, they had an interest in pleasing the government: it employed them and always had the power to dismiss them. A further consideration, of most relevance in the troubled early years of the trade, was the wish to achieve a level of returns for the government high enough to ensure repayment of the large contract loans of 1842 and 1846. There was also the possibility then of a share in profits if net proceeds could be raised above £4 10s. per ton. It must be remembered too that the higher the price the greater the unit commission, and possibly also aggregate commission earnings if demand was not excessively price-elastic. The argument relating consignee interest to price depreciation, moreover, rests in part on the assumption that there would be no complicating restrictions in supply. The fact is, of course, that Gibbs frequently found themselves in a position where supply *was* limited and where income maximization lay in selling the available quantities at the highest possible price.

As for the government's approval of moderation in pricing policy, this relates in part to its seeming indifference to the notion of preserving its wasting asset through high prices and slow-tempo sales. Its main objective appears almost invariably to have been the maximization of income in the short term: this sought cautiously up to the early 1850s and somewhat more daringly in 1855 and 1856. The combination of high prices and slow sales in the late 1850s looks like the enactment of a long-term conservationist policy, and in this sense perhaps had something to commend it, but it almost certainly was not intended as such. The whole financial history of Peru in our period, as MacQueen, Bonilla and others have documented, displays great profligacy, an absence of advance planning, and an apparently untroubled disposition to mortgage the future. There is hardly any evidence to suggest that price policies for guano were related to sober and thrifty concern for the country's long-term economic well-being. There was of course a national interest to be served, but a clear distinction has to be drawn between the abstraction which was Peru and the reality which was a governmental system sunk in debt and chronically beset by urgent political and financial pressures. A government with some concern for the future would, for one thing, probably have adopted a rotational system in the working of the deposits, thereby permitting some replenishment of stocks. Guano was not quite the finite resource that it was sometimes made out to be.[2] It would also have directed some of its profits towards the improvement of loading facilities and the reduction of guano wastage (16% according to Zevallos) at the Chincha islands.[3] Fear of exhaustion may well have flitted across the minds of Castilla and his ministers, and may have strengthened their resolve to push up prices, but there is no evidence to hand to indicate that it was a primary preoccupation.

Motives apart, the government had the clear ability to implement a policy of price elevation and in doing so ran into no disputes with Gibbs. Indeed, Gibbs acted mainly as a source of encouragement, offering only occasional limp and highly generalized caveats on the dangers of competition. Taking market circumstances into account, it is more appropriate to fault the contractors for applying upward, rather than downward, pressures. They did so in the mid-1850s and the trade received a massive setback within a year or two. They also did so in the mid-1840s, with the consequence that the short-run problems arising from African competition were substantially magnified.

On intermediate costs, as on prices, the facts as presented do not give much support to the arguments advanced by Levin and others. In the 1850s Gibbs did have an incentive to raise these inasmuch as interest was earned on payments made in advance of sales and commissions were taken from shipowners. (Incentives relating to commissions on costs from the government are of little account, for these were paid out only for a year or two, and only for charters). All the evidence suggests that there was no notable response by Gibbs to these incentives. They were probably more eager to avoid offending the government than to increase marginally their already wholesome income from freights and other payments made on behalf of their employers. Nowhere in their private correspondence does one get the slightest hint of even a wish for higher costs. There was no sustained upward trend in freights, and the monopoly-export system appears in general to have kept rates lower than they would have been had a variety of guano merchants been bidding for ships. As for other charges connected with docking, unloading and warehousing, the facts to hand show Gibbs pressing for reductions, not advances — in 1844, 1845, 1849 and 1861.

Despite this, however, and their widely-acclaimed labours of market building, one cannot view their conduct as achieving quite the

---

[2]See Levin, pp. 28, 112; Marie Robinson Wright, *The Old and the New Peru* (Philadelphia, 1908), p. 283.

[3]See Mathew, 'Primitive Export Sector', pp. 49-51.

purity that Zevallos, Rivero and Gibbs themselves claimed for it. There was little they did that could be described as downright fraudulent, and they faced the various allegations levelled against them by Barroilhet and others with impressive confidence and much righteous indignation. They did not believe themselves to be sinners and saw their attackers as either malicious or ill-informed, and sometimes both. Nevertheless, in certain respects they did pursue their own interests in ways that may have run contrary to the interests of Peru.

There was, for example, the commission charged to shipowners or brokers on the hiring of vessels for the trade. The Peruvian government did not object to this, no doubt viewing it as a convenient way of reducing its own payments to the consignees. The levies, however, may have caused shipowners to make compensatory upward adjustments to their rates. This is what contemporary critics believed. Whether it happened or not we cannot tell for sure, and it is probable that the 2½ per cent commission was of little consequence by itself as an elevating factor when shippers were competing for guano cargoes in normal conditions of underemployment. Gibbs, however, were also giving offence through their vessel inspection system after 1854 and their use of the so-called 'continental clause' in charters, and this, combined with the other aggravations which were the government's responsibility, almost certainly helped push up rates when the shipping market was tight.[4] A question mark also hangs over their delcredere commissions. These appear to have been largely unnecessary by the 1850s, if not before. And the European and colonial sales commissions might well be judged excessive, considering how little Gibbs were required to do. To give, for example, the men who actually did the importing and selling in France 1 per cent, and Gibbs 2 per cent for merely presiding over the business, seems an unfair allocation of reward. As for the commissions Gibbs received through their own selling activities, however, it would be difficult to argue that these were, by the standards of the time, notably inflated. If the false 1 per cent delcredere is deducted from the 3½ per cent which Gibbs earned for most of the 1850s, we are left with a fairly normal 2½ per

---

[4]In a letter written by an official of the General Shipowners' Society in London to Daniel Ruzo, the president of the Congressional *Comisión de Delegados Fiscales* in September 1871, it was commented that the typical guano charter had, over the years, become 'the most biased and objectionable contract . . . that has ever been used in this country and probably in the entire world; and it is held in great disfavour by the majority of shipowners'. If the terms of charters were improved for shippers — and this included the removal of the persisting 2½ per cent commission — it was suggested that freights could fall by as much as 10s. per ton. *Informe Circunstanciado,* pp. 249-51. It is impossible to estimate with any precision what the balance was between these elevating factors and the downward pressures resulting from monopoly hiring.

cent. Rates, however, were somewhat higher in 1850-1 and in the 1840s, and there was the period early in that decade when Gibbs and Myers pocketed an amount considerably in excess of what had been agreed with the government and consigners. This was an offence, and was clearly viewed as such in Lima.

Gibbs's conduct can also be criticized on the matter of guano distribution. Direct importing from Peru was not spread around a sufficient number of British and European ports, considering the bulk of the commodity and the expense of inland carriage. The consignees' wish to maximize their own commission earnings meant that too much guano came initially to London. The results were unnecessarily high retail prices and the undersupplying of much of the European market. Some flexibility was almost certainly gained, but the advantages here were probably more than offset by impaired consumption. There is also the issue of excessive exporting in 1860-1. By their own admission Gibbs were at this point vigorously advancing their own interests at the expense of all other considerations. Stock-piling failed to win them a fresh contract, but it did ensure that they had guano to sell after the end of 1861 and it complicated the transfer of control from Gibbs to the new contractors. There was, moreover, one allegation of fraudulent practice which may well have had some truth to it, that concerning bag charges. Henry Gibbs was clearly troubled by this and the Lima accounts for 1852-5 show that when Gibbs were not given a commission which they thought they were entitled to, for the purchase of sacks, they simply created one for themselves by overdebiting the government's account.[5]

There was, finally, Gibbs participation in some hastily conceived and secretly negotiated contracts. On occasions in the 1850s official announcements about contracts either were not made at all or were offered belatedly. The 1853 *prórroga* was, in terms of the scale of the award, the most notable instance and Gibbs must have known that they were party to an agreement which went against the spirit of the 1849 law on contract allocation, and possibly its letter as well if one treats a six-year arrangement of this sort not as the *prórroga* that it was called but, for all practical purposes, a fresh contract. It must have been heartening for them when the *Comisión Especial* in 1856 let them off with little more than a mild rebuke and the government declared its intention, on this matter at least, to ignore the misdemeanours of its predecessor.

A further enormously important feature of the prevailing export system that requires summarizing comment is the facility for borrow-

[5]This is not discussed in the text, but is dealt with in footnote 98, p.202.

232

ing that it afforded the Peruvian government. The association of monopoly contracts with the mounting indebtedness of the Peruvian government is a very intimate and obvious one. It permitted borrowing from the contractors. It also allowed borrowing from internal and foreign bondholders. Arguably, the principal reason for the implementation and maintenance of the system was to enable the government to have access to loanable funds of cash. Indebtedness, of course, is not necessarily problematical and debilitating, but there are very obvious dangers. Interest has to be paid and rates may be burdensomely high. If the debtor's normal revenues are low or irregular and debt repayment rapidly soaks these up, fresh loans may be required, indebtedness therefore becoming entrenched and self-perpetuating. The money may not be put to good productive use. If borrowed money is easily obtained, it may be resorted to excessively and spurious needs may arise to match the opportunities. Such facilities, moreover, may reduce the onus on the debtor to sustain or develop alternative and more regular sources of income and economize on unproductive expenditures. Continual borrowing, finally, may place an undesirable degree of power in the hands of the creditor. There can be little doubt in the Peruvian case that the habit did become entrenched, that the scale of borrowing was very large and its frequency very marked, that the money was almost invariably used unproductively and that it permitted the run-down of the internal tax structure: all this at considerable cost, since interest rates were usually 5 per cent or higher. Governments were never prepared merely to sit back and receive a regular and steady inflow of income from the sale of their guano. They usually wanted to take as much as they could as early as they could. MacQueen, writing of these anticipatory advances, comments on 'the paradoxical situation . . . in which the greater the public income, the more penurious the fiscal situation.' By the end of 1861 there was a floating debt of 13,000,000 pesos, made up in the main of money owing to guano contractors.[6]

The relationship between the loan requirements of the Peruvian government and the official belief in the virtue of retaining the monopoly-contract system is shown very clearly in late 1841 and early 1842 when the second and third guano contracts were drawn up and funds sought for the prosecution of the Bolivian war. The larger the loan a merchant could offer, the more likely he was to be accepted into the trade. Gibbs's appeal for the government probably lay more in their command of large resources of liquid capital than in any special merits they displayed as sellers of guano. The government's partiality for borrowing, more than anything else, explains the tardy fashion in

[6]MacQueen, p. 38.

which the *'hijos del Perú'* provisions of the 1849 congressional law were carried into effect. It was, commented the foreign minister, Gómez Sánchez, in a defence of the prevailing exporting arrangements in 1854, very important for a country like Peru, which 'lacks the great resources which old, rich Nations have at their disposal for use in times of conflict', to be able to come by 'substantial loans' to meet exigencies. These 'involve no delay and avoid the evils consequent on the system of loans obtained on onerous conditions, or forcibly secured from the citizenry'.[7] It is not surprising to discover Henry Gibbs writing in 1859 that he was 'inclined to trust . . . to a large advance' as the best means to ensure his house's continued participation in the trade.[8] And, as we have seen, the confusions and delays surrounding the arrangement of the British contract in the early 1860s were very much centred on the difficulties encountered by local merchants in raising loan money for the government.

The government also viewed contracts with Gibbs as a means of strengthening the national credit in foreign money markets. Castilla told the British charge d'affaires in October 1849 that his main reason for persisting with the Gibbs monopoly was his wish to see Peru's credit established on a firm basis. The contract arranged in London earlier that year had made Gibbs responsible for diverting a portion of guano proceeds to the English bondholders. The fact that the funds due to them came from a reputable London merchant house and not from exposed government coffers in Lima gave them great confidence in Peruvian paper. Advantage of this trust was taken in 1852 and 1853, and again in the early 1860s (when Gibbs's departure from the trade may also have *necessitated* further stock-exchange borrowing). In 1858 Castilla wanted a speedy transfer of the French business to Gibbs 'so as to get out of the embarrassing situation in which the unreliability of Sr. Vivero has placed our credit'.[9]

Did the creditors and their representatives in any way force Peru to expand her debt? Was the seepage of guano funds to foreign merchants and bondholders the result of external pressure as much as of internal exigency? Both questions must be answered in the negative. There is no evidence to support the contention that Gibbs deliberately sought to keep the government so poor that borrowing became obligatory.[10] One finds no reference in their correspondence

[7]FO 61/148, Gómez Sánchez to Sulivan, 10 October 1854.

[8]HHGC, 2, Henry Gibbs to William Gibbs, 6 January 1859.

[9]Castilla to Zevallos, 6 February 1858, *loc. cit.* Vivero was the Peruvian official who took over the direction of selling in France immediately after Montané's dismissal.

[10.]See, for example, Barroilhet, *Opúsculo,* p. 33; Bonilla, 'Aspects', pp. 248-9.

to such an objective, or to any effort to create lending opportunities prior to some appeal from the government itself. On occasions — in 1842, 1846, 1849 and frequently in the 1850s — the scale of the government's requirements was in excess of what Gibbs thought desirable. Loans to the Peruvian government did not necessarily provide the most profitable outlets for surplus money and there was occasionally the danger that lending could strain the firm's liquidity. As for the extension of the internal bonded debt, this clearly had nothing to do with external pressure, although it was made possible by external opportunity in the form of guano sales abroad. The settlement of the foreign bonded debt in 1849 and the taking on of fresh obligations in 1853 was again based on Peruvian initiative. This point must be stressed, for the 1849 settlement with the bondholders bit deeply into guano profits. Money was being paid out by Peru more than a quarter of a century after the original funds had been received and spent. It has been assumed by other authors that Peru was pushed into an accommodation by the British government.[11] Foreign Office documents, however, show that British pressure was relatively weak and that Peru came to an agreement basically because she wished to restore her credit on the London money market, thereby opening the way to fresh borrowing.[12] Castilla spoke in 1847 of his wish 'to revive the credit which the Republic lost in Europe almost at the same time as it came into existence'. The only reason Henry Witt gave in his diary for the settlement was the government's desire 'to raise the credit of the country'.[13] In 1854 Gómez Sánchez noted how Peru had made use of her guano funds to honour her debt obligations 'following her own instincts and without any outside pressure'.[14] Had it wished, the government could probably have ignored this debt. The only direct power the bondholders could have brought to bear would have been through their refusal to subscribe to any future Peruvian issues. It is very unlikely that they would have been able to win effective diplomatic or physical support from the British government.

Why, then, was the Peruvian government so eager to enlarge these various categories of indebtedness? The bonded debt had assumed quite massive proportions by the early 1870s, latterly because of the government's ambitious and potentially rewarding (but in the end financially disastrous) programme of railway building.[15] In our

[11] See, for example, Bonilla, 'Aspects', p. 222; Levin, pp. 61-2; Pásara, p. 14; Yepes, p. 62.

[12] Mathew, 'Debt', *passim.*

[13] Witt Diaries, IV, 11 March 1849.

[14] FO 61/148, Gómez Sánchez to Sulivan, 10 October 1848.

[15] Hunt, 'Guano', pp. 107-9; Levin, pp. 99-108; MacQueen, pp. 38-9.

period, however, there was no developmental aspect to the borrowing. Money was directed almost exclusively to military and bureacratic expenditures and the servicing, redemption and consolidation of earlier debts.[16] Bonilla offers the interesting suggestion that in an economy hollowed by foreign intrusion and confined to an international role of 'market for the realisation of surplus value', the government had no opportunity to make effective and productive use of its guano income and was forced instead to employ it merely as a basis for credit-strengthening and debt-extension.[17] 'Not being able to use these [guano revenues] for the internal generation of capital, the State found itself obliged to use guano as a guarantee for the successive and surprising loans contracted from abroad'.[18] The foreigner, in short, was responsible after all, albeit in indirect fashion. The argument, however, is presented with inadequate supporting evidence, and begs a number of questions. Imports from Europe and North America certainly caused problems for certain industries, in particular textiles in the coastal towns, but their overall scale and cheapness was not such as to obliterate all significant manufacturing activity. In the interior especially, indigenous producers could retain a competitive edge through varying degrees of tariff protection, low factor-costs, peculiarities of local markets, and high freights from the coast. Belford Wilson noted in the 1830s that although there was some decline in native industry, the bulk of the population, coastal as well as Andean, was still dressed in clothing of local production.[19] Peru, in fact, was not a large-scale importer of goods from the metropolitan economies. Before guano she had a very low exchange-earning capacity and, of course, the very debts under discussion mopped up, through interest and amortization payments, a good deal of the extra foreign exchange provided by guano sales after the 1840s.

The annual average declared value of British exports to Peru was well under half a million pounds in the 1830s, still below three quarters of a million in the 1840s, and only just over one million in the 1850s. The figure for 1860 (£1,381,357) was only 73 per cent up on that for 1840 (£799,991), and that for 1859 (£857,568) only 7 per cent up — despite the great expansion of the guano trade over the intervening years. In 1855-9 Britain was importing on average

[16]Hunt, 'Guano', pp. 73, 78, 80 and 83; MacQueen, pp. 37-8. The armed forces and the bonded debt alone accounted for 71 per cent of government expenditures in Gibbs's last full contract year, 1861. Hunt, 'Guano', p. 73.

[17]Bonilla, *Guano*, pp. 163-5.

[18]*Ibid.*, p. 165.

[19]FO 61/126, Wilson to Palmerston, 15 January 1834; FO 61/53, Wilson to Palmerston, 29 September 1838.

£3,482,567 worth of goods (excluding bullion and specie) each year from Peru: more than three times the commodity flow in the reverse direction (£1,104,751).[20] Hunt, it should be noted, lends his authority to at least part of Bonilla's argument when he writes of an 'import flood' in the 1850s and of Peru 'importing virtually all manufactured products' by then.[21] Using Bonilla's figures for French and British exports to Peru he shows that there was indeed a rapid expansion after the 1840s, but he does not specify their absolute scale. French exports to Peru, in fact, rose from the extremely low level of £58,373 in 1835-9 to £1,041,793 in 1855-9. The intervening five-year averages were, in sequence, £108,636, £262,700 and £627,932. Over the 1850s as a whole the figure stood at £834,862[22] which, added to the British £1,077,768, gives £1,911,630. For the two main centres of advanced capitalism to be sending less than £2 million worth of goods per annum to Peru in the 1850s, and just a fraction over £1 million in the 1840s, was not indicative of large-scale commercial intrusion. For a great many artisans in the Peruvian coastal cities it was certainly a disturbing and dislocative amount, but it was hardly a flood, washing over the country as a whole and destroying all indigenous industrial production. It is revealing that the French and British averages were so close in the 1850s (and virtually identical in 1855-9), with France ahead in 1858 and 1859. There was a strong bias towards expensive items in the commodity structure of French exports, and the relative popularity of French goods in Peru suggests that a lot of trade was being directed towards a small number of wealthy consumers rather than to the mass market. According to Hunt's figures, one fifth of Callao's imports in 1857 comprised furniture, silks, wines and liquors.[23] French imports, as Bonilla acknowledges, *'ne pouvaient être destiné qu'à la consommation des couches sociales les plus riches'*.[24] Hunt, moreover, suggests the presence within Peru of certain compensatory forces deriving from guano and working towards the *benefit* of local industry. 'Income generated by guano', he writes, 'must have created a substantial demand for goods and

[20]G. R. Porter, *The Progress of the Nation* (London, 1851), pp. 302-5; *PP*, 1854-55, LII, p. 503; 1856, LVI, p. 277; 1859, XXVIII, p. 332; 1860, LX, p. 337; 1861, LX, p. 337; 1866, LXVIII, p. 309. For further detail and comment on these figures, see Mathew, 'Anglo-Peruvian Relations', chs. 1 and 2, *passim*.

[21]Hunt, 'Guano', p. 105.

[22]Statistics from Bonilla's 'Aspects', p. 85, and franc/sterling exchange rate from Hunt's 'Guano', p. 97.

[23]Hunt, 'Guano', p. 99.

[24]Bonilla, 'Aspects', p. 89. In Hunt's words, 'France's share of total Peruvian imports seems reasonable proxy for the luxury share'. 'Guano', p. 98.

services produced by the domestic economy'.[25] And even if there had been massive destruction of local manufacturing, and little surviving industry for the government to assist, the remaining choices were not confined to the single, mindless exercise of debt accumulation. Export sectors like sugar, cotton, silver, and guano itself were all badly in need of capital to increase productivity, raise quality, or reduce inefficiency and waste. Substantial social overhead investment could also have been attempted.[26]

The notion of a state forced into indebtedness for want of any opportunities to capitalize productively on guano earnings also ignores both the fact that governments had their own quite compelling reasons for borrowing, and that their developmental inclinations were very modest in the first place.[27] Debt, it is submitted here, grew partly through habit, partly through built-in momentum, and partly through frequent and often unpredictable upswings in expenditure. The habit had begun in the pre-guano years in a state where tax-raising capacity and general fiscal organization were primitive in the extreme. It was consolidated by the opportunities presented by the guano trade. The premature claiming of funds from one contract, furthermore, meant that there was often little guano revenue coming in when the next one came to be drawn up, thus aggravating the need for a fresh cash injection. 'The importance of Huano', wrote the Peruvian foreign minister in 1854, 'having been discovered in foreign countries at a time when Peru was involved in a National War, the Government was forced to enter into a contract with the propagators of that manure to meet the urgencies of that situation. The first step having been taken, the increasing necessities of the Country obliged it to proceed without stopping in this new and untried line and to contract on each occasion fresh obligations; and although it is true that in the course of fourteen years, the revenue of the Country has considerably improved, the method employed up to the present day has taken such deep root and the obligations of the Government with each one of the Consigners are so complicated and so important that if they were to attempt to make an immediate change in this respect the entire Nation would be placed in a Crisis which perhaps it would not overcome although it might exercise all its energy'.[28] Military and naval activity, real or anticipated, was, as has been noted in the preceding chapters, a continuing and powerful factor ensuring that the habit would not be broken. It was

[25] Hunt, 'Guano', p. 85.

[26] Pike suggests that Castilla believed in 'laissez-faire development prescriptions' and that his success in providing Peru with greater political order blinded him to 'economic problems that lurked beneath the surface . . .'. *Andean Republics,* p. 86.

[27] See, for example, Hunt, 'Guano', p. 111.

[28] FO 61/144, Gómez Sánchez to Sulivan, 10 October 1854.

also so easy to borrow from the foreign merchants, and with the fiscal liberality of the mid-1850s and subsequent years, the reliance on guano to meet sudden increases in state expenditure was, of course, intensified.[29]

If one reflects on the various reasons for guano-backed borrowing one can identify at least two fundamental factors — certainly related over the long run to foreign intrusions represented by Spanish colonialism, but hardly at all to the nineteenth-century commercial incursions of European capitalism which Bonilla views as so crucial. One was the fiscal backwardness already referred to and the failure of the *caudillos* to develop controlled, sophisticated budgetary practices.[30] The other was the insecurity of the military, post-colonial state, as exemplified in the struggles against rebellion, the wars with neighbouring countries, and the bid for popularity that partly underlay the tax reductions of the 1850s. MacQueen stated the central truth more than half a century ago. 'The economic and political organization of the country had not reached a stage where the bountiful revenues might have been applied to constructive purposes'.[31]

We can look next at the contracts themselves. Questions of indebtedness aside, what do the successive arrangements for the export of guano tell us about the relative power of the merchants and the government, and the distribution of guano spoils between them? In 1840 the government was tricked by the new guano traders into awarding a contract which gave it only minimal returns. Within little more than a year, however, it had managed to turn the tables and devise an arrangement which made its own position greatly more profitable and secure, and exposed the merchants to very considerable risks for only modest recompense. It had made full use of the powers of patronage it possessed as owner of the guano, and continued to do so in the years that followed. In 1845 the agreement whereby the existing contract was to be extended by three years was torn up and replaced in 1846 by a one-year *prórroga* in return for a loan of 300,000 pesos. The new contracts arranged in 1847 removed the right of the merchants to claim a small share of the profits of the trade. From that year on every last peso of profit went to the government. In 1849 Gibbs certainly won a contract which paid them a very generous range of commissions and interest rates, but they also lost the advantage of providing part of the proceeds due to the

---

[29] According to Pike, expenditures on the armed forces rose four-fold between 1852 and 1858. *Peru,* p. 113.

[30] The first Peruvian budget was not put into effect until 1846. See MacQueen, pp. 4, 5, 33-4, 36-8; also Pike, *Peru,* pp. 97-8, 111-3.

[31] MacQueen, p. 37.

government in debt paper at face value.[32] In 1850, under the threat of the business being taken from them, Gibbs agreed to a reduction in earnings, and, despite the secrecy and lack of competition in the *prórroga* arrangement of 1853, they were unable to get rates pushed up again. Finally, of course, the challenge from other merchants took solid form in the early 1860s, and Gibbs were dislodged.

Further evidence of the distribution of power within the trade lies in the way returns were apportioned. Gibbs, needless to say, did very well. Alone, or with Myers, they usually had command of the bulk of overseas sales, they received a variety of commission and interest payments, and in the 1840s they had the remunerative opportunity to pass funds over to the government in the form of depreciated debt paper. They were, moreover, in a position where they could play the foreign exchanges to their advantage. Their contract lending posed few problems, liquidity crises being very rare and repayment coming from the sales proceeds which they themselves collected. From the late 1840s on the loans were just about as risk-free as was possible for large-scale financial operations of this sort. There was normally enough guano on hand or afloat to ensure reimbursement in the event of a contract being torn up. They earned adecent interest rate, normally 5 or 6 per cent, but sometimes higher if it was paid in free guano or if part of the advance could be made in the first instance in debt paper. Rates were not extortionate, either by Peruvian or by European standards, but they certainly can be judged as high in relation to risk. The tables in Appendix III show how very substantial was the improvement in the firm's fortunes during the guano years. Net earnings from commissions and brokerage, for example, stood at an annual average of £73,672 in the 1850s, compared with only £6,296 in the 1830s. The expenses of running the establishment — paying rents, salaries and so on — also rose, but only from £1,377 a year in the 1830s to £7,381 in the 1850s. Overall profits, as already noted, increased from an annual average of £11,480 in the 1830s to £26,828 in the 1840s and to £91,984 in the 1850s. In the 1860s they fell back to £60,984. Gibbs, then, secured good returns, although only notably so in the 1850s. The London house's best year in the preceding decade was 1840: well ahead of their entry into the trade. And the books of the Lima firm in the 1840s show a succession of unprofitable guano accounts up to 1847 and a marked dependence on bond speculation for their contract income. 'Keep us supplied with Bonds', Gibbs Crawley asked their parent house in 1843, 'for our profit mainly depends on the rate you buy them at'.[33]

[32] This privilege, however, would have counted for much less with the settlement of the English debt and the consequent rise in the market value of external bonds.

[33] GGC, 28 October 1843.

The 1850s, however, was a good enough decade to turn them into a commercial house of wealth and substance, with an average income three-and-a-half times what it had been in the 1830s. It is, however, rather unlikely that they secured the 12 per cent of gross guano income from their 1849-61 contracts as suggested by Hunt.[34] Indeed, by writing of the possibility that as much as half of the intermediate costs were 'excess charges that really hid contractor profits' Hunt points to a figure as high as 24 per cent, with a government/contractor income ratio of 2.7:1.[35] Accounts of sales given in Basagoitia's *Oficio*[36] show that from 301,464 tons sold in the mid-1850s Gibbs gained a total of £125,817 for commissions, brokerage, delcredere, and interest on various outlays (*ex*cluding direct loans to the government), representing 8s. 4d. per ton. The Peruvian government took £4 16s. — 11.5 times as much. For the Basagoitia figures to fit even Hunt's lower percentage (12), the Gibbs income would have to be 17s. 9d. per ton. The only possible explanation for the difference, discounting any significant atypicality in Basagoitia's narrow period, is interest on direct loans (which Hunt includes), but a figure of 9s. 5d. per ton — 13 per cent more than all the rest of the earnings taken together — is far too large, especially considering how short-term the advances tended to be. It would be surprising if Gibbs earned as much as 1s. a ton on average from their loans. Interestingly enough, Hunt's figures for 15 other contracts arranged in the 1850-9 period show the government earning 10.7 times more than the contractors: a multiple much closer to Basagoitia's 11.5 than to the 2.7 —5.4 indicated by his own calculations and suggestions for the Gibbs operations.[37]

Whatever the precise ratios, the Peruvian government's levels of renumeration (1841 apart) were always a great deal higher than the contractors'. A lot of this income, of course, was immediately soaked up by the creditors, but only because there had been prior borrowing. Official figures for 1841-56 show an average net return to the government of £4. 16s. 6d. or just over 24 pesos on the 1,650,290 tons of guano sold over these years:[38] nearly £8,000,000 in aggregate. In 1862 Gibbs calculated that the government's receipts on each ton of guano sold in Britain and the colonies in the period 1854-61 averaged £6 8s. or 32

---

[34] Unfortunately, the accounts are not arranged in such a way as to permit precise calculation.

[35] Hunt, 'Guano', pp. 61-2.

[36] Statistical appendix.

[37] The whole thrust of the argument in this part of Hunt's paper is, incidentally, towards demonstrating how *high* the government's returns were. To query his figures, as above, is to add weight to his thesis.

[38] Dávalos y Lissón, IV, p. 118.

pesos.[39] At the going exchange rate in the 1860 season Rivero calculated net returns at around 43½ pesos per ton.[40] MacQueen suggests a total of roughly £18,000,000 for 1850-61: 'a figure very large for the times . . .'.[41] However much one may talk of the debilitations caused by guano and of dubious practice by contractors, the fact remains that the share-out of guano proceeds between government and merchants was very heavily weighted in the former's favour. This, of course, was entirely proper. The government, nominally at least, represented a country; the merchants represented only themselves. But it was, for a large trade, unique by nineteenth century standards, and very unusual by present-day norms as well. Such high levels of return to a government, Hunt observes, are 'approached today only by the most heavily taxed export industries, and only after several recent decades of rising rates'.[42]

Considering the likely scale of their aggregate earnings, Gibbs's lack of enthusiasm for continuing in the trade in the early 1860s remains — despite the suggestions offered in the last chapter — something of a mystery. Underlying it, perhaps, was an element of pique, of perverse pleasure at handing the business over to men whom they regarded as unscrupulous and incompetent. Such an appraisal may have been justified, and it is possible that the highly unfavourable assessment of contractor behaviour that other historians have presented is based (though this is not made explicit) more on the events of the 1860s than of the two decades preceding. Detailed research on this period has not yet been attempted, so it would be quite out of order to cast the indigenous merchants in unambiguously villainous roles. Some clue as to possible findings, however, may come from the remarks of the members of a Peruvian commission, charged in the early 1870s with examining the guano sales system. Looking back on the 1850 Barreda contract, they observed: 'The Commission wishes to discuss, with respect to this contract, the preference ordered for native Peruvians; because in its judgement, sad as it may be, it has to be said that possibly irreparable damage has resulted from this preference. Nor could it have been otherwise; for the preference, dictated by sentiment dressed in the raiments of patriotism, is inevitably self-regarding; and since it is accordingly odious in principle it could not fail to be disastrous in practice, especially in a country such as Peru which lacked men with sufficient love or habit of

[39] Gibbs to Rodulfo, 19 March 1862, *loc. cit.*
[40] Rivero, p. 214.
[41] MacQueen, p. 6.
[42] Hunt, 'Guano', p. 61.

work, with sufficient capital for large undertakings and, in view of these defects, with sufficient credit or commercial contacts for administering effectively and honestly such an extensive business . . .'.[43] Bonilla, who in the past has taken a highly critical view of Gibbs's performance in the guano trade,[44] largely ignores them in his recent book and writes instead of the local mercantile groups who consolidated their position in the 1860s by 'speculation and unscrupulous financial manipulations'[45] in the guano trade and used their new wealth in ways that contributed virtually nothing to the growth of the economy at large.[46] By the beginning of the 1870s they had lost the trade in its entirety to the French firm of Dreyfus Bros. & Co.[47] It must be remembered, moreover, that Barreda and his colleagues, despite all the furore of the 1850s, were given the British market in 1862 on terms almost identical to those of the recent Gibbs contracts. It is quite possible that Peruvian merchants, because of their more slender capital resources, their more uncertain access to funds in the metropolitan money markets, and their inevitable exposure to the borrowing proclivites of the government, would (as Henry Gibbs surmised) be under greater pressure to resort to irregular means of gaining profit than the wealthier, more confident, more secure English merchants. Gibbs's base was the London money market, and therein they were attempting, with substantial long-run success, to build up a large acceptance business.[48] Progress in this field had to do with the marketability of one's name and reputation. Manifestly devious and unethical practices could have an adverse effect on one's prospects of expanding such work. (This may have been one reason why Gibbs were so eager in the early 1860s that the Peruvian government publicly denounce their critics). And when one considers the terms of the Gibbs contracts — the monopoly rights, the marketable commodity, the virtually risk-free loans — one can see that there was little point in dishonest treatment of the Peruvian government. Already, very substantial returns were guaranteed. Why place these at risk by the sort of malpractice that might cost one the whole business? The business, of course, *was* lost, but Gibbs did hold tenure for 20 years, and the reasons for their departure had more to do with pressures

---

[43] *Informe Circunstanciado,* p. xvii.

[44] Bonilla, 'Aspects', *passim.*

[45] *Ibid., Guano,* p. 43.

[46] *Ibid.,* pp. 24, 40.

[47] *Inter alia, ibid.,* ch. 2; MacQueen, pp. 6-8; Hunt, 'Guano', pp. 65-6.

[48] Maude, pp. 34, 67-8; Mathew, 'Anglo-Peruvian Relations', Appendix I, in particular pp. 392-6.

generated within Peru itself than with any foolish irregularities committed by the English monopolists.

Gibbs's expulsion from the trade is quite impressive as a Peruvian achievement. There remains, nevertheless, the question as to whether or not they had delayed or minimised participation by indigenous merchants. Keith Griffin writes, with reference to Spanish America generally, that 'large scale participation in an economy by foreigners ... is likely to frustrate the growth of an entrepreneurial class. ... The potential native investor is unable to compete on equal terms with his foreign counterpart; he lacks the experience and knowledge plus the tremendous financial and physical resources the latter can command'.[49] One must judge the relevance of this observation to our particular case in somewhat ambivalent terms. There seems little doubt that Gibbs did use their very substantial experience and financial strength to good personal effect and that the government's wish to borrow so frequently, and on such a large scale, encouraged the amassing of contracts, and thereby markets, in Gibbs hands, giving them in fact a range of territories greater than they were able or willing adequately to supply. It limited the range of choice open to the government over possible alternative modes of export and restricted the number of merchants able to participate within the prevailing export system. This reduced the degree of competitive bidding for contracts and made it difficult for indigenous groups to break into the main stream of the trade. All this, however, must be qualified by three points: that there was already some Peruvian participation prior to 1862; that the Peruvians did capture the British business in that year, when there was still a good deal of life left in the trade; and that the funds which permitted this coup seem to have been derived, in important measure, from the profits that Gibbs were earning for the government abroad, these being channelled back into the Peruvian mercantile community through the consolidation and conversion operations of the early 1850s. It is difficult to weigh this up. The judgement offered here, however, is that the qualifications are relatively minor and that the third in particular is rather strained. On balance, Griffin's observations would seem to have considerable applicability to Gibbs and guano.

What we have been dealing with, clearly, was a mutually convenient, occasionally rather cosy, relationship between ministers and traders, with the Peruvian nation as a whole largely neglected and

---

[49] Keith Griffin, *Underdevelopment in Spanish America* (London, 1969), pp. 132, 134.

ignored.[50] Some benefits did pass its way,[51] but as often by accident as by intent. Castilla raged occasionally in the 1840s, and seemed prepared to consider the scrapping of the Gibbs *prórroga* in 1855, but when Barroilhet came to see him in 1856 with tales of Gibbs's misdemeanours he was dismissed with angry remarks about charlatans wasting his time and trying his patience. Zevallos vigorously defended Gibbs against their critics in 1857 and two or three years later the ex-Peruvian minister in London enthusiastically extolled their virtues. Official approval of Gibbs's conduct in the business, however, seems not to have been the product of any specifically corrupt relationship, but rather of the realisation that the contractors effectively served government interests, especially through their liberal provision of loans and their long experience in the trade. They had also come to know each other well and presumably had devised an easy, friendly and trusting way of working together. Gibbs, in turn, were eager to please their masters, knowing as they did that what power they possessed largely depended on government patronage. They had no interest, however, in the welfare of Peru as such, and looked on fiscal inspectors, congressional resolutions and indigenous capitalists alike with contempt.

It has not been the purpose of this study to offer any general conclusions about the operations of foreign capitalists in the export sectors of backward economies. The Peruvian case is rather a special one,[52] largely because of government ownership of the export

[50] There was also, of course, the labour force which produced the guano. The question of its share of the spoils, and its treatment generally, lies outside our frame of reference and has been dealt with elsewhere. See Mathew, 'Primitive Export Sector'. (One of the arguments of this paper, incidentally, is that guano production [as distinct from the trade] was also very peripheral to the economy and that its positive impact was negligible. See also Levin, pp.85-91.).

[51] See, *inter alia*, Hunt, 'Guano', in particular pp. 80-96; Pike, *Peru*, p. 112; Bill Albert, *An Essay on the Peruvian Sugar Industry, 1880-1920* (Norwich, 1976), p. 11a; Macera, pp. Lxvi-iii.

[52] The notion of uniqueness, however, can be exaggerated. D.C.M. Platt has suggested that there was a general imbalance of economic power in nineteenth-century Latin America between the commonly small-scale foreign enterprises and the governments of individual countries. The foreigner, he writes, 'was constantly outmanoeuvred by experienced politicians . . . . His only real safeguard was his indispensability, and when local substitutes developed he was soon displaced'. ('Economic imperialism and the businessman: Britain and Latin America before 1914', in Roger Owen and Bob Sutcliffe, *Studies in the Theory of Imperialism* [London, 1972], p. 305.). For more extended treatment of these issues, see D.C.M. Platt (ed.), *Business Imperialism, 1840-1930: an enquiry based on British experience in Latin America* (Oxford, 1977).

commodity. This was no mere formality. It meant that very real limits could be set on the power and profit-making capacity of the foreign merchants and that the great bulk of sales receipts could be directed towards the national treasury. This, it should be stressed, was not fortuitous. It was the outcome of two things in particular: the primitive nature of guano production, and the monopoly-contract system of exports. The first meant that foreign participation, and therefore enrichment, could be confined almost exclusively to the mercantile and financial sides of the business. Production did not require any expensive recruitment of overseas capital and entrepreneurial skill.[53] The second meant that merchants, individually controlling large volumes of trade, could receive attractively high aggregate returns to compensate for low unit returns.

Despite the fact that the government commanded the bulk of the income from guano sales, however, there was still a substantial seepage of income from Peru to Britain. The merchants were mainly foreign and took away interest as well as commission earnings. The shippers were almost exclusively foreign,[54] and freights comprised the largest of all charges on guano. From its profits the government paid out considerable sums to foreign bondholders. Such transfers were the result of pre-existing disparities of economic power between Peru and Britain. An additional problem resulting from the economic strength of the foreign trading partners were the limits imposed on the full exploitation of the Peruvian guano monopoly. Britain had the capacity, mercantile and industrial, to provide its farmers with alternative fertilizers when price and supply problems in guano became acute, and this, as we have seen, was quite vigorously employed. It also had powers of physical coercion, although chose not to use them. Had Peru been able to exploit her monopoly more effectively British farmers would, *ipso facto,* have had to pay more for guano. In this sense, disparities in economic power led to a sort of invisible seepage to foreign agriculturalists. On this question, Gibbs's performance is largely irrelevant. They may have aggravated matters by creating supply problems in overseas markets through ill-timed or inadequate chartering, or through sheer lack of effort in some areas, but the more basic problem seems to have been slow and wasteful loading at the Chincha islands. As for price policy, we have already suggested that the contractors cannot really be accused of selling at

[53] For a fuller discussion of this point see Mathew, 'Primitive Export Sector', *passim.*

[54] The *London Customs Bills of Entry,* examined for 1842, 1847, 1852, 1857 and 1862, reveal only three Peruvian-registered ships carrying guano into Britain: the *Constancia* and the *Rosa de Lima* in 1842 and the *Petronila* in 1852 and 1857.

unnecessarily low levels. If the monopoly was not exploited to the full, the reason lay essentially with structural imbalance in the international economy.

There was nothing much that Peru could have done to prevent foreigners compromising her monopoly, short of keeping her prices lower. Likewise, it was impossible in the short run to dent British and North American dominance of the world shipping industry. Losses overseas in the form of payments to foreign contractors and bondholder could, however, have been avoided, or at least reduced. British merchants were employed in the trade and British bondholders repaid out of guano receipts principally because ministers and officials in Lima saw the fertilizer as a means of extending the range of loan-raising facilities open to them. Guano exporting was, in the last resort, in the hands of insecure and inadequately-financed governments, operating within a shaky, immature body politic. Such governments manifested, over guano, a paradoxical combination of power and penury. The penury dictated the way in which the power was used; and the power, being badly used, served in the end to aggravate the penury.

APPENDIX I

PRESIDENTS OF PERU IN THE EARLY GUANO PERIOD

(*Sources:* Santa-Cruz, pp. 88-98; Pike, *Perú*, pp. 83-114; Marett, pp. 90-9).

Gran Mariscal Augustín Gamarra	1839-41
Manuel Menéndez	1841-2
General Juan Crisóstomo Torrico	1842
General Francisco de Vidal	1842-3
Justo Figuerola	1843
General Manuel Ignacio de Vivanco	1843-4
Domingo Elías	1844
Manuel Menéndez	1844
Justo Figuerola	1844
Manuel Menéndez	1844-5
Gran Mariscal Ramón Castilla	1845-51
General José Rufino Echenique	1851-4
Gran Mariscal Ramón Castilla	1855-62
General Miguel San Román	1862-3
General Juan Antonio Pezet	1863-5

APPENDIX II

GIBBS FAMILY TREE, EIGHTEENTH AND NINETEENTH CENTURIES

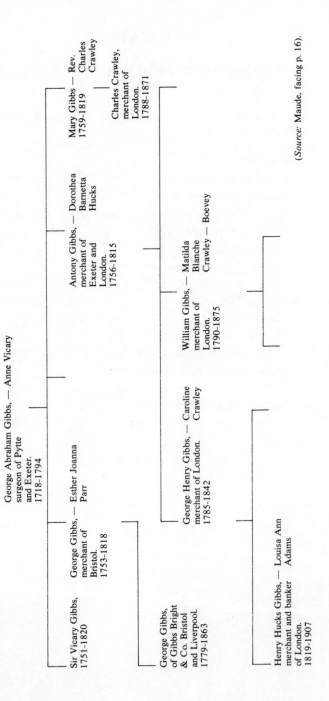

George Abraham Gibbs, — Anne Vicary
surgeon of Pytte
and Exeter.
1718-1794

Mary Gibbs — Rev.
1759-1819   Charles
             Crawley

Charles Crawley,
merchant of
London.
1788-1871

Antony Gibbs, — Dorothea
merchant of   Barnetta
Exeter and   Hucks
London.
1756-1815

William Gibbs, — Matilda
merchant of   Blanche
London.   Crawley — Boevey
1790-1875

George Gibbs, — Esther Joanna
merchant of   Parr
Bristol.
1753-1818

George Henry Gibbs, — Caroline
merchant of London.   Crawley
1785-1842

Sir Vicary Gibbs,
1751-1820

George Gibbs,
of Gibbs Bright
& Co. Bristol
and Liverpool.
1779-1863

Henry Hucks Gibbs, — Louisa Ann
merchant and banker   Adams
of London.
1819-1907

(*Source:* Maude, facing p. 16).

APPENDIX III

STATISTICS FOR ANTONY GIBBS & SONS, 1820-79

(*Source:* LGL, first ser. 3-27).

All figures to nearest pound sterling, with five-year averages and percentage increases or decreases between the successive periods.

Table 1: Profit and loss balances

Year	Value	Avg		Year	Value	Avg
1820	5,882			1850	41,311	
1821	6,660			1851	60,095	
1822	6,750	5,617		1852	74,043	66,977
1823	2,769			1853	51,091	(+156%)
1824	6,025			1854	108,345	
1825	5,592			1855	115,530	
1826	3,923			1856	109,148	
1827	5,400	4,053		1857	135,268	116,992
1828	3,185	(-28%)		1858	125,562	(+75%)
1829	2,167			1859	99,450	
1830	-1,308			1860	22,783	
1831	2,196			1861	150,264	
1832	3,312	1,778		1862	146,199	137,244
1833	5,187	(-56%)		1863	115,203	(+17%)
1834	-498			1864	251,772	
1835	14,538			1865	-3,982	
1836	23,530			1866	-60,798	
1837	17,962	21,183		1867	-71,105	-15,276
1838	22,536	(+1091%)		1868	49,540	
1839	27,350			1869	9,967	
1840	44,500			1870	-55,324	
1841	34,000			1871	23,456	
1842	29,420	27,454		1872	55,008	3,979
1843	14,850	(+30%)		1873	28,772	
1844	14,500			1874	-32,019	
1845	20,744			1875	-24,404	
1846	35,373			1876	6,120	
1847	28,188	26,202		1877	27,492	27,806
1848	17,156	(-5%)		1878	-25,636	(+599%)
1849	29,550			1879	155,458	

Table 2: Aggregate balances of commission and brokerage accounts

1820	4,180		1850	34,633	
1821	4,437		1851	46,830	
1822	5,022	4,441	1852	57,535	55,136
1823	3,565		1853	58,126	(+188%)
1824	5,001		1854	78,558	
1825	6,005		1855	100,609	
1826	2,841		1856	97,526	
1827	4,120	4,009	1857	92,629	92,207
1828	4,088	(-10%)	1858	95,920	(+67%)
1829	2,992		1859	74,349	
1830	2,420		1860	60,008	
1831	3,161		1861	75,965	
1832	3,693	3,736	1862	75,611	81,355
1833	4,572	(-7%)	1863	58,015	(-12%)
1834	4,833		1864	137,178	
1835	7,185		1865	72,888	
1836	7,050		1866	54,869	
1837	7,284	8,856	1867	49,900	52,194
1838	9,706	(+137%)	1868	46,441	(-36%)
1839	13,055		1869	36,873	
1840	16,206		1870	28,388	
1841	14,399		1871	40,478	
1842	14,932	14,810	1872	61,603	40,216
1843	15,781	(+67%)	1873	39,455	(-23%)
1844	12,732		1874	31,155	
1845	14,420		1875	22,815	
1846	18,969		1876	25,525	
1847	19,940	19,149	1877	25,053	28,842
1848	18,780	(+29%)	1878	29,316	(-28%)
1849	23,637		1879	41,503	

Table 3: Aggregate balances of unprofitable accounts, bad debts, gross losses on adventures and investment, and all remaining debit items in profit and loss accounts (excluding counting house expenses).

1820	1,189		1850	5,686	
1821	1,166		1851	973	
1822	4,141	3,613	1852	1,882	8,366
1823	5,644		1853	32,140	(+773%)
1824	5,924		1854	1,147	
1825	6,358		1855	9,629	
1826	2,734		1856	20,849	
1827	1,611	3,004	1857	7,485	8,837
1828	2,660	(-17%)	1858	1,392	(+6%)
1829	1,659		1859	4,830	
1830	3,252		1860	54,367	
1831	564		1861	15,214	
1832	1,384	2,901	1862	11,502	33,196
1833	2,039	(-3%)	1863	39,546	(+276%)
1834	7,265		1864	45,353	
1835	11,929		1865	314,066	
1836	8,939		1866	196,022	
1837	3,696	6,269	1867	202,035	169,893
1838	622	(+116%)	1868	76,499	(+412%)
1839	6,158		1869	60,844	
1840	1,640		1870	116,191	
1841	4,405		1871	86,257	
1842	9,016	7,841	1872	71,111	82,560
1843	8,529	(+25%)	1873	57,668	(-51%)
1844	15,613		1874	81,574	
1845	109		1875	69,213	
1846	1,124		1876	34,898	
1847	2,347	958	1877	19,821	48,895
1848	697	(-88%)	1878	73,490	(-41%)
1849	511		1879	47,055	

APPENDIX IV

BRITISH IMPORTS AND SALES OF PERUVIAN GUANO, 1841-80

Table I: Gross imports of guano from Peru, 1841-80 (in tons)

(*Source:* Commercial statistics in *PP*. Figures up to 1845 refer to Bolivian as well as Peruvian guano).

1841	2,062		1861	161,566
1842	14,123		1862	69,390
1843	1,589		1863	196,704
1844	16,475		1864	113,086
1845	14,101		1865	210,784
1846	22,410		1866	109,142
1847	57,762		1867	164,112
1848	61,055		1868	155,766
1849	73,567		1869	199,122
1850	95,083		1870	243,434
1851	199,732		1871	142,365
1852	86,293		1872	74,401
1853	106,312		1873	135,895
1854	221,747		1874	94,346
1855	255,535		1875	86,042
1856	177,016		1876	156,864
1857	264,230		1877	111,835
1858	302,207		1878	127,813
1859	49,064		1879	44,325
1860	122,459		1880	55,530

Table 2: Sales of Peruvian guano in Britain, 1849-61 (in tons).

(*Sources: Estado Comparativo De Las Ventas De Huano,* in Rivero; letter from Antony Gibbs & Sons to S. A. Rodulfo, 19 March 1862, quoted in *Fenn's Compendium of the English and Foreign Funds* (London, 9th edn., 1867), pp. 377-8).

1 July 1849 to 30 June 1850	77,098
1850-1	96,145
1851-2	112,638
1852-3	188,286
1853-4	135,524
1854	154,271
1855	161,852
1856	211,647
1857	110,490
1858	122,819
1859	132,082
1860	146,145
1861	161,707

254

BIBLIOGRAPHY

I. PRIMARY

A. Manuscript

Archivo Nacional, Lima
Ministerio de Hacienda. Archivo Histórico.

Private Collections, Lima
Diaries of Henry Witt (in possession of Sra. Eloyda Garland Melián
de Montero).
Memorias de Manuel de Argumaniz Muñoz (in possession of Sr.
Félix Denegri Luna).

Guildhall Library, London
Antony Gibbs & Sons, Ltd., merchants and foreign bankers of 22
Bishopsgate: Family archives and mss.
Business archives.

Public Record Office, London
Foreign Office, General Correspondence and Embassy and Consular
Archives: Peru (FO 61 and 177).
Foreign Office, General Correspondence and Embassy and Consular
Archives: Bolivia (FO 11 and 126)
Foreign Office, General Correspondence: Chile (FO 16).
Board of Trade, Correspondence: In-Letters, Foreign Office (BT 2).

Archives Nationales, Paris
Série F12, dossier 6860.

Archives du Ministère des Affaires Etrangères, Paris
Correspondance Consulaire et Commerciale: Chuquisaca and Lima.

Baker Library, Graduate School of Business Administration,
Harvard University
Prices Current Baltimore 1852, 1858. (Collection on produce prices).

B. Printed

Lima
Anales de la Hacienda Pública del Perú. Leyes, Decretos, Reg-
lamentos y Resoluciones; Aranceles, Presupuestos, Asientos y

Contratos que constituyen la Legislación y la Historia Fiscal de República. Ed. P. E. Dancuart and J. M. Rodriguez (Lima, 1902-20).

Crónica Parlamentaria del Perú. Ed. P. E. Dancuart and N. Benvenutto (Lima, 1906-10, 1926-9).

Dictamen de la Comisión Especial sobre la nulidad de las prórrogas de consignación del huano (Lima, 1856).

Dictamen de la Minoría de la Comisión Especial sobre la nulidad de las prórrogas de consignación del huano (Lima, 1856).

'Documentos' (relating to guano trade) in Francisco de Rivero, *Ojeada sobre el Huano* (Paris, 1860).

Correspondencia de los Signatorios del Contrato de Consignación para la Venta del Guano en la Gran Bretaña y sus Colonias, Dirigida a los SS. J. Thomson, T. Bonar y Compañia (Lima, 1877).

Informe Circunstanciado que la Comisión de Delegados Fiscales eleva al Congreso, en cumplimiento del Artículo 8 de la Ley de 28 de enero de 1869 (London, 1872 [?]).

Archivo Castilla (Instituto 'Libertador Ramón Castilla', Lima).

London

Annual Statement of the Trade and Navigation of the United Kingdom with Foreign Countries and British Possessions in the Year 1858 (London, 1859).

Commercial statistics in sundry volumes of *Parliamentary Accounts and Papers*

Correspondence between Great Britain and Foreign Powers, and Communications from the British Government to Claimants, relative to Loans made by British Subjects, 1823-1837. (Parliamentary Accounts and Papers), 1847, LXIX).

Correspondence between Great Britain and Foreign Powers, and Communications from the British Government to Claimants, relative to Loans made by British Subjects, 1847-1853. (Parliamentary Accounts and Papers, 1854, LXIX).

Correspondence respecting the Guano Islands of Lobos de Tierra and Lobos de Afuera, 1833-1852. (Parliamentary Accounts and Papers, 1852, LIV),

Copies or Extracts of Correspondence with the Colonial Office, respecting a Grant made by the Crown to raise and take away Guano from the Islands of Jibleca, Huskie, and Ghwrzoad, on the South Coast of Arabia; and of the Licence under which the Grant has been made. (Parliamentary Accounts and Papers, 1847, XXXVIII).

Minutes of Evidence taken before the Royal Commission on Unseaworthy Ships. (Parliamentary Accounts and Papers, 1873, XXXVI).

Documents relating to Steam Navigation in the Pacific (Lima, 1836).

Bills A. Customs, London. Ships' Reports (Customs House Library, London).

Lloyd's Register of Shipping

Hansard's Parliamentary Debates

Liverpool

Liverpool Customs Bills of Entry (Liverpool Record Office).

Paris

Oficio informativo que por conducto del Ministerio de Hacienda eleva al Supremo Gobierno del Perú el cuidadano Manuel Mariano Basagoitia, Apoderado Fiscal, enviado a Inglaterra, España, Italia e Islas de Mauricio, en cumplimiento de la resolución legislativa de 9 de setiembre de 1857 (Paris, 1858).

2. SECONDARY

W. Innes Addison (ed.), *The Matriculation Albums of the University of Glasgow, 1728-1858* (Glasgow, 1913).

C.M. Aikman, *Manures and the Principles of Manuring* (Edinburgh, 1894)

Sixty Years of Agricultural Science (Edinburgh, 1896)

Andrew P. Aitken, *Report on the Present State of the Agriculture of Scotland* (Edinburgh, 1878)

Bill Albert, *An Essay on the Peruvian Sugar Industry, 1880-1920* (Norwich, 1976)

Aquiles Allier, *Alcance al Comercio Numero 742 Sobre la Cuestion del Huano* (Lima, 1841)

Thomas Anderson, *Elements of Agricultural Chemistry* (Edinburgh, 1860)

G.H. Andrews, *Modern Husbandry: A Practical and Scientific Treatise on Agriculture* (London, 1853)

Anon., *An Inquiry into the Plans, Progress and Policy of the American Mining Companies* (London, 1825 edn.)

Hints to Farmers on the Nature, Purchase, and Application of Peruvian, Bolivian, and African Guano (Liverpool and London, 1844)

257

Sir W.G. Armstrong, I.L. Bell, John Taylor and Dr. Richardson (eds.), *The Industrial Resources of the District of the Three Northern Rivers* (London and Newcastle, 1864)

R. Balgarnie, *Sir Titus Salt* (London, 1877)

Paul A. Baran, *The Political Economy of Growth* (London and New York, 1968)

Carlos Barroilhet, *Exposición que presenta a la Honorable comisión nombrada por la Convención Nacional* (Lima, 1856)

———— *Opúsculo sobre el huano dedicado a la nación Peruano* (Paris, 1857)

———— *Contestación al Señor Ministro de Hacienda del Perú* (Paris, 1857)

———— *Grandeza y Decadencia del Perú* (Paris, 1858)

———— *Consideraciones sobre la Riqueza del Perú* (Paris, 1859)

———— *Ojeada sobre la Crisis Política y Financiera del Perú* (Paris, 1859)

———— *Examen Crítico de un Opúsculo sobre el Guano* (Paris, 1860)

———— *Examen Crítico de Dos Publicaciones del Sr. Don Francisco Rivero* (Paris, 1861)

Jorge Basadre, *Historia de la República del Perú* (Lima, 1946 and 1969 edns.)

———— *Introducción A Las Bases Documentales Para La Historia De La República Del Perú Con Algunas Reflexiones* (Lima, 1971)

John Bateman, *The great landowners of Great Britain and Ireland* (London, 1878)

A.J. Bernays, *Two Lectures on the Theory of Agriculture and on Farming as Practised in Cheshire* (London, 1844)

———— *A Lecture on the Application of Chemistry to the Details of Practical Farming* (London, 1845)

Louis Bertrand and Sir Charles Petrie, *The History of Spain* (London, 1952)

S.T. Bindoff, E.F. Malcolm Smith, and C.K. Webster, *British Diplomatic Representatives 1789-1852* (London, 1934)

Harold Blakemore, *British Nitrates and Chilean Politics, 1886-1896* (London, 1952)

Heraclio Bonilla, 'Aspects de l'histoire économique et sociale du Pérou au XIXe siècle' (doctoral thesis, Paris, 1970)

———— *Guano y Burguesía en el Perú* (Lima, 1974)

W. and B. Brooke, *Guano: Description of the Nature and Properties of Guano Manure* (London, 1843)

Charles A. Browne, *A Source Book of Agricultural Chemistry* (Waltham, 1944)

258

Thomas Wentworth Buller, *A Reply to a Pamphlet, published by David Ricardo, Esq. M.P., on Protection to Agriculture* (London, 1822)
———— *The Hare and Many Friends. Remarks on the Monopoly of Guano* (London, 1852)
Robert N. Burr, *By Reason or Force. Chile and the Balancing of Power in South America, 1830-1905* (Berkeley and Los Angeles, 1965)
T.A. Bushell, *Royal Mail. A Centenary History of the Royal Mail Line 1839-1939* (London, 1939)
James Caird, *English Agriculture in 1850-51* (London, 1852)
Charles A. Cameron, *Chemistry of Agriculture* (Dublin, 1857)
J.D. Chambers and G.E. Mingay, *The Agricultural Revolution 1750-1880* (London, 1966)
R.H. Chilcote, 'A Critical Synthesis of the Dependency Literature', *LAP*, 1, no. 1 (1974)
G. Kitson Clarke, 'The Repeal of the Corn Laws and the Politics of the Forties', *EHR*, 2nd ser., 4, no. 1 (1951)
Alejandro Cochet, *Al Soberano Congreso* (Lima, 1849)
E.J.T. Collins and E.L. Jones, 'Sectoral Advance in English Agriculture, 1850-80', *AHR*, 15, part 2 (1967)
Roberto Cortés Conde, *The First Stages of Modernization in Spanish America* (New York, 1974)
R. Coupland, *East Africa and its Invaders* (Oxford, 1938)
Robert Craig, 'The African Guano Trade', *MM*, 50 (1964)
Charles Darwin, *Journal of Researches into the Natural History and Geology of the Countries visited during the Voyage of H.M.S. 'Beagle' Round the World* (London, 1890 edn.)
P. Dávalos y Lissón, *La Primera Centuria* (Lima, 1926)
Sir Humphrey Davy, *Elements of Agricultural Chemistry* (London, 1813)
H.W. Dickinson and Arthur Titley, *Richard Trevithick* (Cambridge, 1934)
A.J. Duffield, *The Prospects of Peru* (London, 1881)
José Rufino Echenique, *Memorias Para La Historia Del Perú, 1808-1878* (Lima, 1952)
T.E. Eden, *The Search for Nitre, and the True Nature of Guano* (London, Liverpool and Glasgow, 1846)
Arghiri Emmanuel, *Unequal Exchange: a Study of the Imperialism of Trade* (London and New York, 1972)
Henry English, *A General Guide to the Companies formed for Working Foreign Mines* (London, 1825)
———— *A Complete View of the Joint Stock Companies formed during the Years 1824 and 1825* (London, 1827)

Lord Ernle, *English Farming Past and Present* (London, 1936 edn.)

Susan Fairlie, 'The Corn Laws and British Wheat Production, 1829-76', *EHR*, 2nd ser., 22, no. 1 (1969)

J.P. Faivre, *L'Expansion Française dans le Pacifique de 1800 à 1842* (Paris, 1853)

———— 'Le Début des Exportations du Guano Péruvien', *RHES*, 37 (1959)

Charles Fenn, *A Compendium of the English and Foreign Funds* (London, 9th edn., 1967, re-written by R.L.Nash)

J.R. Fisher, *Silver Mines and Silver Miners in Colonial Peru, 1776-1824* (Liverpool, 1977)

Joseph Foster (ed.), *Alumni Oxonienses: the members of the University of Oxford, 1715-1886* (Oxford, 1891)

Andre Gunder Frank, *Capitalism and Underdevelopment in Latin America* (New York and London, 1967)

Claude Moore Fuess, *Daniel Webster* (Boston, 1930)

Arthur D. Gayer, W.W. Rostow and Anna Jacobsen Schwartz, *The Growth and Fluctuations of the British Economy 1790-1850* (Oxford, 1953)

Antony Gibbs & Sons, *Guano: Its Analysis and Effects; Illustrated by the Latest Experiments* (London, 1843)

———— *Contestación de la Casa Gibbs a los cargos sobre el huano* (London, 1858)

Antony Gibbs & Sons and William Joseph Myers & Co., *Peruvian and Bolivian Guano: Its Nature, Properties and Results* (London, 1844)

Henry H. Gibbs, *Pedigree of the Family of Gibbs* (London, 1890)

John Arthur Gibbs, *The History of Antony and Dorothea Gibbs* (London, 1922)

———— *Pedigree of the Family of Gibbs* (London, 1932)

Dorothy Burne Goebel, 'British Trade to the Spanish Colonies, 1796-1823', *AHR*, 43, no. 2 (1938)

A.N. Gray, *Phosphates and Superphosphates* (London, 1930)

Keith Griffin, *Underdevelopment in Spanish America* (London, 1969)

Samuel Haigh, *Sketches of Buenos Ayres, Chile, and Peru* (London, 1931 edn.)

Basil Hall, *Extracts from a Journal written on the Coasts of Chile, Peru, and Mexico, in the years 1820, 1821, 1822* (Edinburgh, 1824)

E.J. Hobsbawm, *The Age of Capital, 1848-1875* (London, 1977 edn.)

W.G. Hoskins, *Industry, Trade and People in Exeter 1688-1800* (Manchester, 1935)

R.A. Humphreys, *British Consular Reports on the Trade and Politics of Latin America, 1824-26* (London, 1940)

Shane J. Hunt, 'Price and Quantum Estimates of Peruvian Exports, 1830-1962' (discussion paper, Woodrow Wilson School, Princeton University, January 1973)

―――――― 'Growth and Guano in Nineteenth Century Peru' (discussion paper, Woodrow Wilson School, Princeton University, February 1973)

L.H. Jenks, *The Migration of British Capital to 1875* (London, 1938)

C.W. Johnson, *The Use of Crushed Bones as Manure* (London, 1836 edn.)

―――――― *The Farmer's Encyclopaedia* (London, 1842)

―――――― *Modern Agricultural Improvements* (London, 1847)

James Johnston (ed.), *The Potato Disease in Scotland* (Edinburgh, 1845)

Colin Jones, *Antony Gibbs & Sons Limited. A Record of 150 Years of Merchant Banking, 1808-1958* (London, 1958)

E.L. Jones, 'The Changing Basis of English Agricultural Prosperity, 1853-73', *AgHR,* 10, part 2 (1962)

―――――― *The Development of English Agriculture, 1815-1873* (London, 1968)

Wilbur Devereaux Jones, *Lord Derby and Victorian Conservatism* (Oxford, 1956)

David Joslin, *A Century of Banking in Latin America* (London, 1963)

L.C. Kendall, 'Andrés de Santa Cruz and the Peru-Bolivian Confederation', *HAHR,* 16 (1936)

Eric Kerridge, *The Agricultural Revolution* (London, 1967)

Pierre Larousse, *Dictionnaire Universel du XIXe Siècle* (Paris, 1866)

Léonce de Lavergne, *The Rural Economy of England, Scotland and Ireland* (Edinburgh and London, 1855)

J.V. Levin, *The Export Economies* (Cambridge, Mass., 1960)

Justus Liebig, *Organic Chemistry in its Applications to Agriculture and Physiology* (London, 1840)

J.C. Loudon, *An Encyclopaedia of Agriculture* (London, 1825)

John MacGregor, *Commercial Statistics* (London, 1843-50)

C.A. MacQueen, *Peruvian Public Finance* (Washington, 1926)

Pablo Macera, *Las Plantaciones Azucareras en el Perú* (Lima, 1974)

Juan Maiguashca, 'A Reinterpretation of the Guano Age 1840-1880' (doctoral thesis, Oxford, 1967)

Sir Robert Marett, *Peru* (London, 1969)

Clements R. Markham, *Travels in Peru and India* (London, 1862)
———— *A History of Peru* (London, 1892)
W.M. Mathew, 'Anglo-Peruvian Commercial and Financial Relations, 1820-62' (doctoral thesis, London, 1964)
———— 'The Imperialism of Free Trade: Peru, 1820-70', *EHR*, 2nd ser., 21, no. 3 (1968)
———— 'Peru and the British Guano Market, 1840-1870', *EHR*, 2nd ser., 23, no. 1 (1970)
———— 'The First Anglo-Peruvian Debt and Its Settlement, 1822-49', *JLAS*, 2, part 1 (1970)
———— 'Foreign Contractors and the Peruvian Government at the Outset of the Guano Trade', *HAHR*, 52 (1972)
———— 'A Primitive Export Sector: Guano Production in Mid-Nineteenth Century Peru', *JLAS*, 9, part 1 (1977)
Wilfred Maude, *Antony Gibbs & Sons Limited, Merchants and Bankers, 1808-1958* (London, 1958)
Luis Mesones, *El Ministerio de Hacienda del Perú en sus relaciones con los administradores del huano en Europa* (Besançon, 1859)
John Miers, *Travels in Chile and La Plata* (London, 1826)
Rory M. Miller and Robert G. Greenhill, 'The Peruvian Government and the Nitrate Trade, 1873-1879', *JLAS*, 5, part 1 (1973)
B.R. Mitchell with Phyllis Deane, *Abstract of British Historical Statistics* (Cambridge, 1971)
D.C. Moore, 'The Corn Laws and High Farming', *EHR*, 2nd ser., 18, no. 3 (1965)
Benjamin Morrell, *A Narrative of Four Voyages* (New York, 1832)
John C. Morton (ed.), *A Cyclopedia of Agriculture* (Glasgow, Edinburgh, and London, 1855)
Robert Cushman Murphy, *Bird Islands of Peru* (New York and London, 1925)
Gunnar Myrdal, *Economic Theory and Underdeveloped Regions* (London, 1957)
J.C. Nesbit, *Lecture on the Application of Chemistry to Agriculture* (London, 1849)
———— *On Peruvian Guano* (London, 1852)
Luis Pásara, *El Rol del Derecho en la época del guano* (Lima, 1970)
Jean Piel, 'The Place of the Peasantry in the National Life of Peru in the Nineteenth Century, *P&P*, no. 46 (1970)
Nicolás de Piérola, *Informe sobre el estado del carguio de huano en las Islas de Chincha, y sobre el cumplimiento del contrato celebrado con D. Domingo Elías* (Lima, 1853)
Fredrick B. Pike, *The Modern History of Peru* (London, 1967)
———— *The United States and the Andean Republics: Peru,*

Bolivia, and Ecuador (Cambridge, Mass. and London, 1977)

Gustave Planchon, *Des Quinquinas* (Paris et Montpellier, 1864)

D.C.M. Platt, 'Economic imperialism and the businessman: Britain and Latin America before 1914', in Roger Owen and Bob Sutcliffe, *Studies in the Theory of Imperialism* (London, 1972)

_____ *Latin America and British Trade 1806-1914* (London, 1972)

D.C.M.Platt (ed.), *Business Imperialism, 1840-1930: an inquiry based on British experience in Latin America* (Oxford, 1977)

Francisco Quiros and Aquiles Allier, *Exposición que Don Francisco Quiros y Don Aquiles Allier Elevan al Soberano Congreso* (Lima, 1845)

Alexander Ramsay, *History of the Highland and Agricultural Society of Scotland* (Edinburgh and London, 1879)

J. Fred Rippy, *British Investments in Latin America, 1822-1949* (Minneapolis, 1959)

Francisco de Rivero, *Ojeada Sobre El Huano* (Paris, 1860)

_____ *Reflexiones Sobre Una Carta Del Doctor Luis Mesones* (Lima, 1861)

Emilio Romero, *Historia Ecónomica Del Perú* (Buenos Aires, 1949)

Sir E. John Russell, *History of Agricultural Science* (London, 1966)

L.E.S., *Estudios Sobre El Huano* (Lima, 1851)

Andrés de Santa-Cruz, Schuhkrafft, *Cuadros Sinópticos De Los Gobernantes De La República De Bolivia . . . Y De la Del Perú* (La Paz, 1956)

Edward Shann, *An Economic History of Australia* (Cambridge, 1930)

J.H. Sheppard, *A Practical Treatise on the Use of Peruvian and Ichaboe African Guano* (London, 1844)

Jack Simmons (ed.), *The Birth of the Great Western Railway. Extracts from the Diary and Correspondence of George Henry Gibbs* (Bath, 1971)

W.A. Smeaton, *Fourcroy, Chemist and Revolutionary 1755-1809* (Cambridge, 1962)

Archibald Smith, *Peru as it is* (London, 1839)

W.C. Spooner, *On the Most Economic and Profitable Method of Growing and Consuming Root Crops* (London, 1854)

Lytton Strachey and Roger Fulford (eds.), *The Greville Memoirs, 1814-1860* (London, 1838)

Edmond Temple, *Travels in Various Parts of Peru, Including a Year's Residence in Potosi* (London, 1830)

Joan Thirsk (ed.), *The Agrarian History of England and Wales*, IV (Cambridge, 1967)

F.M.L. Thompson, *English Landed Society in the Nineteenth Century (London, 1963)*

―――― 'The Second Agricultural Revolution, 1815-1880', *EHR*, 2nd ser., 21, no. 1 (1968)

Thomas Tooke, *A History of Prices, and of the State of the Circulation, from 1839 to 1847 inclusive* (London, 1848)

Joshua Trimmer, *Practical Chemistry for Farmers and Landowners* (London, 1842)

J.J. von Tschudi, *Travels in Peru During the Years 1838-1842* (London, 1847)

José Casimiro Ulloa, *Huano (Apuntes económicos y administrativos)* (Lima, 1859)

J. and J.A. Venn (eds.), *Alumni Cantabrigienses . . . from the earliest times to 1900* (Cambridge, 1922-54)

Jaime Vicens Vives, *An Economic History of Spain* (transl. Frances M. Lopez-Morillas, Princeton, 1969)

C.N. Ward-Perkins, 'The Commercial Crisis of 1847', in E.M. Carus-Wilson (ed.), *Essays in Economic History,* III (London, 1962)

Arthur C. Wardle, *Steam Conquers the Pacific* (London, 1940)

J.A. Scott Watson, *The History of the Royal Agricultural Society of England 1839-1969* (London, 1939)

John M. Wilson (ed.), *The Rural Cyclopedia* (Edinburgh, 1847)

Cecil Woodham-Smith, *The Great Hunger. Ireland 1845-9* (London, 1962)

Marie Robinson Wright, *The Old and the New Peru* (Philadelphia, 1908)

Ernesto Yepes del Castillo, *Perú 1820-1920; un siglo de desarrollo capitalista* (Lima, 1972)

INDEX

Other volumes in this series

Copies obtainable on order from
Swift Printers (Sales) Ltd., 1-7 Albion Place, Britton Street, London EC1M 5RE